W9-AAR-639

The Applause of Heaven

When God Whispers Your Name

In the Grip of Grace

THOMAS NELSON
Since 1798

NASHVILLE DALLAS MEXICO CITY RIO DE JANEIRO BEIJING

Published in Nashville, Tennessee, by Thomas Nelson. Thomas Nelson is a trademark of Thomas Nelson, Inc.

Thomas Nelson, Inc., titles may be purchased in bulk for educational, business, fund-raising, or sales promotional use. For information, please e-mail SpecialMarkets@thomasnelson.com.

ISBN 978-0-8499-2049-3

Printed in the United States of America
07 08 09 10 11 BVG 6 5 4 3 2 1

MAX LUCADO

The Applause of Heaven

THOMAS NELSON
Since 1798

NASHVILLE DALLAS MEXICO CITY RIO DE JANEIRO BEIJING

To Stanley Shipp,

my father in the faith

Contents

Publisher's Preface

Since *The Applause of Heaven* first appeared in the fall of 1990, Max Lucado has truly become a household name in Christian America. Over the years his books have touched the hearts of millions of men and women around the world. Enthusiastic response to this book—including reviews in many periodicals—makes it clear that the work has become a modern classic. It is a book that will be treasured for generations to come.

What readers find in these pages is a series of soul-stirring insights into some of Christ's most provocative teachings in the New Testament. It is not a theological treatise, however, but a heart-to-heart conversation. By offering a fresh look at the Beatitudes—as they appear in the Gospel of Matthew—Lucado's narrative opens our eyes to old truths in compelling new ways. It allows is to see ideas and images we may have missed, no matter how many times we have read them before.

In the hands of this gifted writer, words and phrases become instruments of wonder and imagination. Max Lucado's personal examples and his stories from real life reveal the sparkling facets of the biblical text in a penetrating and colorful light. Every page offers new treasures and new moments of joy. The work, as a whole, is a re-examination of heaven's value system. No wonder *The Applause of Heaven* has become one of the most successful Christian books of our time.

This handsome new gift edition is a celebration of the book's remarkable success. To add to the overall enjoyment of the work, we have chosen eighteen dramatic illustrations by several great masters, each one representing in some way the theme or message of the accompanying chapter. The cover illustration of the American Rockies by the nineteenth-century German artist, Albert Bierstadt, is a classic of Western art which we believe expresses very well the mood of this volume. It is not simply a breathtaking scene, but an image inspired by the sheer beauty of God's creation.

We hope you agree that that pictures, in a variety of styles and media, are a natural complement to the remarkable breadth and versatility of Max Lucado's poetic vision. The special gift size, the text styling, and the look and feel of the book are designed to make this an important addition to every book lover's collection.

Max Lucado reminds us that "Matthew, chapter five is not a list of proverbs or a compilation of independent sayings, but rather a step-by-step description of how God rebuilds the believer's heart." In the Beatitudes, Jesus promises "blessings" to all who come after Him—to all who decide to live their lives each day by His example. This new edition of *The Applause of Heaven* shows us how to have that kind of life, and how to live it more abundantly.

THE PUBLISHER

Foreword

God says all the big words in our lives. Still, it is ofttimes the little words that make the Big Word sing. Max Lucado is a rare and welcome talent who is dedicated to the Word made flesh, but is also a spellbinding spinner of such smaller words as may ornament God's Word.

I first discovered Lucado when I casually took *No Wonder They Call Him the Savior* off a bookstore shelf. Nothing was casual after his first line hooked my eye. Lucado has become popular for two reasons: He reveres Christ, and he loves the world around him. This double love binds our minds and beckons us to follow closely to see where his paragraphs may lead.

It is because Max Lucado loves his Lord that he turns from the muddlesome and thumbworn language so common in the church. To Lucado, Jesus is no ordinary noun to be theologized into dullness. Rather, all holy relationships are glorious, and only the best, most creative English is worthy. So he weaves anew the Shroud of Turin, leaving us no doubt that this splendid cloth has touched the body of our Lord and been forever marked by the imprimatur of Lucado's reverence. Where no ordinary words will serve, here's how he bids us know the Christ:

"Sacred delight derives from stubborn joy," he exults.

"If you have time to read this chapter, you probably don't need to," he calls to those who think they're too busy for the spiritual disciplines.

On and on his wisdom flows: "Show a man his failures without Jesus, and the result will be found in the roadside gutter. Give a man religion without reminding him of his filth, and the result will be arrogance in a three-piece suit."

He counsels the arrogant that facing Christ is like entering the church of the nativity: "The door is so low, you can't go in standing up."

He rebukes the bitter: "Hatred is the rabid dog that turns on its owner. . . . The very word grudge starts with . . . GRRR . . . a growl!"

This book introduces the Beatitudes, which introduce the Sermon on the Mount. The Beatitudes fly at us, but in the simple metaphors of ordinary life. So you'll meet Christ even as you meet the *Exxon Valdez* that dark March night in 1989, when she spilled her crude venom on Bligh Reef in Alaska. The Christ of communion will come to you as you meet Gayaney Petroysan, an Armenian four years old who begged her mother's blood to live. And any number of great Bible heroes come and go in this book to make real the introduction to Jesus' great Sermon on the Mount.

Max and I are friends. I may have overpressed him to be my friend, and I will admit the friendship was originally my idea. But, I confess, I wanted to know Christ as Max does. I want to feel the April wind that breathed upon the cross, as he does. I want to fall like Thomas before Christ and cry, "My Lord and my God!" as he does. I need Max to give me lessons on obedience and spiritual need.

Read this book in a quiet place and you may feel a wounded hand fall lightly on your shoulder. Be not afraid of the nearness you will feel to Christ, but go on and walk his paragraphs. Then you will know by experience that Lucado travels the high country of the Galilee of the heart.

CALVIN MILLER

Before You Begin

This book was almost as difficult to title as it was to write. We went through list after list of options. Dozens of titles were suggested and dozens were discarded. Carol Bartley, Dave Moberg, Kip Jordon and others at Word Publishing spent hours searching for the appropriate phrase that would describe the heart of the book.

In my mind, the scales were tipped in favor of *The Applause of Heaven* when my editor, Carol, read part of the manuscript to some of the Word executives. She read a portion of the book that describes our final journey into the city of God. She read some thoughts I wrote about God's hunger to have his children home, about how he longs to welcome us and may even applaud when we enter the gates.

After Carol read this section, she noticed one of the men was brushing away a tear. He explained his emotion by saying, "It's hard for me to imagine God applauding for me."

Can you relate?

I can. Certain things about God are easy to imagine. I can imagine him creating the world and suspending the stars. I can envision him as almighty, all-powerful, and in control. I can fathom a God who knows me, who made me, and I can even fathom a God who hears me. But a God who is in love with me? A God who is crazy for me? A God who cheers for me?

But that is the message of the Bible. Our Father is relentlessly in pursuit of his children. He has called us home with his word, paved the path with his blood, and is longing for our arrival.

God's love for his children is the message of the Bible. And that is the message of this book.

Indulge me as I say thank-you to some dear friends who made this project possible.

First, to Calvin Miller. In 1977, a dear friend gave me a rectangular-shaped book called *The Singer* and urged me to read it. I did . . . several times. I was amazed. Never had I seen such word crafting. Never had I seen such passion. I still have the book on my shelf. It is dog-eared, weather-worn, and coffee stained.

But I will never discard it. For through it, Calvin Miller introduced me to a new caliber of writing—a fruitful hybrid of faith and creativity.

Thank you, Calvin, for what you've meant to thousands of readers over the last two decades. Thank you for sitting patiently until God gave you a fresh way to tell the ancient tale. And thank you for ushering this writer into a new palace of possibilities.

Thanks, also:

To Kip Jordon and Byron Williamson, two dear brothers who help Word Publishing to be a ministry as well as a business.

To Ernie Owen, a Christian sage with one eye on Him and the other on His children. Thanks for the counsel.

To Carol Bartley and Anne Christian Buchanan. Thanks for editing and editing and editing and editing and. . . You did a great job. (All my mistakes are our little secret, OK?)

To Mary Stain. Because of your secretarial skills and remarkable flexibility, another manuscript is completed. I'm grateful.

To the rest of the Oak Hills Church staff. What would I do without friends like you? Thank you so much.

To Tim Kimmel and John Trent. One conversation with you guys gives me enough encouragement for a whole month.

To the Oak Hills elders and church. I never dreamed I would have the privilege of serving with such a faithful family. I thank God for what he is doing.

To Dave Moberg, Nancy Guthrie, and David Edmonson, for making me look better than I really do.

To Michael Card, a troubadour of truth whose heart touches mine.

And lastly, two special people.

To my wife, Denalyn. Thank you for making coming home the highlight of my day.

And thanks to you, the reader, for spending your time and money in hopes of seeing Jesus. May he honor the desire of your heart.

> Now when he saw the crowds, he went up on a mountainside and sat down. His disciples came to him, and he began to teach them, saying:
>
> *Blessed are the poor in spirit,*
> *for theirs is the kingdom of heaven.*
> *Blessed are those who mourn,*
> *for they will be comforted.*
> *Blessed are the meek,*
> *for they will inherit the earth.*
> *Blessed are those who hunger and thirst for righteousness,*
> *for they will be filled.*
> *Blessed are the merciful,*
> *for they will be shown mercy.*
> *Blessed are the pure in heart,*
> *for they will see God.*
> *Blessed are the peacemakers,*
> *for they will be called sons of God.*
> *Blessed are those who are persecuted because of righteousness,*
> *for theirs is the kingdom of heaven.*
>
> Matthew 5:1–10

Blessed . . .

One

Sacred Delight

SHE HAS EVERY REASON TO BE BITTER.

Though talented, she went unrecognized for years. Prestigious opera circles closed their ranks when she tried to enter. American critics ignored her compelling voice. She was repeatedly rejected for parts for which she easily qualified. It was only after she went to Europe and won the hearts of tough-to-please European audiences that stateside opinion leaders acknowledged her talent.

Not only has her professional life been a battle, her personal life has been marked by challenge. She is the mother of two handicapped children, one of whom is severely retarded. Years ago, in order to escape the pace of New York City, she purchased a home on Martha's Vineyard. It burned to the ground two days before she was to move in.

Professional rejection. Personal setbacks. Perfect soil for

the seeds of bitterness. A receptive field for the roots of resentment. But in this case, anger found no home.

Her friends don't call her bitter; they call her "Bubbles."

Beverly Sills. Internationally acclaimed opera singer. Retired director of the New York City Opera.

Her phrases are sugared with laughter. Her face is softened with serenity. Upon interviewing her, Mike Wallace stated that "she is one of the most impressive—if not *the* most impressive—ladies I've ever interviewed."

How can a person handle such professional rejection and personal trauma and still be known as Bubbles? "I choose to be cheerful," she says. "Years ago I knew I had little or no choice about success, circumstances or even happiness; but I knew I could choose to be cheerful."

♔

"We have prayed for healing. God has not given it. But he has blessed us."

Glyn spoke slowly. Partly because of her conviction. Partly because of her disease. Her husband, Don, sat in the chair next to her. The three of us had come together to plan a funeral—hers. And now, with that task done, with the hymns selected and the directions given, Glyn spoke.

"He has given us strength we did not know.

He gave it when we needed it and not before." Her words were slurred, but clear. Her eyes were moist, but confident.

I wondered what it would be like to have my life taken from me at age forty-five. I wondered what it would be like to say good-bye to my children and spouse. I wondered what it would be like to be a witness to my own death.

"God has given us peace in our pain. He covers us all the time. Even when we are out of control, he is still there."

It had been a year since Glyn and Don had learned of Glyn's condition—amyotrophic lateral sclerosis (Lou Gehrig's disease). The cause and the cure remain a mystery.

But the result doesn't. Muscle strength and mobility steadily deteriorate, leaving only the mind and the faith.

And it was the coming together of Glyn's mind and faith that caused me to realize I was doing more than planning a funeral. I was beholding holy jewels she had quarried out of the mine of despair.

"We can use any tragedy as a stumbling block or a stepping stone. . . .

"I hope this will not cause my family to be bitter. I hope I can be an example that God is wanting us to trust in the good times and the bad. For if we don't trust when times are tough, we don't trust at all."

Don held her hand. He wiped her tears. He wiped his own.

"Who are these two?" I asked myself as I watched him touch a tissue to her cheek. "Who are these, who, on the edge of life's river, can look across with such faith?"

The moment was solemn and sweet. I said little. One is not bold in the presence of the sacred.

♔

"I have everything I need for joy!" Robert Reed said. "Amazing!" I thought.

His hands are twisted and his feet are useless. He can't bathe himself. He can't feed himself. He can't brush his teeth, comb his hair, or put on his underwear. His shirts are held together by strips of Velcro®. His speech drags like a worn-out audio cassette.

Robert has cerebral palsy.

The disease keeps him from driving a car, riding a bike, and going for a walk. But it didn't keep him from graduating from high school or attending Abilene Christian University, from which he graduated with a degree in Latin. Having cerebral palsy didn't keep him from teaching at a St. Louis junior college or from venturing overseas on five mission trips.

And Robert's disease didn't prevent him from becoming a missionary in Portugal.

He moved to Lisbon, alone, in 1972. There he rented a hotel room and began studying Portuguese. He found a restaurant owner who would feed him after the rush hour and a tutor who would instruct him in the language.

Then he stationed himself daily in a park, where he distributed brochures about Christ. Within six years he led seventy people to the Lord, one of whom became his wife, Rosa.

I heard Robert speak recently. I watched other men carry him in his wheelchair onto the platform. I watched them lay a Bible in his lap. I watched his stiff fingers force open the pages. And I watched people in the audience wipe away tears of admiration from their faces. Robert could have asked for sympathy or pity, but he did just the opposite. He held his bent hand up in the air and boasted, "I have everything I need for joy."

His shirts are held together by Velcro®, but his life is held together by joy.

♛

No man had more reason to be miserable than this one—yet no man was more joyful.

His first home was a palace. Servants were at his fingertips. The snap of his fingers changed the course of history. His name was known and loved. He had everything—wealth, power, respect.

And then he had nothing.

Students of the event still ponder it. Historians stumble as they attempt to explain it. How could a king lose everything in one instant?

One moment he was royalty; the next he was in poverty.

His bed became, at best, a borrowed pallet—and usually the hard earth. He never owned even the most basic mode of transportation and was dependent upon handouts for his income. He was sometimes so hungry he would eat raw grain or pick fruit off a tree. He knew what it was like to be rained on, to be cold. He knew what it meant to have no home.

His palace grounds had been spotless; now he was exposed to filth. He had never known disease, but was now surrounded by illness.

In his kingdom he had been revered; now he was ridiculed. His neighbors tried to lynch him. Some called him a lunatic. His family tried to confine him to their house.

Those who didn't ridicule him tried to use him. They wanted favors. They wanted tricks. He was a novelty. They wanted to be seen with him—that is, until being with him was out of fashion. Then they wanted to kill him.

He was accused of a crime he never committed. Witnesses were hired to lie. The jury was rigged. No lawyer was assigned to his defense. A judge swayed by politics handed down the death penalty.

They killed him.

He left as he came—penniless. He was buried in a borrowed grave, his funeral financed by compassionate friends. Though he once had everything, he died with nothing.

He should have been miserable. He should have been bitter. He had every right to be a pot of boiling anger. But he wasn't.

He was joyful.

Sourpusses don't attract a following. People followed him wherever he went.

Children avoid soreheads. Children scampered after this man.

Crowds don't gather to listen to the woeful. Crowds clamored to hear him.

Why? He was joyful. He was joyful when he was poor. He was joyful when he was abandoned. He was joyful when he was betrayed. He was even joyful as he hung on a tool of torture, his hands pierced with six-inch Roman spikes.

Jesus embodied a stubborn joy. A joy that refused to bend in the wind of hard times. A joy that held its ground against pain. A joy whose roots extended deep into the bedrock of eternity.

Perhaps that's where Beverly Sills learned it. Without doubt, that is where Glyn Johnson and Robert Reed learned it. And that is where we can learn it.

What type of joy is this? What is this cheerfulness that dares to wink at adversity? What is this bird that sings while it is still dark? What is the source of this peace that defies pain?

I call it sacred delight.

It is sacred because it is not of the earth. What is sacred is God's. And this joy is God's.

It is delight because delight can both satisfy and surprise.

Delight is the Bethlehem shepherds dancing a jig outside a cave. Delight is Mary watching God sleep in a feed trough. Delight is white-haired Simeon praising God, who is about to be circumcised. Delight is Joseph teaching the Creator of the world how to hold a hammer.

Delight is the look on Andrew's face at the lunch pail that never came up empty. Delight is the dozing wedding guests who drank the wine that had been water. Delight is Jesus walking through waves as casually as you walk through curtains. Delight is a leper seeing a finger where there had been only a nub . . . a widow hosting a party with food made for a funeral . . . a paraplegic doing somersaults. Delight is Jesus doing impossible things in crazy ways: healing the blind with spit, paying taxes with a coin found in a fish's mouth, and coming back from the dead disguised as a gardener.

What is sacred delight? It is God doing what gods would be doing only in your wildest dreams—wearing diapers, riding donkeys, washing feet, dozing in storms.

Delight is the day they accused God of having too much fun, attending too many parties, and spending too much time with the Happy Hour crowd.

Delight is the day's wage paid to workers who had worked only one hour . . . the father scrubbing the pig smell off his son's back . . . the shepherd throwing a party because the sheep was found. Delight is a discovered pearl, a multiplied talent, a heaven-bound beggar, a criminal in the kingdom. Delight is the surprise on the faces of street folks who have been invited to a king's banquet.

Delight is the Samaritan woman big-eyed and speechless, the adulteress walking out of the stone-cluttered courtyard, and a skivvy-clad Peter plunging into cold waters to get close to the one he'd cursed.

Sacred delight is good news coming through the back door of your heart. It's what you'd always dreamed but never expected. It's the too-good-to-be-true coming true. It's having God as your pinch-hitter, your lawyer, your dad, your biggest fan, and your best friend. God on your side, in your heart, out in front, and protecting your back. It's hope where you least expected it: a flower in life's sidewalk.

It is *sacred* because only God can grant it. It is a *delight* because it thrills. Since it is sacred, it can't be stolen. And since it is delightful, it can't be predicted.

It was this gladness that danced through the Red Sea. It was this joy that blew the trumpet at Jericho. It was this secret that made Mary sing. It was this surprise that put the springtime into Easter morning.

It is God's gladness. It's sacred delight.

And it is this sacred delight that Jesus promises in the Sermon on the Mount.

Nine times he promises it. And he promises it to an unlikely crowd:

- *"The poor in spirit."* Beggars in God's soup kitchen.

- *"Those who mourn."* Sinners Anonymous bound together by the truth of their introduction: "Hi, I am me. I'm a sinner."
- *"The meek."* Pawnshop pianos played by Van Cliburn. (He's so good no one notices the missing *keys.*)
- *"Those who hunger and thirst."* Famished orphans who know the difference between a TV dinner and a Thanksgiving feast.
- *"The merciful."* Winners of the million-dollar lottery who share the prize with their enemies.
- *"The pure in heart."* Physicians who love lepers and escape infection.
- *"The peacemakers."* Architects who build bridges with wood from a Roman cross.
- *"The persecuted."* Those who manage to keep an eye on heaven while walking through hell on earth.

It is to this band of pilgrims that God promises a special blessing. A heavenly joy. A sacred delight.

But this joy is not cheap. What Jesus promises is not a gimmick to give you goose bumps nor a mental attitude that has to be pumped up at pep rallies. No, Matthew 5 describes God's radical reconstruction of the heart.

Observe the sequence. First, we recognize we are in need (we're poor in spirit). Next, we repent of our self-sufficiency (we mourn). We quit calling the shots and surrender control to God (we're meek). So grateful are we for his presence that we yearn for more of him (we hunger and thirst). As we grow closer to him, we become more like him. We forgive others (we're merciful). We change our outlook (we're pure in heart). We love others (we're peacemakers). We endure injustice (we're persecuted).

It's no casual shift of attitude. It is a demolition of the

old structure and a creation of the new. The more radical the change, the greater the joy. And it's worth every effort, for this is the joy of God.

It's no accident that the same word used by Jesus to promise sacred delight is the word used by Paul to describe God:

> "*The blessed God . . .*" [1]

> "*God, the blessed and only Ruler . . .*" [2]

Think about God's joy. What can cloud it? What can quench it? What can kill it? Is God ever in a bad mood because of bad weather? Does God get ruffled over long lines or traffic jams? Does God ever refuse to rotate the earth because his feelings are hurt?

No. His is a joy which consequences cannot quench. His is a peace which circumstances cannot steal.

There is a delicious gladness that comes from God. A holy joy. A sacred delight.

And it is within your reach. You are one decision away from Joy.

Now when he saw the crowds, he went up on a mountainside and sat down.

TWO

His Summit

IF YOU HAVE TIME TO READ THIS CHAPTER, you probably don't need to.

If you are reading slowly in order to have something to occupy your time . . . if your reading hour is leisurely sandwiched between a long stroll and a good nap . . . if your list of things to do today was done an hour after you got up . . . then you might want to skip over to the next chapter. You probably have mastered the message of the next few pages.

If, however, you are reading in your car with one eye on the stoplight . . . or in the airport with one ear listening for your flight . . . or in the baby's room with one hand rocking the crib . . . or in bed late at night, knowing you have to get up early in the morning . . . then read on, friend. This chapter is for you.

You are in a hurry. America is in a hurry. Time has

skyrocketed in value. The value of any commodity depends on its scarcity. And time that once was abundant now is going to the highest bidder.

A man in Florida bills his ophthalmologist ninety dollars for keeping him waiting one hour.

A woman in California hires someone to do her shopping for her—out of a catalog.

Twenty bucks will pay someone to pick up your cleaning.

Fifteen hundred bucks will buy a fax machine . . . for your car.

Greeting cards can be purchased to express to your children things you want to say, but don't have time to: "Have a great day at school" or "I wish I were there to tuck you in."

America—the country of shortcuts and fast lanes. (We're the only nation on earth with a mountain called "Rushmore.")

"Time," according to pollster Louis Harris, "may have become the most precious commodity in the land."

Do we really have less time? Or is it just our imagination?

In 1965 a testimony before a Senate subcommittee claimed the future looked bright for free time in America. By 1985, predicted the report, Americans would be working twenty-two hours a week and would be able to retire at age thirty-eight.

The reason? The computer age would usher in a gleaming array of advances that would do our work for us while stabilizing our economy.

Take the household, they cited. Microwaves, quickfix foods, and food processors will pave the way into the carefree future. And the office? Well, you know that old stencil machine? It'll be replaced by a copier. And the files? Computers are the files of the future. And that electric typewriter? Don't get too attached to it; a computer will do its work, too.

And now, years later, we have everything the report

promised. The computers are byting, the VCRs are recording, the fax machines are faxing. Yet the clocks are still ticking, and people are still running. The truth is, the average amount of leisure time has shrunk 37 percent since 1973. The average work week has increased from forty-one to forty-seven hours. (And, for many of you, forty-seven hours would be a calm week.) [1]

Why didn't the forecast come true? What did the committee overlook? They misjudged the appetite of the consumer. As the individualism of the sixties led to the materialism of the eighties, the free time gained for us by technology didn't make us relax; it made us run. Gadgets provided more time . . . more time meant more potential money . . . more potential money meant more time needed . . . and round and round it went. Lives grew louder as demands became greater. And as demands became greater, lives grew emptier.

"I've got so many irons in the fire, I can't keep any of them hot," complained one young father.

Can you relate?

When I was ten years old, my mother enrolled me in piano lessons. Now, many youngsters excel at the keyboard. Not me. Spending thirty minutes every afternoon tethered to a piano bench was a torture just one level away from swallowing broken glass. The metronome inspected each second with glacial slowness before it was allowed to pass.

Some of the music, though, I learned to enjoy. I hammered the staccatos. I belabored the crescendos.

The thundering finishes I kettle-drummed. But there was one instruction in the music I could never obey to my teacher's satisfaction. The rest. The zigzagged command to do nothing. Nothing! What sense does that make? Why sit at the piano and pause when you can pound?

"Because," my teacher patiently explained, "music is always sweeter after a rest."

It didn't make sense to me at age ten. But now, a few

decades later, the words ring with wisdom—divine wisdom. In fact, the words of my teacher remind me of the convictions of another Teacher.

"When he saw the crowds, he went up on a mountainside. . . ."

Don't read the sentence so fast you miss the surprise. Matthew didn't write what you would expect him to. The verse doesn't read, "When he saw the crowds, he went into their midst." Or "When he saw the crowds, he healed their hurts." Or "When he saw the crowds, he seated them and began to teach them." On other occasions he did that . . . but not this time.

Before he went to the masses, he went to the mountain. Before the disciples encountered the crowds, they encountered the Christ. And before they faced the people, they were reminded of the sacred.

♔

I often write late at night. Not necessarily because I want to, but because sanity only comes to our house after the ten o'clock news.

From the moment I get home in the afternoon to the minute I sit down at this computer some five hours later, the motion is nonstop. Within thirty seconds of my entering the door, both of my knees are attacked by two squealing girls. A fuzzy-headed infant is placed in my arms and a welcome-home kiss is placed on my lips.

"The cavalry is here," I announce.

"And none too soon," my wife, Denalyn, replies with a grateful smile.

The next few hours bring a chorus of family noises: giggles, clanging dishes, rumbles on the floor, screams of agony over stumped toes, splashes in the bath, and thuds from toys tossed in the basket. The conversation is as continuous as it is predictable.

"Can I have more pie?"

"Jenna has my doll!"

"Can I hold the baby?"

"Honey, where is the pacifier?"

"Are there any clean gowns in the dryer?"

"Girls, it's time to go to bed.

"One more song?"

Then, eventually, the nightly hurricane passes, and the roar subsides. Mom looks at Dad. The day's damage is surveyed and cleaned up. Mom goes to bed, and Dad goes into the playroom to write.

That's where I am now. I sit in the stillness accompanied by the tap of a computer keyboard, the aroma of coffee, and the rhythm of the dishwasher. What was a playroom thirty minutes ago is now a study. And, what is a study now may—just may—become a sanctuary. For what may happen in the next few minutes borders on the holy.

The quietness will slow my pulse, the silence will open my ears, and something sacred will happen. The soft slap of sandaled feet will break the stillness, a pierced hand will extend a quiet invitation, and I will follow.

I wish I could say it happens every night; it doesn't. Some nights he asks and I don't listen. Other nights he asks and I just don't go. But some nights I hear his poetic whisper, "Come to me, all you who are weary and burdened . . ."[2] and I follow. I leave behind the budgets, bills, and deadlines and walk the narrow trail up the mountain with him.

You've been there. You've escaped the sandy foundations of the valley and ascended his grand outcropping of granite. You've turned your back on the noise and sought his voice. You've stepped away from the masses and followed the Master as he led you up the winding path to the summit.

His summit. Clean air. Clear view. Crisp breeze. The roar of the marketplace is down there, and the perspective of the peak is up here.

Gently your guide invites you to sit on the rock above the tree line and look out with him at the ancient peaks that will never erode. "What is necessary is still what is sure," he confides. "just remember:

"You'll go nowhere tomorrow that I haven't already been.

"Truth will still triumph.

"Death will still die.

"The victory is yours.

"And delight is one decision away— seize it."

The sacred summit. A place of permanence in a world of transition.

Think about the people in your world. Can't you tell the ones who have been to his mountain? Oh, their problems aren't any different. And their challenges are just as severe. But there is a stubborn peace that enshrines them. A confidence that life isn't toppled by unmet budgets or rerouted airplanes. A serenity that softens the corners of their lips. A contagious delight sparkling in their eyes.

And in their hearts reigns a fortresslike confidence that the valley can be endured, even enjoyed, because the mountain is only a decision away.

I read recently about a man who had breathed the summit air. His trips up the trail began early in his life and sustained him to the end. A few days before he died, a priest went to visit him in the hospital. As the priest entered the room, he noticed an empty chair beside the man's bed. The priest asked him if someone had been by to visit. The old man smiled, "I place Jesus on that chair, and I talk to him."

The priest was puzzled, so the man explained. "Years ago a friend told me that prayer was as simple as talking to a good friend. So every day I pull up a chair, invite Jesus to sit, and we have a good talk."

Some days later, the daughter of this man came to the parish house to inform the priest that her father had just died. "Because he seemed so content," she said, "I left him in his room alone for a couple of hours. When I got back to the room, I found him dead. I noticed a strange thing, though: His head was resting, not on the pillow, but on an empty chair that was beside his bed."[3]

Learn a lesson from the man with the chair. Make note of the music teacher and the rest. Take a trip with the King to the mountain peak. It's pristine, uncrowded, and on top of the world. Stubborn joy begins by breathing deep up there before you go crazy down here.

Oops, I think I hear someone calling your flight. . . .

Blessed are the
poor in spirit . . .

Three

The Affluent Poor

WE COULD BEGIN WITH SARAI LAUGHING. HER wrinkled face buried in bony hands. Her shoulders shaking. Her lungs wheezing. She knows she shouldn't laugh; it's not kosher to laugh at what God says. But just as she catches her breath and wipes away the tears, she thinks about it again—and a fresh wave of hilarity doubles her over.

We could begin with Peter staring. It's a stunned stare. His eyes are the size of grapefruits. He's oblivious to the fish piled to his knees and to the water lapping over the edge of the boat. He's deaf to the demands that he snap out of it and help. Peter is numb, absorbed in one thought—a thought too zany to say aloud.

We could begin with Paul resting. For three days he has wrestled; now he rests. He sits on the floor, in the corner. His face is haggard. His stomach is empty.

His lips are parched. Bags droop beneath the blinded eyes. But there is a slight smile on his lips. A fresh stream is flowing into a stagnant pool, and the water is sweet.

But let's not begin with these. Let's begin elsewhere.

Let's begin with the New Testament yuppie negotiating.

♔

He's rich. Italian shoes. Tailored suit. His money is invested. His plastic is golden. He lives like he flies—first class.

He's young. He pumps away fatigue at the gym and slam-dunks old age on the court. His belly is flat, his eyes sharp. Energy is his trademark, and death is an eternity away.

He's powerful. If you don't think so, just ask him. You got questions? He's got answers. You got problems? He's got solutions. You got dilemmas? He's got opinions. He knows where he's going, and he'll be there tomorrow. He's the new generation. So the old had better pick up the pace or pack their bags.

He has mastered the three "Ps" of yuppiedom. Prosperity. Posterity. Power. He's the rich . . . young . . . ruler.[1]

Till today, life for him has been a smooth cruise down a neon avenue. But today he has a question. A casual concern or a genuine fear? We don't know. We do know he has come for some advice.

For one so used to calling the shots, calling on this carpenter's son for help must be awkward. For a man of his pedigree to seek the counsel of a country rube is not standard procedure. But this is no standard question.

"Teacher," he asks, "what good thing must I do to get eternal life?" The wording of his question betrays his misunderstanding. He thinks he can get eternal life as he gets everything else—by his own strength.

"What must I do?"

What are the requirements, Jesus? What's the break-even point? No need for chitchat; go straight to the bottom line. How much do I need to invest to be certain of my return?

Jesus' answer is intended to make him wince. "If you want to enter life, obey the commandments."

A man with half a conscience would have thrown up his hands at that point. "Keep the commandments? Keep the commandments! Do you know how many commandments there are? Have you read the Law lately? I've tried—honestly, I've tried—but I can't."

That is what the ruler should say, but confession is the farthest thing from his mind. Instead of asking for help, he grabs a pencil and paper and asks for the list.

"Which ones?" He licks his pencil and arches an eyebrow.

Jesus indulges him. "Do not murder, do not commit adultery, do not steal, do not give false testimony, honor your father and mother, and love your neighbor as yourself."

"Great!" thinks the yuppie as he finishes the notes. "Now I've got the quiz. Let's see if I pass.

"Murder? Of course not. Adultery? Well, nothing any red-blooded boy wouldn't do. Stealing? A little extortion, but all justifiable. False testimony? Hmmmm . . . let's move on. Honor your father and mother? Sure, I see them on holidays. Love your neighbor as yourself . . . ?

"Hey," he grins, "a piece of cake. I've done all of these. In fact, I've done them since I was a kid." He swaggers a bit and hooks a thumb in his belt. "Got any other commandments you want to run past me?"

How Jesus keeps from laughing—or crying—is beyond me. The question that was intended to show the ruler how he falls short only convinces him that he stands tall. He's a child dripping water on the floor while telling his mom he hasn't been in the rain.

Jesus gets to the point. "If you want to be perfect, then go sell your possessions and give to the poor, and you will have treasure in heaven."

The statement leaves the young man distraught and the disciples bewildered.

Their question could be ours: "Who then can be saved?"

Jesus' answer shell-shocks the listeners, "With man this is impossible. . . .

Impossible.

He doesn't say improbable. He doesn't say unlikely. He doesn't even say it will be tough. He says it is "impossible." No chance. No way. No loopholes. No hope. Impossible. It's impossible to swim the Pacific. It's impossible to go to the moon on the tail of a kite. You can't climb Mount Everest with a picnic basket and a walking stick. And unless somebody does something, you don't have a chance of going to heaven.

Does that strike you as cold? All your life you've been rewarded according to your performance. You get grades according to your study. You get commendations according to your success. You get money in response to your work.

That's why the rich young ruler thought heaven was just a payment away. It only made sense. You work hard, you pay your dues, and "zap"—your account is credited as paid in full. Jesus says, "No way." What you want costs far more than what you can pay. You don't need a system, you need a Savior. You don't need a resume, you need a Redeemer. For "what is impossible with men is possible with God."[2]

Don't miss the thrust of this verse: You cannot save yourself. Not through the right rituals. Not through the right doctrine. Not through the right devotion. Not through the right goose bumps. Jesus' point is crystal clear. It is impossible for human beings to save themselves.

You see, it wasn't the money that hindered the rich man; it was the self-sufficiency. It wasn't the possessions; it was the pomp. It wasn't the big bucks; it was the big head. "How hard it is for the rich to enter the kingdom of God!"[3] It's not just the rich who have difficulty. So do the educated, the strong, the good-looking, the popular, the religious. So do you if you think your piety or power qualifies you as a kingdom candidate.

And if you have trouble digesting what Jesus said to the rich young ruler, then his description of the judgment day will stick in your throat.

It's a prophetic picture of the final day: "Many will say to me on that day, 'Lord, Lord, did we not prophesy in your name, and in your name drive out demons and perform many miracles?'"[4]

Astounding. These people are standing before the throne of God and bragging about themselves. The great trumpet has sounded, and they are still tooting their own horns. Rather than sing his praises, they sing their own. Rather than worship God, they read their resumes. When they should be speechless, they speak. In the very aura of the King they boast of self. What is worse—their arrogance or their blindness?

You don't impress the officials at NASA with a paper airplane. You don't boast about your crayon sketches in the presence of Picasso. You don't claim equality with Einstein because you can write "H2O."

And you don't boast about your goodness in the presence of the Perfect.

"Then I will tell them plainly, 'I never knew you. Away from me, you evildoers.'"[5]

Mark it down. God does not save us because of what we've done. Only a puny god could be bought with tithes. Only an egotistical god would be impressed with our pain. Only a temperamental god could be satisfied by sacrifices. Only a heartless god would sell salvation to the highest bidders.

And only a great God does for his children what they can't do for themselves.

That is the message of Paul: "For what the law was powerless to do . . . God did."[6]

And that is the message of the first beatitude.

"Blessed are the poor in spirit. . . ."

The jewel of joy is given to the impoverished spirits, not the affluent.[7] God's delight is received upon surrender, not awarded upon conquest. The first step to joy is a plea for help, an acknowledgment of moral destitution, an admission of inward paucity. Those who taste God's presence have declared spiritual bankruptcy and are aware of their spiritual crisis. Their cupboards are bare. Their pockets are empty. Their options are gone. They have long since stopped demanding justice; they are pleading for mercy.[8]

They don't brag; they beg.

They ask God to do for them what they can't do without him. They have seen how holy God is and how sinful they are and have agreed with Jesus' statement, "Salvation is impossible."

Oh, the irony of God's delight—born in the parched soil of destitution rather than the fertile ground of achievement.

It's a different path, a path we're not accustomed to taking. We don't often declare our impotence. Admission of failure is not usually admission into joy. Complete confession is not commonly followed by total pardon. But then again, God has never been governed by what is common.

. . . for theirs is the
kingdom of heaven.

Four

The Kingdom of the Absurd

THE KINGDOM OF HEAVEN. ITS CITIZENS ARE DRUNK on wonder.

Consider the case of Sarai.[1] She is in her golden years, but God promises her a son. She gets excited. She visits the maternity shop and buys a few dresses. She plans her shower and remodels her tent . . . but no son. She eats a few birthday cakes and blows out a lot of candles . . . still no son. She goes through a decade of wall calendars . . . still no son.

So Sarai decides to take matters into her own hands. ("Maybe God needs me to take care of this one.")

She convinces Abram that time is running out. ("Face it, Abe, you ain't getting any younger, either.") She commands her maid, Hagar, to go into Abram's tent and see if he needs anything. ("And I mean 'anything'!") Hagar goes in a maid. She comes out a mom. And the problems begin.

Hagar is haughty. Sarai is jealous. Abram is dizzy from the dilemma. And God calls the baby boy a "wild donkey"—an appropriate name for one born out of stubbornness and destined to kick his way into history.

It isn't the cozy family Sarai expected. And it isn't a topic Abram and Sarai bring up very often at dinner.

Finally, fourteen years later, when Abram is pushing a century of years and Sarai ninety . . . when Abram has stopped listening to Sarai's advice, and Sarai has stopped giving it . . . when the wallpaper in the nursery is faded and the baby furniture is several seasons out of date . . . when the topic of the promised child brings sighs and tears and long looks into a silent sky . . . God pays them a visit and tells them they had better select a name for their new son.

Abram and Sarai have the same response: laughter. They laugh partly because it is too good to happen and partly because it might. They laugh because they have given up hope, and hope born anew is always funny before it is real.

They laugh at the lunacy of it all.

Abram looks over at Sarai—toothless and snoring in her rocker, head back and mouth wide open, as fruitful as a pitted prune and just as wrinkled. And he cracks up. He tries to contain it, but he can't. He has always been a sucker for a good joke.

Sarai is just as amused. When she hears the news, a cackle escapes before she can contain it. She mumbles something about her husband's needing a lot more than what he's got and then laughs again.

They laugh because that is what you do when someone says he can do the impossible. They laugh a little *at* God, and a lot *with* God—for God is laughing, too. Then, with the smile still on his face, he gets busy doing what he does best—the unbelievable.

He changes a few things—beginning with their names. Abram, the father of one, will now be Abraham, the father of a multitude. Sarai, the barren one, will now be Sarah, the mother.

But their names aren't the only things God changes. He changes their minds. He changes their faith. He changes the number of their tax deductions. He changes the way they define the word *impossible*.

But most of all, he changes Sarah's attitude about trusting God. Were she to hear Jesus' statement about being poor in spirit, she could give a testimony: "He's right. I do things my way, I get a headache. I let God take over, I get a son. You try to figure that out. All I know is I am the first lady in town to pay her pediatrician with a Social Security check."

♛

Two thousand years later, here's another testimony[2]:

"The last thing I wanted to do was fish. But that was exactly what Jesus wanted to do. I had fished all night. My arms ached. My eyes burned. My neck was sore. All I wanted was to go home and let my wife rub the knots out of my back.

"It had been a long night. I don't know how many times we had thrown that net into the blackness and heard it slap against the sea. I don't know how many times we had held the twine rope as the net sank into the water. All night we had waited for that bump, that tug, that jerk that would clue us to haul in the catch . . . but it had never come. At daybreak, I was ready to go home.

"Just as I was about to leave the beach, I noticed a crowd coming toward me. They were following a lanky fellow who walked with a broad swing and wide gait. He saw me and called my name. 'Morning, Jesus!' I called back. Though he was a hundred yards away, I could see his white smile. 'Quite a crowd, eh?' he yelled, motioning at the mass behind him. I nodded and sat down to watch.

"He stopped near the edge of the water and began to speak. Though I couldn't hear much, I could see a lot. I could see more and more people coming. With all the pressing and shoving, it's a wonder Jesus didn't get pushed down into the water. He was already knee-deep when he looked at me.

"I didn't have to think twice. He climbed into my boat, and John and I followed. We pushed out a bit. I leaned back against the bow, and Jesus began to teach.

"It seemed that half of Israel was on the beach. Men had left their work, women their household chores. I even recognized some priests. How they all listened! They scarcely moved, yet their eyes danced as if they were in some way seeing what they could be.

"When Jesus finished, he turned to me. I stood and had begun to pull anchor when he said, 'Push out into the deep, Peter. Let's fish.'

"I groaned. I looked at John. We were thinking the same thing. As long as he wanted to use the boat for a platform, that was fine. But to use it for a fishing boat—that was our territory. I started to tell this carpenter-teacher, 'You stick to preaching, and I'll stick to fishing.' But I was more polite: 'We worked all night. We didn't catch a thing.'

"He just looked at me. I looked at John. John was waiting for my cue . . .

"I wish I could say I did it because of love. I wish I could say I did it out of devotion. But I can't. All I can say is there is a time to question and a time to listen. So, as much with a grunt as with a prayer, we pushed out.

"With every stroke of the oar, I muttered. With every pull of the paddle, I grumbled. 'No way. No way. Impossible. I may not know much, but I know fishing. And all we're going to come back with are some wet nets.'

"The noise on the beach grew distant, and soon the only sound was the smack of the waves against the hull. Finally we cast anchor. I picked up the heavy netting, held it waist-high, and started to throw it. That's when I caught a glimpse of Jesus out of the corner of my eye. His expression stopped me in midmotion.

"He was leaning out over the edge of the boat, looking

out into the water where I was about to throw the net. And, get this, he was smiling. A boyish grin pushed his cheeks high and turned his round eyes into half-moons—the kind of smile you see when a child gives a gift to a friend and watches as it is unwrapped.

"He noticed me looking at him, and he tried to hide the smile, but it persisted. It pushed at the corners of his mouth until a flash of teeth appeared. He had given me a gift and could scarcely contain himself as I opened it.

"'Boy, is he in for a disappointment,' I thought as I threw the net. It flew high, spreading itself against the blue sky and floating down until it flopped against the surface, then sank. I wrapped the rope once around my hand and sat back for the long wait.

"But there was no wait. The slack rope yanked taut and tried to pull me overboard. I set my feet against the side of the boat and yelled for help. John and Jesus sprang to my side.

"We got the net in just before it began to tear. I'd never seen such a catch. It was like plopping down a sack of rocks in the boat. We began to take in water. John screamed for the other boat to help us.

"It was quite a scene: four fishermen in two boats, knee-deep in fish, and one carpenter seated on our bow, relishing the pandemonium.

"That's when I realized who he was. And that's when I realized who I was: I was the one who told God what he couldn't do!

"'Go away from me, Lord; I'm a sinful man.' There wasn't anything else I could say.

"I don't know what he saw in me, but he didn't leave. Maybe he thought if I would let him tell me how to fish, I would let him tell me how to live.

"It was a scene I would see many times over the next couple of years—in cemeteries with the dead, on hillsides with the hungry, in storms with the frightened, on roadsides with the sick. The characters would change, but the theme wouldn't. When we would say, 'No way,' he would say, 'My way.' Then the ones who doubted would scramble to salvage the blessing. And the One who gave it would savor the surprise."

♔

"My power shows up best in weak people."[3]

God said those words. Paul wrote them down. God said he was looking for empty vessels more than strong muscles. Paul proved it.

Before he encountered Christ, Paul had been somewhat of a hero among the Pharisees. You might say he was their Wyatt Earp. He kept the law and order—or, better said, revered the Law and gave the orders. Good Jewish moms held him up as an example of a good Jewish boy. He was given the seat of honor at the Jerusalem Lions' Club Wednesday luncheon. He had a "Who's Who in Judaism" paperweight on his desk and was selected "Most Likely to Succeed" by his graduating class. He was quickly establishing himself as the heir apparent to his teacher, Gamaliel.

If there is such a thing as a religious fortune, Paul had it. He was a spiritual billionaire, born with one foot in heaven, and he knew it:

> If anyone ever had reason to hope that he could save himself, it would be I. If others could be saved by what they are, certainly I could! For I went through the Jewish initiation ceremony when I was eight days old, having been born into a pure-blooded Jewish home that was a branch of the old original Benjamin family. So I was a real Jew if there ever was one! What's more, I was a member of the Pharisees who demand the strictest obedience to every Jewish law and custom. And sincere? Yes, so much so that I greatly persecuted the Church; and I tried to obey every Jewish rule and regulation down to the very last point.[4]

Blue-blooded and wild-eyed, this young zealot was hell-bent on keeping the kingdom pure—and that meant keeping the Christians out. He marched through the countryside like a general demanding that backslidden Jews salute the flag of the motherland or kiss their family and hopes good-bye.

All this came to a halt, however, on the shoulder of a highway. Equipped with subpoenas, handcuffs, and a posse, Paul was on his way to do a little personal evangelism in Damascus. That's when someone slammed on the stadium lights, and he heard the voice.

When he found out whose voice it was, his jaw hit the ground, and his body followed. He braced himself for the worst. He knew it was all over. He felt the noose around his neck. He smelled the flowers in the hearse. He prayed that death would be quick and painless.

But all he got was silence and the first of a lifetime of surprises.

He ended up bewildered and befuddled in a borrowed bedroom. God left him there a few days with scales on his eyes so thick that the only direction he could look was inside himself. And he didn't like what he saw.

He saw himself for what he really was—to use his own words, the worst of sinners.[5] A legalist. A killjoy. A bumptious braggart who claimed to have mastered God's code. A dispenser of justice who weighed salvation on a panscale.

That's when Ananias found him. He wasn't much to look at—haggard and groggy after three days of turmoil. Sarai wasn't much to look at either, nor was Peter. But what the three have in common says more than a volume of systematic theology. For when they gave up, God stepped in, and the result was a rollercoaster ride straight into the kingdom.

Paul was a step ahead of the rich young ruler. He knew better than to strike a deal with God. He didn't make any excuses; he just pleaded for mercy. Alone in the room with his sins on his conscience and blood on his hands, he asked to be cleansed.

Ananias' instructions to Paul are worth reading: "What are you waiting for? Get up, be baptized and wash your sins away, calling on his name."[6]

He didn't have to be told twice. The legalist Saul was buried, and the liberator Paul was born. He was never the same afterwards. And neither was the world.

Stirring sermons, dedicated disciples, and six thousand miles of trails. If his sandals weren't slapping, his pen was writing. If he wasn't explaining the mystery of grace, he was articulating the theology that would determine the course of Western civilization.

All of his words could be reduced to one sentence. "We preach Christ crucified."[7] It wasn't that he lacked other sermon outlines; it was just that he couldn't exhaust the first one.

The absurdity of the whole thing kept him going. Jesus should have finished him on the road. He should have left him for the buzzards. He should have sent him to hell. But he didn't. He sent him to the lost.

Paul himself called it crazy. He described it with phrases like "stumbling block" and "foolishness," but chose in the end to call it "grace."[8]

And he defended his unquenchable loyalty by saying, "The love of Christ leaves [me] no choice."[9]

Paul never took a course in missions. He never sat in on a committee meeting. He never read a book on church growth. He was just inspired by the Holy Spirit and punch-drunk on the love that makes the impossible possible: salvation.

The message is gripping: Show a man his failures without Jesus, and the result will be found in the roadside gutter. Give a man religion without reminding him of his filth, and the result will be arrogance in a three-piece suit. But get the two in the same heart—get sin to meet Savior and Savior to meet sin—and the result just might be another Pharisee turned preacher who sets the world on fire.

Four people: the rich young ruler, Sarah, Peter, Paul. A curious thread strings the four together—their names.

The final three had their names changed—Sarai to Sarah, Simon to Peter, Saul to Paul. But the first one, the young yuppie, is never mentioned by name.

Perhaps that's the clearest explanation of the first beatitude. The one who made a name for himself is nameless. But the ones who called on Jesus' name—and his name only—got new names and, even more, new life.

Blessed are
those who mourn . . .

Five

The Prison of Pride

AS BRAZILIAN JAIL CELLS GO THIS ONE WASN'T too bad. There was a fan on the table. The twin beds each had a thin mattress and a pillow. There was a toilet and a sink.

No, it wasn't too bad. But, then again, I didn't have to stay.

Anibal did. He was there to stay.

Even more striking than his name (pronounced "uh-nee-ball") was the man himself. The tattooed anchor on his forearm symbolized his personality—cast-iron. His broad chest stretched his shirt. The slightest movement of his arm bulged his biceps. His face was as leathery in texture as it was in color. His glare could blister a foe. His smile was an explosion of white teeth.

But today the glare was gone and the smile was forced. Anibal wasn't on the street where he was the boss; he was in a jail where he was the prisoner.

He'd killed a man—a "neighborhood punk," as Anibal called him, a restless teenager who sold marijuana to the kids on the street and made a nuisance of himself with his mouth. One night the drug dealer had used his mouth one time too many and Anibal had decided to silence it. He'd left the crowded bar where the two of them had been arguing, gone home, taken a pistol out of a drawer, and walked back to the bar. Anibal had entered and called the boy's name. The drug dealer had turned around in time to take a bullet in the heart.

Anibal was guilty. Period. His only hope was that the judge would agree that he had done society a favor by getting rid of a neighborhood problem. He would be sentenced within the month.

I came to know Anibal through a Christian friend, Daniel. Anibal had lifted weights at Daniel's gym. Daniel had given Anibal a Bible and had visited him several times. This time Daniel took me with him to tell Anibal about Jesus.

Our study centered on the cross. We talked about guilt. We talked about forgiveness. The eyes of the murderer softened at the thought that the one who knows him best loves him most. His heart was touched as we discussed heaven, a hope that no executioner could take from him.

But as we began to discuss conversion, Anibal's face began to harden. The head that had leaned toward me in interest now straightened in caution. Anibal didn't like my statement that the first step in coming to God is an admission of guilt. He was uneasy with words like "I've been wrong" and "forgive me." Saying "I'm sorry" was out of character for him. He had never backed down before any man, and he wasn't about to do it now—even if the man were God.

In one final effort to pierce his pride, I asked him, "Don't you want to go to heaven?"

"Sure," he grunted.

"Are you ready?"

Earlier he might have boasted yes, but now he'd heard too many verses from the Bible. He knew better.

He stared at the concrete floor for a long time, meditating on the question. For a moment I thought his stony heart was cracking. For a second, it appeared that burly Anibal would for the first time admit his failures.

But I was wrong. The eyes that lifted to meet mine weren't tear-filled; they were angry. They weren't the eyes of a repentant prodigal; they were the eyes of an angry prisoner.

"All right," he shrugged. "I'll become one of your Christians. But don't expect me to change the way I live."

The conditional answer left my mouth bitter. "You don't draw up the rules," I told him. "It's not a contract that you negotiate before you sign. It's a gift—an undeserved gift! But to receive it, you have to admit that you need it."

"OK." He ran his thick fingers through his hair and stood up. "But don't expect to see me at church on Sundays."

I sighed. How many knocks in the head does a guy need before he'll ask for help?

As I watched Anibal pace back and forth in the tiny cell, I realized that his true prison was not made of bricks and mortar, but of pride. He was twice imprisoned. Once because of murder, and once because of stubbornness. Once by his country, and once by himself.

The prison of pride. For most of us it isn't as blatant as it was with Anibal, but the characteristics are the same. The upper lip is just as stiff. The chin ever protrudes upward, and the heart is just as hard.

A prison of pride is filled with self-made men and women determined to pull themselves up by their own bootstraps even if they land on their rear ends. It doesn't matter what they did or to whom they did it or where they will end up; it only matters that "I did it my way."

You've seen the prisoners. You've seen the alcoholic who won't admit his drinking problem. You've seen the woman who refuses to talk to anyone about her fears. You've seen the businessman who adamantly rejects help, even when his dreams are falling apart.

Perhaps to see such a prisoner all you have to do is look in the mirror.

"*If* we confess our sins, he is faithful and just . . ."[1] The biggest word in Scripture just might be that two-letter one, *if*. For confessing sins—admitting failure—is exactly what prisoners of pride refuse to do.

You know the lingo:

"Well, I may not be perfect, but I'm better than Hitler and certainly kinder than Idi Amin!"

"Me a sinner? Oh, sure, I get rowdy every so often, but I'm a pretty good ol' boy."

"Listen, I'm just as good as the next guy. I pay my taxes. I coach the Little League team. I even make donations to Red Cross. Why, God's probably proud to have somebody like me on his team."

Justification. Rationalization. Comparison. These are the tools of the jailbird. They sound good. They sound familiar. They even sound American. But in the kingdom, they sound hollow.

"Blessed are those who mourn . . ."

To mourn for your sins is a natural outflow of poverty of spirit. The second beatitude should follow the first. But that's not always the case. Many deny their weakness. Many know they are wrong, yet pretend they are right. As a result, they never taste the exquisite sorrow of repentance.

Of all the paths to joy, this one has to be the strangest. True blessedness, Jesus says, begins with deep sadness.

"Blessed are those who know they are in trouble and have enough sense to admit it."[2]

Joy through mourning? Freedom through surrender? Liberty through confession?

Want a model? Let me introduce you to one.

He was nitroglycerin; if you bumped him the wrong way, he blew up. He made a living with his hands and got in trouble with his mouth. In some ways, he had a lot in common with Anibal. If he had had a tattoo, it would have been a big, black anchor on his forearm. If they had had bumper stickers, his would have read, "I don't get mad; I get even."

He was a man among men on the Galilean sea. His family called him Simon, but his master called him "Rocky." You know him as Peter.

And though he might not have known everything about self-control, he knew one thing about being a fisherman. He knew better than to get caught in a storm. . . .

And this night, Peter knows he is in trouble.

The winds roar down onto the Sea of Galilee like a hawk on a rat. Lightning zigzags across the black sky. The clouds vibrate with thunder. The rain taps, then pops, then slaps against the deck of the boat until everyone aboard is soaked and shaking. Ten-foot waves pick them up and slam them down again with bonejarring force.

These drenched men don't look like a team of apostles who are only a decade away from changing the world. They don't look like an army that will march to the ends of the earth and reroute history. They don't look like a band of pioneers who will soon turn the world upside down. No, they look more like a handful of shivering sailors who are wondering if the next wave they ride will be their last.

And you can be sure of one thing. The one with the widest eyes is the one with the biggest biceps—Peter. He's seen these storms before. He's seen the wreckage and bloated bodies float to shore. He knows what the fury of wind and wave can do. And he knows that times like this are not times to make a name for yourself; they're times to get some help.

That is why, when he sees Jesus walking on the water toward the boat, he is the first to say, "Lord, if it's you . . . tell me to come to you on the water."[3]

Now, some say this statement is a simple request for verification. Peter, they suggest, wants to prove that the one they see is really Jesus and not just anyone who might be on a stroll across a storm-tossed sea in the middle of the night. (You can't be too careful, you know.)

So, Peter consults his notes, removes his glasses, clears his throat, and asks a question any good attorney would. "Ahem, Jesus, if you would kindly demonstrate your power and prove your divinity by calling me out on the water with you, I would be most appreciative."

I don't buy that. I don't think Peter is seeking clarification; I think he's trying to save his neck. He is aware of two facts: He's going down, and Jesus is staying up. And it doesn't take him too long to decide where he would rather be.

Perhaps a better interpretation of his request would be, "Jeeeeeeeesus. If that is you, then get me out of here!"

"Come on" is the invitation.

And Peter doesn't have to be told twice. It's not every day that you walk on water through waves that are taller than you are. But when faced with the alternative of sure death or possible life, Peter knows which one he wants.

The first few steps go well. But a few strides out onto the water, and he forgets to look to the One who got him there in the first place, and down he plunges.

At this point we see the major difference between Anibal and Peter—the difference between a man who hides his problem and one who admits it.

Anibal would be more concerned about his image than about his neck. He would prefer to go under rather than let his friends hear him ask for help. He would rather go down "his way" than get out "God's way."

Peter, on the other hand, knows better than to count the teeth in the mouth of a gift horse. He knows better than to bite the hand that can save him. His response may lack class—it probably wouldn't get him on the cover of *Gentleman's Quarterly* or even *Sports Illustrated*—but it gets him out of some deep water:

"Help me!"

And since Peter would rather swallow pride than water, a hand comes through the rain and pulls him up.

The message is clear.

As long as Jesus is one of many options, he is no option. As long as you can carry your burdens alone, you don't need a burden bearer. As long as your situation brings you no grief, you will receive no comfort. And as long as you can take him or leave him, you might as well leave him, because he won't be taken half-heartedly.

But when you mourn, when you get to the point of sorrow for your sins, when you admit that you have no other option but to cast all your cares on him, and when there is truly no other name that you can call, then cast all your cares on him, for he is waiting in the midst of the storm.

. . . for they will
be comforted.

Six

Touches of Tenderness

BEING A PARENT IS BETTER THAN A THEOLOGY course.

Two ten-year-old boys walked up to my five-year-old daughter on the bus yesterday, scowled at her, and demanded that she scoot over.

When I came home from work, she told me about it. "I wanted to cry, but I didn't. I just sat there—afraid."

My immediate impulse was to find out the names of the boys and punch their dads in the nose. But I didn't. I did what was more important. I pulled my little girl up into my lap and let her get lost inside my arms and told her not to worry about those old bullies because her daddy was here, and I'd make sure if any thugs ever got close to my princess they'd be taking their lives in their own hands, yessir.

And that was enough for Jenna. She bounded down and ran outside.

She came back a few minutes later, crying. Her elbow was scraped.

I picked her up and carried her into the bathroom for first aid. She tried to tell me what happened.

"I"—sniff, sniff—"was turning in circles"—sniff, sniff—"like a helicopter"—sniff, sniff—"and then I fell doaaaaawwwn," she wailed.

"It's gonna be OK," I said as I set her on the bathroom counter.

"Can I have a Band-Aid®?"

"Of course."

"A big one?"

"The biggest."

"Really?"

I stretched the adhesive bandage over the scrape and held her arm up in the mirror so she could see her badge of courage.

"Wow. Can I go show Mommy?"

"Sure." I smiled.

And that was enough for Jenna.

"Daddy."

The voice was coming from another world—the world of the awake. I ignored it and stayed in the world of slumber.

"Daddy." The voice was insistent.

I opened one eye. Andrea, our three-year-old, was at the edge of my bed only a few inches from my face.

"Daddy, I'm scared."

I opened the other eye. It was three in the morning.

"What's wrong?"

"I need a fwashwight in my woom.

"What?"

"I need a fwashwight in my woom."

"Why?"

" 'Cause it's dark."

I told her the lights were on. I told her the night light was on and the hall light was on.

"But Daddy," she objected, "what if I open my eyes and can't see anything?"

"Say that again."

"What if I open my eyes and can't see anything?"

Just as I was about to tell her that this was not the best time for questions on affliction, my wife interrupted. She explained to me that there was a power failure around midnight and Andrea must have awakened in the dark. No night light. No hall light. She had opened her eyes and had been unable to see anything. Just darkness.

Even the hardest of hearts would be touched by the thought of a child waking up in a darkness so black she couldn't find her way out of her room.

I climbed out of bed, picked Andrea up, got a flashlight out of the utility room, and carried her to her bed. All the while, I told her that Mom and Dad were here and that she didn't need to be afraid. I tucked her in and gave her a kiss.

And that was enough for Andrea.

♔

My child's feelings are hurt. I tell her she's special. My child is injured. I do whatever it takes to make her feel better.

My child is afraid. I won't go to sleep until she is secure.

I'm not a hero. I'm not a superstar. I'm not unusual. I'm a parent. When a child hurts, a parent does what comes naturally. He helps.

And after I help, I don't charge a fee. I don't ask for a favor in return. When my child cries, I don't tell her to buck up, act tough, and keep a stiff upper lip. Nor do I consult a list and ask her why she is still scraping the same elbow or waking me up again.

I'm not brilliant, but you don't have to be to remember that a child is not an adult. You don't have to be a child psychologist to know that kids are "under construction." You don't have to have the wisdom of Solomon to realize that they didn't ask to be here in the first place and that spilled milk can be wiped up and broken plates can be replaced.

I'm not a prophet, nor the son of one, but something tells me that in the whole scheme of things the tender moments described above are infinitely more valuable than anything I do in front of a computer screen or congregation. Something tells me that the moments of comfort I give my child are a small price to pay for the joy of someday seeing my daughter do for her daughter what her dad did for her.

Moments of comfort from a parent. As a father, I can tell you they are the sweetest moments in my day. They come naturally. They come willingly. They come joyfully.

If all of that is true, if I know that one of the privileges of fatherhood is to comfort a child, then why am I so reluctant to let my heavenly Father comfort me?

Why do I think he wouldn't want to hear about my problems? ("They are puny compared to people starving in India.")

Why do I think he is too busy for me? ("He's got a whole universe to worry about.")

Why do I think he's tired of hearing the same old stuff?

Why do I think he groans when he sees me coming?

Why do I think he consults his list when I ask for forgiveness and asks, "Don't you think you're going to the well a few too many times on this one?"

Why do I think I have to speak a holy language around him that I don't speak with anyone else?

Why do I think he won't do in a heartbeat to the Father of Lies what I thought about doing to the fathers of those bullies on the bus?

Do I think he was just being poetic when he asked me if the birds of the air and the grass of the field have a worry? (No sir.) And if they don't, why do I think I will? (Duh. . . .)[1]

Why do I not take him seriously when he questions, "If you, then, though you are evil, know how to give good gifts to your children, how much more will your Father in heaven give good gifts to those who ask him!"[2]

Why don't I let my Father do for me what I am more than willing to do for my own children?

I'm learning, though. Being a parent is better than a course on theology. Being a father is teaching me that when I am criticized, injured, or afraid, there is a Father who is ready to comfort me. There is a Father who will hold me until I'm better, help me until I can live with the hurt, and who won't go to sleep when I'm afraid of waking up and seeing the dark.

Ever.

And that's enough.

Blessed are

the meek . . .

Seven

The Glory in the Ordinary

THERE IS ONE WORD THAT DESCRIBES THE NIGHT he came—ordinary.

The sky was ordinary. An occasional gust stirred the leaves and chilled the air. The stars were diamonds sparkling on black velvet. Fleets of clouds floated in front of the moon.

It was a beautiful night—a night worth peeking out your bedroom window to admire—but not really an unusual one. No reason to expect a surprise. Nothing to keep a person awake. An ordinary night with an ordinary sky.

The sheep were ordinary. Some fat. Some scrawny. Some with barrel bellies. Some with twig legs. Common animals. No fleece made of gold. No history makers. No blue-ribbon winners. They were simply sheep—lumpy, sleeping silhouettes on a hillside.

And the shepherds. Peasants they were. Probably wearing all the clothes they owned. Smelling like sheep and looking just as woolly. They were conscientious, willing to spend the night with their flocks. But you won't find their staffs in a museum nor their writings in a library. No one asked their opinion on social justice or the application of the Torah. They were nameless and simple.

An ordinary night with ordinary sheep and ordinary shepherds. And were it not for a God who loves to hook an "extra" on the front of the ordinary, the night would have gone unnoticed. The sheep would have been forgotten, and the shepherds would have slept the night away.

But God dances amidst the common. And that night he did a waltz.

The black sky exploded with brightness. Trees that had been shadows jumped into clarity. Sheep that had been silent became a chorus of curiosity. One minute the shepherd was dead asleep, the next he was rubbing his eyes and staring into the face of an alien.

The night was ordinary no more.

The angel came in the night because that is when lights are best seen and that is when they are most needed. God comes into the common for the same reason.

His most powerful tools are the simplest.

♔

Consider the rod of Moses.[1] By this time in his life, Moses had been a shepherd as long as he had been a prince, and he'd grown accustomed to it. Herding sheep wasn't as lively as living with Egyptian royalty, but it had its moments, especially the moment God spoke to him through a burning bush that didn't burn up. God announced that Moses was his man to deliver the Israelites. Moses wasn't convinced he was the one for the job. God said that who Moses was didn't matter; what mattered was who God was. And God set out to demonstrate.

"Moses," spoke the voice from the bush, "throw down your staff."

Moses, who had walked this mountain for forty years, was not comfortable with the command.

"God, you know a lot about a lot of things, but you may not know that out here, well, you just don't go around throwing down your staff. You never know when . . ."

"Throw it down, Moses."

Moses threw it down. The rod became a snake, and Moses began to run.

"Moses!"

The old shepherd stopped.

"Pick up the snake."

Moses peered over his shoulder, first at the snake and then the bush, and then he gave the most courageous response he could muster.

"What?"

"Pick up the snake . . . by the tail." (God had to be smiling at this point.)

"God, I don't mean to object. I mean, you know a lot of things, but out here in the desert, well, you don't pick up snakes too often, and you *never* pick up snakes by the tail."

"Moses!"

"Yessir."

Just as Moses' hand touched the squirmy scales of the snake, it hardened. And Moses lifted up the rod. The same rod he would lift up in Pharaoh's court. The same rod he would lift up to divide the water and guide two million people through a desert. The rod that would remind Moses that if God can make a stick become a snake, then become a stick again—then perhaps he can do something with stubborn hearts and a stiff-necked people.

Perhaps he can do something with the common.

♔

Or consider another shepherd from Bethlehem.[2]

There are certain things anyone knows not to do. You don't try to lasso a tornado. You don't fight a lion with a toothpick. You don't sneeze into the wind. You don't go bear hunting with a cork gun. And you don't send a shepherd boy to battle a giant.

You don't, that is, unless you are out of options. Saul was. And it is when we are out of options that we are most ready for God's surprises.

Was Saul ever surprised!

The king tried to give David some equipment. "What do you want, boy? Shield? Sword? Grenades? Rifles? A helicopter? We'll make a Rambo out of you."

David had something else in mind. Five smooth stones and an ordinary leather sling.

The soldiers gasped. Saul sighed. Goliath jeered.

David swung. And God made his point. "Anyone who underestimates what God can do with the ordinary has rocks in his head."

♛

Or what about the blind man Jesus and the disciples discovered?[3]

The followers thought he was a great theological case study.

"Why do you think he's blind?" one asked.

"He must have sinned."

"No, it's his folks' fault."

"Jesus, what do you think? Why is he blind?"

"He's blind to show what God can do."

The apostles knew what was coming; they had seen this look in Jesus' eyes before. They knew what he was going to do, but they didn't know how he was going to do it. "Lightning? Thunder? A shout? A clap of the hands?" They all watched.

Jesus began to work his mouth a little. The onlookers stared. "What is he doing?" He moved his jaw as if he were chewing on something.

Some of the people began to get restless. Jesus just chewed. His jaw rotated around until he had what he wanted. Spit. Ordinary saliva.

If no one said it, somebody had to be thinking it: "Yuk!"

Jesus spat on the ground, stuck his finger into the puddle, and stirred. Soon it was a mud pie, and he smeared some of the mud across the blind man's eyes.

The same One who'd turned a stick into a scepter and a pebble into a missile now turned saliva and mud into a balm for the blind.

Once again, the mundane became majestic. Once again the dull became divine, the humdrum holy. Once again God's power was seen not through the ability of the instrument, but through its availability.

"Blessed are the meek," Jesus explained. Blessed are the available. Blessed are the conduits, the tunnels, the tools. Deliriously joyful are the ones who believe that if God has used sticks, rocks, and spit to do his will, then he can use us.

We would do well to learn a lesson from the rod, the rock, and the saliva. They didn't complain. They didn't question God's wisdom. They didn't suggest an alternative plan. Perhaps the reason the Father has used so many inanimate objects for his mission is that they don't tell him how to do his job!

It's like the story of the barber who became an artist. When asked why he changed professions, he replied, "A canvas doesn't tell me how to make it beautiful."

Neither do the meek.

That's why the announcement went first to the shepherds. They didn't ask God if he was sure he knew what he was doing. Had the angel gone to the theologians, they would have first consulted their commentaries. Had he gone to the elite, they would have looked around to see if anyone was watching. Had he gone to the successful, they would have first looked at their calendars.

So he went to the shepherds. Men who didn't have a reputation to protect or an ax to grind or a ladder to climb. Men who didn't know enough to tell God that angels don't sing to sheep and that messiahs aren't found wrapped in rags and sleeping in a feed trough.

♔

A small cathedral outside Bethlehem marks the supposed birthplace of Jesus. Behind a high altar in the church is a cave, a little cavern lit by silver lamps.

You can enter the main edifice and admire the ancient church. You can also enter the quiet cave where a star embedded in the floor recognizes the birth of the King. There is one stipulation, however. You have to stoop. The door is so low you can't go in standing up.

The same is true of the Christ. You can see the world standing tall, but to witness the Savior, you have to get on your knees.

So . . .

while the theologians were sleeping
and the elite were dreaming
and the successful were snoring,
the meek were kneeling.

They were kneeling before the One only the meek will see. They were kneeling in front of Jesus.

. . . for they will
inherit the earth.

Eight

The Bandit of Joy

HE WAS A PROFESSIONAL THIEF. HIS NAME STIRRED fear as the desert wind stirs tumbleweeds. He terrorized the Wells Fargo stage line for thirteen years, roaring like a tornado in and out of the Sierra Nevadas, spooking the most rugged frontiersmen. In journals from San Francisco to New York, his name became synonymous with the danger of the frontier.

During his reign of terror between 1875 and 1883, he is credited with stealing the bags and the breath away from twenty-nine different stagecoach crews. And he did it all without firing a shot.

His weapon was his reputation. His ammunition was intimidation.

A hood hid his face. No victim ever saw him. No artist ever sketched his features. No sheriff could ever track his trail. He never fired a shot or took a hostage.

He didn't have to. His presence was enough to paralyze.

Black Bart. A hooded bandit armed with a deadly weapon.

He reminds me of another thief—one who's still around. You know him. Oh you've never seen his face, either. You couldn't describe his voice or sketch his profile. But when he's near, you know it in a heartbeat.

If you've ever been in the hospital, you've felt the leathery brush of his hand against yours.

If you've ever sensed someone was following you, you've felt his cold breath down your neck.

If you've awakened late at night in a strange room, it was his husky whisper that stole your slumber.

You know him.

It was this thief who left your palms sweaty as you went for the job interview.

It was this con man who convinced you to swap your integrity for popularity.

And it was this scoundrel who whispered in your ear as you left the cemetery, "You may be next."

He's the Black Bart of the soul. He doesn't want your money. He doesn't want your diamonds. He won't go after your car. He wants something far more precious. He wants your peace of mind—your joy.

His name?

Fear.

His task is to take your courage and leave you timid and trembling. His *modus operandi is* to manipulate you with the mysterious, to taunt you with the unknown. Fear of death, fear of failure, fear of God, fear of tomorrow—his arsenal is vast. His goal? To create cowardly, joyless souls.

He doesn't want you to make the journey to the mountain. He figures if he can rattle you enough, you will take your eyes off the peaks and settle for a dull existence in the flatlands.

♔

A legend from India tells about a mouse who was terrified of cats until a magician agreed to transform him into a cat. That resolved his fear . . . until he met a dog, so the magician changed him into a dog. The mouse-turned-cat-turned-dog was content until he met a tiger—so, once again, the magician changed him into what he feared. But when the tiger came complaining that he had met a hunter, the magician refused to help. "I will make you into a mouse again, for though you have the body of a tiger, you still have the heart of a mouse."

Sound familiar? How many people do you know who have built a formidable exterior, only to tremble inside with fear? We tackle our anxieties by taking on the appearance of a tiger. We face our fears with force. Military power, security systems, defense strategy—all reflect a conviction that muscle creates security.

Or if we don't use force, we try other methods. We stockpile wealth. We seek security in things. We cultivate fame and seek status.

But do these approaches work? Can power, possessions, or popularity really deliver us from our fears?

If power could, then Joseph Stalin should have been fearless. Instead, this infamous Russian premier was afraid to go bed. He had seven different bedrooms. Each could be locked as tightly as a safe. In order to foil any would-be assassins, he slept in a different one each night. Five chauffeur-driven limousines transported him wherever he went, each with curtains closed so no one would know which contained Stalin. So deep-seated were his apprehensions that he employed a servant whose sole task was to monitor and protect his tea bags.[1]

If possessions conquered fear, the late billionaire Howard Hughes would have been fearless. But you probably know his story. His distrust of people and his paranoia of germs led this billionaire to Mexico, where he died a lonely death as a cadaverous hermit with a belly-length beard and corkscrew fingernails.[2]

What about popularity? Beatle John Lennon's fame as a singer, songwriter, and pop icon made him a household word, but his fears brought him misery. His biographers describe him as a frightened man, unwilling to sleep with the lights off and afraid to touch anything because of its filth.[3]

Though Stalin, Hughes, and Lennon are extreme cases, they are indicative ones. "Though you have the body of a tiger, you still have the heart of a mouse."

Parallel their stories with the life of a little-known but gutsy young man named Paul Keating. On a cold night in February 1980, twenty-seven-year-old Keating was walking home in Manhattan's Greenwich Village when he saw two armed muggers robbing a college student. Keating, a gentle, much-admired photographer for *Time* magazine, had every reason to avoid trouble. He didn't know the student. No one knew he saw the crime. He was outnumbered. He had nothing to gain and much to lose by taking the risk, and yet he jumped on the muggers. The victim escaped and ran to a nearby deli to call for help. Moments later, two shots cracked the night, and the muggers fled. Paul Keating was found dead on the pavement.

The city of New York posthumously awarded him a medal of heroism. I think you'll agree with the commentary offered by Mayor Edward Koch at the ceremony: "Nobody was watching Paul Keating on the street that night. Nobody made him step forward in the time of crisis. He did it because of who he was."[4]

Well put.

Courage is an outgrowth of who we are. Exterior supports may temporarily sustain, but only inward character creates courage.

And it is those inward convictions that Jesus is building in the Beatitudes. Remember, Matthew 5 is not a list of proverbs or a compilation of independent sayings, but rather a step-by-step description of how God rebuilds the believer's heart.

The first step is to ask for help—to become "poor in spirit" and admit our need for a Savior.

The next step is sorrow: "Blessed are those who mourn. . . ." Those who mourn are those who know they are wrong and say they are sorry. No excuses. No justification. Just tears.

The first two steps are admittance of inadequacy and repentance for pride. The next step is the one of renewal: "Blessed are the meek. . . ." Realization of weakness leads to the source of strength—God. And renewal comes when we become meek—when we give our lives to God to be his tool.

The first two beatitudes pass us through the fire of purification; the third places us in the hands of the Master.

The result of this process? Courage: ". . . they shall inherit the earth." No longer shall the earth and its fears dominate us, for we follow the one who dominates the earth.

♛

Could you use some courage? Are you backing down more than you are standing up? If so, let the Master lead you up the mountain again. Let him remind you why you should "fear not." Listen to the time Jesus scattered the butterflies out of the stomachs of his nervous disciples and see if his words help you.[5]

We need to remember that the disciples were common men given a compelling task. Before they were the stained-glassed saints in the windows of cathedrals, they were somebody's next-door-neighbors trying to make a living and raise a family. They weren't cut from theological cloth or raised on supernatural milk. But they were an ounce more devoted than they were afraid and, as a result, did some extraordinary things.

They would have done nothing, however, had they not

learned to face their fears. Jesus knew that. That is why he spoke his words of courage.

The disciples are being sent out on their own. For a limited time they will go into the cities and do what Jesus has done—but without Jesus. Jesus assembles them to give them the final instructions. Perhaps the disciples look nervous, for they have reason to be nervous. What Jesus tells them would raise the pulse rate of the stoutest heart.

First Jesus tells them not to take any extra money or extra clothing on their journey.

"No money?"

Then he assures them that they are being sent out "like sheep among wolves."

"Uh, what do you mean, Jesus?"

His answer is not reassuring. He tells them they will be taken before the authorities, (uh-oh), flogged, (ouch), and arrested (groan).

And it gets worse before it gets better.

Jesus goes on to describe the impact their mission will have on people: "Brother will betray brother to death, and a father his child; children will rebel against their parents and have them put to death. All men will hate you because of me, but he who stands firm to the end will be saved."[6]

Some eyes duck. Some eyes widen. Someone swallows. Feet shift. A brow is wiped. And though no one says it, you know someone is thinking, "Is it too late to get out of this?"

That's the setting for Jesus' paragraph on courage. Three times in five verses[7] he says, "Do not be afraid. Read the words and see his call and cause for courage. See the reason you should sleep well tonight:

"So do not be afraid of them. There is nothing concealed that will not be disclosed, or hidden that will not be made known."[8]

On the surface, those words would seem like a reason for panic rather than a source of peace. Who of us would like to have our secret thoughts made public? Who would want our private sins published? Who would get excited over the idea that every wrong deed we've ever done will be announced to everyone?

You're right, no one would. But we're told over and over that such a thing *will* happen:

> Nothing in all creation is hidden from God's sight. Everything is uncovered and laid bare before the eyes of him to whom we must give account.
>
> He reveals deep and hidden things;
> he knows what lies in darkness,
> and light dwells with him.
>
> But I tell you that men will have to give account on the day of judgment for every careless word they have spoken.
>
> You have set our iniquities before you,
> our secret sins in the light of your presence.
>
> He will bring to light what is hidden in darkness
> and will expose the motives of men's hearts.[9]

To think of the disclosure of my hidden heart conjures up emotions of shame, humiliation, and embarrassment in me. There are things I've done that I want no one to know. There are thoughts I've thought I would never want to be revealed. So why does Jesus point to the day of revelation as a reason for *courage*? How can I take strength in what should be a moment of anguish?

The answer is found in Romans 2:16. Let out a sigh of relief as you underline the last three words of the verse: "This will take place on the day when God will judge men's secrets *through Jesus Christ*."

Did you see it? Jesus is the screen through which God

looks when he judges our sins. Now read another chorus of verses and focus on their promise:

> Therefore, there is now no condemnation for those who are in Christ Jesus.
>
> [God] justifies those who have faith in Jesus.
>
> Through him everyone who believes is justified from everything.
>
> For I will forgive their wickedness
> and will remember their sins no more.
>
> For you died, and your life is now hidden with Christ in God.[10]

If you are in Christ, these promises are not only a source of joy. They are also the foundations of true courage. You are guaranteed that your sins will be filtered through, hidden in, and screened out by the sacrifice of Jesus. When God looks at you, he doesn't see you; he sees the One who surrounds you. That means that failure is not a concern for you. Your victory is secure. How could you not be courageous?

Picture it this way. Imagine that you are an ice skater in competition. You are in first place with one more round to go. If you perform well, the trophy is yours. You are nervous, anxious, and frightened.

Then, only minutes before your performance, your trainer rushes to you with the thrilling news: "You've already won! The judges tabulated the scores, and the person in second place can't catch you. You are too far ahead."

Upon hearing that news, how will you feel? Exhilarated!

And how will you skate? Timidly? Cautiously? Of course not. How about courageously and confidently? You bet you will. You will do your best because the prize is yours. You will skate like a champion because that is what you are! You will hear the applause of victory.

Hence, these words from Hebrews: "Therefore, brothers, since we have *confidence* to enter the Most Holy Place by the blood of Jesus . . . let us draw near to God with a sincere heart in *full assurance* of faith." [11]

The point is clear: the truth will triumph. The Father of truth will win, and the followers of truth will be saved.

As a result, Jesus says, don't be afraid:

> What I tell you in the dark, speak in the daylight; what is whispered in your ear, proclaim from the roofs. Do not be afraid of those who kill the body but cannot kill the soul. Rather, be afraid of the One who can destroy both soul and body in hell.[12]

Earthly fears are no fears at all. All the mystery is revealed. The final destination is guaranteed. Answer the big question of eternity, and the little questions of life fall into perspective.

And by the way, remember Black Bart? As it turns out, he wasn't anything to be afraid of, either. When the hood came off, there was nothing to fear. When the authorities finally tracked down the thief, they didn't find a bloodthirsty bandit from Death Valley; they found a mild-mannered druggist from Decatur, Illinois. The man the papers pictured storming through the mountains on horseback was, in reality, so afraid of horses he rode to and from his robberies in a buggy. He was Charles E. Boles—the bandit who never once fired a shot, because he never once loaded his gun.[13]

Any false hoods in your world?

Blessed are those who
hunger and thirst
for righteousness . . .

Nine

A Satisfied Thirst

MOMMY, I'M SO THIRSTY. I WANT A DRINK."

Susanna Petroysan heard her daughter's pleas, but there was nothing she could do. She and four-year-old Gayaney were trapped beneath tons of collapsed concrete and steel. Beside them in the darkness lay the body of Susanna's sister-in-law, Karine, one of the fifty-five thousand victims of the worst earthquake in the history of Soviet Armenia.

Calamity never knocks before it enters, and this time, it had torn down the door.

Susanna had gone to Karine's house to try on a dress. It was December 7, 1988, at 11:30 A.M. The quake hit at 11:41. She had just removed the dress and was clad in stockings and a slip when the fifth-floor apartment began to shake. Susanna grabbed her daughter but had taken only a few steps before the floor opened up and they tumbled in. Susanna, Gayaney, and Karine fell into the basement with the nine-story apartment house crumbling around them.

"Mommy, I need a drink. Please give me something."

There was nothing for Susanna to give.

She was trapped flat on her back. A concrete panel eighteen inches above her head and a crumpled water pipe above her shoulders kept her from standing. Feeling around in the darkness, she found a twenty-four ounce jar of blackberry jam that had fallen into the basement. She gave the entire jar to her daughter to eat. It was gone by the second day.

"Mommy, I'm so thirsty."

Susanna knew she would die, but she wanted her daughter to live. She found a dress, perhaps the one she had come to try on, and made a bed for Gayaney. Though it was bitter cold, she took off her stockings and wrapped them around the child to keep her warm.

The two were trapped for eight days.

Because of the darkness, Susanna lost track of time. Because of the cold, she lost the feeling in her fingers and toes. Because of her inability to move, she lost hope. "I was just waiting for death."

She began to hallucinate. Her thoughts wandered. A merciful sleep occasionally freed her from the horror of her entombment, but the sleep would be brief. Something always awakened her: the cold, the hunger, or—most often—the voice of her daughter.

"Mommy, I'm thirsty."

At some point in that eternal night, Susanna had an idea. She remembered a television program about an explorer in the Arctic who was dying of thirst. His comrade slashed open his hand and gave his friend his blood.

"I had no water, no fruit juice, no liquids. It was then I remembered I had my own blood."

Her groping fingers, numb from the cold, found a piece of shattered glass. She sliced open her left index finger and gave it to her daughter to suck.

The drops of blood weren't enough. "Please, Mommy, some more. Cut another finger." Susanna has no idea how many times she cut herself. She only knows that if she hadn't, Gayaney would have died. Her blood was her daughter's only hope.

♔

"This cup is the new covenant in my blood," Jesus explained, holding up the wine.[1]

The claim must have puzzled the apostles. They had been taught the story of the Passover wine. It symbolized the lamb's blood that the Israelites, enslaved long ago in Egypt, had painted on the doorposts of their homes. That blood had kept death from their homes and saved their firstborn. It had helped deliver them from the clutches of the Egyptians.

For thousands of generations the Jews had observed the Passover by sacrificing the lambs. Every year the blood would be poured, and every year the deliverance would be celebrated.

The law called for spilling the blood of a lamb. That would be enough.

It would be enough to fulfill the law. It would be enough to satisfy the command. It would be enough to justify God's justice.

But it would not be enough to take away sin.

". . . because it is impossible for the blood of bulls and goats to take away sins."[2]

Sacrifices could offer temporary solutions, but only God could offer the eternal one.

So he did.

Beneath the rubble of a fallen world, he pierced his hands. In the wreckage of a collapsed humanity, he ripped open his side. His children were trapped, so he gave his blood.

It was all he had. His friends were gone. His strength was waning. His possessions had been gambled away at his feet. Even his Father had turned his head. His blood was all he had. But his blood was all it took.

"If anyone is thirsty," Jesus once said, "let him come to me and drink."[3]

Admission of thirst doesn't come easy for us. False fountains pacify our cravings with sugary swallows of pleasure. But there comes a time when pleasure doesn't satisfy. There comes a dark hour in every life when the world caves in and we are left trapped in the rubble of reality, parched and dying.

Some would rather die than admit it. Others admit it and escape death.

"God, I need help."

So the thirsty come. A ragged lot we are, bound together by broken dreams and collapsed promises. Fortunes that were never made. Families that were never built. Promises that were never kept. Wide-eyed children trapped in the basement of our own failures.

And we are very thirsty.

Not thirsty for fame, possessions, passion, or romance. We've drunk from those pools. They are salt water in the desert. They don't quench—they kill.

"Blessed are those who hunger and thirst for righteousness. . . ."

Righteousness. That's it. That's what we are thirsty for. We're thirsty for a clean conscience. We crave a clean slate. We yearn for a fresh start. We pray for a hand which will enter the dark cavern of our world and do for us the one thing we can't do for ourselves—make us right again.[4]

♔

"Mommy, I'm so thirsty," Gayaney begged.

"It was then I remembered I had my own blood," Susanna explained.

And the hand was cut, and the blood was poured, and the child was saved.

"God, I'm so thirsty," we pray.

"It is my blood, the blood of the new agreement," Jesus stated, "shed to set many free from their sins."[5]

And the hand was pierced,
and the blood was poured,
and the children are saved.

. . . for they will
be filled.

Ten

Life in the Pits

I TOOK MY TWO OLDEST DAUGHTERS TO SEA WORLD recently. My wife was out of town, so Jenna, Andrea, and I went to spend the day watching the dolphins dip, the walruses waddle, and the penguins paddle.

We had a great day. Hot dogs. Ice cream. Stuffed whales. Toys, toys, and toys. The girls know their dad is a pushover for a thirteen-letter "Pleeeeeeeease." I should have known better. The average interest in amusement park memorabilia is twelve minutes and thirty-two seconds. Then it is, "Daddy, can you hold this? It's too heavy."

"Now, I told you not to buy it if you couldn't hold on to it.

"Pleeeeeeeease."

So by the end of the day I was carrying two pen-and-pencil sets, one set of sunglasses, an inflated penguin, a shark's tooth (complete with shark), a life-sized stuffed version of Shamu the killer whale, six balloons, and a live turtle. (OK, I'm exaggerating; there were only five balloons.) Add to that the heat, the rash from getting splashed with salt water, and the Eskimo Pie®;' that melted down my shirt, and I was ready for a break.

That's why I was glad to see the plastic ball pit. This one activity is enough to convince you to keep your season pass current. It's a large, covered, shady, cool, soothing pavilion. Under the awning is a four-foot-deep pit the size of a backyard pool. But rather than being filled with water, it is loaded with balls—thousands and thousands of plastic, colorful, lightweight balls.

In the center of the pit is a sort of table with holes through which blow jets of air. Kids climb through the pit, grab balls, place them over the holes, and "Whee!"—up fly the balls.

The greatest part of the pit is the parents' area. While the kids roll and romp in the balls, the parents sit on the carpeted floor next to the pit and rest.

My oldest daughter, Jenna, did great. She dove in and made a beeline to the table.

Three-year-old Andrea, however, had a few difficulties. As soon as she took one step into the pit, she filled her arms with balls.

Now, it is hard enough to walk through the waisthigh pit of balls with your arms spread to keep your balance. It is *impossible* to do it with your arms full.

Andrea took a step and fell. She tried to wrestle her way up without releasing the balls. She couldn't. She began to cry. I walked over to the edge of the pit.

"Andrea," I said gently, "let go of the balls, and you can walk."

"No!" she screamed, wiggling and submerging herself beneath the balls. I reached in and pulled her up. She was still clutching her armful of treasures.

"Andrea," her wise, patient father said, "if you'll let the balls go, you'll be able to walk. Besides, there are plenty of balls near the table."

"No!"

She took two steps and fell again.

Parents aren't supposed to go into the pit. I tried to reach her from the edge, but I couldn't. She was somewhere under the balls, so I spoke toward the area where she had fallen. "Andrea, let go of the balls so you can get up."

I saw a movement under the balls. "Nooo!!"

"Andrea," spoke her slightly agitated father. "You could get up if you would let go of . . ."

"Nooooo!!!!!"

"Jenna, come here and help your sister up."

By now the other parents were beginning to look at me. Jenna waded through the balls toward her little sister. She reached down into the pit and tried to help Andrea onto her feet. Jenna wasn't strong enough, and Andrea couldn't help because she was still clutching the same balls she had grabbed when she first stepped into the pit.

Jenna straightened up and shook her head at me. "I can't get her up, Daddy."

"Andrea," her increasingly irritated father said loudly, "let go of the balls so you can get up!"

The cry from beneath the balls was muffled, but distinct. "Nooooo!!!!!"

"Great," I thought to myself. "She's got what she wants, and she's going to hold on to it if it kills her."

"Jenna," her visibly angered father said sternly. "Take those balls away from your sister."

Down Jenna dove, digging through the balls like a puppy digging through the dirt. I knew she had found her little sister and that the two were engaged in mortal combat when waves of balls began to move on the surface of the pit.

By now the other parents were whispering and pointing. I looked forlornly at the employee who was monitoring the pit. I didn't even have to say a word. "Go on in," he told me.

I waded through the balls to my two angels, broke the death-locks they had on each other, put one under each arm, and carried them to the center of the pit. I dropped them next to the table (all the other kids scrambled away when they saw me coming). Then I marched back to the side of the pit and sat down.

As I watched the girls play with the balls, I asked myself, "What is it that makes children immobilize themselves by clutching toys so tightly?"

I winced as a response surfaced. "Whatever it is, they learned it from their parents."

Andrea's determination to hold those balls is nothing compared to the vice-grips we put on life. If you think Jenna's job of taking the balls away from Andrea was tough, try prying our fingers away from our earthly treasures. Try taking a retirement account away from a fifty-five-year-old. Or try convincing a yuppie to give up her BMW®. Or test your luck on a clotheshorse and his or her wardrobe. The way we clutch our possessions and our pennies, you'd think we couldn't live without them.

Ouch.

♔

Jesus' promise is comprehensive: "Blessed are those who hunger and thirst for righteousness, for they will be filled."

We usually get what we hunger and thirst for. The problem is, the treasures of earth don't satisfy. The promise is, the treasures of heaven do.

Blessed are those, then, who hold their earthly possessions in open palms. Blessed are those who, if everything they own were taken from them, would be, at most, inconvenienced, because their true wealth is elsewhere. Blessed are those who are totally dependent upon Jesus for their joy.

"Andrea," her father pleaded, "there are more than

enough balls to play with at the table. Concentrate on walking."

"Max," the heavenly Father pleads, "there are more riches than you could ever dream at the banquet table. Concentrate on walking."

Our resistance to our Father is just as childish as Andrea's. God, for our own good, tries to loosen our grip from something that will cause us to fall. But we won't let go.

"No, I won't give up my weekend rendezvous for eternal joy."

"Trade a life addicted to drugs and alcohol for a life of peace and a promise of heaven? Are you kidding?"

"I don't want to die. I don't want a new body. I want this one. I don't care if it is fat, balding, and destined to decay. I want this body."

And there we lie, submerged in the pits, desperately clutching the very things that cause us grief.

It's a wonder the Father doesn't give up.

Blessed are the merciful,
for they will be
shown mercy.

Eleven

♔

The Father in the Face of the Enemy

MARCH 24, 1989. A COLD NIGHT OFF THE COAST of Alaska.

The captain of a tanker barked orders to a second mate. The orders were vague, the night was black, and the collision was disastrous. The tanker ship *Exxon Valdez* ran hard aground on Bligh Reef, dumping eleven million gallons of crude oil into one of the most scenic bodies of water in the world. Petroleum blackened everything from the surface of the sea, to beaches, to otters, to sea gulls. Alaska was infuriated, and Exxon, the company which owned the tanker, was humiliated.

The collision, terrible as it was, was mild compared to the ones that occur daily in our relationships. You've been there. Someone doesn't meet your expectations. Promises go unfulfilled. Verbal pistols are drawn, and a round of words is fired.

The result? A collision of the hull of your heart against the reef of someone's actions. Precious energy escapes, coating the surface of your soul with the deadly film of resentment. A black blanket of bitterness darkens your world, dims your sight, sours your outlook, and suffocates your joy.

Do you have a hole in your heart?

Perhaps the wound is old. A parent abused you. A teacher slighted you. A mate betrayed you. A business partner bailed out, leaving you a choice of bills or bankruptcy.

And you are angry.

Or perhaps the wound is fresh. The friend who owes you money just drove by in a new car. The boss who hired you with promises of promotions has forgotten how to pronounce your name. Your circle of friends escaped on a weekend getaway, and you weren't invited. The children you raised seem to have forgotten you exist.

And you are hurt.

Part of you is broken, and the other part is bitter. Part of you wants to cry, and part of you wants to fight. The tears you cry are hot because they come from your heart, and there is a fire burning in your heart. It's the fire of anger. It's blazing. It's consuming. Its flames leap up under a steaming pot of revenge.

And you are left with a decision. "Do I put the fire out or heat it up? Do I get over it or get even? Do I release it or resent it? Do I let my hurts heal, or do I let hurt turn into hate?"

That's a good definition of resentment: Resentment is when you let your hurt become hate. Resentment is when you allow what is eating you to eat you up. Resentment is when you poke, stoke, feed, and fan the fire, stirring the flames and reliving the pain.

Resentment is the deliberate decision to nurse the offense until it becomes a black, furry, growling grudge.

♔

Grudge is one of those words that defines itself. Its very sound betrays its meaning.

Say it slowly: "Grr-uuuud-ge."

It starts with a growl. "Grr . . ." Like a bear with bad breath coming out of hibernation or a mangy mongrel defending his bone in an alley. "Grrr . . ."

Being near a resentful person and petting a growling dog are equally enjoyable.

Don't you just love being next to people who are nursing a grudge? Isn't it a delight to listen to them sing their songs of woe? They are so optimistic! They are so full of hope. They are bubbling with life.

You know better. You know as well as I that if they are bubbling with anything it is anger. And if they are full of anything, it is poisonous barbs of condemnation for all the people who have hurt them. Grudge bearers and angry animals are a lot alike. Both are irritable. Both are explosive. Both can be rabid. Someone needs to make a sign that can be worn around the neck of the resentful: "Beware of the Grrrrudge Bearer."

Add an M to the second part of the word, and you will see what grudge bearers throw. Mud. It's not enough to accuse; the other person's character must be attacked. It's insufficient to point a finger; a rifle must be aimed. Slander is slung. Names are called. Circles are drawn. Walls are built. And enemies are made.

Remove a GR from the word *grudge* and replace it with *SL* and you have the junk that grudge bearers trudge through. Sludge. Black, thick, ankle-deep resentment that steals the bounce from the step. No joyful skips through the meadows. No healthy hikes up the mountain. Just day after day of walking into the storm, shoulders bent against the wind, and feet dragging through all the muck life has delivered.

Is this the way you are coping with your hurts? Are you allowing your hurts to turn into hates? If so, ask yourself: Is it working? Has your hatred done you any good? Has your resentment brought you any relief, any peace? Has it granted you any joy?

Let's say you get even. Let's say you get him back. Let's say she gets what she deserves. Let's say your fantasy of fury runs its ferocious course and you return all your pain with interest. Imagine yourself standing over the corpse of the one you have hated. Will you now be free?

The writer of the following letter thought she would be. She thought her revenge would bring release. But she learned otherwise.

> I caught my husband making love to another woman. He swore it would never happen again. He begged me to forgive him, but I could not—would not. I was so bitter and so incapable of swallowing my pride that I could think of nothing but revenge. I was going to make him pay and pay dearly. I'd have my pound of flesh.
>
> I filed for divorce, even though my children begged me not to.
>
> Even after the divorce, my husband tried for two years to win me back. I refused to have anything to do with him. He had struck first; now I was striking back. All I wanted was to make him pay.
>
> Finally he gave up and married a lovely young widow with a couple of small children. He began rebuilding his life—without me.
>
> I see them occasionally, and he looks so happy. They all do. And here I am—a lonely, old, miserable woman who allowed her selfish pride and foolish stubbornness to ruin her life.

Unfaithfulness is wrong. Revenge is bad. But the worst part of all is that, without forgiveness, bitterness is all that is left.

♔

Resentment is the cocaine of the emotions. It causes our blood to pump and our energy level to rise.

But, also like cocaine, it demands increasingly larger and more frequent dosages. There is a dangerous point at which anger ceases to be an emotion and becomes a driving force. A person bent on revenge moves unknowingly further and further away from being able to forgive, for to be without the anger is to be without a source of energy.

That explains why the bitter complain to anyone who will listen. They want—they need—to have their fire fanned. That helps explain the existence of the KKK, the Skinheads, and other hate organizations. Members of these groups feed each other's anger. And that is why the resentful often appear unreasonable. They are addicted to their bitterness. They don't want to surrender their anger, for to do so would be to surrender their reason to live.

Take bigotry from the racist, and what does he have left? Remove revenge from the heart of the zealot, and her life is empty. Extract chauvinism from the radical sexist, and what remains?

Resentment is like cocaine in another way, too. Cocaine can kill the addict. And anger can kill the angry.

It can kill physically. Chronic anger has been linked with elevated cholesterol, high blood pressure, and other deadly conditions. It can kill emotionally, in that it can raise anxiety levels and lead to depression.[1]

And it can be spiritually fatal, too. It shrivels the soul.

Hatred is the rabid dog that turns on its owner. Revenge is the raging fire that consumes the arsonist. Bitterness is the trap that snares the hunter.

And mercy is the choice that can set them all free.

♔

"Blessed are the merciful," said Jesus on the mountain. Those who are merciful to others are the ones who are truly blessed. Why? Jesus answered the question: ". . . they will be shown mercy."

The merciful, says Jesus, are shown mercy. They witness grace. They are blessed because they are testimonies to a greater goodness. Forgiving others allows us to see how God has forgiven us. The dynamic of giving grace is the key to understanding grace, for it is when we forgive others that we begin to feel what God feels.

Jesus told the story of a king who decided to close out all his accounts with those who worked for him.[2] He called in his debtors and told them to pay. One man owed an amount too great to return—a debt that could never be repaid. But when the king saw the man and heard his story, his heart went out to him, and he erased the debt.

As the man was leaving the palace grounds, he encountered a fellow employee who owed him a small sum. He grabbed the debtor and choked him, demanding payment. When the fellow begged for mercy, no mercy was granted. Instead, the one who had just been forgiven had his debtor thrown into jail.

When word of this got to the king, he became livid. And Jesus says, "In anger his master turned him over to the jailers to be tortured, until he should pay back all he owed."[3]

Could someone actually be forgiven a debt of millions and be unable to forgive a debt of hundreds? Could a person be set free and then imprison another?

You don't have to be a theologian to answer those questions; you only have to look in the mirror. Who among us has not begged God for mercy on Sunday and then demanded justice on Monday? Who hasn't served as a bottleneck instead of a conduit of God's love? Is there anyone who doesn't, at one time or the other, "show contempt for the riches of his [God's] kindness, tolerance and patience, not realizing that God's kindness leads you towards repentance?"[4]

Notice what God does when we calibrate our compassion. He turns us over to be tortured. Tortured by anger. Choked by bitterness. Consumed by revenge.

Such is the punishment for one who tastes God's grace but refuses to share it.

But for the one who tastes God's grace and then gives it to others, the reward is a blessed liberation. The prison door is thrown open, and the prisoner set free is yourself.

Earlier in the book I mentioned Daniel, a dear friend of mine in Brazil. (Daniel was the one who took me to meet Anibal in prison.)

Daniel is big. He used to make his living by lifting weights and teaching others to do the same. His scrapbook is colorful with ribbons and photos of him in his prime, striking the muscle-man pose and flexing the bulging arms.

The only thing bigger than Daniel's biceps is his heart. Let me tell you about a time his heart became tender.

Daniel was living in the southern city of Porto Alegre. He worked at a gym and dreamed of owning his own. The bank agreed to finance the purchase if he could find someone to cosign the note. His brother agreed.

They filled out all the applications and awaited the approval. Everything went smoothly, and Daniel soon received a call from the bank telling him he could come and pick up the check. As soon as he got off work, he went to the bank.

When the loan officer saw Daniel, he looked surprised and asked Daniel why he had come.

"To pick up the check," Daniel explained.

"That's funny," responded the banker. "Your brother was in here earlier. He picked up the money and used it to retire the mortgage on his house."

Daniel was incensed. He never dreamed his own brother would trick him like that. He stormed over to his brother's house and pounded on the door. The brother answered the door with his daughter in his arms. He knew Daniel wouldn't hit him if he was holding a child.

He was right. Daniel didn't hit him. But he promised his brother that if he ever saw him again he would break his neck.

Daniel went home, his big heart bruised and ravaged by the trickery of his brother. He had no other choice but to go back to the gym and work to pay off the debt.

A few months later, Daniel met a young American missionary named Allen Dutton. Allen befriended Daniel and taught him about Jesus Christ. Daniel and his wife soon became Christians and devoted disciples.

But though Daniel had been forgiven so much, he still found it impossible to forgive his brother. The wound was deep. The pot of revenge still simmered. He didn't see his brother for two years. Daniel couldn't bring himself to look into the face of the one who had betrayed him. And his brother liked his own face too much to let Daniel see it.

But an encounter was inevitable. Both knew they would eventually run into each other. And neither knew what would happen then.

The encounter occurred one day on a busy avenue. Let Daniel tell you in his own words what happened:

> I saw him, but he didn't see me. I felt my fists clench and my face get hot. My initial impulse was to grab him around the throat and choke the life out of him.
>
> But as I looked into his face, my anger began to melt. For as I saw him, I saw the image of my father. I saw my father's eyes. I saw my father's look. I saw my father's expression. And as I saw my father in his face, my enemy once again became my brother.

Daniel walked toward him. The brother stopped, turned, and started to run, but he was too slow. Daniel reached out and grabbed his shoulder. The brother winced, expecting the worst. But rather than have his throat squeezed by Daniel's hands, he found himself hugged by Daniel's big arms. And the two brothers stood in the middle of the river of people and wept.

Daniel's words are worth repeating: "When I saw the image of my father in his face, my enemy became my brother."

The Father in the Face of the Enemy

Seeing the father's image in the face of the enemy. Try that. The next time you see or think of the one who broke your heart, look twice. As you look at his face, look also for His face—the face of the One who forgave you. Look into the eyes of the King who wept when you pleaded for mercy. Look into the face of the Father who gave you grace when no one else gave you a chance. Find the face of the God who forgives in the face of your enemy. And then, because God has forgiven you more than you'll ever be called on to forgive in another, set your enemy—and yourself—free.

And allow the hole in your heart to heal.

Blessed are the
pure in heart . . .

Twelve

The State of the Heart

I CAN STILL REMEMBER THE FIRST TIME I SAW one. I had gone to work with my dad—a big thrill for a ten-year-old whose father worked in the oil fields. I sat in the cab of the pickup as tall as I could, stretching to see the endless West Texas plain. The countryside was flat and predictable, boasting nothing taller than pumpjacks and windmills. Maybe that is why the thing seemed so colossal. It stood out on the horizon like a science-fiction city.

"What's that?"

"It's a refinery," Dad answered.

A jungle of pipes and tanks and tubes and generators—heaters, pumps, pipes, filters, valves, hoses, conduits, switches, circuits. It looked like a giant Tinker-Toy® set.

The function of that maze of machinery is defined by its name: It refines. Gasoline, oil, chemicals—the refinery takes whatever comes in and purifies it so that it's ready to go out.

The refinery does for petroleum and other products what your "heart" should do for you. It takes out the bad and utilizes the good.

We tend to think of the heart as the seat of emotion. We speak of "heartthrobs," "heartaches," and "broken hearts."

But when Jesus said, "Blessed are the pure in heart," he was speaking in a different context. To Jesus' listeners, the heart was the totality of the inner person—the control tower, the cockpit. The heart was thought of as the seat of the character—the origin of desires, affections, perceptions, thoughts, reasoning, imagination, conscience, intentions, purpose, will, and faith.

Thus a proverb admonished, "Above all else, guard your heart, for it is the wellspring of life."[1]

To the Hebrew mind, the heart is a freeway cloverleaf where all emotions and prejudices and wisdom converge. It is a switch house that receives freight cars loaded with moods, ideas, emotions, and convictions and puts them on the right track.

And just as a low-grade oil or alloyed gasoline would cause you to question the performance of a refinery, evil acts and impure thoughts cause us to question the condition of our hearts.

> But the things that come out of the mouth come from the heart, and these make a man "unclean." For out of the heart come evil thoughts, murder, adultery, sexual immorality, theft, false testimony, slander.[2]

> The good man brings good things out of the good stored up in his heart, and the evil man brings evil things out of the evil stored up in his heart. For out of the overflow of his heart his mouth speaks.[3]

These verses hammer home the same truth: The heart is the center of the spiritual life. If the fruit of a tree is bad, you don't try to fix the fruit; you treat the roots. And if a person's actions are evil, it's not enough to change habits;

you have to go deeper. You have to go to the heart of the problem, which is the problem of the heart.

That is why the state of the heart is so critical. What's the state of yours?

When someone barks at you, do you bark back or bite your tongue? That depends on the state of your heart.

When your schedule is too tight or your to-do list too long, do you lose your cool or keep it? That depends on the state of your heart.

When you are offered a morsel of gossip marinated in slander, do you turn it down or pass it on? That depends on the state of your heart.

Do you see the bag lady on the street as a burden on society or as an opportunity for God? That, too, depends on the state of your heart.

The state of your heart dictates whether you harbor a grudge or give grace, seek self-pity or seek Christ, drink human misery or taste God's mercy.

No wonder, then, the wise man begs, "Above all else, guard your heart."

David's prayer should be ours: "Create in me a pure heart, O God."[4]

And Jesus' statement rings true: "Blessed are the pure in heart, for they shall see God."

Note the order of this beatitude: *first,* purify the heart, *then you* will see God. Clean the refinery, and the result will be a pure product.

We usually reverse the order. We try to change the inside by altering the outside. Let me give you an example.

♔

When my family lived in Rio de Janeiro, I owned a ham radio. I kept it in the utility room on top of the freezer. When we traveled, I always unplugged the radio and disconnected the antenna.

Once, when we were leaving for a week-long trip, I remembered I hadn't unplugged the radio. I ran back in the house, pulled the plug, and dashed out again.

But I pulled the wrong plug. I unplugged the freezer. It was summertime, and summer in Rio redefines the word *hot*. Our apartment was on the top of a fourteen-floor apartment building, which adds another degree of intensity to the word *hot*. For seven days, then, a freezer full of food sat in a sweltering apartment with the power off. (Why are you groaning?)

When we came home, Denalyn decided to get some meat out of the freezer. As she opened the freezer door—well, I won't go into details as to what she saw, but I will say it was a moving experience.

Guess who got fingered as the one who had unplugged the freezer—and who therefore would be responsible for cleaning it? You got it. So I got to work.

What is the best way to clean out a rotten interior? I knew exactly what to do. I got a rag and a bucket of soapy water and began cleaning the outside of the appliance. I was sure the odor would disappear with a good shine, so I polished and buffed and wiped. When I was through, the freezer could have passed a Marine boot-camp inspection. It was sparkling.

But when I opened the door, that freezer was revolting.

(Are you wondering, "Now what kind of fool would do that?" Read on and you'll see.)

No problem, I thought. I knew what to do. This freezer needs some friends. I'd stink, too, if I had the social life of a machine in a utility room. So, I threw a party. I invited all the appliances from the neighborhood kitchens. It was hard work, but we filled our apartment with refrigerators, stoves, microwaves, and washing machines. It was a great party. A couple of toasters recognized each other from the appliance store. Everyone played pin the plug on the socket and had a few laughs about limited warranties.

The blenders were the hit, though; they really mixed well.

I was sure the social interaction would cure the inside of my freezer, but I was wrong. I opened it up, and the stink was even worse!

Now what?

I had an idea. If a polish job wouldn't do it and a social life didn't help, I'd give the freezer some status!

I bought a Mercedes® sticker and stuck it on the door. I painted a paisley tie down the front. I put a "Save the Whales" bumper sticker on the rear and installed a cellular phone on the side. That freezer was classy. It was stylish. It was . . . cool. I splashed it with cologne and gave it a credit card for clout.

Then I backed away and admired the high-class freezer. "You just might make the cover of *Popular Mechanics*," I told it. It blushed. Then I opened the door, expecting to see a clean inside, but what I saw was putrid—a stinky and repulsive interior.

I could think of only one other option. My freezer needed some high-voltage pleasure! I immediately bought it some copies of *Playfridge* magazine—the publication that displays freezers with their doors open. I rented some films about foxy appliances. (My favorite was *The Big Chill.*) I even tried to get my freezer a date with the Westinghouse® next door, but she gave him the cold shoulder.

After a few days of supercharged, after-hours entertainment, I opened the door. And I nearly got sick.

I know what you're thinking. The only thing worse than Max's humor is his common sense. Who would concentrate on the outside when the problem is on the inside?

Do you really want to know?

A homemaker battles with depression. What is the solution suggested by some well-meaning friend? Buy a new dress.

A husband is involved in an affair that brings him as

much guilt as it does adventure. The solution? Change peer groups. Hang out with people who don't make you feel guilty!

A young professional is plagued with loneliness. His obsession with success has left him with no friends. His boss gives him an idea: Change your style. Get a new haircut. Flash some cash.

Case after case of treating the outside while ignoring the inside—polishing the case while ignoring the interior. And what is the result?

The homemaker gets a new dress, and the depression disappears . . . for a day, maybe. Then the shadow returns.

The husband finds a bunch of buddies who sanction his adultery. The result? Peace . . . until the crowd is gone. Then the guilt is back.

The young professional gets a new look and the people notice . . . until the styles change. Then he has to scurry out and buy more stuff so he won't appear outdated.

The exterior polished; the interior corroding. The outside altered; the inside faltering. One thing is clear: Cosmetic changes are only skin deep.

By now you could write the message of the beatitude. It's a clear one: You change your life by changing your heart.

♔

How do you change your heart? Jesus gave the plan on the mountain. Back away from the beatitudes once more and view them in sequence.

The first step is an admission of poverty: "Blessed are the poor in spirit. . . ." God's gladness is not received by those who earn it, but by those who admit they *don't* deserve it. The joy of Sarah, Peter, and Paul came when they surrendered, when they pleaded for a lifeguard instead of a swimming lesson, when they sought a savior instead of a system.

The second step is sorrow: "Blessed are those who mourn. . . ." Joy comes to those who are sincerely sorry for their sin. We discover gladness when we leave the prison of pride and repent of our rebellion.

Sorrow is followed by meekness. The meek are those who are willing to be used by God. Amazed that God would save them, they are just as surprised that God could use them. They are a junior-high-school clarinet section playing with the Boston Pops. They don't tell the maestro how to conduct; they're just thrilled to be part of the concert.

The result of the first three steps? Hunger. Never have you seen anything like what is happening! You admit sin—you get saved. You confess weakness—you receive strength. You say you are sorry—you find forgiveness. It's a zany, unpredictable path full of pleasant encounters. For once in your life you're addicted to something positive—something that gives life instead of draining it. And you want more.

Then comes mercy. The more you receive, the more you give. You find it easier to give grace because you realize you have been given so much. What has been done to you is nothing compared to what you did to God.

For the first time in your life, you have found a permanent joy, a joy that is not dependent upon your whims and actions. It's a joy from God, a joy no one can take away from you.

A sacred delight is placed in your heart.

It is sacred because only God can grant it.

It is a delight because you would never expect it.

And though your heart isn't perfect, it isn't rotten. And though you aren't invincible, at least you're plugged in. And you can bet that he who made you knows just how to purify you—from the inside out.

. . . for they will
see God.

Thirteen

Nice Palace but No King

THE LEGENDS OF THE TAJ MAHAL. THEY ALL fascinate, but there is one that haunts.

The favorite wife of the Mogul emperor Shah Jahan died. Devastated, he resolved to honor her by constructing a temple that would serve as her tomb. Her coffin was placed in the center of a large parcel of land, and construction of the temple began around it. No expense would be spared to make her final resting place magnificent.

But as the weeks turned into months, the Shah's grief was eclipsed by his passion for the project. He no longer mourned her absence. The construction consumed him. One day, while walking from one side of the construction site to the other, his leg bumped against a wooden box. The prince brushed the dust off his leg and ordered the worker to throw the box out.

Shah Jahan didn't know he had ordered the disposal of

the coffin—now forgotten—hidden beneath layers of dust and time.

The one the temple was intended to honor was forgotten, but the temple was erected anyway.

Difficult to believe? Perhaps. But eerie nonetheless.

Could someone build a temple and forget why? Could someone construct a palace, yet forget the king? Could someone sculpt a tribute and forget the hero?

You answer those questions. Answer them in a church. The next time you enter an assembly of worship, position yourself where you can see the people. Then decide.

You can tell the ones who remember the slain one. They're wide-eyed and expectant. They're children watching the unwrapping of a gift. They're servants standing still as a king passes. You don't doze in the presence of royalty. And you don't yawn while receiving a gift, especially when the giver is the king himself!

You can also tell the ones who see only the temple. Their eyes wander. Their feet shuffle. Their hands doodle, and their mouths open—not to sing, but to yawn For no matter how hard they try to stay amazed, their eyes start to glaze over. All temples, even the Taj Mahal, lose their luster after a while.

The temple gazers don't mean to be bored. They love the church. They can cite its programs and praise its pastors. They don't mean to grow stale. They put on hats and hose and coats and ties and come every week. But still, something is missing. The one they once planned to honor hasn't been seen in a while.

But those who have seen him can't seem to forget him. They find him, often in spite of the temple rather than because of it. They brush the dust away and stand ever impressed before his tomb—his empty tomb.

The temple builders and the Savior seekers. You'll find them both in the same church, on the same pew—at times, even in the same suit. One sees the structure and says,

"What a great church." The other sees the Savior and says, "What a great Christ!"

Which do you see?

Blessed are
the peacemakers . . .

Fourteen

Seeds of Peace

WANT TO SEE A MIRACLE? TRY THIS.

Take a seed the size of a freckle. Put it under several inches of dirt. Give it enough water, light, and fertilizer. And get ready. A mountain will be moved. It doesn't matter that the ground is a zillion times the weight of the seed. The seed will push it back.

Every spring, dreamers around the world plant tiny hopes in overturned soil. And every spring, their hopes press against impossible odds and blossom.

Never underestimate the power of a seed.

As far as I know, James, the epistle writer, wasn't a farmer. But he knew the power of a seed sown in fertile soil.

"Those who are peacemakers will plant seeds of peace and reap a harvest of goodness."[1]

The principle for peace is the same as the principle for crops: Never underestimate the power of a seed.

The story of Heinz is a good example. Europe, 1934. Hitler's plague of anti-Semitism was infecting a continent. Some would escape it. Some would die from it. But eleven-year-old Heinz would learn from it. He would learn the power of sowing seeds of peace.

Heinz was a Jew.

The Bavarian village of Furth, where Heinz lived, was being overrun by Hitler's young thugs. Heinz's father, a schoolteacher, lost his job. Recreational activities ceased. Tension mounted on the streets.

The Jewish families clutched the traditions that held them together—the observance of the Sabbath, of Rosh Hashanah, of Yom Kippur. Old ways took on new significance. As the clouds of persecution swelled and blackened, these ancient precepts were a precious cleft in a mighty rock.

And as the streets became a battleground, such security meant survival.

Hitler youth roamed the neighborhoods looking for trouble. Young Heinz learned to keep his eyes open. When he saw a band of troublemakers, he would step to the other side of the street. Sometimes he would escape a fight—sometimes not.

One day, in 1934, a pivotal confrontation occurred. Heinz found himself face-to-face with a Hitler bully. A beating appeared inevitable. This time, however, he walked away unhurt—not because of what he did, but because of what he said. He didn't fight back; he spoke up. He convinced the troublemakers that a fight was not necessary. His words kept battle at bay.

And Heinz saw firsthand how the tongue can create peace.

He learned the skill of using words to avoid conflict. And for a young Jew in Hitler-ridden Europe, that skill had many opportunities to be honed.

Fortunately, Heinz's family escaped from Bavaria and made their way to America. Later in life, he would downplay the impact those adolescent experiences had on his development.

But one has to wonder. For after Heinz grew up, his name became synonymous with peace negotiations. His legacy became that of a bridge builder. Somewhere he had learned the power of the properly placed word of peace. And one has to wonder if his training didn't come on the streets of Bavaria.

You don't know him as Heinz. You know him by his Anglicized name, Henry. Henry Kissinger.[2]

Never underestimate the power of a seed.

♛

How good are you at sowing seeds of peace?

You may not be called on to ward off international conflict, but you will have opportunities to do something more vital: to bring *inner* peace to troubled hearts.

Jesus modeled this. We don't see him settling many disputes or negotiating conflicts. But we *do* see him cultivating inward harmony through acts of love:

washing the feet of men he knew would betray him,

having lunch with a corrupt tax official,

honoring the sinful woman whom society had scorned.

He built bridges by healing hurts. He prevented conflict by touching the interior. He cultivated harmony by sowing seeds of peace in fertile hearts.

Do me a favor. Pause for a moment and think about the people who make up your world. Take a stroll through the gallery of faces that are significant to you. Mentally flip through the scrapbook of snapshots featuring those you deal with often.

Can you see their faces? Your spouse. Your best friend. Your golf buddies. Your friends at PTA. Your kids. Your aunt across the country. Your neighbor across the street. The receptionist at work. The new secretary in the next office.

Freeze-frame those mental images for a moment while I tell you how some of them are feeling.

I went to our family doctor not long ago. I went for my first check-up since the one required for high school football seventeen years ago.

Since I was way overdue, I ordered the works. One nurse put me on a table and stuck little cold suction cups to my chest. Another nurse wrapped a heavy band around my arm and squeezed a black bulb until my arm tingled. Then they pricked my finger (which always hurts) and told me to fill up a cup (which is always awkward). Then, with all the preliminaries done, they put me in a room and told me to take off my shirt and wait on the doctor.

There is something about being poked, pushed, measured, and drained that makes you feel like a head of lettuce in the produce department. I sat on a tiny stool and stared at the wall.

May I tell you something you know, but may have forgotten? Somebody in your world feels like I felt in that office. The daily push and shove of the world has a way of leaving us worked over and worn out. Someone in your gallery of people is sitting on a cold aluminum stool of insecurity, clutching the backside of a hospital gown for fear of exposing what little pride he or she has left. And that person desperately needs a word of peace.

Someone needs you to do for them what Dr. Jim did for me.

Jim is a small-town doctor in a big city. He still remembers names and keeps pictures of babies he delivered on his office bulletin board. And though you know he's busy, he makes you feel you are his only patient.

After a bit of small talk and a few questions about my

medical history, he put down my file and said, "Let me take off my doctor hat for a minute and talk to you as a friend."

The chat lasted maybe five minutes. He asked me about my family. He asked me about my work load. He asked me about my stress. He told me he thought I was doing a good job at the church and that he loved to read my books.

Nothing profound, nothing probing. He went no deeper than I allowed. But I had the feeling he would have gone to the bottom of the pit with me had I needed him to.

After those few minutes, Dr. Jim went about his task of tapping my knee with his rubber hammer, staring down my throat, looking in my ear, and listening to my chest. When he was all done, as I was buttoning up my shirt, he took his doctor hat off again and reminded me not to carry the world on my shoulders. "And be sure to love your wife and hug those kids, because when it all boils down to it, you're not much without them."

"Thanks, Jim," I said.

And he walked out as quickly as he'd come in—a seed sower in a physician's smock.

♛

Want to see a miracle? Plant a word of love heartdeep in a person's life. Nurture it with a smile and a prayer, and watch what happens.

An employee gets a compliment. A wife receives a bouquet of flowers. A cake is baked and carried next door. A widow is hugged. A gas-station attendant is honored. A preacher is praised.

Sowing seeds of peace is like sowing beans. You don't know why it works; you just know it does. Seeds are planted, and topsoils of hurt are shoved away.

Don't forget the principle. Never underestimate the power of a seed.

God didn't. When his kingdom was ravaged and his people had forgotten his name, he planted his seed.

When the soil of the human heart had grown crusty, he planted his seed. When religion had become a ritual and the temple a trading post, he planted his seed.

Want to see a miracle? Watch him as he places the seed of his own self in the fertile womb of a Jewish girl.

Up it grew, "like a tender green shoot, sprouting from a root in dry and sterile ground."[3] The seed spent a lifetime pushing back the stones that tried to keep it underground. The seed made a ministry out of shoving away the rocks that cluttered his father's soil.

The stones of legalism that burdened backs.

The stones of oppression that broke bones.

The stones of prejudice that fenced out the needy.

But it was the final stone that proved to be the supreme test of the seed. The stone of death—rolled by humans and sealed by Satan in front of the tomb. For a moment it appeared the seed would be stuck in the earth. For a moment, it looked like this rock was too big to be budged.

But then, somewhere in the heart of the earth, the seed of God stirred, shoved, and sprouted. The ground trembled, and the rock of the tomb tumbled. And the flower of Easter blossomed.

Never underestimate the power of a seed.

. . . for they will be called sons of God.

F i f t e e n

The Greasy Pole of Power

THE PUSH FOR POWER HAS COME TO SHOVE.

You know the power lingo. You know the power plays. You have a power wardrobe.

You think you have everything you need for power? Think twice and come to dinner. Now there are power table manners.

"Manners will take you where your money can't," states the "Queen of Courtesy," Marjabelle Stewart. This crusader for couth has developed a seminar to help you eat your way to the top. For six thousand dollars you can sit in on a seminar and learn the manners that have clout.

Here are a few examples of what Stewart calls "power failures":

- Never tuck your napkin into your collar.
- Never leave a lipstick mark on the rim of a glass.

- Never mash or stir your food.
- Never haggle over the bill.
- Never, ever, hand your plate to the waiter.
- Never read the menu like a Bible. You aren't there to eat, but to do business.
- Never stoop down to retrieve dropped silver.[1]

In fact, the primary rule of thumb in the quest for power is never to stoop down for anything.

Never stoop to appear weak. Never stoop to admit mistakes. Never stoop to help someone who could never help you. Never stoop to any level that might loosen your grip on your rung of the ladder.

Add "power etiquette" to "name dropping," "card flashing," and "title touting." Put it on the long list of games we play to make a name for ourselves.

"Power moves" are simply "King of the Mountain" on an adult level.

Remember playing that game as a kid? The object of the game is to get high on the heap and stay there. You push, claw, and climb until you get to the top. And once you get there, you fight to hold your position. Don't even think about sitting down. Forget enjoying the view. Slack up for even a minute, and you'll be slapped down to the bottom of the hill. And then you'll have to start all over again.

As grown-ups we still play "King of the Mountain," but now the stakes are higher. Harrison Ford in the movie *Working Girl* put it this way:

> One lost deal is all it takes to get canned these days. The line buttons on my phone all have an inch of little pieces of tape piled on—the names of new guys over the names of old guys—good men who aren't at the other end of the line anymore all because of one lost deal. I don't want to get buried under a little piece of tape.

The push for power has come to shove. And most of us are either pushing or being pushed.

I might point out the difference between a passion for excellence and a passion for power. The desire for excellence is a gift of God, much needed in society. It is characterized by respect for quality and a yearning to use God's gifts in a way that pleases him. Recall the words of Antonio Stradivari, the seventeenth-century violin maker whose name in its Latin form, Stradivarius, has become synonymous with excellence:

> When any master holds 'twixt chin and hand a violin of mine, he will be glad that Stradivari lived, made violins and made them of the best . . . If my hand slacked I should rob God—since he is the fullest good. . . . But he could not make Antonio Stradivari's violins without Antonio.[2]

He was right. God could not make Stradivarius violins without Antonio Stradivari. Certain gifts were given to that craftsman that no other violin maker possessed.

In the same vein, there are certain things you can do that no one else can. Perhaps it is parenting, or constructing houses, or encouraging the discouraged. There are things that *only you* can do, and you are alive to do them. In the great orchestra we call life, you have an instrument and a song, and you owe it to God to play them both sublimely.

But there is a canyon of difference between doing your best to glorify God and doing whatever it takes to glorify yourself. The quest for excellence is a mark of maturity. The quest for power is childish.

It might interest you to know that the first power play happened not on Wall Street nor on a battlefield, but in a garden. The first promise of prestige was whispered with a hiss, a wink, and a snakish grin by a fallen angel.

Standing in the shadow of the tree of the knowledge of good and evil, Satan knew what to offer Eve to convince her to eat the apple. It wasn't pleasure. It wasn't health. It wasn't prosperity. It was . . . well, you read his words and look for his lure:

"God knows that when you eat of it your eyes will be opened, and you will be like God, knowing good and evil."[3]

The words found a soft spot.

"You will be like God. . . ."

Eve stroked her chin as she replayed the promise.

"You will be like God. . . ."

The snake pulled back the curtain to the throne room and invited Eve to take a seat. Put on the crown. Pick up the scepter. Put on the cape. See how it feels to have power. See how it feels to have a name. See how it feels to be in control!

Eve swallowed the hook. The temptation to be *like* God eclipsed her view of God, and the crunch of an apple echoed in the kingdom. You know the rest of the story.

Now, perhaps your flirtations with power haven't been so blatant. No doubt, you were amused at the thought of spending six grand on a table manners seminar. No doubt you've shaken your head in amazement at the buy-outs staged by the barons of Wall Street. No doubt you've been chagrined by the murders ordered by drug lords and king-pins. That type of power play has no attraction for you. If the snake were to woo you with promises of status, you'd send him back to the pit, right?

Or would you? "King of the Mountain" comes in many forms.

It's the boss who won't compliment her employees. After all, workers need to be kept in their place.

It's the husband who refuses to be kind to his wife. He knows if he does he will lose his most powerful weapon—her fear of his rejection.

It's the employee who places personal ambition over personal integrity.

It's the wife who withholds sex both to punish and persuade.

It might be the taking of someone's life, or it might be the taking of someone's turn. It might be manipulation with a pistol, or it might be manipulation with a pout. It might be the takeover of a nation by a politician, or the takeover of a church by a preacher.

But they are all spelled the same: P-O-W-E-R.

All have the same goal: "I will get what I want at your expense."

All have the same game plan: push, shove, take, and lie.

All have listened to the same snake, the same lying Lucifer who whispers into the ears of anyone who will listen, "You will be like God."

And all have the same end: futility. Please note carefully what I am about to say. Absolute power is unreachable. The pole to the top is greasy, and the ladder rungs are made of cardboard. When you stand at the top—if there is a top—the only way to go is down. And the descent is often painful.

Ask Muhammed Ali.

You know Ali, the unprecedented three-time world heavyweight boxing champion. His face has appeared on the cover of *Sports Illustrated* more times than any other athlete. When he was "floating like a butterfly and stinging like a bee," he was king of his profession. An entourage of reporters, trainers, and support staff tailed this comet as he raced around the world.

But that was yesterday. Where is Muhammed Ali today? Sportswriter Gary Smith went to find out.

Ali escorted Smith to a barn next to his farmhouse. On the floor, leaning against the walls, were mementos of Ali in his prime. Photos and portraits of the champ punching and dancing. Sculpted body. Fist punching the air.

Championship belt held high in triumph. "The thrilla in Manila."

But on the pictures were white streaks—bird droppings. Ali looked into the rafters at the pigeons who had made his gym their home. And then he did something significant. Perhaps it was a gesture of closure. Maybe it was a statement of despair. Whatever the reason, he walked over to the row of pictures and turned them, one by one, toward the wall. He then walked to the door, stared at the countryside, and mumbled something so low that Smith had to ask him to repeat it. Ali did.

"I had the world," he said, "and it wasn't nothin'. Look now."[4]

The pole of power is greasy.

The Roman emperor Charlemagne knew that. An interesting story surrounds the burial of this famous king. Legend has it that he asked to be entombed sitting upright in his throne. He asked that his crown be placed on his head and his scepter in his hand. He requested that the royal cape be draped around his shoulders and an open book be placed in his lap.

That was A.D. 814. Nearly two hundred years later, Emperor Othello determined to see if the burial request had been carried out. He allegedly sent a team of men to open the tomb and make a report. They found the body just as Charlemagne had requested. Only now, nearly two centuries later, the scene was gruesome. The crown was tilted, the mantle moth-eaten, the body disfigured. But open on the skeletal thighs was the book Charlemagne had requested—the Bible. One bony finger pointed to Matthew 16:26: "What good will it be for a man if he gains the whole world, yet forfeits his soul?"[5]

You can answer that one.

As these thoughts on power were beginning to take shape, I found myself at a banquet.

Now, on my list of favorite things to do on a free evening, attending a banquet is pretty close to the bottom. The thought conjures up images of cold food, hot rooms, poor sound systems, long-winded speakers, and gravy spots on my tie. Forgive my social maladjustment, but I'll take a good movie or baseball game anytime.

This particular banquet was doing little to change my opinion. It was an awards ceremony that had been overbooked and had begun late. The master of ceremonies was having a hard time keeping everyone's attention. He competed against a squad of waiters that darted in and dashed out every thirteen seconds. The awards were presented with meticulous detail. They were received with explicit—and verbose—gratitude. I began looking at my watch and munching on ice cubes.

That's when the king was introduced.

"A king?" I looked around, thinking I would see a cape and a crown. I didn't. I did see a nicely dressed young man escorted to the platform.

"So that is what a king looks like," I thought. Others must have been just as intrigued. The place was silent.

King Goodwill was his name. He is a seventh-generation king of the Zulu tribe in Africa. Impressive title. But more significant was the fact that King Good will himself had a King. Goodwill was a believer. He had embraced Christ as his Lord and was encouraging his nation to do the same.

Though King Goodwill's entire speech was noteworthy, it was his first phrase that I copied in my date book: "I am a king, but I greet you as my brothers."

A king who considers me his brother. A ruler who welcomes me into his family. Royalty freely granted.

His words reminded me of another King who did the same.

"Blessed are the peacemakers, for they will be called sons of God."

"Be a power broker," the snake lied, "and you will be like God."

"Be a peacemaker," the King promised, "and you will be a son of God."

Which would you prefer? To be king of the mountain for a day? Or to be a child of God for eternity?

There is a side benefit to sonship. If you are a child of God, then what does the world have to offer? Can you have any greater title than the one you have?

Answer this: A thousand years from now, will it matter what title the world gave you? No, but it will make a literal hell of a difference whose child you are.

One final note about that banquet. After it was over, I stuck around, hoping to meet the king. At first I couldn't find him. Then I came across him and his wife and assistants in a side hall. Guess what they were doing? Laughing! Somebody must have told a whopper of a joke, because this group could barely stand up.

A king in stitches. What a delight.

A belly laugh is not what I would call a power play. It could better be described as a good time. I guess when you're a king, you don't have to worry about being proper for the sake of status; you already have all you need.

That goes for children of the King, too.

Next time I eat, I think I'll tuck my napkin in my collar.

Blesssed are those
who are persecuted because
of righteousness . . .

Sixteen

The Dungeon of Doubt

HE WAS A CHILD OF THE DESERT. LEATHERY FACE. Tanned skin. Clothing of animal skins. What he owned fit in a pouch. His walls were the mountains and his ceiling the stars.

But not anymore. His frontier is walled out, his horizon hidden. The stars are memories. The fresh air is all but forgotten. And the stench of the dungeon relentlessly reminds the child of the desert that he is now a captive of the king.[1]

In anyone's book, John the Baptist deserves better treatment than this. After all, isn't he the forerunner of the Christ? Isn't he a relative of the Messiah? At the very least, isn't his the courageous voice of repentance?

But most recently that voice, instead of opening the door of renewal, has opened the door to his own prison cell.

John's problems began when he called a king on the carpet.

On a trip to Rome, King Herod succumbed to the enticements of his brother's wife, Herodias. Deciding

Herodias was better off married to him, Herod divorced his wife and brought his sister-in-law home.

The gossip columnists were fascinated, but John the Baptist was infuriated. He pounced on Herod like a desert scorpion, denouncing the marriage for what it was—adultery.

Herod might have let him get away with it. But not Herodias. This steamy seductress wasn't about to have her social climbing exposed. She told Herod to have John pulled off the speaking circuit and thrown into the dungeon. Herod hemmed and hawed until she whispered and wooed. Then Herod gave in.

But that wasn't enough for this mistress. She had her daughter strut before the king and his generals at a stag party. Herod, who was as easily duped as he was aroused, promised to do anything for the pretty young thing in the G-string.

"Anything?"

"You name it," he drooled.

She conferred with her mother, who was waiting in the wings, then returned with her request.

"I want John the Baptist."

"You want a date with the prophet?"

"I want his head," replied the dancer. And then, reassured by a nod from her mother, she added, "On a silver platter, if you don't mind."

Herod looked at the faces around him. He knew it wasn't fair, but he also knew everyone was looking at him. And he *had* promised "anything." Though he personally had nothing against the country preacher, he valued the opinion polls much more than he valued John's life. After all, what's more important—to save face or to save the neck of an eccentric prophet?

The story reeks with inequity.

John dies because Herod lusts.

The good is murdered while the bad smirk.

A man of God is killed while a man of passion is winking at his niece.

Is this how God rewards his anointed? Is this how he honors his faithful? Is this how God crowns his chosen? With a dark dungeon and a shiny blade?

The inconsistency was more than John could take. Even before Herod reached his verdict, John was asking his questions. His concerns were outnumbered only by the number of times he paced his cell asking them. When he had a chance to get a message to Jesus, his inquiry was one of despair:

"When John heard in prison what Christ was doing, he sent his disciples to ask him, 'Are you the one who was to come, or should we expect someone else?' "[2]

♛

Note what motivated John's question. It was not just the dungeon or even death. It was the problem of unmet expectations—the fact that John was in deep trouble and Jesus was conducting business as usual.

Is this what messiahs do when trouble comes? Is this what God does when his followers are in a bind?

Jesus' silence was enough to chisel a leak into the dam of John's belief. "Are you the one? Or have I been following the wrong Lord?"

Had the Bible been written by a public relations agency, they would have eliminated that verse. It's not good PR strategy to admit that one of the cabinet members has doubts about the president. You don't let stories like that get out if you are trying to present a unified front.

But the Scriptures weren't written by personality agents; they were inspired by an eternal God who knew that every disciple from then on would spend time in the dungeon of doubt.

Though the circumstances have changed, the questions haven't.

They are asked anytime the faithful suffer the consequences of the faithless. Anytime a person takes a step in the right direction, only to have her feet knocked out from under her, anytime a person does a good deed but suffers evil results, anytime a person takes a stand, only to end up flat on his face . . . the questions fall like rain:

"If God is so good, why do I hurt so bad?"

"If God is really there, why am I here?"

"What did I do to deserve this?"

"Did God slip up this time?"

"Why are the righteous persecuted?"

In his book *Disappointment with God,* Philip Yancey quotes a letter that articulates the problem of unmet expectations in all its excruciating reality. Meg Woodson lost two children to cystic fibrosis, and her daughter's death at age twenty-three was particularly traumatic. The following words speak of her pain and doubt as she struggled to cope with what happened:

> I was sitting beside her bed a few days before her death when suddenly she began screaming. I will never forget those shrill, piercing, primal screams. . . . It's against this background of human beings falling apart . . . that God, who could have helped, looked down on a young woman devoted to Him, quite willing to die for Him to give Him glory, and decided to sit on His hands and let her death top the horror charts for cystic fibrosis deaths.[3]

Does God sometimes sit on his hands? Does God sometimes choose to do nothing? Does God sometimes opt for silence even when I'm screaming my loudest?

♛

Some time ago, I took my family to the bicycle store to purchase a bike for five-year-old Jenna. She picked out a shiny "Starlett" with a banana seat and training wheels. And Andrea, age three, decided she wanted one as well.

I explained to Andrea that she was too young. I told her she was still having trouble with a tricycle and was too small for a two-wheeler. No luck; she still wanted a bike. I explained to her that when she was a bit older, she would get a bike, too. She just stared at me. I tried to tell her that a big bike would bring her more pain than pleasure, more scrapes than thrills. She turned her head and said nothing.

Finally I sighed and said this time her daddy knew best. Her response? She screamed it loud enough for everyone in the store to hear:

"Then I want a *new* daddy!"

Though the words were from a child's mouth, they carried an adult's sentiments.

Disappointment demands a change in command. When we don't agree with the One who calls the shots, our reaction is often the same as Andrea's—the same as John's. "Is he the right one for this job?" Or, as John put it, "Are you the one? Should we look for another?"

Andrea, with her three-year-old reasoning powers, couldn't believe that a new bike would be anything less than ideal for her. From her vantage point, it would be the source of eternal bliss. And from her vantage point, the one who could grant that bliss was "sitting on his hands."

John couldn't believe that anything less than his release would be for the best interest of all involved. In his opinion, it was time to exercise some justice and get some action. But the One who had the power was "sitting on his hands."

I can't believe that God would sit in silence while a missionary is kicked out of a foreign country or a Christian loses a promotion because of his beliefs or a faithful wife is abused by an unbelieving husband. These are just three of many items that have made their way onto my prayer list—all prayers that seem to have gone unanswered.

Rule of thumb: Clouds of doubt are created when the

warm, moist air of our expectations meets the cold air of God's silence.

If you've heard the silence of God, if you've been left standing in the dungeon of doubt, then don't put this book down until you read the next chapter. You may learn, as John did, that the problem is not as much in God's silence as it is in your ability to hear.

. . . for theirs is
the kingdom of heaven.

Seventeen

The Kingdom Worth Dying For

GO BACK AND REPORT TO JOHN WHAT YOU HEAR and see: The blind receive sight, the lame walk, those who have leprosy are cured, the deaf hear, the dead are raised, and the good news is preached to the poor."[1]

This was Jesus' answer to John's agonized query from the dungeon of doubt: "Are you the one who was to come, or should we expect someone else?'"[2]

But before you study what Jesus said, note a couple of things he didn't say.

First, he didn't get angry. He didn't throw up his hands in disgust. He didn't scream, "What in the world do I have to do for John? I've already become flesh! I've already been sinless for three decades. I let him baptize me. What else does he want? Go and tell that ungrateful locust eater I am shocked at his disbelief."

He could have done that. (I would have done that.)

But Jesus didn't. Underline that fact: *God has never turned away the questions of a sincere searcher*. Not Job's nor Abraham's nor Moses' nor John's nor Thomas's nor Max's nor yours.

But note also that Jesus didn't save John. The One who had walked on water could have easily walked on Herod's head, but he didn't. The One who cast out the demons had the power to nuke the king's castle, but he didn't. No battle plan. No SWAT teams. No flashing swords. Just a message—a kingdom message.

"Tell John that everything is going as planned. The kingdom is being inaugurated."

Jesus' words are much more than a statement from Isaiah.[3] They are the description of a heavenly kingdom being established.

A unique kingdom. An invisible kingdom. A kingdom with three distinct traits.

♔

First of all, it is a kingdom where the rejected are received.

"The blind receive sight, the lame walk, those who have leprosy are cured, the deaf hear. . . ."

None were more shunned by their culture than the blind, the lame, the lepers, and the deaf. They had no place. No name. No value. Canker sores on the culture. Excess baggage on the side of the road. But those whom the people called trash, Jesus called treasures.

In my closet hangs a sweater that I seldom wear. It is too small. The sleeves are too short, the shoulders too tight. Some of the buttons are missing, and the thread is frazzled. I should throw that sweater away. I have no use for it. I'll never wear it again. Logic says I should clear out the space and get rid of the sweater.

That's what *logic* says.

But *love* won't let me.

Something unique about that sweater makes me keep it. What is unusual about it? For one thing, it has no label.

Nowhere on the garment will you find a tag that reads, "Made in Taiwan," or "Wash in Cold Water." It has no tag because it wasn't made in a factory. It has no label because it wasn't produced on an assembly line. It isn't the product of a nameless employee earning a living. It's the creation of a devoted mother expressing her love.

That sweater is unique. One of a kind. It can't be replaced. Each strand was chosen with care. Each thread was selected with affection.

And though the sweater has lost all of its use, it has lost none of its value. It is valuable not because of its function, but because of its maker.

That must have been what the psalmist had in mind when he wrote, "you knit me together in my mother's womb."[4]

Think on those words. You were knitted together. You aren't an accident. You weren't mass-produced. You aren't an assembly-line product. You were deliberately planned, specifically gifted, and lovingly positioned on this earth by the Master Craftsman.

"For we are God's workmanship, created in Christ Jesus to do good works, which God prepared in advance for us to do."[5]

In a society that has little room for second fiddles, that's good news. In a culture where the door of opportunity opens only once and then slams shut, that is a revelation. In a system that ranks the value of a human by the figures of his salary or the shape of her legs . . . let me tell you something: Jesus' plan is a reason for joy!

Jesus told John that a new kingdom was coming—a kingdom where people have value not because of what they do, but because of *whose* they are.

The second characteristic of the kingdom is as potent as the first: "The dead have life." The grave has no power.

The year 1899 marked the deaths of two well-known men—Dwight L. Moody, the acclaimed evangelist, and Robert Ingersoll, the famous lawyer, orator, and political leader.

The two men had many similarities. Both were raised in Christian homes. Both were skilled orators. Both traveled extensively and were widely respected. Both drew immense crowds when they spoke and attracted loyal followings. But there was one striking difference between them—their view of God.

Ingersoll was an agnostic and a follower of naturalism; he had no belief in the eternal, but stressed the importance of living only in the here and now. Ingersoll made light of the Bible, stating that "free thought will give us truth." To him the Bible was "a fable, an obscenity, a humbug, a sham and a lie."[6] He was a bold spokesman against the Christian faith. He claimed that a Christian "creed [was] the ignorant past bullying the enlightened present."[7]

Ingersoll's contemporary, Dwight L. Moody, had different convictions. He dedicated his life to presenting a resurrected King to a dying people. He embraced the Bible as the hope for humanity and the cross as the turning point of history. He left behind a legacy of written and spoken words, institutions of education, churches, and changed lives.

Two men. Both powerful speakers and influential leaders. One rejected God; the other embraced him. The impact of their decisions is seen most clearly in the way they died. Read how one biographer parallels the two deaths.

> Ingersoll died suddenly. The news of his death stunned his family. His body was kept at home for several days because his wife was reluctant to part with it. It was eventually removed for the sake of the family's health.
>
> Ingersoll's remains were cremated, and the public response to his passing was altogether dismal. For a man who put all his hopes on this world, death was tragic and came without the consolation of hope.

Moody's legacy was different. On December 22, 1899, Moody awoke to his last winter dawn. Having grown increasingly weak during the night, he began to speak in slow measured words. "Earth recedes, heaven opens before me!" Son Will, who was nearby, hurried across the room to his father's side.

"Father, you are dreaming," he said.

"No. This is no dream, Will," Moody said. "It is beautiful. It is like a trance. If this is death, it is sweet. God is calling me, and I must go. Don't call me back."

At that point, the family gathered around, and moments later the great evangelist died. It was his coronation day—a day he had looked forward to for many years. He was with his Lord.

The funeral service of Dwight L. Moody reflected that same confidence. There was no despair. Loved ones gathered to sing praise to God at a triumphant home-going service. Many remembered the words the evangelist had spoken earlier that year in New York City: "Someday you will read in the papers that Moody is dead. Don't you believe a word of it. At that moment I shall be more alive than I am now. . . . I was born of the flesh in 1837, I was born of the Spirit in 1855. That which is born of the flesh may die. That which is born of the Spirit shall live forever."[8]

Jesus looked into the eyes of John's followers and gave them this message. "Report to John . . . the dead are raised." Jesus wasn't oblivious to John's imprisonment. He wasn't blind to John's captivity. But he was dealing with a greater dungeon than Herod's; he was dealing with the dungeon of death.

♛

But Jesus wasn't through. He passed on one other message to clear the cloud of doubt out of John's heart: "The good news is preached to the poor."

Some months ago I was late to catch a plane out of the San Antonio airport. I wasn't terribly late, but I was late enough to be bumped and have my seat given to a stand-by passenger.

When the ticket agent told me that I would have to miss the flight, I put to work my best persuasive powers.

"But the flight hasn't left yet."

"Yes, but you got here too late."

"I got here before the plane left; is that too late?"

"The regulation says you must arrive ten minutes before the flight is scheduled to depart. That was two minutes ago."

"But, ma'am," I pleaded, "I've got to be in Houston by this evening."

She was patient but firm. "I'm sorry, sir, but the rules say passengers must be at the gate ten minutes before scheduled departure time."

"I know what the rules say," I explained. "But I'm not asking for justice; I'm asking for mercy."

She didn't give it to me.

But God does. Even though by the "book" I'm guilty, by God's love I get another chance. Even though by the law I'm indicted, by mercy I'm given a fresh start.

"For it is by grace you have been saved . . . not by works, so that no one can boast."[9]

No other world religion offers such a message. All others demand the right performance, the right sacrifice, the right chant, the right ritual, the right seance or experience. Theirs is a kingdom of trade-offs and barterdom. You do this, and God will give you that.

The result? Either arrogance or fear. Arrogance if you think you've achieved it, fear if you think you haven't.

Christ's kingdom is just the opposite. It is a kingdom for the poor. A kingdom where membership is *granted*, not *purchased*. *You* are placed into God's kingdom. You are "adopted." And this occurs not when you do enough, but when you admit you *can't* do enough. You don't earn it; you simply accept it. As a result, you serve, not out of arrogance or fear, but out of gratitude.

I recently read a story of a woman who for years was married to a harsh husband. Each day he would leave her a list of chores to complete before he returned at the end of the day. "Clean the yard. Stack the firewood. Wash the windows. . . ."

If she didn't complete the tasks, she would be greeted with his explosive anger. But even if she did complete the list, he was never satisfied; he would always find inadequacies in her work.

After several years, the husband passed away. Some time later she remarried, this time to a man who lavished her with tenderness and adoration.

One day, while going through a box of old papers, the wife discovered one of her first husband's lists. And as she read the sheet, a realization caused a tear of joy to splash on the paper.

"I'm still doing all these things, and no one has to tell me. I do it because I love him."

That is the unique characteristic of the new kingdom. Its subjects don't work in order to go to heaven; they work *because* they are going to heaven. Arrogance and fear are replaced with gratitude and joy.

♔

That's the kingdom Jesus proclaimed: a kingdom of acceptance, eternal life, and forgiveness.

We don't know how John received Jesus' message, but we can imagine. I like to think of a slight smile coming over his lips as he heard what his Master said.

"So that's it. That is what the kingdom will be. That is what the King will do."

For now he understood. It wasn't that Jesus was silent; it was that John had been listening for the wrong answer.

John had been listening for an answer to his earthly problems, while Jesus was busy resolving his heavenly ones.

That's worth remembering the next time you hear the silence of God.

If you've asked for a mate, but are still sleeping alone . . . if you've asked for a child, but your womb stays barren . . . if you've asked for healing, but are still hurting . . . don't think God isn't listening. He is. And he is answering requests you are not even making.

Saint Teresa of Avila was insightful enough to pray, "Do not punish me by granting that which I wish or ask.[10]

The apostle Paul was honest enough to write, "We do not know what we ought to pray for."[11]

The fact is, John wasn't asking too much; he was asking too little. He was asking the Father to resolve the temporary, while Jesus was busy resolving the eternal. John was asking for immediate favor, while Jesus was orchestrating the eternal solution.

Does that mean that Jesus has no regard for injustice? No. He cares about persecutions. He cares about inequities and hunger and prejudice. And he knows what it is like to be punished for something he didn't do. He knows the meaning of the phrase, "It's just not right."

For it wasn't right that people spit into the eyes that had wept for them. It wasn't right that soldiers ripped chunks of flesh out of the back of their God. It wasn't right that spikes pierced the hands that formed the earth. And it wasn't right that the Son of God was forced to hear the silence of God.

It wasn't right, but it happened.

For while Jesus was on the cross, God *did* sit on his hands. He did turn his back. He did ignore the screams of the innocent.

He sat in silence while the sins of the world were placed upon his Son. And he did nothing while a cry a million times bloodier than John's echoed in the black sky: "My God, my God, why have you forsaken me?"[12]

Was it right? No.
Was it fair? No.
Was it love? Yes.

In a world of injustice, God once and for all tipped the scales in the favor of hope. And he did it by sitting on his hands so that we could know the kingdom of God.

Rejoice and
be glad, because great
is your reward. . . .

Eighteen

The Applause of Heaven

I'M ALMOST HOME. AFTER FIVE DAYS, FOUR HOTEL beds, eleven restaurants, and twenty-two cups of coffee, I'm almost home. After eight airplane seats, five airports, two delays, one book, and five hundred thirteen packages of peanuts, I'm almost home.

The plane resonates under me. A baby cries behind me. Businessmen converse around me. Cool air blows from a hole above me. But all that matters is what is before me—home.

Home. It was my first thought when I awoke this morning. It was my first thought when I stepped down from the last podium. It was my first thought when I said good-bye to my last host at the last airport.

There's no door like the one to your own house. There's no better place to put your feet than under your own table. There's no coffee like coffee out of your own mug. There's no meal like the one at your own table. And there's no embrace like the one from your own family.

Home. The longest part of going home is the last part—the plane's taxiing to the terminal from the runway. I'm the fellow the flight attendant always has to tell to sit down. I'm the guy with one hand on my briefcase and the other on my seat belt. I have learned that there is a critical split second in which I can bolt down the aisle into the first-class section before the tributaries of people begin emptying into the main aisle.

I don't do that on every flight. Only when I'm going home.

There is a leap of the heart as I exit the plane. I almost get nervous as I walk up the ramp. I step past people. I grip my satchel. My stomach tightens. My palms sweat. I walk into the lobby like an actor walking onto a stage. The curtain is lifted, and the audience stands in a half-moon. Most of the people see that I'm not the one they want and look past me.

But from the side I hear the familiar shriek of two little girls. "Daddy!" I turn and see them—faces scrubbed, standing on chairs, bouncing up and down in joy as the man in their life walks toward them. Jenna stops bouncing just long enough to clap. She applauds! I don't know who told her to do that, but you can bet I'm not going to tell her to stop.

Behind them I see a third face—little Sara, only a few months old. Deeply asleep, she furrows her brow slightly in reaction to the squealing.

And then I see a fourth face—my wife's face. Somehow, she has found time to comb her hair, put on a new dress, put on that extra sparkle. Somehow, though wrung out and done in, she will make me feel that my week is the only week worth talking about.

Faces of home.

That is what makes the promise at the end of the Beatitudes so compelling: "Rejoice and be glad, because great is your reward in heaven.

What is our reward? Home.

♔

The Book of Revelation could be entitled the Book of Homecoming, for in it we are given a picture of our heavenly home.

John's descriptions of the future steal your breath. His depiction of the final battle is graphic. Good clashes with evil. The sacred encounters the sinful. The pages howl with the shrieks of dragons and smolder with the coals of fiery pits. But in the midst of the battlefield there is a rose. John describes it in chapter 21:

> Then I saw a new heaven and a new earth, for the first heaven and the first earth had passed away, and there was no longer any sea. I saw the Holy City, the new Jerusalem, coming down out of heaven from God, prepared as a bride beautifully dressed for her husband. And I heard a loud voice from the throne saying, "Now the dwelling of God is with men, and he will live with them. They will be his people, and God himself will be with them and be their God. He will wipe every tear from their eyes. There will be no more death or mourning or crying or pain, for the old order of things has passed away. He who was seated on the throne said, "I am making everything new!"[1]

John is old when he writes these words. His body is weary. The journey has taken its toll. His friends are gone. Peter is dead. Paul has been martyred. Andrew, James, Nathaniel . . . they are fuzzy figures from an early era.

As he hears the voice from the throne, I wonder, does he remember the day he heard it on the mountain? For it is the same John and the same Jesus. The same feet that followed Jesus up the mount so long ago now stand to follow him again. The same eyes that watched the Nazarene teach on the summit watch for him again. The same ears that heard Jesus first describe sacred delight listen to it revealed again.

In this final mountaintop encounter, God pulls back the curtain and allows the warrior to peek into the homeland. When given the task of writing down what he sees, John chooses the most beautiful comparison earth has to offer. The Holy City, John says, is like "a bride beautifully dressed for her husband."

What is more beautiful than a bride? One of the side benefits of being a minister is that I get an early glimpse of the bride as she stands at the top of the aisle. And I have to say that I have never seen an ugly bride. I've seen some grooms that could use an alteration or two, but never a bride. Maybe it is the aura of whiteness that clings to her as dew clings to a rose. Or perhaps it is the diamonds that glisten in her eyes. Or maybe it's the blush of love that pinks her cheeks or the bouquet of promises she carries. Whatever it is, there is the feeling that when you see a bride you are seeing the purest beauty the world can boast.

A bride. A commitment robed in elegance. "I'll be with you forever." Tomorrow bringing hope to today. Promised purity faithfully delivered.

When you read that our heavenly home is similar to a bride, tell me, doesn't it make you want to go home?

The world I woke up to this morning couldn't be described as a bride beautifully dressed for her husband, could yours?

Part of the world to which I awoke was grieving. A teenager took his life in the predawn darkness. No note. No explanation. Just a dumbstruck mother and a bewildered father who will forever be hounded by questions they cannot answer.

Part of the world to which I awoke was disillusioned. Another national leader has been accused of dishonesty. He blinked back tears and swallowed anger on network news. A generation ago, we would have given him the benefit of the doubt. Not now.

A part of the world to which I awoke this morning was devastated. A three-year-old's throat was cut open by her own father. A pre-med student was butchered and sacrificed by Satan worshipers. A husband of thirty years ran off with another man. (No, not a woman, a man.)

When you look at this world, stained by innocent blood and smudged with selfishness, doesn't it make you want to go home?

Me, too.

The old saint tells us that when we get home, God himself will wipe away our tears.

When I was a young man, I had plenty of people to wipe away my tears. I had two big sisters who put me under their wings. I had a dozen or so aunts and uncles. I had a mother who worked nights as a nurse and days as a mother—exercising both professions with tenderness. I even had a brother three years my elder who felt sorry for me occasionally.

But when I think about someone wiping away my tears, I think about Dad. His hands were callused and tough, his fingers short and stubby. And when my father wiped away a tear, he seemed to wipe it away forever. There was something in his touch that took away more than the drop of hurt from my cheek. It also took away my fear.

John says that someday God will wipe away your tears. The same hands that stretched the heavens will touch your cheeks. The same hands that formed the mountains will caress your face. The same hands that curled in agony as the Roman spike cut through will someday cup your face and brush away your tears. Forever.

When you think of a world where there will be no reason to cry, ever, doesn't it make you want to go home?

"There will be no more death . . ." John declares. Can you imagine it? A world with no hearses or morgues or cemeteries or tombstones? Can you imagine a world with no spades of dirt thrown on caskets? No names chiseled into marble? No funerals? No black dresses? No black wreaths?

If one of the joys of the ministry is a bride descending

the church aisle, one of the griefs is a body encased in a shiny box in front of the pulpit. It's never easy to say good-bye. It's never easy to walk away. The hardest task in this world is to place a final kiss on cold lips that cannot kiss in return. The hardest thing in this world is to say good-bye.

In the next world, John says, "good-bye" will never be spoken.

Tell me, doesn't that make you want to go home?

♔

The most hopeful words of that passage from Revelation are those of God's resolve: "I am making everything new."

It's hard to see things grow old. The town in which I grew up is growing old. I was there recently. Some of the buildings are boarded up. Some of the houses are torn down. Some of my teachers are retired; some are buried. The old movie house where I took my dates has "For Sale" on the marquee, long since outdated by the newer theaters that give you eight choices. The only visitors to the drive-in theater are tumbleweeds and rodents. Memories of first dates and senior proms are weather-worn by the endless rain of years. High school sweethearts are divorced. A cheerleader died of an aneurysm. Our fastest halfback is buried only a few plots from my own father.

I wish I could make it all new again. I wish I could blow the dust off the streets. I wish I could walk through the familiar neighborhood, and wave at the familiar faces, and pet the familiar dogs, and hit one more home run in the Little League park. I wish I could walk down Main Street and call out the merchants that have retired and open the doors that have been boarded up. I wish I could make everything new . . . but I can't.

My mother still lives in the same house. You couldn't pay her to move. The house that seemed so big when I was a boy now feels tiny. On the wall are pictures of Mom in her youth—her hair autumn-brown, her face irresistibly beautiful. I see her now—still healthy, still vivacious, but with wrinkles, graying hair, slower step. Would that I could wave the wand and make everything new again. Would that I could put her once again in the strong embrace of the high-plains cowboy she loved and buried. Would that I could stretch out the wrinkles and take off the bifocals and restore the spring to her step. Would that I could make everything new . . . but I can't.

I can't. But God can. "He restores my soul,"[2] wrote the shepherd. He doesn't reform; he restores. He doesn't camouflage the old; he restores the new. The Master Builder will pull out the original plan and restore it. He will restore the vigor. He will restore the energy. He will restore the hope. He will restore the soul.

When you see how this world grows stooped and weary and then read of a home where everything is made new, tell me, doesn't that make you want to go home?

What would you give in exchange for a home like that? Would you really rather have a few possessions on earth than eternal possessions in heaven? Would you really choose a life of slavery to passion over a life of freedom? Would you honestly give up all of your heavenly mansions for a second-rate sleazy motel on earth?

"Great," Jesus said, "is your reward in heaven." He must have smiled when he said that line. His eyes must have danced, and his hand must have pointed skyward.

For he should know. It was his idea. It was his home.

♔

I'll be home soon. My plane is nearing San Antonio. I can feel the nose of the jet dipping downward. I can see the flight attendants getting ready. Denalyn is somewhere in the parking lot, parking the car and hustling the girls toward the terminal.

I'll be home soon. The plane will land. I'll walk down that ramp and hear my name and see their faces. I'll be home soon.

You'll be home soon, too. You may not have noticed it, but you are closer to home than ever before. Each moment is a step taken. Each breath is a page turned. Each day is a mile marked, a mountain climbed. You are closer to home than you've ever been.

Before you know it, your appointed arrival time will come; you'll descend the ramp and enter the City.

You'll see faces that are waiting for you. You'll hear your name spoken by those who love you. And, maybe, just maybe—in the back, behind the crowds—the One who would rather die than live without you will remove his pierced hands from his heavenly robe and . . . applaud.

Notes

CHAPTER 1 · SACRED DELIGHT

1. 1 Timothy 1:11.
2. 1 Timothy 6:15.

CHAPTER 2 · THE SUMMIT

1. "How Americans Are Running out of Time," *Time*, 24 April 1989, 74–76.
2. Matthew 11:28.
3. Walter Burkhardt, *Tell the Next Generation* (Ramsey, NJ: Paulist, 1982), 80, quoted in Brennan Mannin, *Lion and Lamb* (Old Tappan, NJ: Chosen, Revell, 1986), 129.

CHAPTER 1 · THE AFFLUENT POOR

1. His story is told in Matthew 19, Mark 10, and Luke 18.
2. Luke 18:27.
3. Mark 10:23.
4. Matthew 7:22.
5. Matthew 7:23.
6. Romans 8:3.
7. Frederick Dale Bruner clarifies this as he interprets Matthew 5:3: "Blessed are those who feel their poverty . . . and so cry out to heaven." *The Christbook: Matthew 1–12* (Waco, TX: Word, 1987), 135.
8. The word Jesus used for "poor" is a word which, when used in its most basic sense, "would not indicate the pauper, one so poor that he must daily work for his living, but the beggar, one who is dependent upon others for support." William Hendricksen, *Exposition of the Gospel of Matthew* (Grand Rapids, MI: Baker, 1973), 269.

CHAPTER 4 · THE KINGDOM OF THE ABSURD

1. See Genesis 16–18, 21.
2. See Luke 5.
3. 2 Corinthians 12:9, LB.
4. Philippians 3:4–6, LB.
5. 1 Timothy 1:15.
6. Acts 22:16.
7. 1 Corinthians 1:23.
8. 1 Corinthians 1:23; Ephesians 2:8.
9. 1 Corinthians 5:14, NEB.

CHAPTER 5 · THE PRISON OF PRIDE

1. 1 John 1:9, emphasis mine.
2. Bruner states it admirably: "God helps those who cannot help themselves and he helps those who try to help others, but he does not in any beatitude help those who think they can help themselves—an often ungodly and antisocial conception." *The Christbook*, 152.
3. Matthew 14:28.

CHAPTER 6 · TOUCHES OF TENDERNESS

1. Matthew 6:28–33.
2. Matthew 7:11.

CHAPTER 7 · THE GLORY IN THE ORDINARY

1. See Exodus 4:1–4.
2. See 1 Samuel 17.
3. See John 9:1–6.

CHAPTER 8 · THE BANDIT OF JOY

1. Ian Grey, *Stalin* (Garden City, NY: Doubleday, 1979), 457, and Alex De Jonge, *Stalin and the Shaping of the Soviet Union* (New York: William Morrow, 1986), 450.
2. "The Secret Life of Howard Hughes," *Time*, 13 December 1976, 22–41.
3. "John Lennon: In the Hard Day's Light," *People Weekly*, 15 August 1989, 68–69.

4. "In Praise of Courage," *Quest*, November 1980, 23.
5. See Matthew 10:1–28.
6. Matthew 10:21–22.
7. Matthew 10:26–31.
8. Matthew 10:26.
9. Hebrews 4:13, Daniel 2:22, Matthew 12:36, Psalm 90:8, 1 Corinthians 4:5.
10. Romans 8:1, 3:26, Acts 13:39, Hebrews 8:12, Colossians 3:3.
11. Hebrews 10:19, 22, emphasis mine.
12. Matthew 10:27–28.
13. Paul Harvey, *Paul Harvey's The Rest of the Story* (New York, NY: Bantam, 1977), 117.

CHAPTER 9 · A SATISFIED THIRST

1. Luke 22:20.
2. Hebrews 10:4.
3. John 7:37.
4. "It is not sufficient that we merely want righteousness unless we have a downright famine for it . . . "—St. Jerome, quoted in Bruner, *The Christbook*, 142.
5. Matthew 26:28, PHILLIPS.

CHAPTER 11 · THE FATHER IN THE FACE OF THE ENEMY

1. Archibald Hart, *The Hidden Link between Adrenaline and Stress* (Waco, TX: Word, 1986), 101, 142–45.
2. Matthew 18:21–35.
3. Matthew 18:34.
4. Romans 2:4.

CHAPTER 12 · THE STATE OF THE HEART

1. Proverbs 4:23.
2. Matthew 15:18–19.
3. Luke 6:45.
4. Psalms 51:10.

CHAPTER 14 · SEEDS OF PEACE

1. James 3:18, LB.
2. Paul Harvey, *Paul Harvey's The Rest of the Story* (New York, NY: Bantam, 1977), 49.
3. Isaiah 53:2, LB.

CHAPTER 15 · THE GREASY POLE OF POWER

1. *USA Today*, 22 March 1988, 5D.
2. Henry Emerson Fosdick, quoted in *A Guide to Prayer for Ministers and Other Servants* (Nashville: *The Upper Room*, 1983), 263.
3. Genesis 3:5.
4. Gary Smith, "Ali and His Entourage," *Sports Illustrated*, 16 April 1988, 48–49.
5. Paul Lee Tan, ed., *Encyclopedia of 7700 Illustrations* (Rockville, MD: Assurance Publishers, 1979), 1213–14.

CHAPTER 16 · THE DUNGEON OF DOUBT

1. Matthew 14:1–12.
2. Matthew 11:3–4.
3. Philip Yancey, *Disappointment with God* (Grand Rapids, MI: Zondervan, 1988), 158.

CHAPTER 17 · THE KINGDOM WORTH DYING FOR

1. Matthew 11:4–5.
2. Matthew 11:3–4.
3. Isaiah 35:5; 61:1.
4. Psalm 139:13.
5. Ephesians 2:10.
6. George Sweeting and Donald Sweeting, "The Evangelist and the Agnostic," *Moody Monthly*, July/August 1989, 69.
7. Ibid., 67.
8. Ibid., 69.
9. Ephesians 2:8–9.
10. Quoted in *A Guide to Prayer for Ministers and Other Servants*, 345.
11. Romans 8:26.
12. Matthew 27:46.

CHAPTER 18 · THE APPLAUSE OF HEAVEN

1. Revelation 21:1–5.
2. Psalm 23:3.

Study Guide

Meeting Christ on the Mountain

THIS BOOK IS NOT AN END IN ITSELF. If it does its job, it will lead you toward your own encounter with Christ on the mountain. And the following guide is intended to help you make that connection between reading a book and meeting the Christ.

This, then, is not so much a study of a book but a study of Christ's message and a catalyst for helping the book bring his message into the core of your life. It does not proceed chapter by chapter, but beatitude by beatitude, using the insights of the chapters as springboards for your own study and meditation.

There are ten study "sessions" here. If you are meeting together in a group, you might try to work through one a week. (Note to group leaders: since some of the questions in the guide are very personal, "sharing" answers should always be optional.) If you are studying on your own, go at your own pace, taking the time to let each beatitude work its transforming way into your attitude and character.

To each encounter, I suggest you bring your Bible and a notebook for writing down your own thoughts and observations. More important, bring a prayerful spirit and an expectant attitude. And when you come, plan to be surprised with the sacred delight of meeting Christ on the mountain.

Session 1 · Chapters 1 & 2

Now when he saw the crowds, he went up on a mountainside and sat down. . . . and he began to teach them, saying: Blessed . . .

1. Describe the happiest moment you can remember. Jot down some of the circumstances surrounding it—who was involved, when it happened, how long your happiness lasted. Now, recall the time in your life that you were most miserable. What was happening then? How have the circumstances of your life contributed to your happiness or unhappiness?
2. What is the difference between "choosing to be cheerful," as Beverly Sills describes it, and putting on a cheerful facade to cover up or deny misery? Under what circumstances, if any, could "choosing to be cheerful" be a negative choice?
3. The following Old Testament passages reveal some of the ideas about happiness Jesus' listeners had grown up on. How does each passage describe a happy (blessed) person?

    - Psalm 1:1–6
    - Psalm 2:10–12
    - Psalm 32:1–2, 5–7, 10–11
    - Psalm 41:1–3
    - Psalm 84:4–5, 11–12
    - Psalm 94:12–13
    - Psalm 112:1–9
    - Proverbs 8:1–2, 32–36 (note who is "speaking")

4. Chapter 1 states that the Greek word Jesus used for "blessed" in the Beatitudes (*makarios*) is the same one used by Paul to describe God. It was used in other ancient literature to describe the "happy state of the gods above earthly sufferings" and to denote "a transcendent happiness of a life beyond care, labor and death" (*Theological Dictionary of the New Testament*, 4:362). What does Jesus' use of this powerful word say about the kind of happiness he is promising?
5. Read Matthew 4:23–25. What events in Jesus' ministry immediately preceded Jesus' withdrawing to the mountain? What do you think was the significance of this order of events? Why did Jesus withdraw to the mountain with his disciples at this particular time?
6. What are the best times and places for you to "go to the mountain"? What specific activities and responsibilities tend to stand in the way of your getting there?
7. Chapter 1 states that "you are one decision away from joy." Chapter 2 says that "the mountain is only a decision away." Specifically, what decision is this?

Session 2 · Chapters 3 & 4

Blessed are the poor in spirit,
for theirs is the kingdom of heaven.

1. How does chapter 3 interpret being "poor in spirit"? How does this compare with any previous ideas you had about what this beatitude means?
2. Luke's version of this beatitude (found in Luke 6:20, 24) omits the "in spirit" idea entirely; it simply states that "the rich" have their reward here and therefore cannot expect a reward in heaven. And Jesus tells the rich young ruler directly that "it is hard for a rich man to enter the kingdom of heaven" (Matthew 19:23–24). Do you think the first beatitude applies especially to those who are poor in material possessions? If not, why does Matthew make these specific comments about material wealth? (You may find some ideas in the end notes for this chapter.)
3. List three reasons why being poor in spirit as described in these two chapters is difficult for most of us. Why do we have such a hard time admitting our own inadequacy and failures even to God and ourselves?
4. List what you consider your five greatest strengths and your five greatest weaknesses. Then examine your list in light of chapter 3. Does being poor in spirit mean denying your strengths or not trying to improve your weaknesses? Does it mean being "down on yourself"? Why or why not?
5. Is it possible to be both arrogant and insecure at the same time? What do you think are the

motives behind the rich young ruler's self-justification and overachievement?

6. What is the difference between trying to achieve salvation and trying to please God? Between being poor in spirit and being a poor steward of your God-given gifts?
7. Read the following parables describing the "kingdom of heaven": Matthew 13:24–33, 44–50. What additional insight do these parables give about the nature of the "kingdom" in which the poor in spirit will live?
8. Read Matthew 16:13–20, which tells the circumstances under which Peter's name was changed and he was given the "keys to the kingdom of heaven." What elements of this account point to Peter's being poor in spirit? What does this passage tell you about the nature of the kingdom?
9. What sort of positive change would you like in your life? According to these two chapters, what would be your best strategy for such change?

Session 3 · Chapters 5 & 6

Blessed are those who mourn,
for they will be comforted.

1 After reading these two chapters, complete the sentence: "Blessed are those who mourn for." What specific kind of grief do these chapters speak of?

2. Can you think of cases in which admitting failure can become a cop-out—an excuse to stop trying? What (if any) is the difference between "mourning" and giving in to failure?

3. Most of our everyday situations aren't as dra-matic as that of Anibal or Peter; the life-or-death nature of our decisions isn't as obvious. How can we be more aware of our need for Jesus in noncrisis situations?

4. Read Hosea 7:14 and 2 Corinthians 7:9–11. What kind of mourning do they describe? Is it included under Jesus' blessing in the second beatitude?

5. To what things, people, or activities (adult versions of the hug, the Band-Aid,® the flashlight) do you tend to turn for comfort? Do they work? In your opinion, is anything inherently wrong with such "security blankets"?

6. Practically speaking, what does God's comfort feel like? What form does it take, and how does it come to us? Have you ever felt it? (For ideas, see Genesis 5:29, 24:67; 1 Chronicles 7:22; Job 6:10; Psalms 23:4, 71:21, 77, 119:50–52, 40:1–5; Isaiah 52:70–9, 57:14–19; John 11:19, 15:15–22, 14:1–6; 2 Corinthians 1:3–4, 7:6–7.)

7. Why do you think so many of us come to think that God doesn't want to hear about our problems or gets tired of forgiving us?
8. Read 2 Corinthians 1:3–4. Under what circumstances are we called upon to be agents of God's comfort to those who mourn?
9. List three ways we can comfort others effectively. What are some tactics that do *not* work? Describe a situation in which you were able to provide comfort.
10. What is the relationship between "mourning" and being poor in spirit? How are the two alike? How are they different?

Session 4 · Chapters 7 & 8

Blessed are the meek, for they will inherit the earth.

1. How does chapter 7 interpret the word meek? How does that definition differ from your previous ideas of "meekness."
2. Do you think of yourself as "ordinary"? Why or why not? Do you find that description comforting or insulting?
3. What are some synonyms for the word meek as it is used in the Beatitudes? For ideas, look up Numbers 12:3, Psalm 25:9, Isaiah 11:4, 61:1, Matthew 11:29, and 1 Peter 3:4 in the King James version and another translation.
4. Practically speaking, what does it mean to be meek in the sense of letting God use you? If he doesn't speak through an angel or a burning bush, how do you know what he wants you to do?
5. In practical terms, how do you avoid taking over or "telling God how to do his job"—and still get something done?
6. Chapter 6 interprets "inherit the earth" as not being intimidated or afraid of any earthly power or person. In your mind, is this a satisfactory definition? Would you be more comfortable saying, "Blessed are the meek, for theirs is the kingdom of heaven?" Why do you think Jesus specified "the earth" in this beatitude?
7. Psalm 37:11 also states that the meek will inherit the earth. Read Psalm 37:1–17 to understand this verse in context. What is the message of the psalm? Is its thrust basically similar or different

from the third beatitude? What new perspective does Psalm 37 give to Jesus' statement?

8. Describe one time in your life when you let fear keep you from doing something you knew you should do.
9. According to chapter 8, what are the three ways we seek to handle our fears? To which of these three are you more likely to turn? (Don't be misled by the 'big guy' examples; these defense mechanisms take many forms—major and minor!). Give an example of a time when you have taken refuge in one of these defenses.
10. What reason did Jesus give the disciples for not being afraid? Why can this be taken as a source of courage?
11. What would you do tomorrow if you were guaranteed you couldn't fail and that nothing could hurt you? Write down and/or share one example.

Session 5 · Chapters 9 & 10

Blessed are those who hunger and thirst for righteousness, for they will be filled.

1. A "how to write fiction" computer software program currently on the market begins its instruction with a question: "What does ______ want?" The idea is that all plots (and therefore, all stories) arise from people's basic needs and desires. If you were writing a novel about yourself, how would you answer that starting question? What "hungers and thirsts" motivate you most?
2. How does chapter 9 interpret the idea of righteousness? What would your own definition be?
3. Read Matthew 23:27–28. What was there about the Pharisees' attitude about righteousness that made Jesus so angry?
4. Read Romans 3:10–31. What do this passage and Matthew 23:27–28 tell us about trying to be righteous in our own right, boasting about our righteousness, or assuming we are righteous because we "keep all the rules"? How are these attitudes different from "hungering and thirsting" for righteousness?
5. According to chapters 9 and 10 and Romans 3:21–31, what is the only way our "hunger and thirst for righteousness" can be "satisfied"?
6. According to chapter 9, what is the ultimate reason that those who hunger and thirst after righteousness will be filled?
7. What does "hungering and thirsting after righteousness" have to do with "holding earthly

possessions in open palms" and being dependent on Jesus for joy (chapter 10)?

8. Chapter 10 intimates that our fullest experience of "being filled" will be in heaven. But do we ever experience such satisfaction here on earth? If so, how?
9. Look back over the first three beatitudes. What do they have in common? How is this fourth beatitude like them? How is it different?

Session 6 · Chapter 11

Blessed are the merciful,
for they will be shown mercy.

1. According to chapter 11, what is the opposite of mercy?
2. Read Matthew 6:12 and 7:1–2. What light do these passages from later in the Sermon on the Mount throw on the idea of the merciful receiving mercy?
3. Is mercy synonymous with forgiveness? Why or why not?
4. Why is it so hard to give up resentments? What does mercy cost us?
5. In what ways does resentment harm us? List three specific negative effects.
6. According to chapter 12, what makes it possible for us to be merciful and forgiving?
7. Write one to five things to do in the next week either to make restitution for hurts you have caused or to reach out in forgiveness to those who have hurt you. (Be honest with yourself. If you cannot bring yourself yet to forgive those who have hurt you or to accept God's forgiveness for hurts you have caused, simply write down that you will pray for the ability to do these things.)

Session 7 · Chapters 12 & 13

Blessed are the pure in heart,
for they will see God.

1. Does the fact that "what comes out of us" makes us good or evil mean that what goes in doesn't matter much? Why or why not?
2. Look up 1 Kings 18:26–28 and Acts 22:3. Is purity the same as sincerity or good intentions? Can a person be both pure and wrong?
3. Look up 1 Peter 1:22, 1 Timothy 1:5–8, and John 8:31–32. What principles determine purity of heart?
4. Now back up and read Matthew 22:34. What, according to this passage, is the key to achieving purity of heart?
5. Must we always wait until our "insides are clean" before we start to act right—and before we see God? Why or why not?
6. Look up John 14:5–14. What does John have to say about how we come to 'see God'? What different perspective does that give to the idea of being pure in heart?
7. According to chapter 13, what is the differenc between "temple builders" and "Savior seekers"?
8. Give an example of a time you, or someone you know, got so caught up in a project you forgot the whole point of it. Have you ever been so involved in church or religious activities that you got out of touch with God?
9. At what time in your life have you been most aware of "seeing God"? At what times have you been able to "see" him only in retrospect? What

is the difference between "temple building" and the "dry times" every Christian experiences?

10. If "Savior seekers" often must find Jesus "in spite of " the temple, what is the purpose of the organized church? What can we do better in community that we cannot do as individual seekers?

Session 8 · Chapters 14 & 15

Blessed are the peacemakers,
for they will be called sons of God.

1. How would you define peace as it is portrayed in chapter 14? How does this concept of peace differ from more common ideas about peace?
2. Commentator Dale Bruner writes, "We can almost translate the key word here, 'peacemakers,' with the word 'wholemakers.' . . . Biblical *shalom* conveys the picture of a circle; it means comprehensive well-being in every direction and relation. . . . If we could translate 'blessed are the circle makers' and make sense, we would. To make peace, in Scripture, is to bring community. "Peacemakers are reconcilers" (*The Christbook*, 149). How do the examples of peacemaking given in this chapter fit Bruner's definition?
3. Read at least three of the following scriptures: Numbers 6:24–26, Psalm 29:11, Luke 1:76–79, John 14:27, 16:33, Romans 5:1, 1 Corinthians 14:33, Galatians 5:22, Ephesians 2:14–17, and Philippians 4:7. According to these passages and to chapter 14, what is the ultimate source of peace?
4. Read James 3:13–18. What are some of the "prerequisites" for peacemaking? What must happen inside us before we can be peacemakers?
5. Read Matthew 10:34–39. Are there times when peacemaking in the larger sense involves accepting conflict rather than avoiding it? Does it ever involve *initiating* conflict? If possible, give a biblical or contemporary example.
6. Is it enough simply to plant seeds of peace? Are

there ways we can nurture them and help them grow?

7. Is the "push for power" a basic part of human nature? Can it ever be a positive thing? How can we avoid it?
8. How does power relate to peacemaking? Can power ever be used in the *service* of peacemaking? Why or why not?
9. Write down the names of three people in your life who could use a word or act of peace from you. Beside each person's name, write an idea for a "seed" of peace. Finally, write down a specific date and time to plant your seed and commit to that schedule. If you are meeting in a group, be prepared to share your "peace seed" (not necessarily the results) at the next meeting. If you are on your own, consider sharing your peace initiatives with a friend and asking to be held accountable.

Session 9 · Chapters 16 & 17

Blessed are those who are persecuted because of righteousness, for theirs is the kingdom of God.

1. According to chapter 16, why did John send word to ask Jesus if he was really the Messiah?
2. Name a situation in which you have felt persecuted for doing what was right. What was the outcome of your experience?
3. What are some of the explanations you've heard for times when God seems silent? Which explanations seemed most satisfactory? Which didn't satisfy you?
4. Do persecution and "God's silence" always go hand in hand, or are they two separate things? Why do you think so?
5. What are some ways (subtle and overt) that Christians are persecuted "because of righteousness"?
6. Read Proverbs 21:2 and Jeremiah 17:9. What do these passages suggest about how we can interpret the bad things that happen to us? If we are in trouble, how can we be sure that our persecution is "because of righteousness"—that we are in trouble for the right reasons?
7. Chapter 17 states, "God has never turned away the questions of a sincere searcher." Do you feel comfortable with this idea of questioning God? Why or why not? When you get to heaven, what are some questions you want to ask him?
8. The Book of Job is another biblical account of a person who suffered from God's seeming silence

in the face of injustice. When struck with numerous, undeserved afflictions, he, too, questioned God. But Job's questions were different, as were the answers he received and the outcome of the story.

- Read Job 3:23, 7:20–21, 10:2–7, 13:20–24, 24:1–12. What questions did Job ask God?
- Read Job 38:1–21, 40:1–14, and 42:1–6. What was God's answer? How was it similar to Jesus' answer to John? How was it different?

9. Write down the three characteristics of Christ's kingdom that are implied in Jesus' answer to John. In what ways have you seen these characteristics continuing in your lifetime?
10. Chapter 17 relates this beatitude back to the first one, "Blessed are the poor in spirit," which also states "for theirs is the kingdom of heaven." Why do you think the phrase was repeated? How does being poor in spirit relate to being persecuted for the sake of righteousness?
11. Read Jesus' familiar model prayer cited in Matthew 6:9–13. In your opinion, how do Jesus' instructions on how to pray relate to the way we respond to persecution and doubt?

Session 10 · Chapter 18

Rejoice and be glad, because great is your reward. . . .

1. According to chapter 18, what is the ultimate joy promised to those who follow Jesus?
2. Describe the happiest homecoming you have ever experienced. Who was there? Why were you (or someone else) coming home? Where had you (or the homecomer) been? Why was this particular experience so happy?
3. According to chapter 18, what biblical images does the Book of Revelation use to describe our "homeland"? What do these biblical pictures say about our future with Christ?
4. What kinds of experiences (personal or second hand) in this world make you "want to go home" to a world made new? How do you picture your heavenly home?
5. What do the Beatitudes tell us about how we receive "the applause of heaven" while still on earth?
6. Read Luke's version of the Beatitudes as given in Luke 6:20–26. How do the two versions differ? Where do they agree? What different perspective does Luke's account give to Jesus' picture of sacred delight?
7. Most of us tend to think of the beatitudes as cause-and-effect statements: If you become poor in spirit, then—as a result—you will see God. If you mourn your sins, then you will be comforted. They therefore tend to be thought of as requirements—"rules to live by" that are almost

impossible to live up to. For a different perspective, conclude this study by turning the "cause and effect" idea around a bit. Think of all the beatitudes as effects— descriptions of what happens when we accept Christ. If you look at each beatitude this way, the two parts of each beatitude can be seen as two stages or dimensions: the immediate, earthly effect and the ultimate or spiritual effect. With this idea in mind, fill in the chart for each beatitude, using the chapters of this book for a resource. The first is filled in below to give an example.

Beatitude	Cause	Result	Ultimate Result
Blessed are the poor in spirit, for theirs is the kingdom of heaven.	We truly respond to the reality of who Christ is and who we are . . .	. . . we become acutely aware of where we fall short; we become poor in spirit.	. . . we become citizens of Christ's heavenly kingdom; we receive a new name and identity.

Beatitude	Cause	Result	Ultimate Result
Blessed are those who mourn, for they will be comforted.	We truly respond to the reality of who Christ is and who we are . . .		
Blessed are the meek, for they shall inherit the earth.	We truly respond to the reality of who Christ is and who we are . . .		
Blessed are those who hunger and thirst for right-eousness, for they will be comforted.	We truly respond to the reality of who Christ is and who we are . . .		
Blessed are the merciful, for they they will be shown mercy.	We truly respond to the reality of who Christ is and who we are . . .		
Blessed are the pure in heart, for they will see God.	We truly respond to the reality of who Christ is and who we are . . .		
Blessed are the peacemakers, for they will be called sons of God.	We truly respond to the reality of who Christ is and who we are . . .		
Blessed are those who are perse-cuted because of righteousness.	We truly respond to the reality of who Christ is and who we are . . .		

When God Whispers Your Name

OTHER BOOKS BY MAX LUCADO

On the Anvil
God Came Near
Six Hours One Friday
The Applause of Heaven
Just in Case You Ever Wonder
And the Angels Were Silent
In the Eye of the Storm
He Still Moves Stones
The Crippled Lamb
Tell Me the Secrets
Tell Me the Story
No Wonder They Call Him the Savior

When

God

Whispers

Your

Name

MAX LUCADO

THOMAS NELSON
Since 1798

NASHVILLE DALLAS MEXICO CITY RIO DE JANEIRO BEIJING

Denalyn and I would like to dedicate this book to our alma mater—Abilene Christian University. We salute the board, administration, faculty, and staff. For all you've done and all you do, we applaud you.

So my dear brothers and sisters, stand strong. Do not let anything change you. Always give yourself fully to the work of the Lord, because you know your work in the Lord is never wasted.

1 Corinthians 15:58

CONTENTS

ACKNOWLEDGMENTS

The following people provided the necessary urgings, reminders, compliments, and kicks on the seat of my pants to get this job done.

Thanks to:

Karen Hill, my assistant. You know what I need before I ask for it. You know where it is when I've lost it. You know what it needs when I can't fix it. Are you human or angel?

Liz Heaney, my editor. Here's a toast to good books, long hours, and finished manuscripts. Thanks for another great job.

The Word family. Every single one of you. I'm honored to be your partner.

To Steve and Cheryl Green. For your dedication to UpWords and your loyal friendship.

To Steve Halliday, for writing the discussion guide.

To Terry Olivarri, for lessons on enjoying life.

To Jim Martin, a fine physician. A dear friend.

To my wife Denalyn. I'm having second thoughts about us. Every second I have a thought about how grateful I am for you.

And to you, the reader, may the words of this book guide you to one Word which matters. His.

MAX LUCADO

INTRODUCTION

The sheep listen to the voice of the shepherd. He calls his own sheep by name and leads them out.
John 10:3

When I see a flock of sheep I see exactly that, a flock. A rabble of wool. A herd of hooves. I don't see *a* sheep. I see sheep. All alike. None different. That's what I see.

But not so with the shepherd. To him every sheep is different. Every face is special. Every face has a story. And every sheep has a name. *The one with the sad eyes, that's Droopy. And the fellow with one ear up and the other down, I call him Oscar. And the small one with the black patch on his leg, he's an orphan with no brothers. I call him Joseph.*

The shepherd knows his sheep. He calls them by name.

When we see a crowd, we see exactly that, a crowd. Filling a stadium or flooding a mall. When we see a crowd, we see people, not persons, but people. A herd of humans. A flock of faces. That's what we see.

But not so with the Shepherd. To him every face is different. Every face is a story. Every face is a child. Every child has a name. *The one with the sad eyes, that's Sally. The old fellow with one eyebrow up and the other down, Harry's his name. And the young one with the limp? He's an orphan with no brothers. I call him Joey.*

The Shepherd knows his sheep. He knows each one by name. The Shepherd knows you. He knows your name. And he will never forget it. *I have written your name on my hand* (Isa. 49:16).

Quite a thought, isn't it? Your name on God's hand. Your name on God's lips. Maybe you've seen your name in some special places. On an award or diploma or walnut door. Or maybe you've heard your name from some important people—a coach, a celebrity, a teacher. But to think that your name is on God's hand and on God's lips . . . my, could it be?

Or perhaps you've never seen your name honored. And you can't remember when you heard it spoken with kindness. If so, it may be more difficult for you to believe that God knows your name.

But he does. Written on his hand. Spoken by his mouth. Whispered by his lips. Your name. And not only the name you now have, but the name he has in store for you. A new name he will give you . . . but wait, I'm getting ahead of myself. I'll tell you about your new name in the last chapter. This is just the introduction.

And so may I introduce you to this book? It's a book of hope. A book whose sole aim is to encourage. For the last year I've harvested thoughts from a landscape of fields. And though their size and flavors are varied, their purpose is singular: to provide you, the reader, with a word of hope. I thought you could use it.

You've been on my mind as I've been writing. I've thought of you often. I honestly have. Over the years I've gotten to know some of you folks well. I've read your letters, shaken your hands, and watched your eyes. I think I know you.

You're busy. Time passes before your tasks are finished. And if you get a chance to read, it's a slim chance indeed.

You're anxious. Bad news outpaces the good. Problems outnumber solutions. And you are concerned. What future do your children have on this earth? What future do you have?

You're cautious. You don't trust as easily as you once did.

Politicians lied. The system failed. The minister compromised. Your spouse cheated. It's not easy to trust. It's not that you don't want to. It's just that you want to be careful.

There is one other thing. You've made some mistakes. I met one of you at a bookstore in Michigan. A businessman, you seldom came out of your office at all and never to meet an author. But then you did. You were regretting the many hours at work and the few hours at home and wanted to talk.

And the single mom in Chicago. One kid was tugging, the other crying, but juggling them both, you made your point. "I made mistakes," you explained, "but I really want to try again."

And there was that night in Fresno. The musician sang and I spoke and you came. You almost didn't. You almost stayed home. Just that day you'd found the note from your wife. She was leaving you. But you came anyway. Hoping I'd have something for the pain. Hoping I'd have an answer. Where is God at a time like this?

And so as I wrote, I thought about you. All of you. You aren't malicious. You aren't evil. You aren't hardhearted, (hardheaded occasionally, but not hardhearted). You really want to do what is right. But sometimes life turns south. Occasionally we need a reminder.

Not a sermon.
A reminder.
A reminder that God knows your name.

Many chapters auditioned for this book, but not all were selected. After all, not just any chapter would do. Brevity was required, for you are busy. Hope was needed, for you are anxious. Loyalty to Scripture was a mandate, for you are cautious. I sought to give you a repertoire of chapters that recite well the lyrics of grace and sing well the melody of joy. For you are the guest of the Maestro, and he is preparing a concert you'll never forget.

PART ONE

The Song of the Minstrel

y wife loves antiques. I don't. (I find them a bit old.) But because I love my wife, I occasionally find myself guiding three children through an antique store while Denalyn shops.

Such is the price of love.

The secret to survival in a shop of relics is to find a chair and an old book and settle down for the long haul. That's what I did yesterday. After cautioning the kids to look with their eyes and not with their hands, I sat down in an overstuffed rocker with some Life magazines from the fifties.

That's when I heard the music. Piano music. Beautiful music. Vintage Rogers and Hammerstein. The hills were alive with the sound of someone's skill at the keyboard.

I turned to see who was playing, but couldn't see anyone. I stood and walked closer. A small group of listeners had gathered at the old upright piano. Between the furniture I could see the small back of the pianist. Why, it's only a child! With a few more steps I could see her hair. Short, blonde, and cute like . . . My heart, it's Andrea!

Our seven-year-old was at the piano, her hands racing up and down the keyboard. I was stunned. What gift of heaven is this that she can play in such a way? Must be a time-released gene she got from my side of the family. But as I drew closer, I saw the real reason. Andrea was "playing" a player piano. She wasn't making the music; she was following it. She wasn't commanding the keyboard; she was trying to keep up with it. Though it appeared she was playing the song, in reality, she was only trying to keep up with one already written. When a key would dip, her hands would dash.

Oh, but if you could have seen her little face, delighted with laughter! Eyes dancing as would her feet had she been able to stand and play at the same time.

I could see why she was so happy. She sat down to attempt "Chopsticks" but instead played "The Sound of Music." What's more, she couldn't fail. One greater than she was dictating the sound. Andrea was free to play as much as she wanted, knowing the music would never suffer.

It's no wonder she rejoiced. She had every reason to. And so do we.

Hasn't God promised the same to us? We sit at the

keyboard, willing to play the only song we know, only to discover a new song. A sublime song. And nobody is more surprised than we are when our meager efforts are converted into melodious moments.

You have one, you know, a song all your own. Each of us does. The only question is, will you play it?

By the way, as I watched Andrea "play" that day in the antique store I observed a couple of things.

I noticed the piano got all the credit. The gathered crowd appreciated Andrea's efforts, but they knew the real source of the music. When God works, the same is true. We may applaud the disciple, but no one knows better than the disciple who really deserves the praise.

But that doesn't keep the disciple from sitting at the bench. It sure didn't keep Andrea from sitting at the piano. Why? Because she knew she couldn't fail. Even though she didn't understand how it worked, she knew it did.

So she sat at the keyboard—and had the time of her life.

Even though you may not understand how God works, you know he does.

So go ahead. Pull up a bench, take your seat at the piano, and play.

CHAPTER ONE

The Voice from the Mop Bucket

THE HALLWAY is silent except for the wheels of the mop bucket and the shuffle of the old man's feet. Both sound tired.

Both know these floors. How many nights has Hank cleaned them? Always careful to get in the corners. Always careful to set up his yellow caution sign warning of wet floors. Always chuckling as he does. "Be careful everyone," he laughs to himself, knowing no one is near.

Not at three A.M.

Hank's health isn't what it used to be. Gout keeps him awake. Arthritis makes him limp. His glasses are so thick his eyeballs look twice their size. Shoulders stoop. But he does his work. Slopping soapy water on linoleum. Scrubbing the heel marks left by the well-heeled lawyers. He'll be finished an hour before quitting time. Always finishes early. Has for twenty years.

When finished he'll put away his bucket and take a seat outside the office of the senior partner and wait. Never leaves early. Could. No one would know. But he doesn't.

He broke the rules once. Never again.

Sometimes, if the door is open, he'll enter the office. Not for long. Just to look. The suite is larger than his apartment. He'll run his finger over the desk. He'll stroke the soft leather couch. He'll stand at the window and watch the gray sky turn gold. And he'll remember.

He once had such an office.

Back when Hank was Henry. Back when the custodian was an executive. Long ago. Before the night shift. Before the mop bucket. Before the maintenance uniform. Before the scandal.

Hank doesn't think about it much now. No reason to. Got in trouble, got fired, and got out. That's it. Not many people know about it. Better that way. No need to tell them.

It's his secret.

Hank's story, by the way, is true. I changed the name and a detail or two. I gave him a different job and put him in a different century. But the story is factual. You've heard it. You know it. When I give you his real name, you'll remember.

But more than a true story, it's a common story. It's a story of a derailed dream. It's a story of high hopes colliding with harsh realities.

Happens to all dreamers. And since all have dreamed, it happens to us all.

In Hank's case, it was a mistake he could never forget. A grave mistake. Hank killed someone. He came upon a thug beating up an innocent man, and Hank lost control. He killed the mugger. When word got out, Hank got out.

Hank would rather hide than go to jail. So he ran. The executive became a fugitive.

True story. Common story. Most stories aren't as extreme as Hank's. Few spend their lives running from the law. Many, however, live with regrets.

"I could have gone to college on a golf scholarship," a fellow told me just last week on the fourth tee box. "Had an offer right out of school. But I joined a rock-and-roll band. Ended up never going. Now I'm stuck fixing garage doors."

"Now I'm stuck." Epitaph of a derailed dream.

Pick up a high school yearbook and read the "What I want to do" sentence under each picture. You'll get dizzy breathing the thin air of mountaintop visions:

"Ivy league school."
"Write books and live in Switzerland."
"Physician in a Third World country."
"Teach inner-city kids."

Yet, take the yearbook to a twentieth-year reunion and read the next chapter. Some dreams have come true, but many haven't. Not that all should, mind you. I hope the little guy who dreamed of being a sumo wrestler came to his senses. And I hope he didn't lose his passion in the process. Changing direction in life is not tragic. Losing passion in life is.

Something happens to us along the way. Convictions to change the world downgrade to commitments to pay the bills. Rather than make a difference, we make a salary. Rather than look forward, we look back. Rather than look outward, we look inward.

And we don't like what we see.

Hank didn't. Hank saw a man who'd settled for the mediocre. Trained in the finest institutions of the world, yet working the night shift in a minimum-wage job so he wouldn't be seen in the day.

But all that changed when he heard the voice from the mop bucket. (Did I mention that his story is true?)

At first he thought the voice was a joke. Some of the fellows on the third floor play these kinds of tricks.

"Henry, Henry," the voice called.

Hank turned. No one called him Henry anymore.

"Henry, Henry."

He turned toward the pail. It was glowing. Bright red. Hot red. He could feel the heat ten feet away. He stepped closer and looked in. The water wasn't boiling.

"This is strange," Hank mumbled to himself as he took another step to get a closer look. But the voice stopped him.

"Don't come any closer. Take off your shoes. You are on holy tile."

Suddenly Hank knew who was speaking. "God?"

I'm not making this up. I know you think I am. Sounds crazy. Almost irreverent. God speaking from a hot mop bucket to a janitor named Hank? Would it be believable if I said God was speaking from a burning bush to a shepherd named Moses?

Maybe that one's easier to handle—because you've heard it before. But just because it's Moses and a bush rather than Hank and a bucket, it's no less spectacular.

It sure shocked the sandals off Moses. We wonder what amazed the old fellow more: that God spoke in a bush or that God spoke at all.

Moses, like Hank, had made a mistake.

You remember his story. Adopted nobility. An Israelite reared in an Egyptian palace. His countrymen were slaves, but Moses was privileged. Ate at the royal table. Educated in the finest schools.

But his most influential teacher had no degree. She was his mother. A Jewess who was hired to be his nanny. "Moses," you can almost hear her whisper to her young son, "God has put you here on purpose. Someday you will set your people free. Never forget, Moses. Never forget."

Moses didn't. The flame of justice grew hotter until it blazed. Moses saw an Egyptian beating a Hebrew slave. Just like Hank killed the mugger, Moses killed the Egyptian.

The next day Moses saw the Hebrew. You'd think the slave would say thanks. He didn't. Rather than express gratitude, he expressed anger. "Will you kill me too?" he asked (see Exod. 2:14).

Moses knew he was in trouble. He fled Egypt and hid in the wilderness. Call it a career shift. He went from dining with the heads of state to counting heads of sheep.

Hardly an upward move.

And so it happened that a bright, promising Hebrew began herding sheep in the hills. From the Ivy League to the cotton patch. From the Oval Office to a taxicab. From swinging a golf club to digging a ditch.

Moses thought the move was permanent. There is no indication he ever intended to go back to Egypt. In fact, there is every indication he wanted to stay with his sheep. Standing barefoot before the bush, he confessed, "I am not a great man! How can I go to the king and lead the Israelites out of Egypt?" (Exod. 3:11).

I'm glad Moses asked that question. It's a good one. Why Moses? Or, more specifically, why eighty-year-old Moses?

The forty-year-old version was more appealing. The Moses we saw in Egypt was brash and confident. But the Moses we find four decades later is reluctant and weather-beaten.

Had you or I looked at Moses back in Egypt, we would have said, "This man is ready for battle." Educated in the finest system in the world. Trained by the ablest soldiers. Instant access to the inner circle of the Pharaoh.

Moses spoke their language and knew their habits. He was the perfect man for the job.

Moses at forty we like. But Moses at eighty? No way. Too old. Too tired. Smells like a shepherd. Speaks like a foreigner. What impact would he have on Pharaoh? He's the wrong man for the job.

And Moses would have agreed. "Tried that once before," he would say. "Those people don't want to be helped. Just leave me here to tend my sheep. They're easier to lead."

Moses wouldn't have gone. You wouldn't have sent him. I wouldn't have sent him.

But God did. How do you figure? Benched at forty and suited up at eighty. Why? What does he know now that he didn't know then? What did he learn in the desert that he didn't learn in Egypt?

The ways of the desert, for one. Forty-year-old Moses was a city boy. Octogenarian Moses knows the name of every snake and the location of every watering hole. If he's going to lead thousands of Hebrews into the wilderness, he better know the basics of desert life 101.

Family dynamics, for another. If he's going to be traveling with families for forty years, it might help to understand how they work. He marries a woman of faith, the daughter of a Midianite priest, and establishes his own family.

But more than the ways of the desert and the people, Moses needed to learn something about himself.

Apparently he has learned it. God says Moses is ready.

And to convince him, God speaks through a bush. (Had to do something dramatic to get Moses' attention.)

"School's out," God tells him. "Now it's time to get to work." Poor Moses. He didn't even know he was enrolled.

But he was. And, guess what. So are you. The voice from the bush is the voice that whispers to you. It reminds you that God is not finished with you yet. Oh, you may think he is. You may think you've peaked. You may think he's got someone else to do the job.

If so, think again.

"God began doing a good work in you, and I am sure he will continue it until it is finished when Jesus Christ comes again."[1]

Did you see what God is doing? *A good work in you.*

Did you see when he will be finished? *When Jesus comes again.*

May I spell out the message? *God ain't finished with you yet.*

Your Father wants you to know that. And to convince you, he may surprise you. He may speak through a bush, a mop bucket, or stranger still, he may speak through this book.

CHAPTER TWO

Why Jesus Went to Parties

I WAS PLANNING to write a chapter on twelve verses this week, but I never got past the second verse. Not supposed to do that. Supposed to present the entire story. I meant to, I really did. But I got stuck. The second verse wouldn't release me—it took me hostage—so I spent the whole lesson on one verse. Captivating little phrase, it was.

I'll tell you about it, after I set the stage.

Picture six men walking on a narrow road. The gold dawn explodes behind them, stretching shadows ahead. Early-morning chill has robes snugly sashed. Grass sparkles with diamonds of dew.

The men's faces are eager, but common. Their leader is confident, but unknown. They call him Rabbi; he looks more like a laborer. And well he should, for he's spent far more time building than teaching. But this week the teaching has begun.

Where are they going? To the temple to worship? To the synagogue to teach? To the hills to pray? They haven't been told, but they each have their own idea.

John and Andrew expect to be led into the desert. That's where their previous teacher had taken them. John the Baptist would guide them into the barren hills and for hours they would pray. For days they would fast. For the Messiah they would yearn. And now, the Messiah is here.

Surely he will do the same.

Everybody knows that a Messiah is a holy man. Everybody knows that self-denial is the first step to holiness. Surely God's voice is first heard by hermits. *Jesus is leading us into solitude.* At least that's what John and Andrew think.

Peter has another opinion. Peter is a man of action. A roll-up-your-sleeves kind of guy. A stand-up-and-say-it sort of fellow. He likes the idea of going somewhere. God's people need to be on the move. *Probably taking us somewhere to preach,* he is thinking to himself. And as they walk, Peter is outlining his own sermon, should Jesus need a breather.

Nathanael would disagree. *Come and see,* his friend Philip had invited. So he came. And Nathanael liked what he saw. In Jesus he saw a man of deep thought. A man of meditation. A heart of contemplation. A man who, like Nathanael, had spent hours under the fig tree reflecting on the mysteries of life. Nathanael was convinced that Jesus was taking them to a place to ponder.

A quiet house on a distant mountain, that's where we are going.

And what about Philip? What was he thinking? He was the only apostle with a Gentile name. When the Greeks came looking for Jesus, it was Philip they approached. Perhaps he had Greek connections. Maybe Philip had a heart for Gentiles. If so, he was hoping this journey was a missionary one—out of Galilee. Out of Judea. Into a distant land.

Did such speculation occur? Who knows? I know it does today.

I know Jesus' followers often enlist with high aspirations and expectations. Disciples step in line with unspoken yet heartfelt agendas. Lips posed to preach to thousands. Eyes fixed on foreign shores. *I know where Jesus will take me,* the young disciples claim, and so they, like the first five, follow.

And they, like the first five, are surprised.

Maybe it was Andrew who asked it. Perhaps Peter. Could be that all approached Jesus. But I wager that at some point in the journey, the disciples expressed their assumptions.

"So Rabbi, where are you taking us? To the desert?"

"No," opines another, "he's taking us to the temple."

"To the temple?" challenges a third. "We're on our way to the Gentiles!"

Then a chorus of confusion breaks out and ends only when Jesus lifts his hand and says softly, "We're on our way to a wedding."

Silence. John and Andrew look at each other. "A wedding?" they say. "John the Baptist would have never gone to a wedding. Why, there is drinking and laughter and dancing . . ."

"And noise!" Philip chimes in. "How can you meditate in a noisy wedding?"

"Or preach in a wedding?" Peter adds.

"Why would we go to a wedding?"

Good question. Why would Jesus, on his first journey, take his followers to a party? Didn't they have work to do? Didn't he have principles to teach? Wasn't his time limited? How could a wedding fit with his purpose on earth?

Why did Jesus go to the wedding?

The answer? It's found in the second verse of John 2 (the verse I could not pass). "Jesus and his followers were also invited to the wedding."

When the bride and groom were putting the guest list together, Jesus' name was included. And when Jesus showed up with a half-dozen friends, the invitation wasn't rescinded. Whoever was hosting this party was happy to have Jesus present.

"Be sure and put Jesus' name on the list," he might have said. "He really lightens up a party."

Jesus wasn't invited because he was a celebrity. He wasn't one yet. The invitation wasn't motivated by his miracles. He'd yet to perform any. Why did they invite him?

I suppose they liked him.

Big deal? I think so. I think it's significant that common folk in a little town enjoyed being with Jesus. I think it's noteworthy that the Almighty didn't act high and mighty. The Holy One wasn't holier-than-thou. The One who knew it all wasn't a know-it-all. The One who made the stars didn't keep his head in them. The One who owns all the stuff of earth never strutted it.

Never. He could have. Oh, how he could have!

He could have been a name-dropper: *Did I ever tell you of the time Moses and I went up on the mountain?*"

He could have been a showoff: *Hey, want me to beam you into the twentieth century?*"

He could have been a smart-aleck: *I know what you're thinking. Want me to prove it?*"

He could have been highbrow and uppity: *I've got some property on Jupiter . . .*

Jesus could have been all of these, but he wasn't. His purpose was not to show off but to show up. He went to great pains to be as human as the guy down the street. He didn't need to study, but still went to the synagogue. He had no need for income, but still worked in the workshop. He had known the fellowship of angels and heard the harps of heaven, yet still went to parties thrown by tax collectors. And upon his shoulders rested the challenge of redeeming creation, but he still took time to walk ninety miles from Jericho to Cana to go to a wedding.

As a result, people liked him. Oh, there were those who chaffed at his claims. They called him a blasphemer, but they never called him a braggart. They accused him of heresy, but never arrogance. He was branded as a radical, but never called unapproachable.

There is no hint that he ever used his heavenly status for personal gain. Ever. You just don't get the impression that his neighbors grew sick of his haughtiness and asked, "Well, who do you think made you God?"

His faith made him likable, not detestable. Would that ours would do the same!

Where did we get the notion that a good Christian is a solemn Christian? Who started the rumor that the sign of a disciple is a long face? How did we create this idea that the truly gifted are the heavy-hearted?

May I state an opinion that may raise an eyebrow? May I tell you why I think Jesus went to the wedding? I think he went to the wedding to—now hold on, hear me out, let me say it before you heat the tar and pluck the feathers—I think Jesus went to the wedding to have fun.

Think about it. It's been a tough season. Forty days in the desert. No food or water. A standoff with the devil. A week breaking in some greenhorn Galileans. A job change. He's left home. It hasn't been easy. A break would be welcome. Good meal with some good wine and some good friends . . . well, it sounds pretty nice.

So off they go.

His purpose wasn't to turn the water to wine. That was a favor for his friends.

His purpose wasn't to show his power. The wedding host didn't even know what Jesus did.

His purpose wasn't to preach. There is no record of a sermon.

Really leaves only one reason. Fun. Jesus went to the wedding because he liked the people, he liked the food, and heaven forbid, he may have even wanted to swirl the bride around the dance floor a time or two. (After all, he's planning a big wedding himself. Maybe he wanted the practice?)

So, forgive me, Deacon Drydust and Sister Somberheart. I'm sorry to rain on your dirge, but Jesus was a likable fellow. And his disciples should be the same. I'm not talking debauchery, drunkenness, and adultery. I'm not endorsing compromise, coarseness, or obscenity. I am simply crusading for the freedom to enjoy a good joke, enliven a dull party, and appreciate a fun evening.

Maybe these thoughts catch you by surprise. They do me. It's been awhile since I pegged Jesus as a party-lover. But he was. His foes accused him of eating too much, drinking too much, and hanging out with the wrong people! (See Matt. 11:19.) I must confess: It's been awhile since I've been accused of having too much fun. How about you?

We used to be good at it. What has happened to us? What happened to clean joy and loud laughter? Is it our neckties that choke us? Is it our diplomas that dignify us? Is it the pew that stiffens us?

Couldn't we learn to be children again?

Bring out the marbles—(so what if the shoes get scuffed?).

Bring out the bat and glove—(so what if the muscles ache?).

Bring out the taffy—(so what if it sticks to your teeth?).

Be a child again. Flirt. Giggle. Dip your cookie in your milk. Take a nap. Say you're sorry if you hurt someone. Chase a butterfly. Be a child again.

Loosen up. Don't you have some people to hug, rocks to skip, or lips to kiss? Someone needs to laugh at Bugs Bunny; might as well be you. Someday you're going to learn to paint; might as well be now. Someday you are going to retire; why not today?

Not retire from your job, just retire from your attitude. Honestly, has complaining ever made the day better? Has grumbling ever paid the bills? Has worrying about tomorrow ever changed it?

Let someone else run the world for a while.

Jesus took time for a party . . . shouldn't we?

CHAPTER THREE

Hidden Heroes

True heroes are hard to identify. They don't look like heroes. Here's an example.

Step with me into a dank dungeon in Judea. Peer through the door's tiny window. Consider the plight of the man on the floor. He has just inaugurated history's greatest movement. His words have triggered a revolution that will span two millenniums. Future historians will describe him as courageous, noble, and visionary.

At this moment he appears anything but. Cheeks hollow. Beard matted. Bewilderment etched on his face. He leans back against the cold wall, closes his eyes, and sighs.

John had never known doubt. Hunger, yes. Loneliness, often. But doubt? Never. Only raw conviction, ruthless pronouncements, and rugged truth. Such was John the Baptist. Conviction as fierce as the desert sun.

Until now. Now the sun is blocked. Now his courage wanes. Now the clouds come. And now, as he faces death, he doesn't raise a fist of victory; he raises only a question. His final act is not a proclamation of courage, but a confession of confusion: "Find out if Jesus is the Son of God or not."

The forerunner of the Messiah is afraid of failure. *Find out if I've told the truth. Find out if I've sent people to the right Messiah. Find out if I've been right or if I've been duped.* [1]

Doesn't sound too heroic, does he?

We'd rather John die in peace. We'd rather the trailblazer catch a glimpse of the mountain. Seems only right that the sailor be granted a sighting of the shore. After all, didn't Moses get a view of the valley? Isn't John the cousin of Jesus? If anybody deserves to see the end of the trail, doesn't he?

Apparently not.

The miracles he prophesied, he never saw. The kingdom he announced, he never knew. And the Messiah he proclaimed, he now doubts.

John doesn't look like the prophet who would be the transition between law and grace. He doesn't look like a hero.

Heroes seldom do.

Can I take you to another prison for a second example?

This time the jail is in Rome. The man is named Paul.

What John did to present Christ, Paul did to explain him. John cleared the path; Paul erected signposts.

Like John, Paul shaped history. And like John, Paul would die in the jail of a despot. No headlines announced his execution. No observer recorded the events. When the ax struck Paul's neck, society's eyes didn't blink. To them Paul was a peculiar purveyor of an odd faith.

Peer into the prison and see him for yourself: bent and frail, shackled to the arm of a Roman guard. Behold the apostle of God. Who knows when his back last felt a bed or his mouth knew a good meal? Three decades of travel and trouble, and what's he got to show for it?

There's squabbling in Phillipi, competition in Corinth, the legalists are swarming in Galatia. Crete is plagued by money-grabbers. Ephesus is stalked by womanizers. Even some of Paul's own friends have turned against him.

Dead broke. No family. No property. Nearsighted and worn out.

Oh, he had his moments. Spoke to an emperor once, but couldn't convert him. Gave a lecture at an Areopagus men's club, but wasn't asked to speak there again. Spent a few days with Peter and the boys in Jerusalem, but they couldn't seem to get along, so Paul hit the road.

And never got off. Ephesus, Thessalonica, Athens, Syracuse, Malta. The only list longer than his itinerary was his misfortune. Got stoned in one city and stranded in another. Nearly drowned as many times as he nearly starved. If he spent more than one week in the same place, it was probably a prison.

He never received a salary. Had to pay his own travel expenses. Kept a part-time job on the side to make ends meet.

Doesn't look like a hero.

Doesn't sound like one either. He introduced himself as the worst sinner in history. He was a Christian-killer before he was a Christian leader. At times his heart was so heavy, Paul's pen drug itself across the page. "What a miserable man I am! Who will save me from this body that brings me death?" (Rom. 7:24).

Only heaven knows how long he stared at the question before he found the courage to defy logic and write, "I thank God for saving me through Jesus Christ our Lord!" (Rom. 7:25).

One minute he's in charge; the next he's in doubt. One day he's preaching; the next he's in prison. And that's where I'd like you to look at him. Look at him in the prison.

Pretend you don't know him. You're a guard or a cook or a friend of the hatchet man, and you've come to get one last look at the guy while they sharpen the blade.

What you see shuffling around in his cell isn't too much. But what I lean over and tell you is: "That man will shape the course of history."

You chuckle, but I continue.

"Nero's fame will fade in this man's light."

You turn and stare. I continue.

"His churches will die. But his thoughts? Within two hundred years his thoughts will influence the teaching of every school on this continent."

You shake your head.

"See those letters? Those letters scribbled on parchment? They'll be read in thousands of languages and will impact every major creed and constitution of the future. Every major figure will read them. Every single one."

That would be your breaking point. "No way. He's an old man with an odd faith. He'll be killed and forgotten before his head hits the floor."

Who could disagree? What rational thinker would counter?

Paul's name would blow like the dust his bones would become.

Just like John's. No level-headed observer would think otherwise. Both were noble, but passing. Courageous, but small. Radical, yet unnoticed. No one—I repeat, no one—bade farewell to these men thinking their names would be remembered more than a generation.

Their peers simply had no way of knowing—and neither do we.

For that reason, a hero could be next door and you wouldn't know it. The fellow who changes the oil in your car could be one. A hero in coveralls? Maybe. Maybe as he works he prays, asking God to do with the heart of the driver what he does with the engine.

The day-care worker where you drop off the kids? Perhaps. Perhaps her morning prayers include the name of each child and the dream that one of them will change the world. Who's to say God isn't listening?

The parole officer downtown? Could be a hero. She could be the one who challenges the ex-con to challenge the teens to challenge the gangs.

I know, I know. These folks don't fit our image of a hero. They look too, too, . . . well, normal. Give us four stars, titles, and headlines. But something tells me that for every hero in the spotlight, there are dozens in the shadows. They don't get press. They don't draw crowds. They don't even write books!

But behind every avalanche is a snowflake.

Behind a rock slide is a pebble.

An atomic explosion begins with one atom.

And a revival can begin with one sermon.

History proves it. John Egglen had never preached a sermon in his life. Never.

Wasn't that he didn't want to, just never needed to. But then one morning he did. The snow left his town of Colchester, England, buried in white. When he awoke on that January Sunday in 1850, he thought of staying home. Who would go to church in such weather?

But he reconsidered. He was, after all, a deacon. And if the deacons didn't go, who would? So he put on his boots, hat, and coat and walked the six miles to the Methodist Church.

He wasn't the only member who considered staying home. In fact, he was one of the few who came. Only thirteen people were present. Twelve members and one visitor. Even the minister was snowed in. Someone suggested they go home. Egglen would hear none of that. They'd come this far; they would have a service. Besides, they had a visitor. A thirteen-year-old boy.

But who would preach? Egglen was the only deacon. It fell to him.

And so he did. His sermon lasted only ten minutes. It drifted and wandered and made no point in an effort to make several. But at the end, an uncharacteristic courage settled upon the man. He lifted his eyes and looked straight at the boy and challenged: "Young man, look to Jesus. Look! Look! Look!"

Did the challenge make a difference? Let the boy, now a man, answer. "I did look, and then and there the cloud on my heart lifted, the darkness rolled away, and at that moment I saw the sun."

The boy's name? Charles Haddon Spurgeon. England's prince of preachers.[2]

Did Egglen know what he'd done? No.

Do heroes know when they are heroic? Rarely.

Are historic moments acknowledged when they happen?

You know the answer to that one. (If not, a visit to the manger will remind you.) We seldom see history in the making, and we seldom recognize heroes. Which is just as well, for if we knew either, we might mess up both.

But we'd do well to keep our eyes open. Tomorrow's Spurgeon might be mowing your lawn. And the hero who inspires him might be nearer than you think.

He might be in your mirror.

CHAPTER FOUR

You Might've Been in the Bible

THERE ARE a few stories in the Bible where everything turns out right. This is one. It has three characters.

The first is Philip—a disciple in the early church who had a penchant for lost people. One day he was instructed by God to go to the road that leads to Gaza from Jerusalem. It was a desert road. He went. When he arrived he came upon a ruler from Ethiopia.

Must have been a bit intimidating for Philip. It would be similar to your hopping on a motor scooter and following the secretary of the treasury. At a stoplight you notice he is reading the Bible, and you volunteer your services.

That is what Philip did.

"Do you understand what you are reading?"

"How can I unless someone explains it to me?"

And so Philip did. They have a Bible study in the chariot. The study is so convicting that the Ethiopian is baptized that day. And then they separate. Philip goes one way, and the Ethiopian goes another. The story has a happy ending. Philip teaches, the Ethiopian obeys, and the gospel is sent to Africa.

But that's not all the story. Remember I said there were three characters. The first was Philip; the second was the Ethiopian. Did you see the third? There is one. Read these verses and take note.

"An angel of the Lord said to Philip, 'Get ready and go south. . . .' So Philip got ready and went" (Acts 8: 26–27).

"The Spirit said to Philip, 'Go to that chariot and stay near it.' So . . . Philip ran toward the chariot" (Acts 8: 29–30).

The third character? God! *God* sent the angel. The Holy Spirit instructed Philip; God orchestrated the entire moment! He saw this godly man coming from Ethiopia to worship. He saw his confusion. So he decided to resolve it.

He looked in Jerusalem for a man he could send. He found Philip.

Our typical response when we read these verses is to think Philip was a special guy. He had access to the Oval Office. He carried a first-century pager that God doesn't pass out anymore.

But don't be too quick. In a letter to Christians just like us, Paul wrote, "Live by following the Spirit" (Gal. 5:16).

"The true children of God are those who let God's Spirit lead them" (Rom. 8:14).

To hear many of us talk, you'd think we didn't believe these verses. You'd think we didn't believe in the Trinity. We talk about the Father and study the Son—but when it comes to the Holy Spirit, we are confused at best and frightened at worst. Confused because we've never been taught. Frightened because we've been taught to be afraid.

May I simplify things a bit? The Holy Spirit is the presence of God in our lives, carrying on the work of Jesus. The Holy Spirit helps us in three directions—inwardly (by granting us the fruits of the Spirit, Gal. 5:22–24), upwardly (by praying for us, Rom. 8:26) and outwardly (by pouring God's love into our hearts, Rom. 5:5).

In evangelism the Holy Spirit is on center stage. If the disciple teaches, it is because the Spirit teaches the disciple (Luke 12:12). If the listener is convicted, it is because the Spirit has penetrated (John 16:10). If the listener is converted, it is by the transforming power of the Spirit (Rom. 8:11). If the new believer matures, it is because the Spirit makes him or her competent (2 Cor. 3:6).

You have the same Spirit working with you that Philip did. Some of you don't believe me. You're still cautious. I can hear you mumbling under your breath as you read, "Philip had something I don't. I've never heard an angel's voice." To which I counter, "How do you know Philip did?"

We assume he did. We've been taught he did. The flannelboard figures say he did. An angel puts his trumpet in Philip's ear, blares the announcement, and Philip has no choice. Flashing lights and fluttering wings are nothing to deny. The deacon had to go. But could our assumption be wrong? Could it be that the angel's voice was every bit as miraculous as the one you and I hear?

What?

You've heard the voice whispering your name, haven't you? You've felt the nudge to go and sensed the urge to speak. Hasn't it occurred to you?

You invite a couple over for coffee. Nothing heroic, just a nice evening with old friends. But from the moment they enter, you can feel the tension. Colder than glaciers, they are. You can tell something is wrong. Typically you're not one to inquire, but you feel a concern that won't be silent. So you ask.

You are in a business meeting where one of your coworkers gets raked over the coals. Everyone else is thinking, *I'm glad that wasn't me.* But the Holy Spirit is leading you to think, *How hard this must be.* So, after the meeting you approach the employee and express your concern.

You notice the fellow on the other side of the church auditorium. He looks a bit out of place, what with his strange clothing and all. You learn that he is from Africa, in town on business. The next Sunday he is back. And the third Sunday he is present. You introduce yourself. He tells you how he is fascinated by the faith and how he wants to learn more. Rather than offer to teach him, you simply urge him to read the Bible.

Later in the week, you regret not being more direct. You call the office where he is consulting and learn that he is leaving today for home. You know in your heart you can't let him leave. So you rush to the airport and find him awaiting his flight, with a Bible open on his lap.

"Do you understand what you are reading?" you inquire.

"How can I, unless someone explains it to me?"

And so you, like Philip, explain. And he, like the Ethiopian, believes. Baptism is requested and baptism is offered. He catches a later flight and you catch a glimpse of what it means to be led by the Spirit.

Were there lights? You just lit one. Were there voices? You just were one. Was there a miracle? You just witnessed one. Who knows? If the Bible were being written today, that might be your name in the eighth chapter of Acts.

CHAPTER FIVE

Maxims

HERE'S A TOAST to the simple sentence.

Here's a salute to one-liners.

Join me in applauding the delete key and the eraser. May they feast on the trimmings of the writer's table.

I believe in brevity. Cut the fat and keep the fact. Give us words to chew on, not words to wade through. Thoughts that spark, not lines that drag. More periods. Fewer commas.

Distill it.

Barebone it.

Bareknuckle it.

Concise (but not cute). Clear (but not shallow). Vivid (but not detailed.) That's good writing. That's good reading. But that's hard work!

But, it's what we like. We appreciate the chef who cuts

the gristle before he serves the steak. We salute the communicator who does the same.

Ahhh, brevity. An art apparently unheeded in the realms of insurance brochures and some-assembly-required bicycle manuals.

We learn brevity from Jesus. His greatest sermon can be read in eight minutes (Matthew 5–7). His best-known story can be read in ninety seconds (Luke 15:11–32). He summarized prayer in five phrases (Matt. 6:9–13). He silenced accusers with one challenge (John 8:7). He rescued a soul with one sentence (Luke 23:43). He summarized the Law in three verses (Mark 12:29–31), and he reduced all his teachings to one command (John 15:12).

He made his point and went home.

We preachers would do well to imitate. (What's that old line? "Our speaker today needs no introduction, but he could use a conclusion.")

I believe in brevity. I believe that you, the reader, entrust me, the writer, with your most valued commodity—your time. I shouldn't take more than my share. For that reason, I love the short sentence. Big-time game it is. Hiding in the jungle of circular construction and six-syllable canyons. As I write, I hunt. And when I find, I shoot. Then I drag the treasure out of the trees and marvel.

Not all of my prey make their way into chapters. So what becomes of them? I save them. But I can't keep them to myself. So, may I invite you to see my trophy case? What follows are cuts from this book and a couple of others. Keep the ones you like. Forgive the ones you don't. Share them when you can. But if you do, keep it brief.

Maxims

Pray all the time. If necessary, use words.

Sacrilege is to feel guilt for sins forgiven.

God forgets the past. Imitate him.

Greed I've often regretted. Generosity—never.

Never miss a chance to read a child a story.

Pursue forgiveness, not innocence.

Be doubly kind to the people who bring your food or park your car.

In buying a gift for your wife, practicality can be more expensive than extravagance.

Don't ask God to do what you want. Ask God to do what is right.

Nails didn't hold God to a cross. Love did.

You'll give up on yourself before God will.

Know answered prayer when you see it, and don't give up when you don't.

Flattery is fancy dishonesty.

The right heart with the wrong creed is better than the right creed with the wrong heart.

We treat others as we perceive God is treating us.

Sometimes the most godly thing we can do is take a day off.

Faith in the future begets power in the present.

No one is useless to God. No one.

Conflict is inevitable, but combat is optional.

You will never forgive anyone more than God has already forgiven you.

Succeed in what matters.

You'll regret opening your mouth. You'll rarely regret keeping it shut.

To see sin without grace is despair. To see grace without sin is arrogance. To see them in tandem is conversion.

Faith is the grit in the soul that puts the dare into dreams.

God doesn't keep a clock.

Never underestimate a gesture of affection.

When Jesus went home, he left the front door open.

And to sum it up:

As soon as you can, pay your debts.
As long as you can, give the benefit of the doubt.
As much as you can, give thanks. He's already given us more than we deserve.

CHAPTER SIX

God's Christmas Cards

I'M MONITORING my mailbox.

I don't usually spend time looking at it, but I am today. I don't want it to fall. Just a few days ago that wasn't a concern—but that was before the construction crew started clearing the lot across the street. And that was before the gravel-truck driver forgot to look in his rearview mirror.

Clunk.

So today our mailbox is upright again, propped up by three two-by-fours on three sides. Not too attractive, but functional.

Strange what you think about while posting an eye on the postal receptacle. As I gaze at it, it occurs to me that the mailbox is a lot like a bus terminal—a turnstile for the good and the bad, the wanted and the unwanted. Just for fun, I'm making a list of letters I hope I never receive. (Well, what do *you* think about when you're watching a box on a pole?)

Here's what I've written so far:

Dear Dad,

I'm writing to ask if there is a limitation to the number of cars our liability insurance covers . . .

Dear Max,

You know last summer when you broke the vase my Uncle Bill had left me? Remember I told you a hundred bucks would be fine, but you insisted I get it appraised? Well, boy, am I glad you did. I hope you are sitting down because the museum's curator of thirteenth-century art says . . .

Mr. Lucado,

The purpose of this letter is to inform you that the purebred puppy you were sending to Oakland, California, was inadvertently sent to Auckland, New Zealand . . .

Dear Max,

So why am I writing after all these years? Well, it seems that the university made a mistake. They swapped our transcripts. Isn't that a hoot? And all these years I thought I graduated by the skin of my teeth. And all these years you thought you were summa cum laude!

Dear Mrs. Lucado,

Recently you purchased from us a home pregnancy diagnostic kit. We are writing to inform you that there was a mistake in the instructions, and what you thought you were, you aren't, and what you thought you weren't, you are. . . .

Groan.

I've never read any scientific data on it, but it seems to me that the unnecessary mail has the necessary mail outnumbered. (Maybe you are like me and you sort your mail over a trash can. Maybe you are like me and wonder if there is anything in the world that doesn't have its own catalog. If you are a left-handed, right-winged, Ivy-League fan of jazz music, there is probably an underwear catalog just for you.)

Most mail is unnecessary. So why am I repairing my box?

Simple. It's December.

Were it any other time of the year, I might leave it on its side. Let the postman hang on to my bills for a few days. But I can't do that. Not this time of the year. Not December. Not the week before Christmas!

This is the week that mail is fun. This is the week of red envelopes, green stamps, and Christmas tree stickers. This is the week when your old roomie who married Hazel and moved to Phoenix writes to tell you their fourth child is on the way. This is the week of front-and-back newsletters describing the Grand Canyon, graduations, and gallbladder surgeries.

This is the week of overnighted nuts and packaged fruitcakes and frenzied mailmen. Add to that a gift from Aunt Sophie and a calendar from your insurance agent, and you've got a daily reason to whistle your way to the mailbox.

So, as much for me as for the mailman, I propped up the box.

Only a Scrooge doesn't want a Christmas card.

Some are funny. Got one today with elves pulling books off the "elf-help" shelf.

Others are touching, like the illustration of Mother Mary and the baby resting at the base of the Egyptian sphinx.

And a few are unforgettable. Every Christmas I read this reminder that came in the mail several years ago:

> *If our greatest need had been information, God would have sent an educator. If our greatest need had been technology, God would have sent us a scientist. If our greatest need had been money, God would have sent us an economist. But since our greatest need was forgiveness, God sent us a Savior.*

Christmas cards. Punctuated promises. Phrases filled with the reason we do it all anyway.

He became like us, so we could become like him.
Angels still sing and the star still beckons.
He loves each one of us like there was only one of us to love.

Long after the sender's name is forgotten, the card's message lingers. Words of promise. A handful of seeds and syllables flung upon the fertile soil of December with hope of fruit born in July. For that reason, I keep the mailbox up.

My heart can use all the seeds it can get.

CHAPTER SEVEN

Behind the Shower Curtain

I'M GOING to have to install a computer in my shower. That's where I have my best thoughts.

I had a great one today.

I was mulling over a recent conversation I had with a disenchanted Christian brother. He was upset with me. So upset that he was considering rescinding his invitation for me to speak to his group. Seems he'd heard I was pretty open about who I have fellowship with. He'd read the words I wrote: "If God calls a person his child, shouldn't I call him my brother?" And, "If God accepts others with their errors and misinterpretations, shouldn't we?"[1]

He didn't like that. "Carrying it a bit too far," he told me. "Fences are necessary," he explained. "Scriptures are clear on such matters." He read me a few and then urged me to be careful to whom I give grace.

"I don't give it," I assured. "I only spotlight where God already has."

Didn't seem to satisfy him. I offered to bow out of the engagement (the break would be nice), but he softened and told me to come after all.

That's where I'm going today. That's why I was thinking about him in the shower. And that's why I need a waterproof computer. I had a great thought. A why-didn't-I-think-to-say-that? insight.

I hope to see him today. If the subject resurfaces, I'll say it. But in case it doesn't, I'll say it to you. (It's too good to waste.) Just one sentence:

> I've never been surprised by God's judgment, but I'm still stunned by his grace.

God's judgment has never been a problem for me. In fact, it always seemed right. Lightning bolts on Sodom. Fire on Gomorrah. *Good job, God.* Egyptians swallowed in the Red Sea. *They had it coming.* Forty years of wandering to loosen the stiff necks of the Israelites? *Would've done it myself.* Ananias and Sapphira? *You bet.*

Discipline is easy for me to swallow. Logical to assimilate. Manageable and appropriate.

But God's grace? Anything but.

Examples? How much time do you have?

> David the psalmist becomes David the voyeur, but by God's grace becomes David the psalmist again.

Peter denied Christ before he preached Christ.

Zacchaeus, the crook. The cleanest part of his life was the money he'd laundered. But Jesus still had time for him.

The thief on the cross: hellbent and hung-out-to-die one minute, heaven-bound and smiling the next.

Story after story. Prayer after prayer. Surprise after surprise.

Seems that God is looking more for ways to get us home than for ways to keep us out. I challenge you to find one soul who came to God seeking grace and did not find it. Search the pages. Read the stories. Envision the encounters. Find one person who came seeking a second chance and left with a stern lecture. I dare you. Search.

You won't find it.

You will find a strayed sheep on the other side of the creek. He's lost. He knows it. He's stuck and embarrassed. What will the other sheep say? What will the shepherd say?

You will find a shepherd who finds him.[2]

Oh boy. Duck down. Put hooves over the eyes. The belt is about to fly. But the belt is never felt. Just hands. Large, open hands reaching under his body and lifting the sheep up, up, up until he's placed upon the shepherd's shoulders. He's carried back to the flock and given a party! "Cut the grass and comb the wool," he announces.

"We are going to have a celebration!"

The other sheep shake their heads in disbelief. Just like we will. At our party. When we get home. When we watch the Shepherd shoulder into our midst one unlikely soul after another.

Seems to me God gives a lot more grace than we'd ever imagine.

We could do the same.

I'm not for watering down the truth or compromising the gospel. But if a fellow with a pure heart calls God *Father*, can't I call that same man *Brother?* If God doesn't make doctrinal perfection a requirement for family membership, should I?

And if we never agree, can't we agree to disagree? If God can tolerate my mistakes, can't I tolerate the mistakes of others? If God can overlook my errors, can't I overlook the errors of others? If God allows me with my foibles and failures to call him *Father*, shouldn't I extend the same grace to others?

One thing's for sure. When we get to heaven, we'll be surprised at some of the folks we see. And some of them will be surprised when they see us.

CHAPTER EIGHT

Gabriel's Questions

GABRIEL MUST HAVE scratched his head at this one. He wasn't one to question his God-given missions. Sending fire and dividing seas were all in an eternity's work for this angel. When God sent, Gabriel went.

And when word got out that God was to become man, Gabriel was enthused. He could envision the moment:

The Messiah in a blazing chariot.
The King descending on a fiery cloud.
An explosion of light from which the Messiah would emerge.

That's what he expected. What he never expected, however, was what he got: a slip of paper with a Nazarene address. "God will become a baby," it read. "Tell the mother to name the child Jesus. And tell her not to be afraid."

Gabriel was never one to question, but this time he had to wonder.

God will become a baby? Gabriel had seen babies before. He had been platoon leader on the bulrush operation. He remembered what little Moses looked like.

That's okay for humans, he thought to himself. *But God?*

The heavens can't contain him; how could a body? Besides, have you seen what comes out of those babies? Hardly befitting for the Creator of the universe. Babies must be carried and fed, bounced and bathed. To imagine some mother burping God on her shoulder—why, that was beyond what even an angel could imagine.

And what of this name—what was it—*Jesus?* Such a common name. There's a Jesus in every cul-de-sac. Come on, even *Gabriel* has more punch to it than *Jesus.* Call the baby *Eminence* or *Majesty* or *Heaven-sent.* Anything but *Jesus.*

So Gabriel scratched his head. What happened to the good ol' days? The Sodom and Gomorrah stuff. Flooding the globe. Flaming swords. That's the action he liked.

But Gabriel had his orders. Take the message to Mary. *Must be a special girl,* he assumed as he traveled. But Gabriel was in for another shock. One peek told him Mary was no queen. The mother-to-be of God was not regal. She was a Jewish peasant who'd barely outgrown her acne and had a crush on a guy named Joe.

And speaking of Joe—what does this fellow know? Might as well be a weaver in Spain or a cobbler in Greece. He's a carpenter. Look at him over there, sawdust in his beard and nail apron around his waist. You're telling me God is going to have dinner every night with him? You're telling me the source of wisdom is going to call this guy "Dad"? You're telling me a common laborer is going to be charged with giving food to God?

What if he gets laid off?

What if he gets cranky?

What if he decides to run off with a pretty young girl from down the street? Then where will we be?

It was all Gabriel could do to keep from turning back. "This is a peculiar idea you have, God," he must have muttered to himself.

Are God's guardians given to such musings?

Are we? Are we still stunned by God's coming? Still staggered by the event? Does Christmas still spawn the same speechless wonder it did two thousand years ago?

I've been asking that question lately—to myself. As I write, Christmas is only days away and something just happened that has me concerned that the pace of the holidays may be overshadowing the purpose of the holidays.

I saw a manger in a mall. Correct that. I *barely* saw a manger in a mall. I almost didn't see it. I was in a hurry. Guests coming. Santa dropping in. Sermons to be prepared. Services to be planned. Presents to be purchased.

The crush of things was so great that the crèche of Christ was almost ignored. I nearly missed it. And had it not been for the child and his father, I would have.

But out of the corner of my eye, I saw them. The little boy, three, maybe four years old, in jeans and high-tops staring at the manger's infant. The father, in baseball hat and work clothes, looking over his son's shoulder, gesturing first at Joseph, then Mary, then the baby. He was telling the little fellow the story.

And oh, the twinkle in the boy's eyes. The wonder on his little face. He didn't speak. He just listened. And I didn't move. I just watched. What questions were filling the little boy's head? Could they have been the same as Gabriel's? What sparked the amazement on his face? Was it the magic?

And why is it that out of a hundred or so of God's children only two paused to consider his son? What is this December demon that steals our eyes and stills our tongues? Isn't this the season to pause and pose Gabriel's questions?

The tragedy is not that we can't answer them, but that we are too busy to ask them.

Only heaven knows how long Gabriel fluttered unseen above Mary before he took a breath and broke the news. But he did. He told her the name. He told her the plan. He told her not to be afraid. And when he announced, "With God nothing is impossible!" he said it as much for himself as for her.

For even though he couldn't answer the questions, he knew who could, and that was enough. And even though we can't answer them all, taking time to ask a few would be a good start.

CHAPTER NINE

What Is Your Price?

ATTENDING a game show wasn't your idea of a vacation activity, but your kids wanted to go, so you gave in. Now that you're here, you are beginning to enjoy it. The studio frenzy is contagious. The music is upbeat. The stage is colorful. And the stakes are high.

"Higher than they've ever been!" The show host brags. "Welcome to *What Is Your Price?*" You're just about to ask your spouse if that is his real hair when he announces the pot: "Ten million dollars!"

The audience needs no prompting; they explode with applause.

"It's the richest game in history," the host beams. "Someone today will walk out of here with a check for ten million!"

"Won't be me," you chuckle to your oldest child. "I've never had any luck at luck."

"Shhhh," she whispers, pointing to the stage. "They're about to draw the name."

Guess whose name they call. In the instant it takes to call it, you go from spectator to player. Your kids shriek, your spouse screams, and a thousand eyes watch the pretty girl take your hand and walk you to the stage.

"Open the curtain!" the host commands. You turn and watch as the curtains part and you gasp at the sight. A bright red wheelbarrow full of money—overflowing with money. The same girl who walked you to the stage now pushes the wheelbarrow in your direction, parking it in front of you.

"Ever seen ten million dollars?" asks the pearly toothed host.

"Not in a while," you answer. The audience laughs like you were a stand-up comic.

"Dig your hands in it," he invites. "Go ahead, dive in."

You look at your family. One child is drooling, one is praying, and your mate is giving you two thumbs up. How can you refuse? You burrow in up to your shoulders and rise up, clutching a chestful of one-hundred-dollar bills.

"It can be yours. It can be all yours. The choice is up to you. The only question you have to answer is, 'What is your price?'"

Applause rings again, the band plays, and you swallow hard. Behind you a second curtain opens, revealing a large placard. "What are you willing to give?" is written on the top. The host explains the rules. "All you have to do is agree to one condition and you will receive the money."

"Ten million dollars!" you whisper to yourself.

Not one million or two, but *ten* million. No small sum. Nice nest egg. Ten million bucks would go a long way, right? Tuition paid off. Retirement guaranteed. Would open a few doors on a few cars or a new house (or several).

You could be quite the benefactor with such a sum. Help a few orphanages. Feed a few nations. Build some church buildings. Suddenly you understand: This is the opportunity of a lifetime.

"Take your pick. Just choose one option and the money is yours."

A deep voice from another microphone begins reading the list.

> "Put your children up for adoption."
> "Become a prostitute for a week."
> "Give up your American citizenship."
> "Abandon your church."
> "Abandon your family."
> "Kill a stranger."
> "Have a sex-change operation."
> "Leave your spouse."
> "Change your race."

"That's the list," the host proclaims. "Now make your choice."

The theme music begins, the audience is quiet, and your pulse is racing. You have a choice to make. No one can help you. You are on the stage. The decision is yours. No one can tell you what to pick.

But there is one thing I can tell you. I can tell you what others would do. Your neighbors have given their answers. In a national survey that asked the same question, many said what they would do. Seven percent of those who answered would murder for the money. Six percent would change their race. Four percent would change their sex.[1]

If money is the gauge of the heart, then this study revealed that money is on the heart of most Americans. In exchange for ten million dollars:

25 percent would abandon their family.

25 percent would abandon their church.

23 percent would become a prostitute for a week.

16 percent would give up their American citizenship.

16 percent would leave their spouse.

3 percent would put their children up for adoption.[2]

Even more revealing than what Americans would do for ten million dollars is that most would do *something.* Two-thirds of those polled would agree to at least one—some to several—of the options. The majority, in other words, would not leave the stage empty-handed. They would pay the price to own the wheelbarrow.

What would you do? Or better, what are you doing?

“Get real, Max,” you are saying. “I’ve never had a shot at ten million.”

Perhaps not, but you’ve had a chance to make a thousand or a hundred or ten. The amount may not have been the same but the choices are. Which makes the question even more disturbing. Some are willing to give up their family, faith, or morals for far less than ten million dollars.

Jesus had a word for that: *greed*.

Jesus also had a definition for greed. He called it the practice of measuring life by possessions.[3]

Greed equates a person’s worth with a person’s purse.

1. You got a lot = you are a lot.
2. You got a little = you are little.

The consequence of such a philosophy is predictable. If you are the sum of what you own, then by all means own it all. No price is too high. No payment is too much.

Now, very few would be guilty of blatant greed. Jesus knew that. That’s why he cautioned against “all kinds of greed” (Luke 12:15). Greed wears many faces.

When we lived in Rio de Janeiro, Brazil, I went to visit a member of our church. He had been a strong leader in the congregation, but for several Sundays we didn’t see or hear from him.

Friends told me he had inherited some money and was building a house. I found him at the construction site. He’d inherited three hundred dollars. With the money he'd purchased a tiny lot adjacent to a polluted swamp. The plot of land was the size of a garage. On it he was, by hand, constructing a one-room house. He gave me a tour of the project—it took about twenty seconds.

We sat in front and talked. I told him we'd missed him, that the church needed him back. He grew quiet and turned and looked at his house. When he turned again his eyes were moist.

"You're right, Max," he confessed. "I guess I just got too greedy."

Greedy? I wanted to say. *You're building a hut in a swamp and you call it greed?* But I didn't say anything because he was right. Greed is relative. Greed is not defined by what something costs; it is measured by what it costs you.

If anything costs you your faith or your family, the price is too high.

Such is the point Jesus makes in the parable of the portfolio.[4] Seems a fellow made a windfall profit off an investment. The land produced a bumper crop. He found himself with excess cash and an enviable question, "What will I do with my earnings?"

Doesn't take him long to decide. He will save it. He will find a way to store it so he can live the good life. His plan? Accumulate. His aim? Wine, dine, shine, and recline. Move to the Sunbelt, play golf, kick back, and relax.

Suddenly, the man dies and another voice is heard.

The voice of God. God has nothing kind to say to the man. His initial words are "Foolish man!"

On earth the man was respected. He is honored with a nice funeral and a mahogany casket. Gray flannels fill the auditorium with admiration for the canny businessman. But on the front pew is a family already starting to bicker over their dad's estate. "Foolish man!" God declares. "So who will get those things you have prepared for yourself?" (Luke 12:20).

The man spent his life building a house of cards. He never saw the storm. And now, the wind has blown.

The storm wasn't the only thing he didn't see.

He never saw God. Note his first words after the capital gain. "*What will I do?*" (v. 17). He went to the wrong place and asked the wrong question. What if he'd gone to God and asked, "What would you have me to do?"

The man's sin is not that he planned for the future. His sin was that his plans did not include God.

Imagine if someone treated you like this. Let's say you bring over a housesitter to care for your home over a weekend. You leave her with keys, money, and instructions. And you leave to enjoy your trip.

When you return, you find your house has been painted purple. The locks have been changed, so you ring the doorbell and the housesitter answers. Before you can say anything, she escorts you in proclaiming, "Look how I decorated my house!"

The fireplace has been replaced with an indoor

waterfall. Carpet has been replaced with pink tile, and portraits of Elvis on black velvet line the walls.

"This isn't your house!" you proclaim. "It's mine."

"Those aren't your possessions," God reminds us. "They are mine."

"The LORD owns the world and everything in it—the heavens, even the highest heavens, are his" (Deut. 10:14).

God's foremost rule of finance is: We own nothing. We are managers, not owners. Stewards, not landlords. Maintenance people, not proprietors. Our money is not ours; it is his.

This man, however, gave no thought to that. Please note that Jesus didn't criticize this man's affluence. He criticized his arrogance. The rich man's words testify to his priority.

> This is what I will do:
> I will tear down . . .
> I will store . . .
> Then I can say to myself, "I have enough good things." (Luke 12:18–19)

A schoolboy was once asked to define the parts of speech, *I* and *mine*. He answered, "aggressive pronouns." This rich man was aggressively self-centered. His world was fenced in by himself. He was blind. He didn't see God. He didn't see others. He saw only self.

"Foolish man," God told him. "Tonight your life will be taken from you" (v. 20).

Strange, isn't it, that this man had enough sense to acquire wealth but not enough to get ready for eternity? Stranger still, that we make the same mistake. I mean, it's not as if God kept the future a secret. One glance at a cemetery should remind us; everyone dies. One visit to a funeral should convince us; we don't take anything with us.

Hearses pull no U-Hauls.

Dead men push no ten-million-dollar wheelbarrows.

The game show was pretend, but the facts are real. You are on a stage. You have been given a prize. The stakes are high. Very high.

What is your price?

CHAPTER TEN

Groceries and Grace

THIS STORY made its way to me from a friend who heard it from a friend who heard it from who knows who. Chances are it has suffered through each of the generations—but even if there is only a splinter of fact in what I heard, it's worth retelling.

Seems a fellow is doing some shopping at a commissary on a military base. Doesn't need much, just some coffee and a loaf of bread. He is standing in line at the checkout stand. Behind him is a woman with a full cart. Her basket overflows with groceries, clothing, and a VCR.

At his turn he steps up to the register. The clerk invites him to draw a piece of paper out of a fishbowl. "If you pull out the correct slip, then all your groceries are free," the clerk explains.

"How many 'correct slips' are there?" asks the buyer.

"Only one."

The bowl is full so the chances are slim, but the fellow tries anyway, and wouldn't you know it, he gets the winning ticket! What a surprise. But then he realizes he is only buying coffee and bread. What a waste.

But this fellow is quick. He turns to the lady behind him—the one with the mountain of stuff—and proclaims, "Well, what do you know, Honey? We won! We don't have to pay a penny."

She stares at him. He winks at her. And somehow she has the wherewithal to play along. She steps up beside him. Puts her arm in his and smiles. And for a moment they stand side-by-side, wedded by good fortune. In the parking lot she consummates the temporary union with a kiss and a hug and goes on her way with a grand story to tell her friends.

I know, I know. What they did was a bit shady. He shouldn't have lied and she shouldn't have pretended. But that taken into account, it's still a nice story.

A story not too distant from our own. We, too, have been graced with a surprise. Even more than that of the lady. For though her debt was high, she could pay it. We can't begin to pay ours.

We, like the woman, have been given a gift. Not just at the checkout stand, but at the judgment seat.

And we, too, have become a bride. Not just for a moment, but for eternity. And not just for groceries, but for the feast.

Don't we have a grand story to tell our friends?

CHAPTER ELEVEN

The Choice

IT'S QUIET. It's early. My coffee is hot. The sky is still black. The world is still asleep. The day is coming.

In a few moments the day will arrive. It will roar down the track with the rising of the sun. The stillness of the dawn will be exchanged for the noise of the day. The calm of solitude will be replaced by the pounding pace of the human race. The refuge of the early morning will be invaded by decisions to be made and deadlines to be met.

For the next twelve hours I will be exposed to the day's demands. It is now that I must make a choice. Because of Calvary, I'm free to choose. And so I choose.

I choose love . . .

No occasion justifies hatred; no injustice warrants bitterness. I choose love. Today I will love God and what God loves.

I choose joy . . .

I will invite my God to be the God of circumstance. I will refuse the temptation to be cynical . . . the tool of the lazy thinker. I will refuse to see people as anything less than human beings, created by God. I will refuse to see any problem as anything less than an opportunity to see God.

I choose peace . . .

I will live forgiven. I will forgive so that I may live.

I choose patience . . .

I will overlook the inconveniences of the world. Instead of cursing the one who takes my place, I'll invite him to do so. Rather than complain that the wait is too long, I will thank God for a moment to pray. Instead of clinching my fist at new assignments, I will face them with joy and courage.

I choose kindness . . .

I will be kind to the poor, for they are alone. Kind to the rich, for they are afraid. And kind to the unkind, for such is how God has treated me.

I choose goodness . . .

I will go without a dollar before I take a dishonest one. I will be overlooked before I will boast. I will confess before I will accuse. I choose goodness.

I choose faithfulness . . .

Today I will keep my promises. My debtors will not regret their trust. My associates will not question my word. My wife will not question my love. And my children will never fear that their father will not come home.

I choose gentleness . . .

Nothing is won by force. I choose to be gentle. If I raise my voice may it be only in praise. If I clench my fist, may it be only in prayer. If I make a demand, may it be only of myself.

I choose self-control . . .

I am a spiritual being. After this body is dead, my spirit will soar. I refuse to let what will rot, rule the eternal. I choose self-control. I will be drunk only by joy. I will be impassioned only by my faith. I will be influenced only by God. I will be taught only by Christ. I choose self-control.

Love, joy, peace, patience, kindness, goodness, faithfulness, gentleness, and self-control. To these I commit my day. If I succeed, I will give thanks. If I fail, I will seek his grace. And then, when this day is done, I will place my head on my pillow and rest.

CHAPTER TWELVE

The Prophet

I WANTED BREAKFAST. I got a prophet.

I stopped at the grocery store on the way to the office this morning. Had to run an errand and decided while I was there to run another. I went over to the deli to order some breakfast. For a couple of bucks you can get all the eggs and sausage you can handle. My waistline and the doctor keep me from doing this every day, but since I was in the store anyway and since I hadn't eaten . . .

A prophet had the same idea. Not a prophet *in* the Bible, but a prophet *with* a Bible. A thick, dog-eared blue-bound Bible. He was short and thin—a wispy fellow with cropped, unkempt hair, and a bushy, red beard.

By the time I got there, he was already ordering his food. *Meticulously* ordering his food. "Do you serve a breakfast taco with no meat?"

Yes.

"Just potatoes and eggs?"

Yes.

"Is it salted?"

No.

"How many potatoes?"

The deli lady lifted the pan so he could see.

"And how many tacos?"

Maybe he wanted to be sure he got his money's worth. Maybe he observes a religious diet. Or maybe he was just picky. I couldn't tell. But I could see that he was polite, painfully polite.

He carried a rake. (A modern version of the winnowing fork perhaps?) His robe was blue, and under it was a shirt that looked like a converted towel.

As one was preparing the prophet's food, a second worker appeared. He thought the prophet hadn't been waited on and asked if he needed help.

"No, I've been helped. But since you asked, may I ask you if you are a believer in Jesus Christ? I am his prophet and I am sent to you."

The worker didn't know how to respond. He looked at the deli lady, who looked over her shoulder and shrugged. He looked at me, then looked away. Then he looked back at the prophet and mumbled something like, "Thanks for coming," and asked me if I needed any help.

I did and told him what I wanted. And while I waited, out came the tacos for the prophet. He'd ordered a soft drink—with no ice. And water—in a paper cup. He was surprised at the color of his soft drink.

“I thought it would be orange.”

“No, it’s clear,” the lady responded.

I half-hoped he’d try a miracle—changing the water from clear to orange. He didn’t; he simply interpreted the moment. “In life it really doesn’t matter what color your drinks are, does it?” He smiled at the lady, smiled at the man, and then smiled at me.

We all smiled back.

Since he had a Bible in one hand and a rake in the other, I wondered how he was going to carry the food. So I offered to help. He declined.

“Thank you in the name of Jesus for offering to help, but I can make it.”

He stacked the plate on the top of the soft-drink cup and somehow picked up the water with the rake-holding, Bible-toting hand. In the process he almost lost it all, so I offered to help again.

“No, but in the name of Jesus I bless you for offering to help me.”

“And,” he turned to the deli lady, “I bless you in the name of Jesus Christ for your kind assistance.”

“And,” he caught the glance of the deli man, “I bless you in the name of Jesus Christ.” He didn’t say what for. A generic blessing, I assumed.

Having blessed us, he turned to leave. As far as I know, he made it to the table.

I watched the eyes of the cashier as she rang up my breakfast. Knowing absolutely nothing about her, I wondered what she was thinking. I wondered what her encounter with the prophet had done for her opinion of the One whom the prophet represented.

I wanted to say something, but didn't know what to say. I started to say, "Me and the prophet there, we are on the same team; we just have two different approaches. Being a Christian doesn't really mean carrying a rake."

But before I could think what to say, she'd turned to help someone else. So I turned to leave.

That's when I bumped into Lawrence. Lawrence is a friend from my church. Bumping into Lawrence is no small matter. He's an ex-pro football player. Everything about Lawrence is big, and everything about Lawrence is kind. A strong hug from Lawrence can last you a week.

And that's what he gave me . . . a good hug, a warm handshake, and a genuine question about my well-being. Not much, just a couple of minutes of kind concern. Then he went his way and I went mine.

As I was leaving, I was struck by the contrast of the two encounters. Both the prophet and Lawrence are followers of Christ. Both are unashamed of their faith. Both love to carry a Bible. Both like to bless people. But that's where the similarities end.

One wears sandals and a robe, and the other wears tennis shoes and jeans.

One dresses like Jesus, but the other acts like Jesus.

One introduced himself as an ambassador for Christ; the other didn't have to.

One stirred my curiosity, but the other touched my heart.

And something told me that if Jesus were here, in person, in San Antonio, and I ran into him in a grocery store, I wouldn't recognize him by his rake, robe, and big Bible. But I would know him for his good heart and kind words.

PART TWO

The Touch of the Master

The Touch of the Master

n his later years Beethoven would spend hours playing a broken harpsichord. The instrument was worthless. Keys were missing. Strings were stretched. It was out of tune, harsh on the ears.

Nonetheless the great pianist would play till tears came down his cheeks. To look at him, you'd think he was hearing the sublime. He was. For he was deaf. Beethoven was hearing the sound the instrument should make, not the one it did make.[1]

Ever feel like Beethoven's harpsichord? Out of tune? Inadequate? Your service ill-timed, insignificant?

Ever wonder what God does when the instrument is broken? What happens to the song when the strings are out of tune? How does the Master respond when the keys don't work?

Does he turn and leave? Does he demand a replacement? Does he junk the old? Or does he patiently tune until he hears the song he longs to hear?

If you've asked those questions (and who hasn't?), I've got some thoughts for you to read. I've assembled a curious covey of testimonies I thought you'd enjoy. In the following pages, you'll find:

- *an explanation of why the Wizard of Oz is not in the Bible*
- *an account of a moody moon*
- *an early newspaper interview with Moses and Jehoshaphat.*
- *the message of a cricket and the common diet of pre-chewed food*

Some chapters are funny. Some serious. Some fictional. Some factual. But all have an answer for those who feel like Beethoven's harpsichord. All work together to encourage the tired instrument. All hope to show you how the Master Musician fixes what we can't and hears music when we don't.

CHAPTER THIRTEEN

When Crickets Make You Cranky

FORGIVE ME if this chapter is disjointed. As I write, I am angry. I am angered by a cricket. He's loud. He's obnoxious. He's hidden. And he's in big trouble if I ever find him.

I arrived at my office early. Two hours before my alarm sounded, I was here. Sleeves rolled back and computer humming. *Beat the phones*, I thought. *Get a jump on the morning*, I planned. *Get a leg up on the day.*

But *Get your hands on that cricket* is what I keep mumbling.

Now, I have nothing against nature. The melody of a canary, I love. The pleasant hum of the wind in the leaves, I relish. But the predawn *raack-raack-raack* of a cricket bugs me.

So I get on my knees and follow the sound through the office. I peek under boxes. I pull books off the shelves. I get on my belly and look under my desk. Humbling. I've been sabotaged by a one-inch bug.

What is this insolent irritant that reduces a man to bug-stalker?

Finally, I isolate the culprit.

Rats, he's behind a shelf. Out of my reach. Hidden in a haven of plywood. I can't get to him. All I can do is throw pens at the base of the shelf. So I do. *Pop. Pop. Pop.* One after another. A barrage of Bics. He finally shuts up.

But the silence lasts only a minute.

So forgive me if my thoughts are fragmented, but I'm launching artillery every other paragraph. This is no way to work. This is no way to start the day. My floor is cluttered. My pants are dirty. My train of thought is derailed. I mean, how can you write about anger with a stupid bug in your office?

Oooops. Guess I'm in the right frame of mind after all . . .

Anger. This morning it's easy to define: the noise of the soul. *Anger*. The unseen irritant of the heart. *Anger*. The relentless invader of silence.

Just like the cricket, anger irritates.

Just like the cricket, anger isn't easily silenced.

Just like the cricket, anger has a way of increasing in volume until it's the only sound we hear. The louder it gets the more desperate we become.

When we are mistreated, our animalistic response is to go on the hunt. Instinctively, we double up our fists.

Getting even is only natural. Which, incidentally, is precisely the problem. Revenge is natural, not spiritual. Getting even is the rule of the jungle. Giving grace is the rule of the kingdom.

Some of you are thinking, *Easy for you to say, Max, sitting there in your office with a cricket as your chief irritant. You ought to try living with my wife.* Or, *You ought to have to cope with my past.* Or, *You ought to raise my kids. You don't know how my ex has mistreated me. You don't have any idea how hard my life has been.*

And you're right, I don't. But I have a very clear idea how miserable your future will be unless you deal with your anger.

X-ray the soul of the vengeful and behold the tumor of bitterness: black, menacing, malignant. Carcinoma of the spirit. Its fatal fibers creep around the edge of the heart and ravage it. Yesterday you can't alter, but your reaction to yesterday you can. The past you cannot change, but your response to your past you can.

Impossible, you say? Let me try to show you otherwise.

Imagine you are from a large family—a dozen or so kids. A family more blended than the Brady bunch. All the children are from the same dad, but they have four or five different moms.

Imagine also that your dad is a sneak and has been one for a long time. Everybody knows it. Everybody knows he cheated your uncle out of the estate.

Everybody knows he ran like a coward to avoid getting caught.

Let's also imagine that your great-uncle tricked your dad into marrying your mother's sister. He got your dad drunk before the wedding and had his ugly daughter go to the altar instead of the pretty one your dad thought he was marrying.

That didn't slow down your father, though. He just married them both. The one he loved couldn't have kids, so he slept with her maid. In fact, he had a habit of sleeping with most of the kitchen help; as a result, most of your siblings resemble the cooks.

Finally the bride your dad wanted to marry in the first place gets pregnant . . . and you are born.

You're the favored son . . . and your brothers know it.

You get a car. They don't. You get Armani; they get K-Mart. You get summer camp; they get summer jobs. You get educated; they get angry.

And they get even. They sell you to some foreign service project, put you on a plane for Egypt, and tell your dad you got shot by a sniper. You find yourself surrounded by people you don't know, learning a language you don't understand, and living in a culture you've never seen.

Imaginary tale? No. It's the story of Joseph. A favored son in a bizarre family, he had every reason to be angry.

He tried to make the best of it. He became the chief servant of the head of the Secret Service. His boss's wife tried to seduce him, and when he refused, she pouted and he ended up in prison. Pharaoh got wind of the fact that Joseph could interpret dreams and let him take a shot at some of Pharaoh's own.

When Joseph interpreted them he got promoted out of the prison into the palace as prime minister. The second highest position in all of Egypt. The only person Joseph bowed before was the king.

Meanwhile a famine hits and Jacob, Joseph's father, sends his sons to Egypt for a foreign loan. The brothers don't know it, but they are standing in front of the same brother they sold to the Gypsies some twenty-two years earlier.

They don't recognize Joseph, but Joseph recognizes them. A bit balder and paunchier, but they are the same brothers. Imagine Joseph's thoughts. The last time he saw these faces, he was looking up at them from the bottom of a pit. The last time he heard these voices, they were laughing at him. The last time they called his name, they called him every name in the book.

Now is his chance to get even. He has complete control. One snap of his fingers and these brothers are dead. Better yet, slap some manacles on their hands and feet and let them see what an Egyptian dungeon is like. Let them sleep in the mud. Let them mop floors. Let them learn Egyptian.

Revenge is within Joseph's power. And there is power in revenge. Intoxicating power.

Haven't we tasted it? Haven't we been tempted to get even?

As we escort the offender into the courtroom, we announce, "He hurt me!" The jurors shake their heads in disgust. "He abandoned me!" we explain, and the chambers echo with our accusation. "Guilty!" the judge snarls as he slams the gavel. "Guilty!" the jury agrees. "Guilty!" the audience proclaims. We delight in this moment of justice. We relish this pound of flesh. So we prolong the event. We tell the story again and again and again.

Now let's freeze-frame that scene. I have a question. Not for all of you, but for a few of you. Some of you are in the courtroom. The courtroom of complaint. Some of you are rehashing the same hurt every chance you get with anyone who will listen.

For you, I have this question: Who made you God? I don't mean to be cocky, but why are you doing his work for him?

"Vengeance is Mine," God declared. "I will repay" (Heb. 10:30 NKJV).

"Don't say, 'I'll pay you back for the wrong you did.' Wait for the LORD, and he will make things right" (Prov. 20:22).

Judgment is God's job. To assume otherwise is to assume God can't do it.

Revenge is irreverent. When we strike back we are saying, "I know vengeance is yours, God, but I just didn't think you'd punish enough. I thought I'd better take this situation into my own hands. You have a tendency to be a little soft."

Joseph understands that. Rather than get even, he reveals his identity and has his father and the rest of the family brought to Egypt. He grants them safety and provides them a place to live. They live in harmony for seventeen years.

But then Jacob dies and the moment of truth comes. The brothers have a hunch that with Jacob gone they'll be lucky to get out of Egypt with their heads on their shoulders. So they go to Joseph and plead for mercy.

"Your father gave this command before he died. . . . 'Tell Joseph to forgive you'" (Gen. 50:16–17). (I have to smile at the thought of grown men talking like this. Don't they sound like kids, whining, "Daddy said to be nice to us"?)

Joseph's response? "When Joseph received the message, he cried" (Gen. 50:17). *"What more do I have to do?"* his tears implore. *"I've given you a home. I've provided for your families. Why do you still mistrust my grace?"*

Please read carefully the two statements he makes to his brothers. First he asks, "Can I do what only God can do?" (v. 19).

May I restate the obvious? Revenge belongs to God! If vengeance is God's, then it is not ours. God has not asked us to settle the score or get even. Ever.

Why? The answer is found in the second part of Joseph's statement: "You meant to hurt me, but God turned your evil into good to save the lives of many people, which is being done" (v. 20).

Forgiveness comes easier with a wide-angle lens.

Joseph uses one to get the whole picture. He refuses to focus on the betrayal of his brothers without also seeing the loyalty of his God.

It always helps to see the big picture.

Some time ago I was in an airport lobby when I saw an acquaintance enter. He was a man I hadn't seen in a while but had thought about often. He'd been through a divorce, and I was close enough to it to know that he deserved some of the blame.

I noticed he was not alone. Beside him was a woman. *Why, that scoundrel! Just a few months out and here he has another lady?*

Any thought of greeting him disappeared as I passed judgment on his character. But then he saw me. He waved at me. He motioned me over. I was caught. I was trapped. I'd have to go visit with the reprobate. So I did.

"Max, meet my aunt and her husband."

I gulped. I hadn't noticed the man.

"We're on our way to a family reunion. I know they would really like to meet you."

"We use your books in our home Bible study," my friend's uncle spoke up. "You've got some great insights."

"If only you knew," I said to myself. I had committed a common sin of the unforgiving. I had cast a vote without knowing the story.

To forgive someone is to admit our limitations. We've been given only one piece of life's jigsaw puzzle. Only God has the cover of the box.

To forgive someone is to display reverence. Forgiveness is not saying the one who hurt you was right. Forgiveness is stating that God is fair and he will do what is right.

After all, don't we have enough things to do without trying to do God's work too?

Guess what. I just noticed something. The cricket is quiet. I got so wrapped up in this chapter I forgot him. I haven't thrown a pen for an hour. Guess he fell asleep. Could be that's what he wanted to do all along, but I kept waking him up with my Bics.

He ended up getting some rest. I ended up finishing this chapter. Remarkable what gets accomplished when we let go of our anger.

CHAPTER FOURTEEN

Seeing What Eyes Can't

I STAND six steps from the bed's edge. My arms extended. Hands open. On the bed Sara—all four years of her—crouches, posed like a playful kitten. She's going to jump. But she's not ready. I'm too close.

"Back more, Daddy," she stands and dares.

I dramatically comply, confessing admiration for her courage. After two giant steps I stop. "More?" I ask.

"Yes!" Sara squeals, hopping on the bed.

With each step she laughs and claps and motions for more. When I'm on the other side of the canyon, when I'm beyond the reach of mortal man, when I am but a tiny figure on the horizon, she stops me. "There, stop there."

"Are you sure?"

"I'm sure," she shouts. I extend my arms. Once again she crouches, then springs. Superman without a cape.

Skydiver without a chute. Only her heart flies higher than her body. In that airborne instant her only hope is her father. If he proves weak, she'll fall. If he proves cruel, she'll crash. If he proves forgetful, she'll tumble to the hard floor.

But such fear she does not know, for her father she does. She trusts him. Four years under the same roof have convinced her he is reliable. He is not superhuman, but he is strong. He is not holy, but he is good. He's not brilliant, but he doesn't have to be to remember to catch his child when she jumps.

And so she flies.

And so she soars.

And so he catches her and the two rejoice at the wedding of her trust and his faithfulness.

I stand a few feet from another bed. This time no one laughs. The room is solemn. A machine pumps air into a tired body. A monitor metronomes the beats of a weary heart. The woman on the bed is no child. She was, once. Decades back. She was. But not now.

Like Sara, she must trust. Only days out of the operating room, she's just been told she'll have to return. Her frail hand squeezes mine. Her eyes mist with fear.

Unlike Sara, she sees no father. But the Father sees her. *Trust him,* I say to us both. Trust the voice that whispers your name. Trust the hands to catch.

⁂

I sit across the table from a good man. Good and afraid. His fear is honest. Stocks are down. Inflation is up. He has payroll to meet and bills to pay. He hasn't squandered or gambled or played. He has worked hard and prayed often, but now he's afraid. Beneath the flannel suit lies a timid heart.

He stirs his coffee and stares at me with the eyes of Wile E. Coyote who just realized he's run beyond the edge of a cliff. He's about to fall and fall fast. He's Peter on the water, seeing the storm and not the face. He's Peter in the waves, hearing the wind and not the voice.

Trust, I urge. But the word thuds. He's unaccustomed to such strangeness. He's a man of reason. Even when the kite flies beyond the clouds he still holds the string. But now the string has slipped. And the sky is silent.

⁂

I stand a few feet from a mirror and see the face of a man who failed . . . who failed his Maker. Again. I promised I wouldn't, but I did. I was quiet when I should have been bold. I took a seat when I should have taken a stand.

If this were the first time, it would be different. But it isn't. How many times can one fall and expect to be caught?

Trust. Why is it easy to tell others and so hard to remind self? Can God deal with death? I told the woman so. Can God deal with debt? I ventured as much with the man. Can God hear yet one more confession from these lips? The face in the mirror asks.

∞

I sit a few feet from a man on death row. Jewish by birth. Tentmaker by trade. Apostle by calling. His days are marked. I'm curious about what bolsters this man as he nears his execution. So I ask some questions.

Do you have family, Paul? *I have none.*

What about your health? *My body is beaten and tired.*

What do you own? *I have my parchments. My pen. A cloak.*

And your reputation? *Well, it's not much. I'm a heretic to some, a maverick to others.*

Do you have friends? *I do, but even some of them have turned back.*

Any awards? *Not on earth.*

Then what do you have, Paul? No belongings. No family. Criticized by some. Mocked by others. What do you have, Paul? What do you have that matters?

I sit back quietly and watch. Paul rolls his hand into a fist. He looks at it. I look at it. What is he holding? What does he have?

He extends his hand so I can see. As I lean forward, he opens his fingers. I peer at his palm. It's empty.

I have my faith. It's all I have. But it's all I need. I have kept the faith.

Paul leans back against the wall of his cell and smiles. And I lean back against another and stare into the face of a man who has learned that there is more to life than meets the eye.

For that's what faith is. Faith is trusting what the eye can't see.

Eyes see the prowling lion. Faith sees Daniel's angel.

Eyes see storms. Faith sees Noah's rainbow.

Eyes see giants. Faith sees Canaan.

Your eyes see your faults. Your faith sees your Savior.

Your eyes see your guilt. Your faith sees his blood.

Your eyes see your grave. Your faith sees a city whose builder and maker is God.

Your eyes look in the mirror and see a sinner, a failure, a promise-breaker. But by faith you look in the mirror and see a robed prodigal bearing the ring of grace on your finger and the kiss of your Father on your face.

But wait a minute, someone asks. How do I know this is true? Nice prose, but give me the facts. How do I know these aren't just fanciful hopes?

Part of the answer can be found in Sara's little leaps of faith. Her older sister, Andrea, was in the room watching, and I asked Sara if she would jump to Andrea. Sara refused. I tried to convince her. She wouldn't budge. "Why not?" I asked.

"I only jump to big arms."

If we think the arms are weak, we won't jump.

For that reason, the Father flexed his muscles. "God's power is very great for those who believe," Paul taught. "That power is the same as the great strength God used to raise Christ from the dead" (Eph. 1:19–20).

Next time you wonder if God can catch you, read that verse. The very arms that defeated death are the arms awaiting you.

Next time you wonder if God can forgive you, read that verse. The very hands that were nailed to the cross are open for you.

And the next time you wonder if you will survive the jump, think of Sara and me. If a flesh-and-bone-headed dad like me can catch his child, don't you think your eternal Father can catch you?

CHAPTER FIFTEEN

Overcoming Your Heritage

STEFAN CAN TELL you about family trees. He makes his living from them. He inherited a German forest that has been in his family for 400 years. The trees he harvests were planted 180 years ago by his great-grandfather. The trees he plants won't be ready for market until his great-grandchildren are born.

He's part of a chain.

"Every generation must make a choice," he told me. "They can either pillage or plant. They can rape the landscape and get rich, or they can care for the landscape, harvest only what is theirs, and leave an investment for their children."

Stefan harvests seeds sown by men he never knew.

Stefan sows seeds to be harvested by descendants he'll never see.

Dependent upon the past, responsible for the future: he's part of a chain.

Like us. Children of the past, are we. Parents of the future. Heirs. Benefactors. Recipients of the work done by those before. Born into a forest we didn't seed.

Which leads me to ask, how's your forest?

As you stand on the land bequeathed by your ancestors, how does it look? How do you feel?

Pride at legacy left? Perhaps. Some inherit nourished soil. Deeply rooted trees of conviction. Row after row of truth and heritage. Could be that you stand in the forest of your fathers with pride. If so, give thanks, for many don't.

Many aren't proud of their family trees. Poverty. Shame. Abuse. Such are the forests found by some of you. The land was pillaged. Harvest was taken, but no seed was sown.

Perhaps you were reared in a home of bigotry and so you are intolerant of minorities. Perhaps you were reared in a home of greed, hence your desires for possessions are insatiable.

Perhaps your childhood memories bring more hurt than inspiration. The voices of your past cursed you, belittled you, ignored you. At the time, you thought such treatment was typical. Now you see it isn't.

And now you find yourself trying to explain your past.

I came across a story of a man who must have had such thoughts. His heritage was tragic. His grandfather was a murderer and a mystic who sacrificed his own children in ritual abuse. His dad was a punk who ravaged houses of worship and made a mockery of believers. He was killed at the age of twenty-four . . . by his friends.

The men were typical of their era. They lived in a time when prostitutes purveyed their wares in houses of worship. Wizards treated disease with chants. People worshiped stars and followed horoscopes. More thought went into superstition and voodoo than into the education of the children.

It was a dark time in which to be born. What do you do when your grandfather followed black magic, your father was a scoundrel, and your nation is corrupt?

Follow suit? Some assumed he would. Branded him as a delinquent before he was born, a chip off the old rotten block. You can almost hear the people moan as he passes, "Gonna be just like his dad."

But they were wrong. He wasn't. He reversed the trend. He defied the odds. He stood like a dam against the trends of his day and rerouted the future of his nation. His achievements were so remarkable, we still tell his story twenty-six hundred years later.

The story of King Josiah. The world has seen wiser kings; the world has seen wealthier kings; the world has seen more powerful kings. But history has never seen a more courageous king than young Josiah.

Born some six hundred years before Jesus, Josiah inherited a fragile throne and a tarnished crown. The temple was in disarray, the Law was lost, and the people worshiped whatever god they desired. But by the end of Josiah's thirty-one-year reign, the temple had been rebuilt, the idols destroyed, and the law of God was once again elevated to a place of prominence and power.

The forest had been reclaimed.

Josiah's grandfather, King Manasseh, was remembered as the king who filled "Jerusalem from one end to the other with [the people's] blood" (2 Kings 21:16). His father, King Amon, died at the hands of his own officers. "He did what God said was wrong," reads his epitaph.

The citizens formed a posse and killed the assassins, and eight-year-old Josiah ascended the throne. Early in his reign Josiah made a brave choice. "He lived as his ancestor David had lived, and he did not stop doing what was right" (2 Kings 22:2).

He flipped through his family scrapbook until he found an ancestor worthy of emulation. Josiah skipped his dad's life and bypassed his grandpa's. He leapfrogged back in time until he found David and resolved, "I'm going to be like him."

The principle? We can't choose our parents, but we can choose our mentors.

And since Josiah chose David (who had chosen God), things began to happen.

> The people tore down the altars for the Baal gods as Josiah directed.
>
> Josiah cut down the incense altars.

> Josiah . . . broke up the Asherah idols and . . . beat them into powder.
>
> He burned the bones of the priests.
>
> Josiah broke down the altars.
>
> He cut down all the incense altars in all of Israel. (2 Chron. 34:4–5, 7)

Not what you call a public relations tour. But, then again, Josiah was not out to make friends. He was out to make a statement: "What my fathers taught, I don't teach. What they embraced, I reject."

And he wasn't finished. Four years later, at the age of twenty-six, he turned his attention to the temple. It was in shambles. The people had allowed it to fall into disrepair. But Josiah was determined. Something had happened that fueled his passion to restore the temple. A baton had been passed. A torch had been received.

Early in his reign he'd resolved to serve the God of his ancestor David. Now he chose to serve the God of someone else. Note 2 Chronicles 34:8: "In Josiah's eighteenth year as king, he made Judah and the Temple pure again. He sent Shaphan . . . to repair the Temple of the LORD, *the God of Josiah*" (emphasis mine).

God was *his* God. David's faith was Josiah's faith. He had found the God of David and made him his own. As the temple was being rebuilt, one of the workers happened upon a scroll. On the scroll were the words of God given to Moses nearly a thousand years earlier.

When Josiah heard the words, he was shocked. He wept that his people had drifted so far from God that his Word was not a part of their lives.

He sent word to a prophetess and asked her, "What will become of our people?"

She told Josiah that since he had repented when he heard the words, his nation would be spared the anger of God (see 2 Chron. 34:27). Incredible. An entire generation received grace because of the integrity of one man.

Could it be that God placed him on earth for that reason?

Could it be that God has placed you on earth for the same?

Maybe your past isn't much to brag about. Maybe you've seen raw evil. And now you, like Josiah, have to make a choice. Do you rise above the past and make a difference? Or do you remain controlled by the past and make excuses?

Many choose the latter.

Many choose the convalescent homes of the heart. Healthy bodies. Sharp minds. But retired dreams. Back and forth they rock in the chair of regret, repeating the terms of surrender. Lean closely and you will hear them: "If only." The white flag of the heart.

> "If only . . ."
>
> "If only I'd been born somewhere else . . ."
>
> "If only I'd been treated fairly . . ."

> "If only I'd had kinder parents, more money, greater opportunites . . ."
>
> "If only I'd been potty-trained sooner, spanked less, or taught to eat without slurping."

Maybe you've used those words. Maybe you have every right to use them. Perhaps you, like Josiah, were hearing the ten count before you even got into the ring. For you to find an ancestor worth imitating, you, like Josiah, have to flip way back in your family album.

If such is the case, let me show you where to turn. Put down the scrapbook and pick up your Bible. Go to John's gospel and read Jesus' words: "Human life comes from human parents, but spiritual life comes from the Spirit" (John 3:6).

Think about that. Spiritual life comes from the Spirit! Your parents may have given you genes, but God gives you grace. Your parents may be responsible for your body, but God has taken charge of your soul. You may get your looks from your mother, but you get eternity from your Father, your heavenly Father.

By the way, he's not blind to your problems. In fact, God is willing to give you what your family didn't.

Didn't have a good father? He'll be your Father.

> Through God you are a son; and, if you are a son, then you are certainly an heir. (Gal. 4:7 PHILLIPS)

Didn't have a good role model? Try God.

> You are God's children whom he loves, so try to be like him. (Eph. 5:1)

Never had a parent who wiped away your tears? Think again. God has noted each one.

> You have seen me tossing and turning through the night. You have collected all my tears in your bottle! You have recorded every one in your book. (Ps. 56:8 TLB)

God has not left you adrift on a sea of heredity. Just like Josiah, you cannot control the way your forefathers responded to God. But you can control the way you respond to him. The past does not have to be your prison. You have a voice in your destiny. You have a say in your life. You have a choice in the path you take.

Choose well and someday—generations from now—your grandchildren and great-grandchildren will thank God for the seeds you sowed.

CHAPTER SIXTEEN

The Sweet Song of the Second Fiddle

For thousands of years, the relationship had been perfect. As far back as anyone could remember, the moon had faithfully reflected the sun's rays into the dark night. It was the greatest duo in the universe. Other stars and planets marveled at the reliability of the team. Generation after generation of earthlings were captivated by the reflection. The moon became the symbol of romance, high hopes, and even nursery rhymes.

"Shine on, harvest moon," the people would sing. And he did. Well, in a way he did. You see, the moon didn't actually shine. He reflected. He took the light given to him by the sun and redirected it toward the earth. A simple task of receiving illumination and sharing it.

You would think such a combo would last forever. It almost did. But one day, a nearby star planted a thought in the moon's core.

"It must be tough being a moon," the star suggested.

"What do you mean? I love it! I've got an important job to do. When it gets dark, people look to me for help. And I look to the sun. He gives me what I need and I give the people what they need. People depend on me to light up their world. And I depend on the sun."

"So, you and the sun must be pretty tight."

"Tight? Why, we are like Huntley and Brinkley, Hope and Crosby, Benny and Day . . ."

"Or maybe Edgar Bergen and Charlie McCarthy?"

"Who?"

"You know, the man and the dummy."

"Well, I don't know about the dummy part."

"That's exactly what I mean. You are the dummy. You don't have any light of your own. You depend on the sun. You're the sidekick. You don't have any name for yourself."

"Name for myself?"

"Yeah, you've been playing second fiddle for too long. You need to step out on your own."

"What do you mean?"

"I mean stop reflecting and start generating. Do your own thing. Be your own boss. Get people to see you for who you really are."

"Who am I?"

"Well, you are, uh, well, uh, well, that's what you need to find out. You need to find out who you are."

The moon paused and thought for a moment. What the star said made sense. Though he had never considered it, the moon was suddenly aware of all the inequities of the relationship.

Why should he have to work the night shift all the time? And why should he be the one the astronauts stepped on first? And why should he always be accused of making waves? And why don't the dogs and wolves howl at the sun for a change? And why should it be such an outrage to "moon" while "sunning" is an accepted practice?

"You are right!" asserted the moon. "It's high time we had a solar-lunar equity up here."

"Now you're talking," prodded the star. "Go discover the real moon!"

Such was the beginning of the breakup. Rather than turning his attention toward the sun, the moon began turning his attention toward himself.

He set out on the course of self-enhancement. After all, his complexion was a disgrace, so full of craters and all. His wardrobe was sadly limited to three sizes; full-length, half-cast, and quarter-clad. And his coloring was an anemic yellow.

So, girded with determination, he set out to reach for the moon.

He ordered glacier packs for his complexion. He changed his appearance to include new shapes such as triangular and square. And for coloring he opted for a punk-rock orange. "No one is going to call me cheese-face anymore."

The new moon was slimmed down and shaped up. His surface was as smooth as a baby's bottom. Everything was fine for a while.

Initially, his new look left him basking in his own moonlight. Passing meteors would pause and visit. Distant stars would call and compliment. Fellow moons would invite him over to their orbits to watch "As the World Turns."

He had friends. He had fame. He didn't need the sun—until the trends changed. Suddenly "punk" was out and "prep" was in. The compliments stopped and the giggles began as the moon was slow to realize that he was out of style. Just as he finally caught on and had his orange changed to pinstripe, the style went to "country."

It was the painful poking of the rhinestones into his surface that caused him to finally ask himself, "What's this all for anyway? You're on the cover of the magazine one day and forgotten the next. Living off the praise of others is an erratic diet."

For the first time since he'd begun his campaign to find himself, the moon thought of the sun. He remembered the good ol' millenniums when praise was not a concern. What people thought of him was immaterial since he wasn't in the business of getting people to look at himself. Any praise that came his way was quickly passed on to the boss. The sun's plan was beginning to dawn on the moon. "He may have been doing me a favor."

He looked down upon the earth. The earthlings had been getting quite a show. They never knew what to expect: first punk, then preppie, now country. Oddsmakers in Las Vegas were making bets as to whether the next style would be chic or macho. Rather than be the light of their world he was the butt of their jokes.

Even the cow refused to jump over him.

But it was the cold that bothered him the most. Absence from the sunlight left him with a persistent chill. No warmth. No glow. His full-length overcoat didn't help. It couldn't help; the shiver was from the inside, an icy shiver from deep within his core that left him feeling cold and alone.

Which is exactly what he was.

One night as he looked down upon the people walking in the dark, he was struck by the futility of it all. He thought of the sun. *He gave me everything I needed. I served a purpose. I was warm. I was content. I was . . . I was what I was made to be.*

Suddenly, he felt the old familiar warmth. He turned and there was the sun. The sun had never moved. "I'm glad you're back," the sun said. "Let's get back to work."

"You bet!" agreed the moon.

The coat came off. The roundness returned, and a light was seen in the dark sky. A light even fuller. A light even brighter.

And to this day whenever the sun shines and the moon reflects and the darkness is illuminated, the moon doesn't complain or get jealous. He does what he was intended to do all along.

The moon beams.

CHAPTER SEVENTEEN

Your Sack of Stones

YOU HAVE ONE. A sack. A burlap sack. Probably aren't aware of it, may not have been told about it. Could be you don't remember it. But it was given to you. A sack. An itchy, scratchy burlap sack.

You needed the sack so you could carry the stones. Rocks, boulders, pebbles. All sizes. All shapes. All unwanted.

You didn't request them. You didn't seek them. But you were given them.

Don't remember?

Some were rocks of rejection. You were given one the time you didn't pass the tryout. It wasn't for lack of effort. Heaven only knows how much you practiced. You thought you were good enough for the team. But the coach didn't. The instructor didn't. You thought you were good enough, but they said you weren't.

They and how many others?

You don't have to live long before you get a collection of stones. Make a poor grade. Make a bad choice. Make a mess. Get called a few names. Get mocked. Get abused.

And the stones don't stop with adolescence. I sent a letter this week to an unemployed man who's been rejected in more than fifty interviews.

And so the sack gets heavy. Heavy with stones. Stones of rejection. Stones we don't deserve.

Along with a few we do.

Look into the burlap sack and you see that not all the stones are from rejections. There is a second type of stone. The stone of regret.

Regret for the time you lost your temper.

Regret for the day you lost control.

Regret for the moment you lost your pride.

Regret for the years you lost your priorities.

And even regret for the hour you lost your innocence.

One stone after another, one guilty stone after another.

With time the sack gets heavy. We get tired. How can you have dreams for the future when all your energy is required to shoulder the past?

No wonder some people look miserable. The sack slows the step. The sack chafes. Helps explain the irritation on so many faces, the sag in so many steps, the drag in so many shoulders, and most of all, the desperation in so many acts.

You're consumed with doing whatever it takes to get some rest.

So you take the sack to the office. You resolve to work so hard you'll forget about the sack. You arrive early and stay late. People are impressed. But when it's time to go home, there is the sack—waiting to be carried out.

You carry the stones into happy hour. With a name like that, it must bring relief. So you set the sack on the floor, sit on the stool, and drink a few. The music gets loud and your head gets light. But then it's time to go and you look down and there is the sack.

You drag it into therapy. You sit on the couch with the sack at your feet and spill all your stones on the floor and name them one by one. The therapist listens. She empathizes. Some helpful counsel is given. But when the time is up, you're obliged to gather the rocks and take them with you.

You get so desperate you try a weekend rendezvous. A little excitement. A risky embrace. A night of stolen passion. And for a moment the load is lighter. But then the weekend passes. Sunday's sun sets and awaiting you on Monday's doorstep is—you got it—your sack of regrets and rejections.

Some even take the sack to church. Perhaps religion will help, we reason. But instead of removing a few stones, some well-meaning but misguided preacher may add to the load. God's messengers sometimes give more hurt than help. And you might leave the church with a few new rocks in your sack.

The result? A person slugging his way through life, weighed down by the past. I don't know if you've noticed, but it's hard to be thoughtful when you're carrying a burlap sack. It's hard to be affirming when you are affirmation-starved. It's hard to be forgiving when you feel guilty.

Paul had an interesting observation about the way we treat people. He said it about marriage, but the principle applies in any relationship. "The man who loves his wife loves himself" (Eph. 5:28). There is a correlation between the way you feel about yourself and the way you feel about others. If you are at peace with yourself—if you like yourself—you will get along with others.

The converse is also true. If you don't like yourself, if you are ashamed, embarrassed, or angry, other people are going to know it. The tragic part of the burlap-sack story is we tend to throw our stones at those we love.

Unless the cycle is interrupted.

Which takes us to the question, "How *does* a person get relief?"

Which, in turn, takes us to one of the kindest verses in the Bible, "Come to me, all of you who are tired and have heavy loads, and I will give you rest. Accept my teachings and learn from me, because I am gentle and humble in spirit, and you will find rest for your lives.

The teaching I ask you to accept is easy; the load I give you to carry is light" (Matt. 11:28–29).

You knew I was going to say that. I can see you holding this book and shaking your head. "I've tried that. I've read the Bible, I've sat on the pew—but I've never received relief."

If that is the case, could I ask a delicate but deliberate question? Could it be that you went to religion and didn't go to God? Could it be that you went to a church, but never saw Christ?

"Come to me," the verse reads.

It's easy to go to the wrong place. I did yesterday. I was in Portland, Maine, catching a flight to Boston. Went to the desk, checked my bag, got my ticket, and went to the gate. I went past security, took my seat, and waited for the flight to be called. I waited and waited and waited—

Finally, I went up to the desk to ask the attendant and she looked at me and said, "You're at the wrong gate."

Now, what if I'd pouted and sighed, "Well, there must not be a flight to Boston. Looks like I'm stuck."

You would have said to me, "You're not stuck. You're just at the wrong gate. Go down to the right gate and try again."

It's not that you haven't tried—you've tried for years to deal with your past. Alcohol. Affairs. Workaholism. Religion.

Jesus says he is the solution for weariness of soul.

Go to him. Be honest with him. Admit you have soul secrets you've never dealt with. He already knows what they are. He's just waiting for you to ask him to help. He's just waiting for you to give him your sack.

Go ahead. You'll be glad you did. (Those near to you will be glad as well . . . it's hard to throw stones when you've left your sack at the cross.)

CHAPTER EIGHTEEN

Of Oz and God

YOU, ME, and Dorothy of *The Wizard of Oz*—we have a lot in common.

We all know what it's like to find ourselves in a distant land surrounded by strange people.

Though our chosen path isn't paved with yellow bricks, we still hope it will lead us home.

The witches of the East want more than our ruby slippers.

And Dorothy is not the first person to find herself surrounded by brainless, heartless, and spineless people.

We can relate to Dorothy.

But when Dorothy gets to the Emerald City the comparison is uncanny. For what the Wizard said to her, some think God says to us.

You remember the plot. Each of the chief characters comes to the Wizard with a need. Dorothy seeks a way home. The scarecrow wants wisdom. The tinman desires a heart. The lion needs courage. The Wizard of Oz, they've heard, could grant all four. So they come. Trembling and reverent, they come. They shiver in his presence and gasp at his power. And with all the courage they can muster, they present their requests.

His response? He will help *after* they demonstrate their worthiness. He will help as soon as they overcome the source of evil. Bring me the witch's broom, he says, and I will help you.

So they do. They scale the castle walls and make wax of the witch, and in the process, they make some startling discoveries. They discover they can overcome evil. They discover that, with a little luck, a quick mind can handle the best the worst has to give. And they discover they can do it all without the wizard.

Which is good because when they get back to Oz the foursome learn that the wizard is a wimp. The curtain is pulled back and the almighty is revealed. The one they worshiped and feared is, alas, a balding, pudgy professor who can stage a good light show but can do nothing to solve their problems.

He redeems himself, however, by what he shows this band of pilgrims. (This is the part that makes me think the Wizard may have done a pulpit circuit before he landed the wizard position.) He tells Dorothy and company that all the power they need is the power they already have. He explains that the power to handle their problems was with them all along. After all, didn't the scarecrow display wisdom, the tinman compassion, and the lion courage when they dealt with the witch? And Dorothy doesn't need the help of Oz almighty; all she needs is a good, hot-air balloon.

The movie ends with Dorothy discovering that her worst nightmare was in reality just a bad dream. That her somewhere-over-the-rainbow home was right where she'd always been. And that it's nice to have friends in high places, but in the end, it's up to you to find your own way home.

The moral of *The Wizard of Oz?* Everything you may need, you've already got.

The power you need is really a power you already have. Just look deep enough, long enough, and there's nothing you can't do.

Sound familiar? Sound patriotic? Sound . . . Christian?

For years it did to me. I'm an offspring of sturdy stock. A product of a rugged, blue-collar culture that honored decency, loyalty, hard work, and loved Bible verses like, "God helps those who help themselves." (No, it's not in there.)

"God started it and now we must finish it" was our motto. He's done his part; now we do ours. It's a fifty-fifty proposition. A do-it-yourself curriculum that majors in our part and minors in God's part.

"Blessed are the busy" this theology proclaims, "for they are the true Christians."

No need for the supernatural. No place for the extraordinary. No room for the transcendent. Prayer becomes a token. (The real strength is within you, not "up there.") Communion becomes a ritual. (The true hero is you, not him.) And the Holy Spirit? Well, the Holy Spirit becomes anything from a sweet disposition to a positive mental attitude.

It's a wind-the-world-up-and-walk-away view of God. And the philosophy works . . . as long as you work. Your faith is strong, as long as you are strong. Your position is secure, as long as you are secure. Your life is good, as long as you are good.

But, alas, therein lies the problem. As the Teacher said, "No one is good" (Matt. 19:17 NKJV). Nor is anyone always strong; nor is anyone always secure.

Do-it-yourself Christianity is not much encouragement to the done in and worn out.

Self-sanctification holds little hope for the addict.

"Try a little harder" is little encouragement for the abused.

At some point we need more than good advice; we need help. Somewhere on this journey home we realize that a fifty-fifty proposition is too little. We need more—more than a pudgy wizard who thanks us for coming but tells us the trip was unnecessary.

We need help. Help from the inside out. The kind of help Jesus promised. "I will ask the Father, and he will give you another Helper to be with you forever—the Spirit of truth. The world cannot accept him, because it does not see him or know him. But you know him, because he lives with you and will be *in* you" (John 14:16–17, emphasis mine).

Note the final words of the verse. And in doing so, note the dwelling place of God—"in you."

Not near us. Not above us. Not around us. But in us. In the part of us we don't even know. In the heart no one else has seen. In the hidden recesses of our being dwells, not an angel, not a philosophy, not a genie, but God.

Imagine that.

When my daughter Jenna was six years old, I came upon her standing in front of a full-length mirror. She was looking down her throat. I asked her what she was doing and she answered, "I'm looking to see if God is in my heart."

I chuckled and turned and then overheard her ask him, "Are you in there?" When no answer came, she grew impatient and spoke on his behalf. With a voice deepened as much as a six-year-old can, she said, "Yes."

She's asking the right question. "Are you in there?" Could it be what they say is true? It wasn't enough for you to appear in a bush or dwell in the temple? It wasn't enough for you to become human flesh and walk on the earth? It wasn't enough to leave your word and the promise of your return? You had to go further? You had to take up residence in us?

"Do you not know," Paul penned, "that your body is the temple of the Holy Spirit?" (1 Cor. 6:19 NKJV).

Perhaps you didn't. Perhaps you didn't know God would go that far to make sure you got home. If not, thanks for letting me remind you.

The wizard says look inside yourself and find self. God says look inside yourself and find God. The first will get you to Kansas.

The latter will get you to heaven.

Take your pick.

CHAPTER NINETEEN

An Inside Job

SPRAY PAINT won't fix rust.

A Band-Aid won't remove a tumor.

Wax on the hood won't cure the cough of a motor.

If the problem is inside, you have to go inside.

I learned that this morning. I rolled out of bed early . . . real early. So early that Denalyn tried to convince me not to go to the office. "It's the middle of the night," she mumbled. "What if a burglar tries to break in?"

But I'd been on vacation for a couple of weeks, and I was rested. My energy level was as high as the stack of things to do on my desk, so I drove to the church.

I must confess that the empty streets did look a bit scary. And there was that attempted break-in at the office a few weeks back. So I decided to be careful. I entered the office complex, disarmed the alarm, and then re-armed it so it would sound if anyone tried to enter.

Brilliant, I thought.

I had been at my desk for only a few seconds when the sirens screamed. *Somebody is trying to get in!* I raced down the hall, turned off the alarm, ran back to my office, and dialed 911. After I hung up, it occurred to mc that the thieves could get in before the police arrived. I dashed back down the hall and re-armed the system.

"They won't get me," I mumbled defiantly as I punched in the code.

As I turned to go back to the office, the sirens blared again. I disarmed the alarm and reset it. I could just picture those frustrated burglars racing back into the shadows every time they set off the alarm.

I walked to a window to look for the police. When I did, the alarm sounded a third time. *Hope the police get here soon*, I thought as I again disarmed and reset the alarm.

I was walking back to my office when—that's right—the alarm sounded again. I disarmed it and paused. *Wait a minute; this alarm system must be fouled up.*

I went back to my office to call the alarm company. *Just my luck*, I thought as I dialed, *of all the nights for the system to malfunction.*

"Our alarm system keeps going off," I told the fellow who answered. "We've either got some determined thieves or a malfunction."

Miffed, I drummed my fingers on my desk as he called up our account.

"There could be one other option," he volunteered.

"What else?"

"Did you know that your building is equipped with a motion detector?"

Oh boy.

About that time I saw the lights from the police car. I walked outside. "Uh, I think the problem is on the inside, not the outside," I told them.

They were nice enough not to ask for details, and I was embarrassed enough not to volunteer any. But I did learn a lesson: *You can't fix an inside problem by going outside.*

I spent an hour hiding from thieves who weren't there, faulting a system that hadn't failed, and calling for help I didn't need. I thought the problem was out there. All along it was in here.

Am I the only one to ever do that? Am I the only one to blame an inside problem on an outside source?

Alarms sound in your world as well. Maybe not with bells and horns, but with problems and pain. Their purpose is to signal impending danger. A fit of anger is a red flare. Uncontrolled debt is a flashing light. A guilty conscience is a warning sign indicating trouble within. Icy relationships are posted notices announcing anything from neglect to abuse.

You have alarms in your life. When they go off, how do you respond? Be honest, now. Hasn't there been a time or two when you went outside for a solution when you should have gone inward?

Ever blamed your plight on Washington? (If they'd lower the tax rates, my business would work.) Inculpated your family for your failure? (Mom always liked my sister more.) Called God to account for your problems? (If he is God, why doesn't he heal my marriage?) Faulted the church for your frail faith? (Those people are a bunch of hypocrites.)

Reminds me of the golfer about to hit his first shot on the first hole. He swung and missed the ball. Swung again and whiffed again. Tried a third time and still hit nothing but air. In frustration he looked at his buddies and judged, "Man, this is a tough course."

Now, he may have been right. The course may have been tough. But that wasn't the problem. You may be right, as well. Your circumstances may be challenging, but blaming them is not the solution. Nor is neglecting them. Heaven knows you don't silence life's alarms by pretending they aren't screaming. But heaven also knows it's wise to look in the mirror before you peek out the window.

Consider the prayer of David: "Create *in* me a new heart, O God, and renew a steadfast spirit *within* me" (Ps. 51:10 NIV).

Read the admonition of Paul: "Fix your attention on God. You'll be changed from the *inside out*" (Rom. 12:2 THE MESSAGE).

But most of all, listen to the explanation of Jesus: "I tell you the truth, unless one is born again, he cannot be in God's kingdom" (John 3:3).

Real change is an inside job. You might alter things a day or two with money and systems, but the heart of the matter is and always will be, the matter of the heart.

Allow me to get specific. Our problem is sin. Not finances. Not budgets. Not overcrowded prisons or drug dealers. Our problem is sin. We are in rebellion against our Creator. We are separated from our Father. We are cut off from the source of life. A new president or policy won't fix that. It can only be solved by God.

That's why the Bible uses drastic terms like *conversion, repentance,* and *lost* and *found.* Society may renovate, but only God re-creates.

Here is a practical exercise to put this truth into practice. The next time alarms go off in your world, ask yourself three questions.

1. Is there any unconfessed sin in my life?

"There was a time when I wouldn't admit what a sinner I was. But my dishonesty made me miserable and filled my days with frustration. . . . My strength evaporated like water on a sunny day until I finally admitted all my sins to you and stopped trying to hide them" (Ps. 32:3–5 TLB).

Confession is telling God you did the thing he saw you do. He doesn't need to hear it as much as you need to say it. Whether it's too small to be mentioned or too big to be forgiven isn't yours to decide. Your task is to be honest.)

2. *Are there any unresolved conflicts in my world?*

"If you enter a place of worship and, about to make an offering, suddenly remember a grudge that a friend has against you, abandon your offering, leave immediately, go to this friend and make things right. Then and only then, come back and work things out with God" (Matt. 5:23–24 THE MESSAGE).

(As far as I know, this is the only time God tells you to slip out of church early. Apparently, he'd rather have you give your olive branch than your tithe. If you are worshiping and remember that your mom is hacked-off at you for forgetting her birthday, then get off the pew and find a phone. Maybe she'll forgive you; maybe she won't. But at least you can return to your pew with a clean conscience.)

3. *Are there any unsurrendered worries in my heart?*

"Give all your worries to him, because he cares about you" (1 Pet. 5:7).

(The German word for *worry* means "to strangle." The Greek word means "to divide the mind." Both are accurate. Worry is a noose on the neck and a distraction of the mind, neither of which is befitting for joy.)

Alarms serve a purpose. They signal a problem. Sometimes the problem is out there. More often it's in here. So before you peek outside, take a good look inside.

CHAPTER TWENTY

Late-Night Good News

LATE-NIGHT NEWS is a poor sedative.

Last night it was for me. All I wanted was the allergen count and the basketball scores. But to get them, I had to endure the usual monologue of global misery. And last night the world seemed worse than usual.

Watching the news doesn't usually disturb me so. I'm not a gloom-and-doom sort of fellow. I feel I'm as good as the next guy in taking human tragedy with a spoon of faith. But last night . . . well, the world seemed dark.

Perhaps it was the two youngsters shot in a drive-by shooting—one was six, the other ten.

Perhaps it was the reassuring announcement that twenty-six thousand highway bridges in America are near collapse.

Our surgeon general, who is opposed to tobacco, wants to legalize drugs.

A billionaire rock star is accused of molesting children. One senator is accused of seducing associates, another of tampering with election procedures.

A rising political figure in Russia has earned the nickname of Hitler.

Pistol-packing drivers give rise to a new bumper sticker: "Keep honking. I'm reloading."

The national debt is deeper. Our taxes are higher, the pollen count is up, and the Dallas Mavericks lost their fifteenth game in a row.

"And that's the world tonight!" the well-dressed man announces. I wonder why he's smiling.

On the way to bed, I step into the rooms of my three sleeping daughters. At the bedside of each I pause and ponder the plight of their future. "What in the world awaits you?" I whisper as I brush back hair and straighten blankets.

Their greatest concerns today are math tests, presents, and birthday parties. Would that their world would always be so innocent. It won't. Forests shadow every trail, and cliffs edge every turn. Every life has its share of fear. My children are no exception.

Nor are yours. And as appealing as a desert island or a monastery might be, seclusion is simply not the answer for facing a scary tomorrow.

Then what is? Does someone have a hand on the

throttle of this train, or has the engineer bailed out just as we come in sight of dead-man's curve?

I may have found part of the answer in, of all places, the first chapter of the New Testament. I've often thought it strange that Matthew would begin his book with a genealogy. Certainly not good journalism. A list of who-sired-who wouldn't get past most editors.

But then again, Matthew wasn't a journalist, and the Holy Spirit wasn't trying to get our attention. He was making a point. God had promised he would give a Messiah through the bloodline of Abraham (Gen. 12:3), and he did.

"Having doubts about the future?" Matthew asks. "Just take a look at the past." And with that he opens the cedar chest of Jesus' lineage and begins pulling out the dirty laundry.

Believe me, you and I would have kept some of these stories in the closet. Jesus' lineage is anything but a roll call at the Institute for Halos and Harps. Reads more like the Sunday morning occupancy at the county jail.

It begins with Abraham, the father of the nation, who more than once lied like Pinocchio just to save his neck (Gen. 12:10–20).

Abraham's grandson Jacob was slicker than a Las Vegas card shark. He cheated his brother, lied to his father, got swindled, and then swindled his uncle (Genesis 27, 29).

Jacob's son Judah was so blinded by testosterone that he engaged the services of a streetwalker, not knowing she was his daughter-in-law! When he learned her identity, he threatened to have her burned to death for solicitation (Genesis 38).

Special mention is made of Solomon's mother, Bathsheba (who bathed in questionable places), and Solomon's father, David, who watched the bath of Bathsheba (2 Sam. 11:2–3).

Rahab was a harlot (Josh. 2:1). Ruth was a foreigner (Ruth 1:4).

Manasseh made the list, even though he forced his children to walk through fire (2 Kings 21:6). His son Amon is on the list, even though he rejected God (2 Kings 21:22).

Seems that almost half the kings were crooks, half embezzlers, and all but a handful worshiped an idol or two for good measure.

And so reads the list of Jesus' not-so-great grandparents. Seems like the only common bond between this lot was a promise. A promise from heaven that God would use them to send his son.

Why did God use these people? Didn't have to. Could have just laid the Savior on a doorstep. Would have been simpler that way. And why does God tell us their stories? Why does God give us an entire testament of blunders and stumbles of his people?

Simple. He knew what you and I watched on the

news last night. He knew you would fret. He knew I would worry. And he wants us to know that when the world goes wild, he stays calm.

Want proof? Read the last name on the list. In spite of all the crooked halos and tasteless gambols of his people, the last name on the list is the first one promised—Jesus.

"Joseph was the husband of Mary, and Mary was the mother of Jesus. Jesus is called the Christ" (Matt. 1:16).

Period. No more names are listed. No more are needed. As if God is announcing to a doubting world, "See, I did it. Just like I said I would. The plan succeeded."

The famine couldn't starve it.

Four hundred years of Egyptian slavery couldn't oppress it.

Wilderness wanderings couldn't lose it.

Babylonian captivity couldn't stop it.

Clay-footed pilgrims couldn't spoil it.

The promise of the Messiah threads its way through forty-two generations of rough-cut stones, forming a necklace fit for the King who came. Just as promised.

And the promise remains.

> Those people who keep their faith until the end will be saved (Matt. 24:13), Joseph's child assures.
>
> In this world you will have trouble, but be brave! I have defeated the world. (John 16:33)

The engineer has not abandoned the train. Nuclear war is no threat to God. Yo-yo economies don't intimidate the heavens. Immoral leaders have never derailed the plan.

God keeps his promise.

See for yourself. In the manger. He's there.

See for yourself. In the tomb. He's gone.

CHAPTER TWENTY-ONE

Healthy Habits

I LIKE THE STORY of the little boy who fell out of bed. When his Mom asked him what happened, he answered, "I don't know. I guess I stayed too close to where I got in."

Easy to do the same with our faith. It's tempting just to stay where we got in and never move.

Pick a time in the not-too-distant past. A year or two ago. Now ask yourself a few questions. How does your prayer life today compare with then? How about your giving? Have both the amount and the joy increased? What about your church loyalty? Can you tell you've grown? And Bible study? Are you learning to learn?

> We will in all things *grow up* into him who is the Head, that is, Christ. (Eph. 4:15 NIV, emphasis mine)

> Let us leave the elementary teachings about Christ and go on to *maturity.* (Heb. 6:1 NIV, emphasis mine)

> Like newborn babies, crave pure spiritual milk, so that by it you may *grow up* in your salvation. (1 Pet. 2:2 NIV, emphasis mine)

> But *grow* in the grace and knowledge of our Lord and Savior Jesus Christ. (2 Pet. 3:18 NIV, emphasis mine)

Growth is the goal of the Christian. Maturity is mandatory. If a child ceased to develop, the parent would be concerned, right? Doctors would be called. Tests would be run. When a child stops growing, something is wrong.

When a Christian stops growing, help is needed. If you are the same Christian you were a few months ago, be careful. You might be wise to get a checkup. Not on your body, but on your heart. Not a physical, but a spiritual.

May I suggest one?

At the risk of sounding like a preacher—which is what I am—may I make a suggestion? Why don't you check your habits? Though there are many bad habits, there are also many good ones. In fact, I can find four in the Bible. Make these four habits regular activities and see what happens.

First, the habit of prayer: "Base your happiness on your hope in Christ. When trials come endure them patiently; steadfastly maintain the *habit* of prayer" (Rom. 12:12 PHILLIPS, emphasis mine).

Do you want to know how to deepen your prayer life? Pray. Don't prepare to pray. Just pray. Don't read about prayer. Just pray. Don't attend a lecture on prayer or engage in discussion about prayer. Just pray.

Posture, tone, and place are personal matters. Select the form that works for you. But don't think about it too much. Don't be so concerned about wrapping the gift that you never give it. Better to pray awkwardly than not at all.

And if you feel you should only pray when inspired, that's okay. Just see to it that you are inspired every day.

Second, the habit of study: "The man who looks into the perfect law . . . and makes a *habit* of so doing, is not the man who hears and forgets. He puts that law into practice and he wins true happiness" (James 1:25 PHILLIPS, emphasis mine).

Imagine you are selecting your food from a cafeteria line. You pick your salad, you choose your entrée, but when you get to the vegetables, you see a pan of something that turns your stomach.

"Yuck! What's that?" you ask, pointing.

"Oh, you don't want to know," replies a slightly embarrassed server.

"Yes, I do."

"Well, if you must. It's a pan of pre-chewed food."

"What?"

"Pre-chewed food. Some people prefer to swallow what others have chewed."

Repulsive? You bet. But widespread. More so than you might imagine. Not with cafeteria food, but with God's Word.

Such Christians mean well. They listen well. But they discern little. They are content to swallow whatever they are told. No wonder they've stopped growing.

Third, the habit of giving: "On *every Lord's Day* each of you should put aside something from what you have earned during the week, and use it for this offering. The amount depends on how much the Lord has helped you earn" (1 Cor. 16:2 TLB, emphasis mine).

You don't give for God's sake. You give for your sake. "The purpose of tithing is to teach you to always put God first in your lives" (Deut. 14:23 TLB).

How does tithing teach you? Consider the simple act of writing a check for the offering. First you enter the date. Already you are reminded that you are a time-bound creature and every possession you have will rust or burn. Best to give it while you can.

Then you enter the name of the one to whom you are giving the money. If the bank would cash it, you'd write *God*. But they won't, so you write the name of the church or group that has earned your trust.

Next comes the amount. Ahhh, the moment of truth. You're more than a person with a checkbook. You're David, placing a stone in the sling. You're Peter, one foot on the boat, one foot on the lake. You're a little boy in a big crowd. A picnic lunch is all the Teacher needs, but it's all you have.

What will you do?

Sling the stone?
Take the step?
Give the meal?

Careful now, don't move too quickly. You aren't just entering an amount . . . you are making a confession. A confession that God owns it all anyway.

And then the line in the lower left-hand corner on which you write what the check is for. Hard to know what to put. It's for light bills and literature. A little bit of outreach. A little bit of salary.

Better yet, it's partial payment for what the church has done to help you raise your family . . . keep your own priorities sorted out . . . tune you in to his ever-nearness.

Or, perhaps, best yet, it's for you. For though the gift is to God, the benefit is for you. It's a moment for you to clip yet another strand from the rope of earth so that when he returns you won't be tied up.

And last of all, the habit of fellowship: "Let us not give up the *habit* of meeting together, as some are doing. Instead let us encourage one another" (Heb. 10:25 TEV, emphasis mine).

I'm writing this chapter on a Saturday morning in Boston. I came here to speak at a conference. After I did my part last night, I did something very spiritual: I went to a Boston Celtics basketball game. I couldn't resist. Boston Gardens is a stadium I'd wanted to see since I was a kid. Besides, Boston was playing my favorite team, the San Antonio Spurs.

As I took my seat, it occurred to me that I might be

the only Spurs fan in the crowd. I'd be wise to be quiet. But that was hard to do. I contained myself for a few moments, but that's all. By the end of the first quarter I was letting out solo war whoops every time the Spurs would score.

People were beginning to turn and look. Risky stuff, this voice-in-the-wilderness routine.

That's when I noticed I had a friend across the aisle. He, too, applauded the Spurs. When I clapped, he clapped. I had a partner. We buoyed each other. I felt better.

At the end of the quarter I gave him the thumbs-up. He gave it back. He was only a teenager. No matter. We were united by the higher bond of fellowship.

That's one reason for the church. All week you cheer for the visiting team. You applaud the success of the One the world opposes. You stand when everyone sits and sit when everyone stands.

At some point you need support. You need to be with folks who cheer when you do. You need what the Bible calls *fellowship.* And you need it every week. After all, you can only go so long before you think about joining the crowd.

There they are. Four habits worth having. Isn't it good to know that some habits are good for you? Make them a part of your day and grow. Don't make the mistake of the little boy. Don't stay too close to where you got in. It's risky resting on the edge.

CHAPTER TWENTY-TWO

DFW and the Holy Spirit

THE Dallas-Fort Worth International Airport can be fatal. It doesn't have concourses—it has catacombs. Lobbies empty into labyrinths. People have been known to go into that airport and never come out.

Frequent flyers are easily distinguished from the first-timers. They're the ones with backpacks, compasses, canteens, and walking sticks. The novices bear the haggard faces, hollow eyes, and distant stares.

One of my first times through the maze was on a trip home from Brazil. I'd been flying all night and was a bit anxious about making my connections. I stopped one family of five and asked where I could get information. The parents looked at me as if they were the only survivors of a nuclear disaster.

The mother held up three fingers and gasped, "Three days we have been here, and we still haven't found our connecting flight."

I gulped. The dad asked if I could spare five dollars for a pizza for his kids. I gave him the money, and he pointed me toward a map of the airport.

The map was easy to find; it covered an entire wall. When I found the "You are here" sign, I began looking for the gate of my next flight. When I saw where I was as opposed to where I needed to be, I gulped again. The Appalachian Trail would have been easier.

But I had no choice. I took a deep breath, gripped my satchel in one hand and my garment bag in the other, and set my face toward gate 6,690.

The floor was littered with travel bags discarded by weary pilgrims. People were falling to my right and to my left. Airport migrants hovered around water fountains as they would an oasis. Travelers fought over luggage carts.

I began to doubt if I would make it. Three hours into my trip, my knees began to ache. Five hours into the journey my hands grew raw from my bags. At the seven-hour mark, I began to hallucinate, seeing my gate number appear on the horizon only to have it grow wavy and disappear as I came near.

By the tenth hour, I had discarded my garment bag and was carrying only my briefcase. I was about to chuck it when I heard the cheering.

It was coming from the corridor up ahead. People were shouting. Some were running.

What was it? What could stir the hope of this trail of despairing pilgrims? What sight could strengthen these exhausted legs? A hotel? An empty restaurant? An available flight?

No, it was something far better. As I turned the corner, I saw it. My face lit like the night sky on the Fourth of July. I took the bandana off my head and wiped my brow. I straightened my back. I hastened my pace. My heart soared. Now, I knew, I would make it.

For there, in the distance, covered with lights and plated in gold, was a people-mover.

A people-mover. The Yellow Brick Road of the airport. It's the bridge across the Jordan. It's the downhill run for the marathoner, the fourth quarter for the athlete, the paycheck for the laborer, the final draft for the writer.

The people-mover, a path of progressive rest. Once on the people-mover, you don't have to move, but you still move! And while you are catching your breath, it's carrying your body.

But it's also a path of multiplied movement. For when you begin walking on it, every step is doubled. The propelling trail makes two steps out of your one. What would have taken an hour takes minutes.

And what a difference the people-mover makes on your attitude. You actually whistle as you walk. The fatigue is forgotten. The galumph is gone. Troops of travelers wave to each other.

And most important, you dare to believe again that you will reach your destination.

Now, maybe I overstated my point about the airport.

But I could never overstate the power of discovering

strength for the journey. What I discovered about DFW you've discovered about life. No matter how you travel, the trip can get tiring. Wouldn't it be great to discover a people-mover for your heart?

Paul did. Well, he didn't call it as such. But then, he never went to DFW. He did say, however, that there is a power that works in you as you work. "We proclaim him, admonishing and teaching everyone with all wisdom, so that we may present everyone perfect in Christ. To this end I labor, struggling with all his energy, which so powerfully works in me" (Col. 1:28 NIV).

Look at Paul's aim, *to present everyone perfect in Christ.* Paul dreamed of the day each person would be safe in Christ. What was his method? *Counseling and teaching.* Paul's tools? Verbs. Nouns. Sentences. Lessons. The same equipment you and I have. Not much has changed, has it?

Was it easier then than now? Don't think so. Paul called it work. *To this end I labor,* he wrote. Labor means work. Work means homes visited, people taught, classes prepared.

How did he do it? What was his source of strength? He worked with *all the energy he so powerfully works in me.*

As Paul worked, so did God. As Paul labored, so did the Father. And as you work, so does the Father. Every step multiplied. Divine dividends paid. Like the people-mover, God energizes our efforts. And like the people-mover, God moves us forward. And even when we are too tired to walk, he ensures we are moving ahead.

So the next time you need to rest, go ahead. He'll keep you headed in the right direction. And the next time you make progress—thank him. He's the one providing the power.

And the next time you want to give up? Don't. Please don't. Round the next corner. You may be surprised at what you find.

Besides, you've got a flight home you don't want to miss.

CHAPTER TWENTY-THREE

The God Who Fights for You

HERE IS a big question. What is God doing when you are in a bind? When the lifeboat springs a leak? When the rip cord snaps? When the last penny is gone before the last bill is paid? When the last hope left on the last train? What is God doing?

I know what we are doing. Nibbling on nails like corn on the cob. Pacing floors. Taking pills. I know what we do.

But what does God do? Big question. Real big. If God is sleeping, I'm duck soup. If he is laughing, I'm lost. If he is crossing his arms and shaking his head, then saw off the limb, Honey, it's time to crash.

What *is* God doing?

Well, I decided to research that question. Being the astute researcher that I am, I discovered some ancient writings that may answer this question. Few people are aware—in fact, no one is aware—that newspaper journalists roamed the lands of the Old Testament era.

Yes, it is true that in the days of Noah, Abraham, and Moses, reporters were fast on the scene recording the drama of their days. And now, for the first time, their articles are to be shared.

How did I come upon them? one might ask.

Well, I discovered them pressed between the pages of an in-flight magazine on a red-eye flight out of Sheboygan, Wisconsin. I can only surmise that a courageous archaeologist had hidden them to protect himself from imminent danger of evil spies. We'll never know if he survived. But we do know what he discovered—ancient newspaper interviews with Moses and Jehoshaphat.

So with a salute to his courage and a hunger for the truth, I proudly share with you heretofore undiscovered conversations with two men who will answer the question: What does God do when we are in a bind?

The first interview is between the *Holy Land Press* (HLP) and Moses.

HLP: Tell us about your conflict with the Egyptians.

MOSES: Oh, the Egyptians—big people. Strong fighters. Mean as snakes.

HLP: But you got away.

MOSES: Not before they got washed away.

HLP: You're talking about the Red Sea conflict.

MOSES: You're right. That was scary.

HLP: Tell us what happened.

MOSES: Well, the Red Sea was on one side and the Egyptians were on the other.

HLP: So you attacked?

MOSES: Are you kidding? With a half-a-million rock stackers? No, my people were too afraid. They wanted to go back to Egypt.

HLP: So you told everyone to retreat?

MOSES: Where? Into the water? We didn't have a boat. We didn't have anywhere to go.

HLP: What did your leaders recommend?

MOSES: I didn't ask them. There wasn't time.

HLP: Then what did you do?

MOSES: I told the people to stand still.

HLP: You mean, with the enemy coming, you told them not to move?

MOSES: Yep. I told the people, "Stand still and you will see the Lord save you."

HLP: Why would you want the people to stand still?

MOSES: To get out of God's way. If you don't know what to do, it's best just to sit tight till he does his thing.

HLP: That's odd strategy, don't you think?

MOSES: It is if you are big enough for the battle. But when the battle is bigger than you are and you want God to take over, it's all you can do.

HLP: Can we talk about something else?

MOSES: It's your paper.

HLP: Soon after your escape . . .

MOSES: Our deliverance.

HLP: What's the difference?

MOSES: There is a big difference. When you escape, *you* do it. When you are delivered, someone else does it and you just follow.

HLP: Okay, soon after your deliverance, you battled with the Ammo . . . Amala . . . let's see, I have it here . . .

MOSES: The Amalekites.

HLP: Yeah, the Amalekites.

MOSES: Big people. Strong fighters. Mean as snakes.

HLP: But you won.

MOSES: God won.

HLP: Okay—God won—but you did the work. You fought the battle. You were on the field.

MOSES: Wrong.

HLP: What? You weren't in the battle?

MOSES: Not that one. While the army was fighting, I took my friends Aaron and Hur to the top of a hill and we did our fighting up there.

HLP: With each other?

MOSES: With the darkness.

HLP: With swords?

MOSES: No, in prayer. I just lifted my hands to God, like I did at the Red Sea, only this time I forgot my rod. When I lifted my hands, we would win, but when I would lower my arms we would lose. So I got my friends to hold up my arms until the Amalekites were history and we won.

HLP: Hold on a second. You think that standing on a hill with your hands in the air made a difference?

MOSES: You don't see any Amalekites around, do you?

HLP: Don't you think it strange that the general of the army stays on the mountain while the soldiers fight in the valley?

MOSES: If the battle had been in the valley I would have gone, but that's not where the battle was being fought.

HLP: Odd, this strategy of yours.

MOSES: You mean if your father was bigger than the fellow beating you up, you wouldn't call his name?

HLP: What?

MOSES: If some guy has you on the ground pounding on you and your father is within earshot and tells you to call him anytime you need help, what would you do?

HLP: I'd call my father.

MOSES: That's all I do. When the battle is too great, I ask God to take over. I get the Father to fight for me.

HLP: And he comes?

MOSES: Seen any Jews building pyramids lately?

HLP: Let me see if I've got this straight. Once you defeat the enemy by standing still and another time you win the battle by holding up your hands. Where did you pick all this up?

MOSES: Well, if I told you, you wouldn't believe me.

HLP: Try me.

MOSES: Well, you see, there was this bush on fire and it spoke to me . . .

HLP: Maybe you're right. We'll save that one for another day.

⁂

The second interview moves us ahead in history a couple of centuries. Here is King Jehoshaphat (KJ) in a postwar interview with the *Jerusalem Chronicle* (JC) on the battlefield of Ziz.

JC: Congratulations, King.

KJ: For what?

JC: You just defeated three armies at one time. You defeated the Moabites, Ammonites, and Meunites.

KJ: Oh, I didn't do that.

JC: Don't be so modest. Tell us what you think of these armies.

KJ: Big people. Strong fighters. Mean as snakes.

JC: How did you feel when you heard they were coming?

KJ: I was scared.

JC: But you handled it pretty calmly. That strategy session with your generals must have paid off.

KJ: We didn't have one.

JC: You didn't have a meeting, or you didn't have a strategy?

KJ: Neither.

JC: What did you do?

KJ: I asked God what to do.

JC: What did he say?

KJ: Nothing at first, so I got some people to talk to him with me.

JC: Your cabinet had a prayer session?

KJ: No, my nation went on a fast.

JC: The whole nation?

KJ: Everyone but you, apparently.

JC: Uh, well, what did you tell God?

KJ: Well, we told God that he was the king and whatever he wanted was okay with us, but if he wouldn't mind, we'd like his help on a big problem.

JC: *Then* you had your strategy session.

KJ: No.

JC: What did you do?

KJ: We stood before God.

JC: Who did?

KJ: All of us. The men. The women. The babies. We just stood there and waited.

JC: What was the enemy doing while you were waiting?

KJ: They were getting closer.

JC: Is that when you rallied the people?

KJ: Who told you I rallied the people?

JC: Well, I just assumed . . .

KJ: I never said anything to the people. I just listened. After a while this young fellow named Jahaziel spoke up and said the Lord said not to be discouraged or afraid because the battle wasn't ours, it was his.

JC: How did you know he was speaking for God?

KJ: When you spend as much time talking to God as I do, you learn to recognize his voice.

JC: Incredible.

KJ: No, supernatural.

JC: Then you attacked?

KJ: No, Jahaziel said, "Stand still and you will see the Lord save you."

JC: I've heard that somewhere.

KJ: Vintage Moses.

JC: Then you attacked?

KJ: No, then we sang. Well, some sang. I'm not much with a tune so I fell on my face and prayed. I let the others sing. We've got this group—Levites—who really know how to sing.

JC: Wait a minute. With the army getting closer, you sang?

KJ: A few tunes. Then I told the people to be strong and have faith in God and then we marched out to the battlefield.

JC: And you led the army?

KJ: No, we put the singers out in front. And as we marched they sang. And as we sang, God set ambushes. And by the time we got to the battlefield, the enemy was dead. That was three days ago. It took us that long to clean up the area. We are back today to have another worship service. Come over here; I want you to listen to these Levites sing. I bet you ten shekels you can't keep your seat for five minutes.

JC: Wait. I can't write this story. It's too bizarre. Who'll believe it?

KJ: Just write it. Those with man-sized problems will laugh. And those with God-sized problems will pray. Leave it to them to decide. Come on. The band is tuning up. You won't want to miss the first piece.

So, what do you think? What does God do when we are in a bind? If Moses and Jehoshaphat are any indication, that question can be answered with one word: *fights.* He fights for us. He steps into the ring and points us to our corner and takes over. "Remain calm; the LORD will fight for you" (Exod. 14:14).

His job is to fight. Our job is to trust.

Just trust. Not direct. Or question. Or yank the steering wheel out of his hands. Our job is to pray and wait. Nothing more is necessary. Nothing more is needed.

"He is my defender; I will not be defeated" (Ps. 62:6).

By the way, was it just me, or did I detect a few giggles when I announced my archaeological discovery?

Some of you didn't believe me, did you? Tsk, tsk, tsk . . . Just for that you're going to have to wait until the next book before I tell you about the diary of Jonah I found in a used-book store in Wink, Texas. Still has some whale guts in it.

And you thought I was kidding.[1]

PART THREE

The Guest of the Maestro

The Guest of the Maestro

hat happens when a dog interrupts a concert? To answer that, come with me to a spring night in Lawrence, Kansas.

Take your seat in Hoch Auditorium and behold the Leipzig Gewandhaus Orchestra — the oldest continually operating orchestra in the world. The greatest composers and conductors in history have directed this orchestra. It was playing in the days of Beethoven (some of the musicians have been replaced).

You watch as stately dressed Europeans take their seats on the stage. You listen as professionals carefully tune their instruments. The percussionist puts her ear to the kettle drum. A violinist plucks the nylon sting. A clarinet player tightens the reed. And you sit a bit straighter as the lights dim and the tuning stops. The music is about to begin.

The conductor, dressed in tails, strides onto the stage, springs onto the podium, and gestures for the orchestra to rise. You and two thousand others applaud. The musicians take their seats, the maestro takes his position, and the audience holds its breath.

There is a second of silence between lightning and thunder. And there is a second of silence between the raising of the baton and the explosion of the music. But when it falls the heavens open and you are delightfully drenched in the downpour of Beethoven's Third Symphony.

Such was the power of that spring night in Lawrence, Kansas. That hot, spring night in Lawrence, Kansas. I mention the temperature so you'll understand why the doors were open. It was hot. Hoch Auditorium, a historic building, was not air-conditioned. Combine bright stage lights with formal dress and furious music, and the result is a heated orchestra. Outside doors on each side of the stage were left open in case of a breeze.

Enter, stage right, the dog. A brown, generic, Kansas dog. Not a mean dog. Not a mad dog. Just a curious dog. He passes between the double basses and makes his way through the second violins and into the cellos. His tail wags in beat with the music. As the dog passes between the players, they look at him, look at each other, and continue with the next measure.

The dog takes a liking to a certain cello. Perhaps it was the lateral passing of the bow. Maybe it was the eye-level view of the strings. Whatever it was, it caught the dog's attention and he stopped and watched. The cellist wasn't sure what to do. He'd never played before a canine audience. And music schools don't teach you what dog slobber might do to the lacquer of a sixteenth-century Guarneri cello. But the dog did nothing but watch for a moment and then move on.

Had he passed on through the orchestra, the music might have continued. Had he made his way across the stage into the motioning hands of the stagehand, the audience might have never noticed. But he didn't leave. He stayed. At home in the splendor. Roaming through the meadow of music.

He visited the woodwinds, turned his head at the trumpets, stepped between the flutists, and stopped by the side of the conductor. And Beethoven's Third Symphony came undone.

The musicians laughed. The audience laughed. The dog looked up at the conductor and panted. And the conductor lowered his baton.

The most historic orchestra in the world. One of the most moving pieces ever written. A night wrapped in glory, all brought to a stop by a wayward dog.

The chuckles ceased as the conductor turned. What

fury might erupt? The audience grew quiet as the maestro faced them. What fuse had been lit? The polished, German director looked at the crowd, looked down at the dog, then looked back at the people, raised his hands in a universal gesture and . . . shrugged.

Everyone roared.

He stepped off the podium and scratched the dog behind the ears. The tail wagged again. The maestro spoke to the dog. He spoke in German, but the dog seemed to understand. The two visited for a few seconds before the maestro took his new friend by the collar and led him off the stage. You'd have thought the dog was Pavarotti the way the people applauded. The conductor returned and the music began and Beethoven seemed none the worse for the whole experience.[1]

Can you find you and me in this picture?

I can. Just call us Fido. And consider God the Maestro.

And envision the moment when we will walk onto his stage. We won't deserve it. We will not have earned it. We may even surprise the musicians with our presence.

The music will be like none we've ever heard. We'll stroll among the angels and listen as they sing. We'll gaze at heaven's lights and gasp as they shine. And we'll walk next to the Maestro, stand by his side, and worship as he leads.

These final chapters remind us of that moment. They challenge us to see the unseen and live for that event. They invite us to tune our ears to the song of the skies and long—long for the moment when we'll be at the Maestro's side.

He, too, will welcome. And he, too, will speak. But he will not lead us away. He will invite us to remain, forever his guests on his stage.

CHAPTER TWENTY-FOUR

The Gift of Unhappiness

There dwells inside you, deep within, a tiny whippoorwill. Listen. You will hear him sing. His aria mourns the dusk. His solo signals the dawn.

It is the song of the whippoorwill.

He will not be silent until the sun is seen.

We forget he is there, so easy is he to ignore. Other animals of the heart are larger, noisier, more demanding, more imposing.

But none is so constant.

Other creatures of the soul are more quickly fed. More simply satisfied. We feed the lion who growls for power. We stroke the tiger who demands affection. We bridle the stallion who bucks control.

But what do we do with the whippoorwill who yearns for eternity?

For that is his song. That is his task. Out of the gray

he sings a golden song. Perched in time he chirps a timeless verse. Peering through pain's shroud, he sees a painless place. Of that place he sings.

And though we try to ignore him, we cannot. He is us, and his song is ours. Our heart song won't be silenced until we see the dawn.

"God has planted eternity in the hearts of men" (Eccles. 3:10 TLB), says the wise man. But it doesn't take a wise person to know that people long for more than earth. When we see pain, we yearn. When we see hunger, we question why. Senseless deaths. Endless tears, needless loss. Where do they come from? Where will they lead?

Isn't there more to life than death?

And so sings the whippoorwill.

We try to quiet this terrible, tiny voice. Like a parent hushing a child, we place a finger over puckered lips and request silence. *I'm too busy now to talk. I'm too busy to think. I'm too busy to question.*

And so we busy ourselves with the task of staying busy.

But occasionally we hear his song. And occasionally we let the song whisper to us that there is something more. There *must* be something more.

And as long as we hear the song, we are comforted. As long as we are discontent, we will search. As long as we know there is a far-off country, we will have hope.

The only ultimate disaster that can befall us, I have come to realize, is to feel ourselves to be home on earth. As long as we are aliens, we cannot forget our true homeland.[1]

Unhappiness on earth cultivates a hunger for heaven. By gracing us with a deep dissatisfaction, God holds our attention. The only tragedy, then, is to be satisfied prematurely. To settle for earth. To be content in a strange land. To intermarry with the Babylonians and forget Jerusalem.

We are not happy here because we are not at home here. We are not happy here because we are not supposed to be happy here. We are "like foreigners and strangers in this world" (1 Pet. 2:11).

Take a fish and place him on the beach.[2] Watch his gills gasp and scales dry. Is he happy? No! How do you make him happy? Do you cover him with a mountain of cash? Do you get him a beach chair and sunglasses? Do you bring him a *Playfish* magazine and martini? Do you wardrobe him in double-breasted fins and people-skinned shoes?

Of course not. Then how do you make him happy? You put him back in his element. You put him back in the water. He will never be happy on the beach simply because he was not made for the beach.

And you will never be completely happy on earth simply because you were not made for earth. Oh, you will have your moments of joy. You will catch glimpses of light. You will know moments or even days of peace. But they simply do not compare with the happiness that lies ahead.

Thou hast made us for thyself and our hearts are restless until they rest in thee.[3]

Rest on this earth is a false rest. Beware of those who urge you to find happiness here; you won't find it. Guard against the false physicians who promise that joy is only a diet away, a marriage away, a job away, or a transfer away. The prophet denounced people like this, "They tried to heal my people's serious injuries as if they were small wounds. They said, 'It's all right, it's all right.' But really, it is not all right" (Jer. 6:14).

And it won't be all right until we get home.

Again, we have our moments. The newborn on our breast, the bride on our arm, the sunshine on our back. But even those moments are simply slivers of light breaking through heaven's window. God flirts with us. He tantalizes us. He romances us. Those moments are appetizers for the dish that is to come.

"No one has ever imagined what God has prepared for those who love him" (1 Cor. 2:9).

What a breathtaking verse! Do you see what it says? *Heaven is beyond our imagination.* We cannot envision it. At our most creative moment, at our deepest thought, at our highest level, we still cannot fathom eternity.

Try this. Imagine a perfect world. Whatever that means to you, imagine it. Does that mean peace? Then envision absolute tranquility. Does a perfect world imply joy? Then create your highest happiness. Will a perfect world have love? If so, ponder a place where love has no bounds. Whatever heaven means to you, imagine it. Get it firmly fixed in your mind. Delight in it. Dream about it. Long for it.

And then smile as the Father reminds you, *No one has ever imagined what God has prepared for those who love him.*

Anything you imagine is inadequate. Anything anyone imagines is inadequate. No one has come close. No one. Think of all the songs about heaven. All the artists' portrayals. All the lessons preached, poems written, and chapters drafted.

When it comes to describing heaven, we are all happy failures.

It's beyond us.

But it's also within us. The song of the whippoorwill. Let her sing. Let her sing in the dark. Let her sing at the dawn. Let her song remind you that you were not made for this place and that there is a place made just for you.

But until then, be realistic. Lower your expectations of earth. This is not heaven, so don't expect it to be. There will never be a newscast with no bad news. There will never be a church with no gossip or competition. There will never be a new car, new wife, or new baby who can give you the joy your heart craves. Only God can.

And God will. Be patient. And be listening. Listening for the song of the whippoorwill.

CHAPTER TWENTY-FIVE

On Seeing God

ONE OF MY favorite childhood memories is greeting my father as he came home from work.

My mother, who worked an evening shift at the hospital, would leave the house around three in the afternoon. Dad would arrive home at three-thirty. My brother and I were left alone for that half-hour with strict instructions not to leave the house until Dad arrived.

We would take our positions on the couch and watch cartoons, always keeping one ear alert to the driveway. Even the best "Daffy Duck" would be abandoned when we heard his car.

I can remember running out to meet Dad and getting swept up in his big (often sweaty) arms. As he carried me toward the house, he'd put his big-brimmed straw hat on my head, and for a moment I'd be a cowboy. We'd sit on the porch as he removed his oily work boots (never allowed in the house). As he took them off I'd pull them on, and for a moment I'd be a wrangler. Then we'd go indoors and open his lunch pail. Any leftover snacks, which he always seemed to have, were for my brother and me to split.

It was great. Boots, hats, and snacks. What more could a five-year-old want?

But suppose, for a minute, that is all I got. Suppose my dad, rather than coming home, just sent some things home. Boots for me to play in. A hat for me to wear. Snacks for me to eat.

Would that be enough? Maybe so, but not for long. Soon the gifts would lose their charm. Soon, if not immediately, I'd ask, "Where's Dad?"

Or consider something worse. Suppose he called me up and said, "Max, I won't be coming home anymore. But I'll send my boots and hat over, and every afternoon you can play in them."

No deal. That wouldn't work. Even a five-year-old knows it's the person, not the presents, that makes a reunion special. It's not the frills; it's the father.

Imagine God making us a similar offer:

I will give you anything you desire. Anything. Perfect love. Eternal peace. You will never be afraid or alone. No confusion will enter your mind. No anxiety or boredom will enter your heart. You will never lack for anything.

There will be no sin. No guilt. No rules. No expectations. No failure. You will never be lonely. You will never hurt. You will never die.

Only you will never see my face.[1]

Would you want it? Neither would I. It's not enough. Who wants heaven without God? Heaven is not heaven without God.

A painless, deathless eternity will be nice, but inadequate. A world shot with splendor would stagger us, but it's not what we seek. What we want is God. We want God more than we know. It's not that the perks aren't attractive. It's just that they aren't enough. It's not that we are greedy. It's just that we are his and—Augustine was right—our hearts are restless until they rest in him.

Only when we find him will we be satisfied. Moses can tell you.

He had as much of God as any man in the Bible. God spoke to him in a bush. God guided him with fire. God amazed Moses with the plagues. And when God grew angry with the Israelites and withdrew from them, he stayed close to Moses. He spoke to Moses "as a man speaks with his friend" (Exod. 33:11). Moses knew God like no other man.

But that wasn't enough. Moses yearned for more. Moses longed to see God. He even dared to ask, "Please show me your glory" (Exod. 33:18).

A hat and snack were not enough. A fiery pillar and morning manna were insufficient. Moses wanted to see God himself.

Don't we all?

Isn't that why we long for heaven? We may speak about a place where there are no tears, no death, no fear, no night; but those are just the benefits of heaven.

The beauty of heaven is seeing God. Heaven is God's heart.

And our heart will only be at peace when we see him. "Because I have lived right, I will see your face. When I wake up, I will see your likeness and be satisfied" (Ps. 17:15).

Satisfied? That is one thing we are not. We are not satisfied.

We push back from the Thanksgiving table and pat our round bellies. "I'm satisfied," we declare. But look at us a few hours later, back in the kitchen picking the meat from the bone.

We wake up after a good night's rest and hop out of bed. We couldn't go back to sleep if someone paid us. We are satisfied—for a while. But look at us a dozen or so hours later, crawling back in the sheets.

We take the vacation of a lifetime. For years we planned. For years we saved. And off we go. We satiate ourselves with sun, fun, and good food. But we are not even on the way home before we dread the end of the trip and begin planning another.

We are not satisfied.

As a child we say, "If only I were a teenager." As a teen we say, "If only I were an adult." As an adult, "If only I were married." As a spouse, "If only I had kids." As a parent, "If only my kids were grown." In an empty house, "If only the kids would visit." As a retiree in the rocking chair with stiff joints and fading sight, "If only I were a child again."

We are not satisfied. Contentment is a difficult virtue. Why?

Because there is nothing on earth that can satisfy our deepest longing. We long to see God. The leaves of life are rustling with the rumor that we will—and we won't be satisfied until we do.

We can't be satisfied. Not because we are greedy, but because we are hungry for something not found on this earth. Only God can satisfy. Philip was right when he said, "Lord, show us the Father. That is all we need" (John 14:8).

Alas, therein lies the problem: "But you cannot see my face," God told Moses, "because no one can see me and live" (Exod. 33:20).

The eighteenth-century Hasids understood the risk of seeing God. Rabbi Uri wept every morning as he left his house to pray. He called his children and wife to his side and wept as if he would never see them again. When asked why, he gave this answer. "When I begin my prayers I call out to the Lord. Then I pray, 'Lord have mercy on us.' Who knows what the Lord's power will do to me in that moment after I have invoked it and before I beg for mercy?"[2]

According to legend, the first American Indian to see the Grand Canyon tied himself to a tree in terror. According to Scripture, any man privileged a peek at God has felt the same.

Sheer terror. Remember the words of Isaiah after his vision of God? "Oh, no! I will be destroyed. I am not pure, and I live among people who are not pure, but I have seen the King, the LORD All-Powerful" (Isa. 6:5).

Upon seeing God, Isaiah was terrified. Why such fear? Why did he tremble so? Because he was wax before the sun. A candle in a hurricane. A minnow at Niagara. God's glory was too great. His purity too sterling. His power too mighty.

The holiness of God illuminates the sinfulness of man.

To understand this, let's imagine you are in a theater. You have never visited one before and you are curious. You poke around backstage and look at the lights and play with the curtains and examine the props. Then you see a dressing room.

You enter and sit at the table. You look in the large mirror on the wall. What you see is what you always see when you look at your reflection. No surprises. Then you notice that the mirror is framed in light bulbs. There is a switch on the wall. You flip it on.

A dozen lights shine on your face. Suddenly you see what you had not seen. Blemishes. Wrinkles. Every mole and mark is highlighted. The light has illuminated your imperfections.

That's what happened to Isaiah. When he saw God, he didn't sigh with admiration. He didn't applaud in appreciation. He drew back in horror, crying, "I am unclean and my people are unclean!"

The holiness of God highlights our sins.

Listen to the words of another prophet. "Look, Jesus is coming with the clouds, and everyone will see him, even those who stabbed him. And all peoples of the earth will *cry loudly* because of him. Yes, this will happen!" (Rev. 1:7, emphasis mine).

Read the verse in another translation. "Riding the clouds, he'll be seen by every eye, those who mocked and killed him will see him. People from all nations and all times will tear their clothes in lament. Oh, yes" (Rev. 1:7, THE MESSAGE).

The holiness of God highlights the sin of man.

Then what do we do? If it is true that "Anyone whose life is not holy will never see the Lord" (Heb. 12:14), where do we turn?

We can't turn off the light. We can't flip the switch. We can't return to the gray. By then it will be too late.

So what can we do?

The answer is found in the story of Moses. Read carefully, very carefully, the following verses. Read to answer this question—what did Moses do in order to see God? Read slowly what God says. You may miss it.

"There is a place near me where you may stand on a rock. When my glory passes that place, I will put you in a large crack in the rock and cover you with my hand until I have passed by. Then I will take away my hand, and you will see my back. But my face must not be seen" (Exod. 33:21–23).

Did you see what Moses was to do? Neither did I. Did you note who did the work? So did I.

God did! God is active. God gave Moses a place to stand. God placed Moses in the crevice. God covered

Moses with his hand. God passed by. And God revealed himself.

Please, underscore the point. God equipped Moses to catch a glimpse of God.

(*Holy Moses!*)

All Moses did was ask. But, oh, how he asked.

All we can do is ask. But, oh, we must ask.

For only in asking do we receive. And only in seeking do we find.

And (need I make the application?) God is the one who will equip us for our eternal moment in the Son. Hasn't he given us a rock, the Lord Jesus? Hasn't he given us a cleft, his grace? And hasn't he covered us with his hand, his pierced hand?

And isn't the father on his way to get us?

Just as my dad came at the right hour, so God will come. And just as my father brought gifts and pleasures, so will yours. But, as splendid as are the gifts of heaven, it is not for those we wait.

We wait to see the Father. And that will be enough.

CHAPTER TWENTY-SIX

Orphans at the Gate

I CAME ACROSS a sad story this week, a story about a honeymoon disaster. The newlyweds arrived at the hotel in the wee hours with high hopes. They'd reserved a large room with romantic amenities. That's not what they found.

Seems the room was pretty skimpy. The tiny room had no view, no flowers, a cramped bathroom and worst of all—no bed. Just a foldout sofa with a lumpy mattress and sagging springs. It was not what they'd hoped for; consequently, neither was the night.

The next morning the sore-necked groom stormed down to the manager's desk and ventilated his anger. After listening patiently for a few minutes, the clerk asked, "Did you open the door in your room?"

The groom admitted he hadn't. He returned to the suite and opened the door he had thought was a closet.

There, complete with fruit baskets and chocolates, was a spacious bedroom![1]

Sigh.

Can't you just see them standing in the doorway of the room they'd overlooked? Oh, it would have been so nice . . .

A comfortable bed instead of clumpy sofa.

A curtain-framed window rather than a blank wall.

A fresh breeze in place of stuffy air.

An elaborate restroom, not a tight toilet.

But they missed it. How sad. Cramped, cranky, and uncomfortable while comfort was a door away. They missed it because they thought the door was a closet.

Why didn't you try? I was asking as I read the piece. Get curious. Check it out. Give it a shot. Take a look. Why did you just assume the door led nowhere?

Good question. Not just for the couple but for everyone. Not for the pair who thought the room was all there was, but for all who feel cramped and packed in the anteroom called earth. It's not what we'd hoped. It may have its moments, but it is simply not what we think it should be. Something inside of us groans for more.

We understand what Paul meant when he wrote: "We . . . groan inwardly as we wait eagerly our adoption as sons, the redemption of our bodies" (Rom. 8:23 NIV).

Groan. That's the word. An inward angst. The echo from the cavern of the heart. The sigh of the soul that says the world is out of joint. Awry. Misspelled. Limping.

Something is wrong.

The room is too cramped to breathe, the bed too stiff for rest, the walls too bare for pleasure.

And so we groan.

It's not that we don't try. We do our best with the room we have. We shuffle the furniture, we paint the walls, we turn down the lights. But there's only so much you can do with the place.

And so we groan.

And well we should, Paul argues. We were not made for these puny quarters. "For while we are in this tent, we groan and are burdened" (2 Cor. 5:6).

Our body a tent? Not a bad metaphor. I've spent some nights in tents. Nice for vacation, but not intended for daily use. Flaps fly open. Winter wind creeps from beneath. Summer showers seep from above. Canvas gets raw and tent stakes come loose.

We need something better, Paul argues. Something permanent. Something painless. Something more than flesh and bone. And until we get it, we groan.

I know I'm not telling you anything new. You know the groan of the soul. You didn't need me to tell you it's there.

But maybe you do need me to tell you it's okay. It's all right to groan. It's permissible to yearn. Longing is part of life. It's only natural to long for home when on a journey.

We aren't home yet.

We are orphans at the gate of the orphanage, awaiting our new parents. They aren't here yet, but we know they are coming. They wrote us a letter. We haven't seen them yet, but we know what they look like. They sent us a picture. And we're not acquainted with our new house yet, but we have a hunch about it. It's grand. They sent a description.

And so what do we do? Here, at the gate where the now-already meets the path of the not-yet, what do we do?

We groan. We long for the call to come home. But until he calls, we wait. We stand on the porch of the orphanage and wait. And how do we wait? With patient eagerness.

"We are hoping for something we do not have yet, and we are waiting for it *patiently* (Rom. 8:25, emphasis mine).

"We wait *eagerly* for our adoption as sons" (Rom. 8:23 NIV, emphasis mine). Patient eagerness. Not so eager as to lose our patience, and not so patient as to lose our eagerness.[2]

Yet, we often tend to one or the other.

We grow so patient we sleep! Our eyelids grow heavy. Our hearts grow drowsy. Our hope lapses. We slumber at our post.

Or we are so eager we demand. We demand in this world what only the next world can give. No sickness. No suffering. No struggle. We stomp our feet and shake our fists, forgetting it is only in heaven that such peace is found.

We must be patient, but not so much that we don't

yearn. We must be eager, but not so much that we don't wait.

We'd be wise to do what the newlyweds never did. We'd be wise to open the door. Stand in the entryway. Gaze in the chambers. Gasp at the beauty.

And wait. Wait for the groom to come and carry us, his bride, over the threshold.

CHAPTER TWENTY-SEVEN

View of the High Country

WHILE IN Colorado for a week's vacation, our family teamed up with several others and decided to ascend the summit of a fourteen-thousand-foot peak. We would climb it the easy way. Drive above the timberline and tackle the final mile by foot. You hearty hikers would have been bored, but for a family with three small girls, it was about all we could take.

The journey was as tiring as it was beautiful. I was reminded how the air was thin and my waist was not.

Our four-year-old Sara had it doubly difficult. A tumble in the first few minutes left her with a skinned knee and a timid step. She didn't want to walk. Actually, she *refused* to walk. She wanted to ride. First on my back, then in Mom's arms, then my back, then a friend's back, then my back, then Mom's . . . well, you get the picture.

In fact, you know how she felt. You, too, have tumbled, and you, too, have asked for help. And you, too, have received it.

All of us need help sometimes. This journey gets steep. So steep that some of us give up.

Some stop climbing. Some just sit down. They are still near the trail but aren't on it. They haven't abandoned the trip, but they haven't continued it. They haven't dismounted, but they haven't spurred either. They haven't resigned and yet haven't resolved.

They have simply stopped walking. Much time is spent sitting around the fire, talking about how things used to be. Some will sit in the same place for years. They will not change. Prayers will not deepen. Devotion will not increase. Passion will not rise.

A few even grow cynical. Woe to the traveler who challenges them to resume the journey. Woe to the prophet who dares them to see the mountain. Woe to the explorer who reminds them of their call . . . pilgrims are not welcome here.

And so the pilgrim moves on while the settler settles.

Settles for sameness.

Settles for safety.

Settles for snowdrifts.

I hope you don't do that. But if you do, I hope you don't scorn the pilgrim who calls you back to the journey.

It's worth it to keep moving.

As I tried, unsuccessfully, to convince Sara to walk, I tried describing what we were going to see. "It will be so pretty," I told her. "You'll see all the mountains and the sky and the trees." No luck—she wanted to be carried. Still a good idea, however. Even if it didn't work. Nothing puts power in the journey like a vision of the mountaintop.

By the way, a grand scene awaits you as well. The Hebrew writer gives us a *National Geographic* piece on heaven. Listen to how he describes the mountaintop of Zion. He says when we reach the mountain we will have come to "the city of the living God. . . . To thousands of angels gathered together with joy. . . . To the meeting of God's firstborn children whose names are written in heaven. . . . To God, the judge of all people, . . . and to the spirits of good people who have been made perfect. . . . To Jesus, the One who brought the new agreement from God to his people. . . . To the sprinkled blood that has a better message than the blood of Abel" (Heb. 12:22–24).

What a mountain! Won't it be great to see the angels? To finally know what they look like and who they are? To hear them tell of the times they were at our side, even in our house?

Imagine the meeting of the firstborn. A gathering of all God's children. No jealousy. No competition. No division. No hurry. We will be perfect . . . sinless. No more stumbles. No more tripping. Lusting will cease. Gossip will be silenced. Grudges forever removed.

And imagine seeing God. Finally, to gaze in the face of your Father. To feel the Father's gaze upon you. Neither will ever cease.

He will do what he promised he would do. *I will make all things new,* he promised. *I will restore what was taken. I will restore your years drooped on crutches and trapped in wheelchairs. I will restore the smiles faded by hurt. I will replay the symphonies unheard by deaf ears and the sunsets unseen by blind eyes.*

The mute will sing. The poor will feast. The wounds will heal.

I will make all things new. I will restore all things. The child snatched by disease will run to your arms. The freedom lost to oppression will dance in your heart. The peace of a pure heart will be my gift to you.

I will make all things new. New hope. New faith. And most of all new Love. The Love of which all other loves speak. The Love before which all other loves pale. The Love you have sought in a thousand ports in a thousand nights . . . this Love of mine, will be yours.[1]

What a mountain! Jesus will be there. You've longed to see him. You finally will. Interesting what the writer says we will see. He doesn't mention the face of Jesus, though we will see it. He doesn't refer to the voice of Jesus, though it will shout. He mentions a part of Jesus that most of us wouldn't think of seeing. He says we will see Jesus' blood. The crimson of the cross. The life liquid that seeped from his forehead, dripped from his hands, and flowed from his side.

The human blood of the divine Christ. Covering our sins.

Proclaiming a message: *We have been bought. We cannot be sold. Ever.*

My, what a moment. What a mountain.

Believe me when I say it will be worth it. No cost is too high. If you must pay a price, pay it! No sacrifice too much. If you must leave baggage on the trail, leave it! No loss will compare. Whatever it takes, do it.

For heaven's sake, do it.

It will be worth it. I promise. One view of the peak will justify the pain of the path.

By the way, our group finally made it up the mountain. We spent an hour or so at the top, taking pictures and enjoying the view. Later, on the way down, I heard little Sara exclaim proudly, "I did it!"

I chuckled. *No you didn't,* I thought. *Your mom and I did it. Friends and family got you up this mountain. You didn't do it.*

But I didn't say anything. I didn't say anything because I'm getting the same treatment. So are you. We may think we are climbing, but we are riding. Riding on the back of the Father who saw us fall. Riding on the back of the Father who wants us to make it home. A Father who doesn't get angry when we get weary.

After all, he knows what it's like to climb a mountain.

He climbed one for us.

CHAPTER TWENTY-EIGHT

The Name Only God Knows

HAD A PICTURE given to me after a church service sometime back. A picture of a dog. A snapshot of a scruffy red hound.

It's not often that people show me a picture of their dog. Babies, yes. Grandchildren, often. Spouses, occasionally. But dogs? This was a first. I didn't know what to say.

"Quite a dog," I attempted. The couple looked at each other, snickered, and looked back at me. They knew something I didn't.

"What's the scoop?" I asked. (Poor choice of nouns.)

"We named him Max!" they proclaimed in unison.

Again I was stumped. Was this a joke or an honor? A cut or a compliment?

I took the safe route. "Uh . . . I've never had a dog named after me before."

"We knew you'd be flattered," she explained. "We've enjoyed your books so much that when we got 'Puppy-boo' we thought of you."

(*Puppy-boo?*)

I said thanks and pocketed the photo. Only later did I think of some appropriate replies. "Not the first Max to be in a doghouse," was one. Too bad I didn't think of it in time. A friend later gave me an article reporting that Max is the most popular name for dogs in America. So maybe I'll get another chance.

Can't say I've given a lot of thought to my given name. Never figured it made much difference. I do recall a kid in elementary school wondering if I were German. I said no. "Then why do you have a German name?" I didn't even know Max was German. He assured me it was. So I decided to find out.

"Why did you name me Max?" I asked Mom when I got home.

She looked up from the sink and replied, "You just looked like one."

Like I say, I haven't given much thought to my name. But there is one name that has caught my interest lately. A name only God knows. A name only God gives. A unique, one-of-a-kind, once-to-be-given name.

What am I talking about? Well, you may not have known it, but God has a new name for you. When you get home, he won't call you Alice or Bob or Juan or Geraldo. The name you've always heard won't be the one he uses. When God says he will make all things new, he means it. You will have a new home, a new body, a new life, and you guessed it, a new name.

"I will give some of the hidden manna to everyone who wins the victory. I will also give to each one who wins the victory a white stone with a new name written on it. No one knows this new name except the one who receives it" (Rev. 2:17).

Makes sense. Fathers are fond of giving their children special names. Princess. Tiger. Sweetheart. Bubba. Angel. I have a friend whose father calls her Willy. Her name is Priscilla. Growing up, he teased her by saying Priscilly. That became Silly-willy. Today he calls her Willy. No one else does. Even if they did, no one else could say it the way her dad does.

Now maybe you didn't get a special name. Or maybe you've devoted much of your life to making a name for yourself. Or perhaps your name, like mine, is popular in the animal kingdom. Whatever, any earthly name will soon be forgotten. The only name that matters is the one God has reserved just for you.

Or maybe you have received special names. Names you never sought. Names of derision and hurt. Names like "loser" or "cheat," "cripple," "infected," or "divorced." If so, I'm sorry. You know how a name can hurt. But you can also imagine how a name can heal.

Especially when it comes from the lips of God.

Isn't it incredible to think that God has saved a name just for you? One you don't even know? We've always assumed that the name we got is the name we will keep.

Not so. Imagine what that implies. Apparently your future is so promising it warrants a new title. The road ahead is so bright a fresh name is needed. Your eternity is so special no common name will do.

So God has one reserved just for you. There is more to your life than you ever thought. There is more to your story than what you have read. There is more to your song than what you have sung. A good author saves the best for last. A great composer keeps his finest for the finish. And God, the author of life and composer of hope, has done the same for you.

The best is yet to be.

And so I urge you, don't give up.

And so I plead, finish the journey.

And so I exhort, be there.

Be there when God whispers your name.

NOTES

CHAPTER 1 The Voice from the Mop Bucket

1. Philippians 1:6.

CHAPTER 3 Hidden Heroes

1. See Matthew 11:2.
2. *1,041 Sermon Illustrations, Ideas and Expositions,* compiled and edited by A. Gordon Nasby (Grand Rapids: Baker, 1976), 180–81.

CHAPTER 7 Behind the Shower Curtain

1. These phrases appeared in "A Dream Worth Keeping Alive," *Wineskins Magazine,* January–February 1993, 16–20.
2. See Luke 15:3–7.

CHAPTER 9 What Is Your Price?

1. James Patterson and Peter Kim, *The Day America Told the Truth* (New York: Prentice Hall, 1991), as quoted in *Discipleship Journal*, September–October 1991, 16.

2. Ibid.
3. "Life is not measured by how much one owns" (Luke 12:15).
4. Better known as the Parable of Greed (Luke 12:16–21).

PART 2 The Touch of the Master

1. *1041 Sermon Illustrations, Ideas, and Expositions,* 199.

CHAPTER 15 Overcoming Your Heritage

1. With appreciation to Stefan Richart-Willmes.

PART 3 The Guest of the Maestro

1. With appreciation to Erik Ketcherside for telling me this story.

CHAPTER 23 The God Who Fights for You

1. See Exodus 14:5–31, Exodus chapters 8–15, and 2 Chronicles 20.

CHAPTER 24 The Gift of Unhappiness

1. Augustine, *Confessions I.i,* as quoted in Peter Kreeft, *Heaven: The Heart's Deepest Longing* (San Francisco: Ignatius Press), 1989, 49. The inspiration for this essay about the whippoorwill is drawn from Kreeft's description of "The Nightingale in the Heart," 51–54.
2. With appreciation to Landon Saunders for this idea.

3. Malcolm Muggeridge, *Jesus Rediscovered* (New York: Doubleday, 1979), 47–48 as quoted in Peter Kreeft, *Heaven,* 63.

CHAPTER 25 On Seeing God

1. With acknowledgment to Augustine, *Ennarationes in Psalmos,* 127.9, as quoted in Peter Kreeft, *Heaven,* 49.
2. Annie Dillard, *The Writing Life* (New York: Harper and Row, 1989), 9.

CHAPTER 26 Orphans at the Gate

1. *Leadership*, Winter 1994, 46.
2. With appreciation to John R. W. Stott, *Christian Assurance: The Hope of Glory* (London: All Souls Cassettes), d28 1b.

CHAPTER 27 View of the High Country

1. See Revelation 21:5.

DISCUSSION GUIDE

Prepared by

Steve Halliday

HOW TO USE THIS DISCUSSION GUIDE

Each of these short studies is designed not only to interact with the ideas in *When God Whispers Your Name*, but also to point readers back to Scripture as the wellspring of those ideas.

The first section of each study, Points to Ponder, excerpts portions of each chapter for group discussion. The second section, Wisdom from the Word, helps readers dig a little deeper into scriptural viewpoint on the issue under discussion.

While all of the studies may be completed separately, they may also be considered together with one or more other studies that cover similar themes. A suggested list of complementary studies follows:

- The Voice From the Mop Bucket/Hidden Heroes/You Might've Been in the Bible
- Why Jesus Went to Parties/Maxims
- Behind the Shower Curtain/Groceries and Grace/Of Oz and God
- God's Christmas Cards/Gabriel's Questions
- The Prophet/The Choice
- What Is Your Price?/When Crickets Make You Cranky
- Overcoming Your Heritage/Your Sack of Stones
- The Sweet Sound of the Second Fiddle/ An Inside Job/ On Seeing God
- Late-Night Good News/The God Who Fights for You
- Seeing What Eyes Can't/Healthy Habits
- The Gift of Unhappiness/Orphans at the Gate/View of the High Country
- DFW and the Holy Spirit/The Name Only God Knows

When God Whispers Your Name

Points to Ponder

"Something happens to us along the way. Convictions to change the world downgrade to commitments to pay the bills. Rather than make a difference, we make a salary. Rather than look forward, we look back. Rather than look outward, we look inward. And we don't like what we see."

1 Have your convictions changed as you've grown older? If so, in what way?

2 Do you like what you see? Explain.

"Moses at forty we like. But Moses at eighty? No way. Too old. Too tired. Smells like a shepherd. Speaks like a foreigner. What impact would he have on Pharaoh? He's the wrong man for the job. Moses would have agreed. 'Tried that once before,' he would say. 'Those people don't want to be helped. Just leave me here to tend my sheep. They're easier to lead.' Moses wouldn't have gone. You wouldn't have sent him. I wouldn't have sent him. But God did."

1 Would you have given Moses the job of bringing Israel out of slavery? Explain.

2 What do you think God saw in Moses? What do you think He might see in you?

"The voice from the bush reminds you that God is not

finished with you yet. Oh, you may think he is. You may think you've peaked. You may think he's got someone else to do the job. If so, think again."

1 How does the "voice from the bush" remind you that God isn't finished with you yet?

2 Have you ever had a "burning bush" experience? If so, describe it.

3 What do you think God may still be calling you to do?

Wisdom from the Word

- Read Exodus 6:28–7:6. What did Moses think of himself? What did God think of him? Whose opinion won out?
- Read Hebrews 11:24–28. According to this passage, how did Moses accomplish what he did? How does this relate to you?
- Read Philippians 1:6. What promise is given in this verse? How can it change the way you live? Does it affect the way you live personally? Explain.

∞

CHAPTER 2 WHY JESUS WENT TO PARTIES

Points to Ponder

"I think it's significant that common folk in a little town enjoyed being with Jesus. I think it's noteworthy that the

Almighty didn't act high and mighty. The Holy One wasn't holier-than-thou. The One who knew it all wasn't a know-it-all. The One who made the stars didn't keep his head in them. The One who owns all the stuff of earth never strutted it."

1 Is it important to you that the "common folk" enjoyed being around Jesus? Explain.

2 Use a single word to describe the trait in Jesus' life that's described above.

"Where did we get the notion that a good Christian is a solemn Christian? Who started the rumor that the sign of a disciple is a long face? How did we create this idea that the truly gifted are the heavy-hearted?"

1 Do you think of Christians as "solemn"? Explain.

2 Where do you think the idea of the heavy-hearted Christian came from?

3 Would others see you as a disciple with a long face? Explain.

"Forgive me, Deacon Drydust and Sister Somberheart. I'm sorry to rain on your dirge, but Jesus was a likable fellow. And his disciples should be the same. I'm not talking debauchery, drunkenness, and adultery. I'm not endorsing compromise, coarseness, or obscenity. I am simply crusading for the freedom to enjoy a good joke, enliven a dull party, and appreciate a fun evening."

1 Describe your response to Max's insight above.

2 How do you respond to the Deacon Drydust and Sister Somberhearts you encounter? How do you think Jesus would respond to them?

Wisdom from the Word

- Read John 2:1–11. What impression do you get of Jesus from this passage? Why do you think John included it in his Gospel?
- Read Matthew 11:18–19. Which parts of this accusation against Jesus are true, and which are false? What does this passage tell you about Jesus' lifestyle? How does this relate to Max's point?
- Read 1 Thessalonians 4:16. What does it mean to "rejoice"? Why is it significant that this is a command? How good are you at obeying this command?

CHAPTER 3 HIDDEN HEROES

Points to Ponder

"John doesn't look like the prophet who would be the transition between law and grace. He doesn't look like a hero. Heroes seldom do."

1 In what way do heroes seldom look like heroes?

2 What's your picture of a hero?

"For every hero in the spotlight, there are dozens in the shadows. They don't get press. They don't draw crowds. They don't even write books (!). But behind every avalanche is a snowflake. Behind a rock slide is a pebble. An atomic explosion begins with one atom. And a revival can begin with one sermon."

1 What "heroes out of the spotlight" do you know?

2 What makes them heroes?

"We'd do well to keep our eyes open. Tomorrow's Spurgeon might be mowing your lawn. And the hero who inspires him might be nearer than you think. He might be in your mirror."

1 Have you been a hero to anyone?

2 Could you be a hero to anyone?

Wisdom from the Word

- Read Mark 1:1–8. How would you describe John in modern terms? How did his appearance and lifestyle help him accomplish his mission? In what way was he a hero?
- Read 2 Corinthians 4:7–11; 6:4–10; 11:22–28. What do you learn about Paul from these passages? What in them describes the kind of hero he was? Do these passages encourage or discourage you? Why?

∞

Points to Ponder

"In evangelism the Holy Spirit is on center stage. If the disciple teaches, it is because the Spirit teaches the disciple (Luke 12:12). If the listener is convicted, it is because the Spirit has penetrated (John 16:10). If the listener is converted, it is by the transforming power of the Spirit (Rom. 8:11)."

1 How have you seen the Holy Spirit at work in your own life in the process of evangelism?

2 What difference does it make to you that the Holy Spirit is at work alongside you in evangelism?

"You have the same Spirit working with you that Philip did. Some of you don't believe me. You're still cautious."

1 How is the Spirit's working in your life the same as it was in Philip's? How is it different?

2 Are you one of the "cautious" ones? Explain.

Wisdom from the Word

- Read Acts 8:26–40. List the steps Philip took, directed by the Spirit. What principles of effective evangelism can you glean from this passage? Which ones do you use? Which ones don't you use? Explain.
- Read Romans 8:13–14; Galatians 5:16–18. What do these passages teach about the leading of the Spirit? What is promised? What warnings are given?

When God Whispers Your Name

Points to Ponder

"We learn brevity from Jesus. His greatest sermon can be read in eight minutes. His best-known story can be read in ninety seconds. He summarized prayer in five phrases. He silenced accusers with one challenge. He rescued a soul with one sentence. He summarized the Law in three verses and reduced all his teachings to one command. He made his point and went home."

1 What is so powerful about brevity? What can make it so effective?

2 Which of Max's maxims in this chapter most struck a chord in you? Why?

Wisdom from the Word

- Read Luke 15:11–32. Why do you think this is Jesus' best-known story? What makes it so powerful?
- Read Matthew 6:9–13. List the elements of prayer found in this passage. Do you use these elements in your own prayer life? Explain.
- Read Mark 12:29–31. How do these commands summarize all the Bible's teaching? How do they fit together?

Points to Ponder

"If our greatest need had been information, God would have sent an educator. If our greatest need had been technology, God would have sent us a scientist. If our greatest need had been money, God would have sent us an economist. But since our greatest need was forgiveness, God sent us a Savior."

1 Do you agree that our greatest need was forgiveness?

2 Explain why you think this is true.

"He became like us, so we could become like him."

1 In what way did He become like us?

2 In what way can we become like Him?

Wisdom from the Word

- Read Matthew 1:18–2:12. If you were to write a commercial Christmas-card message based on this passage, what element of the story would you highlight? Why?
- Read Luke 2:1–20. If you were to write a commercial Christmas-card message based on this passage, what element of the story would you highlight? Why?

Points to Ponder

"I've never been surprised by God's judgment, but I'm still stunned by his grace."

1 Have you ever been surprised by God's judgment? By His grace? Explain.

2 Why is grace usually more of a surprise to us than judgment?

"Seems that God is looking more for ways to get us home than for ways to keep us out. I challenge you to find one soul who came to God seeking grace and did not find it."

1 What ways did God use to get you "home"?

2 Accept Max's challenge—can you think of one biblical person who sought God's grace but didn't find it? How significant is this? Why?

"I'm not for watering-down the truth or compromising the gospel. But if a fellow with a pure heart calls God, *Father*, can't I call that same man, *Brother*? If God doesn't make doctrinal perfection a requirement for family membership, should I?"

1 What do you think Max means by "a fellow with a pure heart"?

2 What would happen if "doctrinal perfection" were made "a requirement for family membership"?

Wisdom from the Word

- Read Luke 19:1–10. How did grace change Zacchaeus? Do you think he was surprised by grace? How about those around him? Explain.
- Read Luke 15:3–7. To whom did Jesus direct this parable? Why is that significant? What was His main point? What do you learn about grace from this parable?

CHAPTER 8 GABRIEL'S QUESTIONS

Points to Ponder

"Are we still stunned by God's coming? Still staggered by the event? Does Christmas still spawn the same speechless wonder it did two thousand years ago?"

1 Are you "still stunned by God's coming"?

2 How do you stay ready to allow God to stun you?

"Why is it that out of a hundred or so of God's children only two paused to consider his son? What is this December demon that steals our eyes and stills our tongues? Isn't this the season to pause and pose Gabriel's questions? The tragedy is not that I can't answer them, but that I am too busy to ask them."

1 How do you explain "this December demon that steals our eyes and stills our tongues"?

2 Which of Gabriel's questions most intrigue you? Why?

Wisdom from the Word

- Read Luke 1:5–20; 26–38. Compare verse 18 with verse 34. Why do you think Gabriel reacted so differently to these questions? Do you think Gabriel was a very gracious "personality"? Explain.
- Read Daniel 8:15–19; 9:20–22. What do you learn about Gabriel's personality from these passages? If he were to appear to you, how do you think you'd respond?

CHAPTER 9 WHAT IS YOUR PRICE?

Points to Ponder

"'Take your pick. Just choose one option and the ten million dollars is yours.' A deep voice from another microphone begins reading the list: 'Put your children up for adoption; become a prostitute for a week; give up your American citizenship; abandon your church; abandon your family; kill a stranger; have a sex-change operation; leave your spouse; change your race.' 'That's the list,' the host proclaims. 'Now make your choice.'"

1 If you were a contestant on this show, how would you respond?

2 What is your price?

"A schoolboy was once asked to define the parts of speech *I* and *mine.* He answered 'aggressive pronouns.'"

1 What is the problem with "aggressive pronouns"?

2 What is the cost of selfishness?

Wisdom from the Word

- Read Luke 12:13–21. What point about greed does Jesus make in this passage? What is His main point?
- Read Deuteronomy 10:14–15. According to this passage, why does greed make no sense? What is the connection between verses 14 and 15?
- Read Hebrews 13:5–6. What negative command is given here? What positive command? What reason is given for obeying the commands? What results from obeying the commands?

CHAPTER 10 GROCERIES AND GRACE

Points to Ponder

"We, too, have been graced with a surprise. Even more than that of the lady. For though her debt was high, she could pay it. We can't begin to pay ours. We, like the woman, have been given a gift. Not just at the checkout stand, but at the judgment seat. And we, too, have become a bride. Not just for a moment, but for eternity. And not just for groceries, but for the feast."

1. In what way have we been "graced with a surprise"?
2. Why can't we begin to pay our debt?
3. What gift will we be given at the judgment seat?
4. In what way have we become a bride?
5. What is the feast Max mentions?
6. Do you expect to be at the feast? Explain.

Wisdom from the Word

- Read Romans 5:6–11. For whom did Christ die (v. 6)? Why is this an example of grace? What is the result of embracing grace (v. 11)? Is this characteristic of your experience? Explain.
- Read Revelation 19:6–9. What is the mood of the event described in this passage? Who are the main participants? Do you expect to be there? Why or why not?

∞

CHAPTER 11 THE CHOICE

Points to Ponder

"Love, joy, peace, patience, kindness, goodness, faithfulness, gentleness, and self-control. To these I commit my day. If I succeed, I will give thanks. If I fail, I will seek his grace. And then, when this day is done, I will place my head on my pillow and rest. I choose God."

1 What do you think of the philosophy of life expressed in the paragraph above? Does it work? Explain.

2 What does Max mean, "I choose God." How do you *choose* God?

Wisdom from the Word

- Read Galatians 5:22–23. Why is there no law against the things listed in this passage? To what are these things compared in verses 19–21? Which list do you find yourself in most often?

- Read Deuteronomy 30:19–20 and Joshua 24:14–15. What choices are we given in these two passages? In what way are these choices the same ones we must make? What choice have you made? Explain.

∞

CHAPTER 12 THE PROPHET

Points to Ponder

"One dresses like Jesus, but the other acts like Jesus. One introduced himself as an ambassador for Christ, the other didn't have to. One stirred my curiosity, but the other touched my heart."

1 Which of these two men would you most like to meet? Explain.

2 Which of these two men would you most like to spend a week with? Explain.

"Something told me that if Jesus were here, in person, in San Antonio and I ran into him in a grocery store, I wouldn't recognize him by his rake, robe, and big Bible. But I would know him for his good heart and kind words."

1 How do you think Jesus would dress if he walked the streets of our world today? Could you pick him out of a crowd? Explain.

2 How do you think he would act?

Wisdom from the Word

- Read 1 John 2:3–6. How can we know that we have come to know Jesus (v. 3)? What happens to someone who obeys God's Word (v. 5)? If we claim to know Jesus, what are we to do (v. 6)?
- Read Luke 6:43–45. How can you tell a bad "tree" from a good one? What sort of "fruit" would others say you bear?
- Read Ephesians 5:1–2. What commands are we given in this passage? What example are we given?

CHAPTER 13 WHEN CRICKETS MAKE YOU CRANKY

Points to Ponder

"When we are mistreated, our animalistic response is to go on the hunt. Instinctively we double up our fists.

Getting even is only natural. Which, incidentally, is precisely the problem. Revenge is natural, not spiritual. Getting even is the rule of the jungle. Giving grace is the rule of the kingdom."

Discussion Guide

1 Does the "rule of the jungle" or the "rule of the kingdom" most often characterize your response to mistreatment?

2 Give an example of how you react to mistreatment.

"Revenge is irreverent. When we strike back we are saying, 'I know vengeance is yours, God, but I just didn't think you'd punish enough. I thought I'd better take this situation into my own hands. You have a tendency to be a little soft.'"

1 Have you ever felt the way the paragraph above describes? Explain.

2 If you've ever acted out this feeling, what was the result?

"Forgiveness comes easier with a wide-angle lens. Joseph uses one to get the whole picture. He refuses to focus on the betrayal of his brothers without also seeing the loyalty of his God."

1 How does forgiveness come easier with a "wide-angle lens"?

2 How is it made more difficult with a "telephoto lens"?

Wisdom from the Word

❦ Read Proverbs 20:22. What negative command is given

here? What positive command is given? How do the two work together?

❦ Read Genesis 50:15–21. Did Joseph have a right to be angry about the way his brothers mistreated him? How did he react? What was the result? If you were Joseph, how do you think you would have reacted?

∞

CHAPTER 14 SEEING WHAT EYES CAN'T

Points to Ponder

"There is more to life than meets the eye. For that's what faith is. Faith is trusting what the eye can't see. Eyes see the prowling lion. Faith sees Daniel's angel. Eyes see storms. Faith sees Noah's rainbow. Eyes see giants. Faith sees Canaan."

1 Do you agree that "faith is trusting what the eye can't see"?

2 Is there more to it than that? Explain.

"'I only jump to big arms.' If we think the arms are weak, we won't jump. For that reason, the Father flexed his muscles."

1 How has God demonstrated his "big arms" in your own life?

2 What's the biggest "arm flexing" you've ever experienced?

Wisdom from the Word

- Read Hebrews 11:1–3. How is faith defined in this passage? How would you put this in your own words?
- Read Psalm 20. What lessons of trust do you learn from this passage? What promises are given? What hope is expressed?
- Read Ephesians 1:19–20. Does this passage help build your own faith? Explain. How does Paul use this passage in Ephesians?

∞

CHAPTER 15 OVERCOMING YOUR HERITAGE

Points to Ponder

"We can't choose our parents, but we can choose our mentors."

1 What mentors have you chosen?

2 Why did you choose these particular individuals?

"Maybe your past isn't much to brag about. You saw raw evil. And now you, like Josiah, have to make a choice. Do you rise above the past and make a difference? Or do you remain controlled by the past and make excuses?"

1 Choose one word to describe how you feel about your

past: Grateful? Angry? Discouraged? Proud? Depressed? Blessed?

2 How do we sometimes allow ourselves to be controlled by the past? Have you ever slipped into this mode? Explain.

"Spiritual life comes from the Spirit! Your parents may have given you genes, but God gives you grace. Your parents may be responsible for your body, but God has taken charge of your soul. You may get your looks from your mother, but you get eternity from your Father, your heavenly Father."

1 How does this principle change our whole outlook?

2 What sort of spiritual heritage do you have now? Describe it.

Wisdom from the Word

- Read 2 Kings 21. Describe Josiah's heritage. How do you think he felt about it?
- Read John 3:1–8. How did Jesus explain that we can receive a spiritual heritage? What must we do? How did the Spirit move in your own life? Where did the "wind" come from?
- Read 2 Corinthians 5:17. What does it mean to be "in Christ"? What is gained? What is lost?

CHAPTER 16 THE SWEET SOUND OF THE SECOND FIDDLE

Points to Ponder

"You've been playing second fiddle for too long. You need to step out on your own."

1 Have you ever received advice like the statement above?

2 Have you ever given such advice? What was the result of acting on such advice?

"Living off the praise of others is an erratic diet."

1 What does the statement above mean?

2 In what way is it an "erratic diet"?

"To this day whenever the sun shines and the moon reflects and the darkness is illuminated, the moon doesn't complain or get jealous. He does what he was intended to do all along; the moon beams."

1 What is the result of doing what you were created to do?

2 Do you know this feeling? Explain.

Wisdom from the Word

- Read 1 Corinthians 12:12–30. How could heeding the advice in this passage have saved the moon from a lot of grief? Is there a lesson here for you? If so, what is it?

- Read Romans 12:3–8. How could the advice given in verse 3 have spared the moon some pain? How does it fit in with the guidelines laid out in the rest of the passage?
- Read Isaiah 43:5–7. For what were we created, according to Isaiah? How do we "glorify" God? Are you doing so? Explain.

∞

CHAPTER 17 YOUR SACK OF STONES

Points to Ponder

"Could it be that you went to religion and didn't go to God? Could it be that you went to a church, but never saw Christ?"

1 Have you ever gone to "religion" instead of God? If so, what happened?

2 How is it possible to go to church but not see Christ? Do you see Christ when you go to church? Explain.

"Go to him. Be honest with him. Admit you have soul secrets you've never dealt with. He already knows what they are. He's just waiting for you to ask him to help. He's just waiting for you to give him your sack. Go ahead. You'll be glad you did."

1 How do you go to Jesus? Have you ever gone to him like this?

2 Ask yourself what things are in your sack. Have you brought these things to him? If not, why not?

Wisdom from the Word

- Read 2 Corinthians 7:5–13. What is the connection between sorrow and regret in this passage (see especially verse 10)? What does godly sorrow produce?
- Read Matthew 11:28–30. What does Jesus tell us to do in this passage? How do we do it? What is the result? Have you experienced such "rest"? Explain.

CHAPTER 18 OF OZ AND GOD

Points to Ponder

> "'The power you need is really a power you already have. Just look deep enough, long enough, and there's nothing you can't do.' Sound familiar? Sound patriotic? Sound . . . Christian?"

1 When was the last time you heard a statement similar to the one quoted above? Describe it.

2 Was there ever a time such statements sounded Christian to you? Explain.

> "Do-it-yourself Christianity is not much encouragement to the done-in and worn-out."

1 What does Max mean by "do-it-yourself Christianity"?

2 Why is such Christianity not much encouragement to the "done-in and worn-out"?

"The wizard says look inside yourself and find self. God says look inside yourself and find God. The first will get you to Kansas. The latter will get you to heaven. Take your pick."

1 How could Max's phrase "look inside yourself and find God" be misunderstood?

2 How do you think it should be understood?

Wisdom from the Word

- Read Matthew 19:17. What was Jesus' point in telling the young man this statement? What did He want him to understand? Did the young man "get it"? Explain.
- Read 1 Corinthians 6:9–11. What lie did Paul not want the Corinthians to believe? How had their lives radically changed? Who caused the change?
- Read Romans 1:17. Where does "righteousness" come from, according to this verse? What does faith have to do with it? How is this different from the wizard's message?

CHAPTER 19 AN INSIDE JOB

Points to Ponder

"You can't fix an inside problem by going outside."

1. What "inside problem" is Max talking about?
2. Why can't you fix it from the "outside"?

"Society may renovate, but only God re-creates."

1. Why can't society re-create?
2. Why doesn't God merely renovate?

"The next time alarms go off in your world, ask yourself three questions: (1) Is there any unconfessed sin in my life? (2) Are there any unresolved conflicts in my world? (3) Are there any unsurrendered worries in my heart?"

1. Ask yourself the questions Max lists above.
2. What answers do you come up with? What do you need to do, if anything?

Wisdom from the Word

- Read Psalm 32:1–5. How did David at first deal with his own sin? What happened? How did he then respond? What happened?
- Read Psalm 51:10. How is this a prayer for every believer in every age? Is this a part of your own prayer life? Explain.
- Read 1 Peter 5:7. What command is given? What reason is given for the command? How can we follow this command in a practical sense?

CHAPTER 20 LATE-NIGHT GOOD NEWS

Points to Ponder

"Does someone have a hand on the throttle of this train or has the engineer bailed out just as we come in sight of dead-man's curve?"

1 Have you ever asked yourself a question like the one above?

2 If so, what were the circumstances?

"The promise of the Messiah threads its way through forty-two generations of rough-cut stones, forming a necklace fit for the King who came. Just as promised."

1 Are you surprised at the ancestors in the Messiah's family tree? Why or why not?

2 Why is this genealogy "fit for the King who came"?

3 Why do you think God chose to record his family tree?

"The engineer has not abandoned the train. Nuclear war is no threat to God. Yo-yo economies don't intimidate the heavens. Immoral leaders have never derailed the plan. God keeps his promise."

1 How can a firm belief in the truth expressed above keep our heads above water?

2 What evidence in your own world do you see of its truth?

3 What biblical evidence can you cite?

Wisdom from the Word

- Read John 16:33. What promise does Jesus give us in this passage? What warning does He give? What does it mean to "take heart"? Why should we take heart?
- Read Daniel 4:34–35. What lesson did Nebuchadnezzar learn about God's control of the universe? How did this lesson affect him?
- Read Isaiah 43:11–13. What does God Himself say about His control of the universe? What phrase in this passage is most memorable for you? Why?

∞

CHAPTER 21 HEALTHY HABITS

Points to Ponder

"Pick a time in the not-too-distant past. A year or two ago. Now ask yourself a few questions. How does your prayer life today compare with then? How about your giving? Have both the amount and the joy increased? What about your church loyalty? Can they tell you've grown? And Bible study? Are you learning to learn?"

1 Ask yourself the questions Max lists above.

2 How are you doing in these areas?

"Growth is the goal of the Christian. Maturity is mandatory."

1 In what way is growth the goal of the Christian?

2 How is maturity mandatory?

"There they are: prayer, study, giving, fellowship. Four habits worth having. Isn't it good to know that some habits are good for you? Make them a part of your day and grow. Don't make the mistake of the little boy. Don't stay too close to where you got in. It's risky resting on the edge."

1 Evaluate yourself in your performance of each of the four habits Max lists.

2 Which are your strengths? Your weaknesses?

3 What can you do to improve?

Wisdom from the Word

- Read Colossians 1:9–12. What specific requests did Paul make for the Colossians? How can these requests help shape our own prayer life?
- Read 1 Peter 2:2–3. What command are we given here? What result is promised? What motivation is given?
- Read 2 Peter 3:18. What does it mean to grow in grace? What does it mean to grow in knowledge? How are the two related?

CHAPTER 22 DFW AND THE HOLY SPIRIT

Points to Ponder

"No matter how you travel, the trip can get tiring.

Wouldn't it be great to discover a people-mover for your heart?"

1 What does Max mean by a "people-mover for your heart"?

2 Would you want one? Explain.

"The next time you need to rest, go ahead. He'll keep you headed in the right direction. And the next time you make progress—thank him. He's the one providing the power. And the next time you want to give up? Don't. Please don't. Round the next corner. You may be surprised at what you find. Besides, you've got a flight home you don't want to miss."

1 How does the Holy Spirit accomplish each of the things Max lists above? Have you experienced these things in your own life? Explain.

2 What is this "flight home" Max writes about? How do you book reservations for it?

Wisdom from the Word

- Read Colossians 1:28–29. What was Paul's goal for his ministry? What did it take to accomplish this goal? Is this any different for us? Explain.
- Read Hebrews 10:32–36. How does the writer encourage his readers to not give up? What reasons does he give? What promise does he give? What warning does he give?

Points to Ponder

"If you don't know what to do, it's best just to sit tight till God does his thing."

1 What do you think of this advice?

2 Is this hard for you to act on? Explain.

"If some guy has you on the ground pounding on you and your father is within earshot and tells you to call him anytime you need help, what would you do? I'd call my father. That's all I do. When the battle is too great, I ask God to take over. I get the Father to fight for me."

1 How do we get the Father to fight for us in our day-to-day lives?

2 What does this mean? What can we expect?

"His job is to fight. Our job is to trust. Just trust. Not direct. Or question. Or yank the steering wheel out of his hands. Our job is to pray and wait. Nothing more is necessary. Nothing more is needed."

1 What does it mean for you personally to "trust"?

2 What is the relationship between acting in faith and waiting in prayer?

Wisdom from the Word

- Read Exodus 14. In what ways did Moses trust God in

this chapter? In what ways did God fight for him? What was the result?

- Read 2 Chronicles 20:1–30. In what ways did Jehoshaphat trust God in this passage? In what ways did God fight for him? What was the result? How do you respond to the king's statement in verse 12b?
- Read Psalm 115. What difficulties were the people facing at this time? How did they respond? What did God do? How can their example help us?

CHAPTER 24 THE GIFT OF UNHAPPINESS

Points to Ponder

"Unhappiness on earth cultivates a hunger for heaven. By gracing us with a deep dissatisfaction, God holds our attention. The only tragedy, then, is to be satisfied prematurely. To settle for earth. To be content in a strange land. To intermarry with the Babylonians and forget Jerusalem."

1. In what way can dissatisfaction be called an example of grace?
2. What does it mean to "intermarry with the Babylonians and forget Jerusalem"? Are you ever tempted to do this? Explain.

"You will never be completely happy on earth simply because you were not made for earth. Oh, you will have your moments of joy. You will catch glimpses of light. You will know moments or even days of peace. But they simply do not compare with the happiness that lies ahead."

1 Why does Max say we were not made for earth?

2 What would be the problem with becoming completely happy on earth?

"Lower your expectations of earth. This is not heaven, so don't expect it to be. There will never be a newscast with no bad news. There will never be a church with no gossip or competition. There will never be a new car, new wife, or new baby who can give you the joy your heart craves. Only God can."

1 How can we practically lower our expectations of earth?

2 Give several examples.

Wisdom from the Word

- Read Ecclesiastes 3:11. What does it mean to say that "he set eternity in the hearts of men"? How does this reveal itself?
- Read 1 Peter 2:11. How does an "alien" or a "stranger in the world" live differently than natives? How do sinful desires war against the soul? How does living like an alien help in this battle?
- Read 1 Corinthians 2:9–10. Why is this probably the best picture of heaven we can understand? Does this passage give you hope? Explain.

Points to Ponder

"Who wants heaven without God? Heaven is not heaven without God."

1 Why would heaven cease to be heaven without God?

2 Would you want to live in such a place? Explain.

"Contentment is a difficult virtue. Why? Because there is nothing on earth that can satisfy our deepest longing. We long to see God. The leaves of life are rustling with the rumor that we will—and we won't be satisfied until we do."

1 Do you agree with Max's explanation for why contentment is hard to achieve?

2 Are there any other reasons it may be hard to achieve? Explain.

"Upon seeing God, Isaiah was terrified. Why such fear? Why did he tremble so? Because he was wax before the sun. A candle in a hurricane. A minnow at Niagara. God's glory was too great. His purity too sterling. His power too mighty. The holiness of God illuminates the sinfulness of man."

1 Define God's holiness.

2 Why should it terrify Isaiah?

Wisdom from the Word

❦ Read Exodus 33:12–23. Would you have made Moses'

request recorded in verse 18? What does it mean that he could not see God's "face"? How does this relate to God's holiness?

- Read Isaiah 6:1–7; Hebrews 12:14; Revelation 1:12–18. How do people normally respond to God's unveiled holiness? Why is this so? What does this suggest about the way we should relate to God?
- Read Psalm 17:15. What will finally satisfy us, according to David? Why should this satisfy us?

CHAPTER 26 ORPHANS AT THE GATE

Points to Ponder

"Earth is not what we'd hoped. It may have its moments, but it is simply not what we think it should be. Something inside us groans for more."

1 In what ways is earth not what you'd hoped for?

2 Do you "groan" for something more? Explain.

"We are so eager we demand. We demand in this world what only the next world can give. No sickness. No suffering. No struggle. We stomp our feet and shake our fists, forgetting it is only in heaven that such peace is found."

1 Do you ever find yourself demanding what properly belongs to the next world?

2 If so, what causes this? What is the result?

Wisdom from the Word

- Read Romans 8:18–25. How does the hope of "redemption" make life easier in our "groaning"? How does this groaning display itself? What ultimate hope do we have?
- Read 2 Corinthians 5:1–10. For what purpose did God make us (vs. 4–5)? Where does living by faith come in (v. 7)? What is our goal in the meanwhile (v. 9)? What motivation is given (v. 10)?

CHAPTER 27 VIEW OF THE HIGH COUNTRY

Points to Ponder

"All of us need help sometimes. This journey gets steep. So steep that some of us give up."

1 Are you ever tempted to give up?

2 What circumstances prompt this urge?

"The human blood of the divine Christ covers our sins and proclaims a message: *We have been bought. We cannot be sold. Ever.*"

1 How does the statement above make you feel?

2 Explain why.

"Believe me when I say it will be worth it. No cost is too high. If you must pay a price, pay it! No sacrifice is too much. If you must leave baggage on the trail, leave it! No loss will compare. Whatever it takes, do it."

1 What price might you be asked to pay in your own life? What sacrifices might you have to make?

2 What "baggage" do you need to "leave on the trail"? What baggage can you help others leave?

Wisdom from the Word

- Read Hebrews 12:22–24. How is our future described in this passage? What picture do you get of it? Does this encourage you? If so, how? If not, why not?
- Read 1 Corinthians 6:19–20. To whom do you belong, according to this passage? How did this happen? How are we to respond?
- Read Romans 8:35–39. Are any possible enemies left off this list? How certain is our destiny? How is this destiny made certain? How does this make you feel? Why?

CHAPTER 28 THE NAME ONLY GOD KNOWS

Points to Ponder

"Isn't it incredible to think that God has saved a name just for you? One you don't even know? We've always assumed that the name we got is the name we will keep. Apparently your future is so promising that it warrants a new title. Your eternity is so special, no common name will do."

1 Have you ever had a "secret name"? Have you ever given

anyone else one? If so, what was the purpose of these names? How did they make the recipient feel?

2 If you were to be given a "secret name" based on a character trait, what trait would you most want to be known for?

"There is more to your life than you ever thought. There is more to your story than what you have read. There is more to your song than what you have sung. A good author saves the best for last. A great composer keeps his finest for the finish. And God, the author of life and composer of hope, has done the same for you."

1 Is it easy for you to believe that "there is more to your life than you ever thought"? Explain.

2 What are you most looking forward in the world to come? Describe it.

Wisdom from the Word

- Read Isaiah 56:3–5. What problems did God address in these verses? What were the people tempted to think? Have you ever thought this way? If so, explain. What does God promise in verse 5?
- Read Revelation 2:17. What does it mean to be an "overcomer"? What is promised such a person? Do you hope to be such a person? Explain.
- Read Zephaniah 3:17. What role does God play in this verse? What is the mood of this verse? Does this verse give you something to look forward to? Does it encourage you? Explain.

JOHN

INTRODUCTION

He's an old man, this one who sits on the stool and leans against the wall. Eyes closed and face soft, were it not for his hand stroking his beard, you'd think he was asleep.

Some in the room assume he is. He does this often during worship. As the people sing, his eyes will close and his chin will fall until it rests on his chest, and there he will remain motionless. Silent.

Those who know him well know better. They know he is not resting. He is traveling. Atop the music he journeys back, back, back until he is young again. Strong again. There again. There on the seashore with James and the apostles. There on the trail with the disciples and the women. There in the Temple with Caiaphas and the accusers.

It's been sixty years, but John sees him still. The decades took John's strength, but they didn't take his memory. The years dulled his sight, but they didn't dull his vision. The seasons may have wrinkled his face, but they didn't soften his love.

He had been with God. God had been with him. How could he forget?

❁ The wine that moments before had been water—John could still taste it.

❁ The mud placed on the eyes of the blind man in Jerusalem—John could still remember it.

❁ The aroma of Mary's perfume as it filled the room—John could still smell it.

And the voice. Oh, the voice. His voice. John could still hear it.

I am the light of the world, it rang . . . I am the door . . . I am the way, the truth, the life.

I will come back, it promised, and take you to be with me.

Those who believe in me, it assured, will have life even if they die.

John could hear him. John could see him. Scenes branded on his heart. Words seared into his soul. John would never forget. How could he? He had been there.

He opens his eyes and blinks. The singing has stopped. The teaching has begun. John looks at the listeners and listens to the teacher.

If only you could have been there, he thinks.

But he wasn't. Most weren't. Most weren't even born. And most who were there are dead. Peter is. So is James. Nathanael, Martha, Philip. They are all gone. Even Paul, the apostle who came late, is dead.

Only John remains.

He looks again at the church. Small but earnest. They lean forward to hear the teacher. John listens to him. What a task. Speaking of one he never saw. Explaining words he never heard. John is there if the teacher needs him.

But what will happen when John is gone? What will the teacher do then? When John's voice is silent and his tongue stilled? Who will tell them how Jesus silenced the waves? Will they hear how he fed the thousands? Will they remember how he prayed for unity?

How will they know? If only they could have been there.

Suddenly, in his heart he knows what to do.

Later, under the light of a sunlit shaft, the old fisherman unfolds the scroll and begins to write the story of his life . . .

In the beginning there was the Word . . .

LIFE LESSON

John 1:1-51

SITUATION The Greeks and the Jews were familiar with the concept of the *word*. For the Jews it was an expression of God's wisdom, and for the Greeks it meant reason and intellect.

OBSERVATION Leaving his heavenly home, Jesus put on human flesh to bring us God's Good News.

INSPIRATION It all happened in a moment, a most remarkable moment. . . . that was like none other. For through that segment of time a spectacular thing occurred. God became a man. While the creatures of earth walked unaware, Divinity arrived. Heaven opened herself and placed her most precious one in a human womb. . . .

God as a fetus. Holiness sleeping in a womb. The creator of life being created.

God was given eyebrows, elbows, two kidneys, and a spleen. He stretched against the walls and floated in the amniotic fluids of his mother.

God had come near. . . .

The hands that first held him were unmanicured, calloused, and dirty.

No silk. No ivory. No hype. No party. No hoopla.

Were it not for the shepherds, there would have been no reception. And were it not for a group of star-gazers, there would have been no gifts. . . .

Christ Comes to the World

In the beginning there was the Word.[n] The Word was with God, and
the Word was God. [2]He was with God in the beginning. [3]All
things were made by him, and nothing was made without him.
[4]In him there was life, and that life was the light of all people. [5]The
Light shines in the darkness, and the darkness has not overpowered it.
[6]There was a man named John[n] who was sent by God. [7]He came to tell
people the truth about the Light so that through him all people could hear
about the Light and believe. [8]John was not the Light, but he came to tell
people the truth about the Light. [9]The true Light that gives light to all was
coming into the world!
[10]The Word was in the world, and the world was made by him, but the
world did not know him. [11]He came to the world that was his own, but his
own people did not accept him. [12]But to all who did accept him and believe
in him he gave the right to become children of God. [13]They did not become
his children in any human way—by any human parents or human desire.
They were born of God.
[14]The Word became a human and lived among us. We saw his glory
the glory that belongs to the only Son of the Father—and he was full of
grace and truth. [15]John tells the truth about him and cries out, saying,
"This is the One I told you about: 'The One who comes after me is greater
than I am, because he was living before me.' "
[16]Because he was full of grace and truth, from him we all received one gift
after another. [17]The law was given through Moses, but grace and truth
came through Jesus Christ. [18]No one has ever seen God. But God the only
Son is very close to the Father,[n] and he has shown us what God is like.

John Tells People About Jesus

[19]Here is the truth John[n] told when the Jews in Jerusalem sent priests
and Levites to ask him, "Who are you?"
[20]John spoke freely and did not refuse to answer. He said, "I am not the
Christ."
[21]So they asked him, "Then who are you? Are you Elijah?"[n]
He answered, "No, I am not."
"Are you the Prophet?"[n] they asked.
He answered, "No."
[22]Then they said, "Who are you? Give us an answer to tell those who sent
us. What do you say about yourself?"
[23]John told them in the words of the prophet Isaiah:

"I am the voice of one
    calling out in the desert:
'Make the road straight for the Lord.' " *Isaiah 40:3*

Word The Greek word is "logos," meaning any kind of communication; it could be translated "message." Here, it means Christ, because Christ was the way God told people about himself.

John John the Baptist, who preached to people about Christ's coming (Matthew 3, Luke 3).

But . . . Father This could be translated, "But the only God is very close to the Father." Also, some Greek copies say, "But the only Son is very close to the Father."

John John the Baptist, who preached to people about Christ's coming (Matthew 3, Luke 3).

Elijah A man who spoke for God. He lived hundreds of years before Christ and was expected to return before Christ (Malachi 4:5-6).

Prophet They probably meant the prophet that God told Moses he would send (Deuteronomy 18:15-19).

24 Some Pharisees who had been sent asked John: 25 "If you are not the
Christ or Elijah or the Prophet, why do you baptize people?"
26 John answered, "I baptize with water, but there is one here with you
that you don't know about. 27 He is the One who comes after me. I am not
good enough to untie the strings of his sandals."
28 This all happened at Bethany on the other side of the Jordan River,
where John was baptizing people.
29 The next day John saw Jesus coming toward him. John said, "Look, the
Lamb of God,[n] who takes away the sin of the world! 30 This is the One I was
talking about when I said, 'A man will come after me, but he is greater than
I am, because he was living before me.' 31 Even I did not know who he was,
although I came baptizing with water so that the people of Israel would
know who he is."
32-33 Then John said, "I saw the Spirit come down from heaven in the
form of a dove and rest on him. Until then I did not know who the Christ
was. But the God who sent me to baptize with water told me, 'You will see
the Spirit come down and rest on a man; he is the One who will baptize
with the Holy Spirit.' 34 I have seen this happen, and I tell you the truth: This
man is the Son of God."

The First Followers of Jesus

35 The next day John[n] was there again with two of his followers. 36 When
he saw Jesus walking by, he said, "Look, the Lamb of God!"[n]
37 The two followers heard John say this, so they followed Jesus. 38 When
Jesus turned and saw them following him, he asked, "What are you looking for?"
They said, "Rabbi, where are you staying?" ("Rabbi" means "Teacher.")
39 He answered, "Come and see." So the two men went with Jesus and saw
where he was staying and stayed there with him that day. It was about four
o'clock in the afternoon.
40 One of the two men who followed Jesus after they heard John speak
about him was Andrew, Simon Peter's brother. 41 The first thing Andrew did
was to find his brother Simon and say to him, "We have found the
Messiah." ("Messiah" means "Christ.")
42 Then Andrew took Simon to Jesus. Jesus looked at him and said, "You
are Simon son of John. You will be called Cephas." ("Cephas" means
"Peter."[n])
43 The next day Jesus decided to go to Galilee. He found Philip and said
to him, "Follow me."
44 Philip was from the town of Bethsaida, where Andrew and Peter lived.
45 Philip found Nathanael and told him, "We have found the man that
Moses wrote about in the law, and the prophets also wrote about him. He
is Jesus, the son of Joseph, from Nazareth."
46 But Nathanael said to Philip, "Can anything good come from
Nazareth?"
Philip answered, "Come and see."
47 As Jesus saw Nathanael coming toward him, he said, "Here is truly an
Israelite. There is nothing false in him."

For thirty-three years he would feel everything you and I have ever felt. He felt weak. He grew weary. He was afraid of failure. He was susceptible to wooing women. He got colds, burped, and had body odor. His feelings got hurt. His feet got tired. And his head ached.

To think of Jesus in such a light is—well, it seems almost irreverent, doesn't it? It's not something we like to do; it's uncomfortable. It is much easier to keep the humanity out of the incarnation. He's easier to stomach that way. . . .

But don't do it. For heaven's sake, don't. Let him be as human as he intended to be. Let him into the mire and muck of our world. For only if we let him in can he pull us out.

(From *God Came Near* by Max Lucado)

APPLICATION If people want to know what God is like, they can look at Jesus. If they want to know what Jesus is like, they should be able to look at his followers. Can people see Christ in you?

EXPLORATION The Word is Born—John 14:6-7; 1 Corinthians 8:5-6; Galatians 4:4; Philippians 2:7, 8; 1 Timothy 3:16; Hebrews 2:14; 13:8; 1 John 1:1-2; 4:2.

Lamb of God Name for Jesus. Jesus is like the lambs that were offered for a sacrifice to God.
Peter The Greek name "Peter," like the Aramaic name "Cephas," means "rock."

In the Grip of Grace

MAX LUCADO

In the Grip of Grace

THOMAS NELSON
Since 1798

NASHVILLE DALLAS MEXICO CITY RIO DE JANEIRO BEIJING

Dedicated to my editor,
Liz Heaney,
in celebration of ten years
of words and wonder.

Contents

Acknowledgments

Let me say a word of thanks to:

Karen Hill: My assistant and friend, what a gift you are.

Steve and Cheryl Green and the UpWords staff: Thanks for being so faithful.

Charles Prince: Our resident statesman and scholar. We treasure your input.

Charles Swindoll: Your words posted at the intersection kept me on the higher trail.

The elders, staff, and members of the Oak Hills Church of Christ: There is no church I'd rather serve.

Steve Halliday: Thanks for another excellent discussion guide.

Nancy Norris: A special salute to you for the *many* Lucado pages you've endured and improved through the years. I'm grateful.

Sue Ann Jones: May your red ink flow! Thanks for your careful editing.

My pals at Word Publishing: You've done it again! Great job.

Dr. John Stott and his insightful book *Romans: God's Good News for the World*. Your scholarship was invaluable to me as I wrote this book.

Jenna, Andrea, and Sara: I feel sorry for every dad who doesn't have you as his daughters.

And to my wife, Denalyn: Next to God's grace you're the best thing that ever happened to me.

And to you, the reader: I've prayed for you. Long before you held this book, I asked God to prepare your heart. May I ask that you pray for me? Would you offer the prayer of Colossians 4:4 on my behalf? Thank you. I'm honored that you would read these pages.

May God secure you firmly in the grip of his grace.

Introduction

My only qualification for writing a book on grace is the clothing I wear. Let me explain.

For years I owned an elegant suit complete with coat, trousers, even a hat. I considered myself quite dapper in the outfit and was confident others agreed.

The pants were cut from the cloth of my good works, sturdy fabric of deeds done and projects completed. Some studies here, some sermons there. Many people complimented my trousers, and I confess, I tended to hitch them up in public so people would notice them.

The coat was equally impressive. It was woven together from my convictions. Each day I dressed myself in deep feelings of religious fervor. My emotions were quite strong.

So strong, in fact, that I was often asked to model my cloak of zeal in public gatherings to inspire others. Of course I was happy to comply.

While there I'd also display my hat, a feathered cap of knowledge. Formed with my own hands from the fabric of personal opinion, I wore it proudly.

Surely God is impressed with my garments, I often thought. Occasionally I strutted into his presence so he could compliment the self-tailored wear. He never spoke. *His silence must mean admiration*, I convinced myself.

But then my wardrobe began to suffer. The fabric of my trousers grew thin. My best works started coming unstitched. I began leaving more undone than done, and what little I did was nothing to boast about.

No problem, I thought. *I'll work harder*.

But working harder *was* a problem. There was a hole in my coat of convictions. My resolve was threadbare. A cold wind cut into my chest. I reached up to pull my hat down firmly, and the brim ripped off in my hands.

Over a period of a few months, my wardrobe of self-righteousness completely unraveled. I went from tailored gentlemen's apparel to beggars' rags. Fearful that God might be angry at my tattered suit, I did my best to stitch it together and cover my mistakes. But the cloth was so worn. And the wind was so icy. I gave up. I went back to God. (Where else could I go?)

On a wintry Thursday afternoon, I stepped into his presence, not for applause, but for warmth. My prayer was feeble.

"I feel naked."

"You are. And you have been for a long time."

What he did next I'll never forget. "I have something to give you," he said. He gently removed the remaining threads and then picked up a robe, a regal robe, the clothing of his own goodness.

He wrapped it around my shoulders. His words to me were tender. "*My son, you are now clothed with Christ*" (see Gal. 3:27).

Though I'd sung the hymn a thousand times, I finally understood it:

Dressed in his righteousness alone,
faultless to stand before the throne.[1]

I have a hunch that some of you know what I'm talking about. You're wearing a handmade wardrobe yourself. You've sewn your garments, and you're sporting your religious deeds . . . and, already, you've noticed a tear in the fabric. Before you start stitching yourself together, I'd like to share some thoughts with you on the greatest discovery of my life: the grace of God.

My strategy is for us to spend some time walking the mountains of Paul's letter to the Romans. An epistle for the self-sufficient, Romans contrasts the plight of people who choose to dress in self-made garments with those who gladly accept the robes of grace. Romans is the grandest treatise on grace ever written. You'll find the air fresh and the view clear.

Martin Luther called Romans "the chief part of the New Testament and . . . truly the purest gospel."[2] God used the book to change the lives (and the wardrobes) of Luther, John Wesley, John Calvin, William Tyndale, Saint Augustine, and millions of others.

There is every reason to think he'll do the same for you.

MAX LUCADO
MEMORIAL DAY, 1996

1 The Parable of the River

Romans 1:21–32

Once there were five sons who lived in a mountain castle with their father. The eldest was an obedient son, but his four younger brothers were rebellious. Their father had warned them of the river, but they had not listened. He had begged them to stay clear of the bank lest they be swept downstream, but the river's lure was too strong.

Each day the four rebellious brothers ventured closer and closer until one son dared to reach in and feel the waters. "Hold my hand so I won't fall in," he said, and his brothers did. But when he touched the water, the current yanked him and the other three into the rapids and rolled them down the river.

Over rocks they bounced, through the

channels they roared, on the swells they rode. Their cries for help were lost in the rage of the river. Though they fought to gain their balance, they were powerless against the strength of the current. After hours of struggle, they surrendered to the pull of the river. The waters finally dumped them on the bank in a strange land, in a distant country, in a barren place.

Savage people dwelt in the land. It was not safe like their home.

Cold winds chilled the land. It was not warm like their home.

Rugged mountains marked the land. It was not inviting like their home.

Though they did not know where they were, of one fact they were sure: They were not intended for this place. For a long time the four young sons lay on the bank, stunned at their fall and not knowing where to turn. After some time they gathered their courage and reentered the waters, hoping to walk upstream. But the current was too strong. They attempted to walk along the river's edge, but the terrain was too steep. They considered climbing the mountains, but the peaks were too high. Besides, they didn't know the way.

Finally, they built a fire and sat down. "We shouldn't have disobeyed our father," they admitted. "We are a long way from home."

With the passage of time the sons learned to survive in the strange land. They found nuts for food and killed animals for skins. They determined not to forget their homeland nor abandon hopes of returning. Each day they set about the task of finding food and building shelter. Each evening they built a fire and told stories of their father and older brother. All four sons longed to see them again.

Then, one night, one brother failed to come to the fire. The others found him the next morning in the valley with the savages. He was building a hut of grass and mud. "I've grown tired of our talks," he told them. "What good does it do to remember? Besides, this land isn't so bad. I will build a great house and settle here."

"But it isn't home," they objected.

"No, but it is if you don't think of the real one."

"But what of Father?"

"What of him? He isn't here. He isn't near. Am I to spend forever awaiting his arrival? I'm making new friends; I'm learning new ways. If he comes, he comes, but I'm not holding my breath."

And so the other three left their hut-building brother and walked away. They continued to meet around the fire, speaking of home and dreaming of their return.

Some days later a second brother failed to appear at the campfire. The next morning his siblings found him on a hillside staring at the hut of his brother.

"How disgusting," he told them as they approached. "Our brother is an utter failure. An insult to our family name. Can you imagine a more despicable deed? Building a hut and forgetting our father?"

"What he's doing is wrong," agreed the youngest, "but what we did was wrong as well. We disobeyed. We touched the river. We ignored our father's warnings."

"Well, we may have made a mistake or two, but compared to the sleaze in the hut, we are saints. Father will dismiss our sin and punish him."

"Come," urged his two brothers, "return to the fire with us."

"No, I think I'll keep an eye on our brother. Someone needs to keep a record of his wrongs to show Father."

And so the two returned, leaving one brother building and the other judging.

The remaining two sons stayed near the fire, encouraging each other and speaking of home. Then one morning the youngest son awoke to find he was alone. He searched for his brother and found him near the river, stacking rocks.

"It's no use," the rock-stacking brother explained as he worked.

"Father won't come for me. I must go to him. I offended him. I insulted him. I failed him. There is only one option. I will build a path back up the river and walk into our father's presence. Rock upon rock I will stack until I have enough rocks to travel upstream to the castle. When he sees how hard I have worked and how diligent I have been, he will have no choice but to open the door and let me into his house."

The last brother did not know what to say. He returned to sit by the fire, alone. One morning he heard a familiar voice behind him. "Father has sent me to bring you home."

The youngest lifted his eyes to see the face of his oldest brother. "You have come for us!" he shouted. For a long time the two embraced.

"And your brothers?" the eldest finally asked.

"One has made a home here. Another is watching him. The third is building a path up the river."

And so Firstborn set out to find his siblings. He went first to the thatched hut in the valley.

"Go away, stranger!" screamed the brother through the window. "You are not welcome here!"

"I have come to take you home."

"You have not. You have come to take my mansion."

"This is no mansion," Firstborn countered. "This is a hut."

"It is a mansion! The finest in the lowlands. I built it with my own hands. Now, go away. You cannot have my mansion."

"Don't you remember the house of your father?"

"I have no father."

"You were born in a castle in a distant land where the air is warm and the fruit is plentiful. You disobeyed your father and ended up in this strange land. I have come to take you home."

The brother peered through the window at Firstborn as if recognizing a face he'd remembered from a dream. But the pause was brief, for suddenly the savages in the house filled the window as well. "Go away, intruder!" they demanded. "This is not your home."

"You are right," responded the firstborn son, "but neither is it his."

The eyes of the two brothers met again. Once more the hut-building brother felt a tug at his heart, but the savages had won his trust. "He just wants your mansion," they cried. "Send him away!"

And so he did.

Firstborn sought the next brother. He didn't have to walk far. On the hillside near the hut, within eyesight of the savages, sat the fault-finding son. When he saw Firstborn approaching, he shouted, "How good that you are here to behold the sin of our brother! Are you aware that he turned his back on the castle? Are you aware that he never speaks of home? I knew you would come. I have kept careful account of his deeds. Punish him! I will applaud your anger. He deserves it! Deal with the sins of our brother."

Firstborn spoke softly, "We need to deal with your sins first."

"My sins?"

"Yes, you disobeyed Father."

The son smirked and slapped at the air. "My sins are nothing. *There* is the sinner," he claimed, pointing to the hut. "Let me tell you of the savages who stay there . . ."

"I'd rather you tell me about yourself."

"Don't worry about me. Let me show you who needs help," he said, running toward the hut. "Come, we'll peek in the windows. He never sees me. Let's go together." The son was at the hut before he noticed that Firstborn hadn't followed him.

Next, the eldest son walked to the river. There he found the last brother, knee-deep in the water, stacking rocks.

"Father has sent me to take you home."

The brother never looked up. "I can't talk now. I must work."

"Father knows you have fallen. But he will forgive you . . ."

"He may," the brother interrupted, struggling to keep his balance against the current, "but I have to get to the castle first. I must build a pathway up the river. First I will show him that I am worthy. Then I will ask for his mercy."

"He has already given his mercy. I will carry you up the river. You will never be able to build a pathway. The river is too long. The task is too great for your hands. Father sent me to carry you home. I am stronger."

For the first time the rock-stacking brother looked up. "How dare you speak with such irreverence! My father will not simply forgive. I have sinned. I have sinned greatly! He told us to avoid the river, and we disobeyed. I am a great sinner. I need much work."

"No, my brother, you don't need much work. You need much grace. The distance between you and our father's house is too great. You haven't enough strength nor the stones to build the road. That is why our father sent me. He wants me to carry you home."

"Are you saying I can't do it? Are you saying I'm not strong enough? Look at my work. Look at my rocks. Already I can walk five steps!"

"But you have five million to go!"

The younger brother looked at Firstborn with anger. "I know who you are. You are the voice of evil. You are trying to seduce me from my holy work. Get behind me, you serpent!" He hurled at Firstborn the rock he was about to place in the river.

"Heretic!" screamed the path-builder. "Leave this land. You can't stop me! I will build this walkway and stand before my father, and he will have to forgive me. I will win his favor. I will earn his mercy."

Firstborn shook his head. "Favor won is no favor. Mercy earned is no mercy. I implore you, let me carry you up the river."

The response was another rock. So Firstborn turned and left.

The youngest brother was waiting near the fire when Firstborn returned.

"The others didn't come?"

"No. One chose to indulge, the other to judge, and the third to work. None of them chose our father."

"So they will remain here?"

The eldest brother nodded slowly. "For now."

"And we will return to Father?" asked the brother.

"Yes."

"Will he forgive me?"

"Would he have sent me if he wouldn't?"

And so the younger brother climbed on the back of the Firstborn and began the journey home.

* * *

All four brothers heard the same invitation. Each had an opportunity to be carried home by the elder brother. The first said no, choosing a grass hut over his father's house. The second said no, preferring to analyze the mistakes of his brother rather than admit his own. The third said no, thinking it wiser to make a good impression than an honest confession. And the fourth said yes, choosing gratitude over guilt.

"I'll indulge myself," resolves one son.

"I'll compare myself," opts another.

"I'll save myself," determines the third.

"I'll entrust myself to you," decides the fourth.

May I ask a vital question? As you read of the brothers, which describes your relationship to God? Have you, like the fourth son, recognized your helplessness to make the journey home alone? Do you take the extended hand of your Father? Are you caught in the grip of his grace?

Or are you like one of the other three sons?

MAPPING THE PARABLE

	The Hut-Building Hedonist Romans 1:18–32	The Fault-Finding Judgmentalist Romans 2:1–11
Strategy	indulge myself	compare myself
Goal	satisfy my passions	monitor my neighbor
Description	fun-lover	finger-pointer
Personality	laid back	stuck-up
Self-analysis	I may be bad, but so what?	I may be bad, but I'm better than . . .
Theology	disregard God	distract God
Bumper sticker	"Life is short. Play hard."	"God's watching you and so am I."
Complaint	I can't play enough.	I can't see enough.
Favorite animal	tomcat	watchdog
Spends time looking	over the menu at the options	over the fence at the neighbor
View of grace	Who, me?	Yes, you!
View of sin	No one is guilty.	He is guilty.
Work ethic	What I do is my business.	What you do is my business.
Favorite phrase	Live it up!	Straighten up!
Boundaries	If it feels good, do it.	If he feels good, note it.
Condition	bored	bitter
Paul's pronouncements	You have no excuse for the things you do.	You have no authority for the judgments you make.
Key verse	"God left them and let them go their sinful way." (1:24)	"If you think you can judge others, you are wrong. When you judge them, you are really yourself guilty because you do the same things they do." (2:1)

MAPPING THE PARABLE

The Rock-Stacking Legalist Romans 2:17–3:20	The Grace-Driven Christian Romans 3:21–25
save myself	entrust myself to Christ
measure my merits	know my father
burden-bearer	God-lover
stressed-out	peaceful
I may be bad, but if I work harder . . .	I may be bad, but I'm forgiven.
reimburse God	seek God
"I owe, I owe, it's off to work I go."	"I'm not perfect, but I'm forgiven."
I can't work enough.	I can't thank Him enough.
beaver	eagle
over the list of requirements	over the abundance of God's blessings
Not me!	Yes, me.
I'm always guilty.	I was guilty.
What God demands is my business.	What God does is my business.
Get to work!	Thank you!
If it feels good, stop it.	If it feels good, examine it.
weary	grateful
You have no solution for the problem you have.	You have no reason to fear.
". . . people cannot do any work that will make them right with God." (4:5)	". . . those who are right with God will live by trusting him." (1:17)

A hedonist. A judgmentalist. A legalist. All occupied with self to the exclusion of their father. Paul addresses these three in the first three chapters of Romans. Let's look at each one.

The Hut-Building Hedonist
Romans 1:21–32

Can you relate to the hut-builder? He traded his passion for the castle for a love of the lowland. Rather than long for home, he settled for a hut. The aim of his life is pleasure. Such is the definition of hedonism, and such is the practice of this son.

The hedonist navigates his life as if there is no father in his past, present, or future. There may have been, somewhere in the somewhat distant past, a once-upon-a-time father, but as far as the here and now? The son will live without him. There may be, in the faraway future, a father who comes and claims him, but as for today? The son will forge out his life on his own. Rather than seize the future, he's content to seize the day.

Paul had such a person in mind when he said, "They traded the glory of God who lives forever for the worship of idols made to look like earthly people, birds, animals, and snakes. . . . They worshiped and served what had been created instead of the God who created these things" (Rom. 1:23, 25). Hedonists make poor swaps; they trade mansions for huts and their brother for a stranger. They exchange their father's house for a hillside ghetto and send his son away.

The Fault-Finding Judgmentalist
Romans 2:1–11

The approach of the second brother was simple: "Why deal with my mistakes when I can focus on the mistakes of others?"

He is a judgmentalist. *I may be bad, but as long as I can find someone worse, I am safe.* He fuels his goodness with the failures of others. He is the self-appointed teacher's pet in elementary school. He tattles on the sloppy work of others, oblivious to the F on his own paper. He's the neighborhood watchdog, passing out citations for people to clean up their act, never noticing the garbage on his own front lawn.

"Come on God, let me show you the evil deeds of my neighbor," the moralist invites. But God won't follow him into the valley. "If you think you can judge others, you are wrong. When you judge them, you are really judging yourself guilty, because you do the same things they do" (Rom. 2:1). It's a shallow ploy, and God won't fall for it.

The Rock-Stacking Legalist
Romans 2:17–3:20

And then there is the brother in the river. Ahhh, now here is a son we respect. Hard-working. Industrious. Zealous. Intense. Here is a fellow who sees his sin and sets out to resolve it by himself. Surely he is worthy of our applause. Surely he is worthy of our emulation. And, most surely, he is worthy of the father's mercy. Won't the father throw open the castle doors when he sees how hard the son has worked to get home?

With no help from the father, the legalist is tackling the odds and fording the river of failure. Surely, the father will be happy to see him. That is, if the father ever does.

You see, the problem is not the affection of the father but the strength of the river. What sucked the son away from his father's house was no gentle stream but rather a roaring torrent. Is the son strong enough to build an upriver path to the father's house?

Doubtful. We certainly can't. "There is no one who always does what is right, not even one" (Rom. 3:10). Oh, but we try. We don't stack rocks in a river, but we do good deeds on earth.

We think: *If I do this God will accept me.*

If I teach this class . . . and we pick up a rock.

If I go to church . . . and we put the rock in the stream.

If I give this money . . . another rock.

If I endure a Lucado book . . . ten big rocks.

If I read my Bible, have the right opinion on the right doctrine, if I join this movement . . . rock upon rock upon rock.

The problem? You may take five steps, but you have five million to go. The river is too long. What separates us from God is not a shallow stream but a tumbling, cascading, overwhelming river of sin. We stack and stack and stack only to find we can barely keep our footing, much less make progress.

The impact on the rock-stackers is remarkably predictable: either despair or arrogance. They either give up or become stuck-up. They think they'll never make it, or they think they are the only ones who'll ever make it. Strange, how two people can look at the same stacked rocks and one hang his head and the other puff out his chest.

Call the condition a *religious* godlessness. It's the theme behind Paul's brazen pronouncement: "We're sinners, every one of us, in the same sinking boat with everyone else" (3:19 MSG).

Godless or Godly?

Quite a trio, don't you think?

The first on a barstool.

The second in the judge's chair.

The third on the church pew.

Though they may appear different, they are very much alike. All are separated from the Father. And none is asking for help. The first indulges his passions, the second monitors his neighbor, and the third measures his merits. Self-satisfaction. Self-justification. Self-salvation. The operative word is *self*. Self-sufficient. "They never give God the time of day" (3:18 MSG).

Paul's word for this is *godlessness* (Rom. 1:18 NIV). *Godlessness*. The word defines itself. A life minus God. Worse than a disdain for God, this is a disregard for God. A disdain at least acknowledges his presence. Godlessness doesn't. Whereas disdain will lead people to act with irreverence, disregard causes them to act as if God were irrelevant, as if he is not a factor in the journey.

How does God respond to godless living? Not flippantly. "The wrath of God is being revealed from heaven against all godlessness and wickedness" (Rom. 1:18 NIV). Paul's main point is not a light one. God is justly angered over the actions of his children.

I might as well prepare you: The first chapters of Romans are not exactly upbeat. Paul gives us the bad news before he gives the good news. He will eventually tell us that we are all equal candidates for grace but not before he proves that we are all desperately sinful. We have to see the mess we are in before we can appreciate the God we have. Before presenting the grace of God, we must understand the wrath of God.

And since that is where Paul begins, that is where we will begin.

PART ONE

WHAT A MESS!

The loss of mystery has led to the loss of majesty.

The more we know, the less we believe.

No wonder there is no wonder.

We think we've figured it all out.

Strange, don't you think?

Knowledge of the workings shouldn't negate wonder.

Knowledge should stir wonder.

Who has more reason to worship than the

astronomer who has seen the stars?

Than the surgeon who has held a heart?

Than the oceanographer who has pondered the depths?

2 God's Gracious Anger

Romans 1:18–20

God's anger is shown from heaven against all the evil and wrong things people do. By their own evil lives they hide the truth. God shows his anger because some knowledge of him has been made clear to them. Yes, God has shown himself to them. ROMANS 1:18–19

"And you discovered that your boyfriend had been sleeping with your mother?" The audience snickered. The teenage girl on the stage ducked her head at the burst of attention.

The mother was a middle-aged woman in a too-tight black dress, sitting with her arm entwined with the skinny one of a boy in a sleeveless T-shirt. She waved to the crowd. He grinned.

Talk-show host Christy Adams wasted no time. "Do the two of you really sleep together?"

The mother, still holding the hand of the boy, looked at him. He grinned, and she smiled. "Yes."

She went on to explain how she'd been

lonely since her divorce. Her daughter's boyfriend hung out at her house all hours of the day and night and, well, one afternoon he plopped beside her on the couch and the two started talking and one thing led to another and the next thing she knew they were . . . Her face flushed, and the boy shrugged as they let the audience complete the sentence.

The girl sat expressionless and silent.

"Aren't you worried what this might teach your daughter?" Christy inquired.

"I'm only teaching her the ways of the world."

"What about you?" Christy asked the boy. "Aren't you being unfaithful to your girlfriend?"

The boy looked honestly amazed. "I still love her," he announced. "I'm only helping her by loving her mother. We are one happy family. There's nothing wrong with that!"

The audience erupted with whistles and applause. Just as the hubbub began to subside, Christy told the lovers, "Not everyone would agree with you. I've invited a guest to react to your lifestyle." With that, the crowd got quiet, anxious to see who Christy had recruited to spice up the dialogue.

"He's the world's most famous theologian. His writings have long been followed by some and debated by others. Making his first appearance on the Christy Adams Show, please welcome controversial theologian, scholar, and author, the apostle Paul!"

Polite applause welcomed a short, balding man with glasses and a tweed jacket. He loosened his tie a bit as he settled his small frame in the stage chair. Christy skipped the welcome. "You have trouble with what these people are doing?"

Paul held his hands in his lap, looked over at the trio, and then back at Christy. "It's not how I feel that matters. It's how God feels."

Christy paused so the TV audience could hear the "ooohs" ripple through the studio.

"Then tell us, please Paul, how does God feel about this creative tryst?"

"It angers him."

"And why?"

"Evil angers God because evil destroys his children. What these people are doing is evil."

The strong words triggered a few hoots, some scattered applause, and an outburst of raised hands. Before Christy could speak, Paul continued. "As a result God has left them and let them go their sinful way. Their thinking is dark, their acts are evil, and God is disgusted."

A lanky fellow in the front shouted out his objection. "It's her body. She can do what she wants!"

"Oh, but that's where you are mistaken. Her body belongs to God and is to be used for him."

"What we're doing is harmless," objected the mother.

"Look at your daughter," Paul urged her, gesturing toward the girl whose eyes were full of tears. "Don't you see you have harmed her? You traded healthy love for lust. You traded the love of God for the love of the flesh. You traded truth for lie. And you traded the natural for the unnatural . . ."

Christy could restrain herself no longer. "Do you know how hokey you sound? All this talk about God and right and wrong and immorality? Don't you feel out of touch with reality?"

"Out of touch? No. Out of place, yes. But out of touch, hardly. God does not sit silently while his children indulge in perversion. He lets us go our sinful way and reap the consequences. Every broken heart, every unwanted child, every war and tragedy can be traced back to our rebellion against God."

People sprang to their feet, the mother put her finger in Paul's face, and Christy turned to the camera, delighting in the pandemonium. "We've got to take a break," she shouted over the noise.

"Don't go away; we've got some more questions for our friend the apostle."

God Hates Evil

How does the above dialogue strike you? Harsh? (Paul was too narrow.) Unreal? (The scene was too bizarre.) Outlandish? (No one would accept such convictions.)

Regardless of your response, it is important to note that though the script is fictional, Paul's words are not.

God is "against all the evil and wrong things that people do" (Rom. 1:18). The One who urges us to "hate what is evil" (Rom. 12:9) hates what is evil.

In three chilling verses Paul states:

> "God left them and let them go . . ." (Rom. 1:24).
> "God left them and let them do . . . " (Rom. 1:26).
> "God left them and allowed them to have their own worthless thinking . . ." (Rom. 1:28).

God is angry at evil.

For many, this is a revelation. Some assume God is a harried high-school principal, too busy monitoring the planets to notice us.

He's not.

Others assume he is a doting parent, blind to the evil of his children.

Wrong.

Still others insist he loves us so much he cannot be angry at our evil.

They don't understand that love is *always* angry at evil.

God Has Every Right to Be Angry

Many don't understand God's anger because they confuse the wrath of God with the wrath of man. The two have little in common. Human anger is typically self-driven and prone to explosions of temper and violent deeds. We get ticked off because we've been overlooked, neglected, or cheated. This is the anger of man. It is not, however, the anger of God.

God doesn't get angry because he doesn't get his way. He gets angry because disobedience always results in self-destruction. What kind of father sits by and watches his child hurt himself?

What kind of God would do the same? Do we think he giggles at adultery or snickers at murder? Do you think he looks the other way when we produce television talk shows based on perverse pleasures? Does he shake his head and say, "Humans will be humans"?

I don't think so. Mark it down and underline it in red. God is rightfully angry. God is a holy God. Our sins are an affront to his holiness. His eyes "are too good to look at evil; [he] cannot stand to see those who do wrong" (Hab. 1:13).

God is angry at the evil that ruins his children. "As long as God is God, he cannot behold with indifference that his creation is destroyed and his holy will trodden underfoot."[1]

We Have No Excuse

My father had a similar hostility toward alcohol. Jack Lucado hated drinking in every form because he knew its power to destroy. His mild nature bristled at the thought of drunkenness. He left no doubt in my mind that he hated drinking and wanted his kids to have nothing to do with it.

But children don't always listen to their fathers. As a fifteen-year-old, I plotted a plan to get drunk and succeeded. I drank beer until I couldn't see straight then came home and vomited until I couldn't stand up. My father came to the bathroom, smelled the beer, threw a towel in my direction, and walked away in disgust. I stumbled back to bed, knowing I was in deep trouble.

He awoke me early the next morning. (There was no way I'd have the pleasure of sleeping off the hangover.) While in the shower I tried to think of an explanation. "My friends made me do it," or "It was an accident," or "Somebody must have put whiskey in the punch." But one option I never considered was ignorance. Never once did I think about saying, "You never told me I shouldn't get drunk."

Not only would that have been a lie, it would have been slander against my father. Had he not told me? Had he not warned me? Had he not tried to teach me? I knew better than to say that I didn't know better.

I was without excuse. According to Paul, we all are. In some of the most arresting words of the Bible he says:

> God shows his anger because some knowledge of him has been made clear to them. Yes, God has shown himself to them. There are things about him that people cannot see—his eternal power and all the things that make him God. But since the beginning of the world those things have been easy to understand by what God has made. *So people have no excuse for the bad things they do.* (Rom. 1:19–20, italics mine)

We are without excuse because God has revealed himself to us through his creation.

The psalmist wrote: "The heavens tell the glory of God, and the skies announce what his hands have made. Day after day they tell their story; night after night they tell it again. They have no speech or words; they have no voice to be heard. But their message goes through all the world; their words go everywhere on earth" (Ps. 19:1–4).

Every star is an announcement. Each leaf a reminder. The glaciers are megaphones, the seasons are chapters, the clouds are banners. Nature is a song of many parts but one theme and one verse: *God is*.

Hundreds of years ago Tertullian stated:

> It was not the pen of Moses that initiated the knowledge of the Creator. . . . The vast majority of mankind, though they had never heard the name of Moses, to say nothing of his books, knew the God of Moses none-the-less. . . . Nature is the teacher; the soul is the pupil. . . . One flower of the hedgerow . . . one shell from any sea you like . . . one feather of a moor fowl . . . will they speak to you of a mean Creator? . . . If I offer you a rose, you will not scorn its Creator.[2]

Creation is God's first missionary. There are those who never held a Bible or heard a scripture. There are those who die before a translator puts God's Word in their tongue. There are millions who lived in ancient times before Christ or live in distant lands far from Christians. There are the simple-minded who are incapable of understanding the gospel. What does the future hold for the person who never hears of God?

Again, Paul's answer is clear. The human heart can know God through the handiwork of nature. If that is all one ever sees, that is enough. One need only respond to what he is given. And if he is given only the testimony of creation, then he has enough.

The problem is not that God hasn't spoken but that we haven't listened. God says his anger is directed against any *thing* and any *one* who suppresses the knowledge of truth. God loves his children, and he hates what destroys them. This doesn't mean that he flies into a rage or loses his temper or is emotionally unpredictable. It means simply that he loves you and hates what you become when you turn from him.

Call it holy hostility. A righteous hatred of wrong. A divine disgust at the evil that destroys his children.

The question is not, "How dare a loving God be angry?" but rather, "How could a loving God feel anything less?"

3 Godless Living

Romans 1:21–32

They traded the glory of God who lives forever for the worship of idols made to look like earthly people, birds, animals, and snakes. . . . They worshiped and served what had been created instead of the God who created those things. ROMANS 1:23, 25

Can a cricket comprehend communion? I've been pondering this question since last Sunday, when both the cricket and the question came my way. The Lord's Supper was being served when I bowed my head and noticed the visitor beneath my pew. Best I can figure, he'd sneaked in a side door, slipped between the deacon's feet, and worked his way to the front of the sanctuary.

The sight of a cricket stirs many emotions within me, not one of them spiritual. Forgive me, all you bug lovers, but I'm not attracted to his beauty nor stunned by his strength. Typically I would have no interest in the insect, but the sight of a bug in an auditorium strikes me as symbolic.

We have something in common, you, me, and the cricket. Limited vision. I hope the parallel doesn't bug you (*ouch!*), but I think it's fair. None of us do too well imagining life beyond the rafters.

You see, as far as the cricket is concerned, his entire universe is an auditorium. I can envision him taking his son out of the wall at night and telling him to look up at the rafters. He wraps his clickers around the boy's back and sighs, "It's a mighty sky we live under, son." Does he know he sees only a fraction?

And then there are the aspirations of a cricket. His highest dream is to find a piece of bread. He falls asleep with visions of pie crumbs and jam drippings.

Or consider the hero of the cricket's world. Crickets lionize bugs. A fast one who can dash across a room full of feet. A gutsy one who has explored the hinterlands of the baptistry. A courageous one who has ventured to the edge of a mighty cabinet or hopped along the precipice of a window sill. Is there, in the legends of cricketdom, a story about Cricket Revere who dashed through the walls yelling, "The bugman is coming! The bugman is coming!"?

Do amazed crickets ever look at each other and proclaim, "Jimminy Human!"?

Perhaps the best question is, who does a cricket worship? Does he acknowledge that there was a hand behind the building? Or does he choose to worship the building itself? Or perhaps a place in the building? Does he assume that since he has never seen the builder there *was* no builder?

The hedonist does. Since he has never seen the hand who made the universe, he assumes there is no life beyond the here and now. He believes there is no truth beyond this room. No purpose beyond his own pleasure. No divine factor. He has no concern for the eternal. Like a cricket who refuses to acknowledge a builder, he refuses to acknowledge his creator.

The hedonist opts to live as if there is no creator at all. Again, Paul's word for this is *godlessness*. He wrote, "People did not think it was important to have a true knowledge of God" (Rom. 1:28).

What happens when a society sees the world through the eyes of a cricket? What happens when a culture settles for grass huts instead of the father's castle? Are there any consequences for a godless pursuit of pleasure? Is there a price to pay for living for today?

The hedonist says, "Who cares? I may be bad, but so what? What I do is my business." He's more concerned about satisfying his passions than in knowing the Father. His life is so desperate for pleasure that he has no time or room for God.

Is he right? Is it OK to spend our days thumbing our noses at God and living it up?

Paul says, "Absolutely not!"

According to Romans 1, we lose more than stained-glass windows when we dismiss God. We lose our standard, our purpose, and our worship. "Their thinking became useless. Their foolish minds were filled with darkness. They said they were wise, but they became fools" (Rom. 1:21–22).

1. We Lose Our Standard

When I was nine years old I complimented a friend's model airplane. He curtly replied, "I stole it." He could tell that I was stunned because he asked, "Do you think that was wrong?"

When I told him I did, he answered simply, "It may be wrong for you. It's not wrong for me. I didn't hurt anyone when I stole the plane. I knew the owner. He is rich. I'm not. He can afford one. I can't."

What do you say to that argument? If you don't believe in life beyond the rafters, you have little to say. If there is no ultimate good *behind* the world, then how do we define "good" *within* the world? If the majority opinion determines good and evil, what happens when the majority is wrong? What do you do when the majority of kids in a certain group say it's all right to steal or raid or even fire pistols from a moving vehicle?

The hedonist's world of no moral absolutes works fine on paper and sounds great in a college philosophy course, but in life? Ask the father of three children whose wife abandoned him, saying, "Divorce may be wrong for you, but it's OK for me." Or get the opinion of the teenage girl, pregnant and frightened, who was told by her boyfriend, "If you have the baby, it's your responsibility." Or the retirees ripped off of their pension by a huckster who believed anything is right if you don't get caught.

A godly view of the world, on the other hand, has something to say to my childhood thief. Faith challenges those with cricket brains to answer to a higher standard than personal opinion: "You may think it's right. Society may think it's OK. But the God who made you said, 'You shall not steal'—and he wasn't kidding."

By the way, follow the godless thinking to its logical extension, and see what you get. What happens when a society denies the importance of right and wrong? Read the answer on a prison wall in Poland: "I freed Germany from the stupid and degrading fallacies of conscience and morality."[1]

Who made the boast? Adolf Hitler. Where are the words posted? In a Nazi death camp. Visitors read the claim and then see its results: a room stuffed with thousands of pounds of women's hair, rooms filled with pictures of castrated children and gas ovens that served as Hitler's final solution. Paul described it best: "Their foolish minds were filled with darkness" (Rom. 1:21).

Come on, Max, you're going too far. Isn't it a stretch to state that what began as a stolen model plane will conclude in a holocaust?

Most of the time it won't. But it could, and what is there to stop it? What dike does the God-denying thinker have to stop the flood? What anchor will the secularist use to keep society from being sucked out to sea? If a society deletes God from the human equation, what sandbags will they stack against the swelling tide of barbarism and hedonism?

As Dostoevsky stated, "If God is dead, then everything is justifiable."

2. *We Lose Our Purpose*

The following conversation occurred between a canary in a cage and a lark on the window sill. The lark looked in at the canary and asked, "What is your purpose?"

"My purpose is to eat seed."

"What for?"

"So I can be strong."

"What for?"

"So I can sing," answered the canary.

"What for?" continued the lark.

"Because when I sing I get more seed."

"So you eat in order to be strong so you can sing so you can get seed so you can eat?"

"Yes."

"There is more to you than that," the lark offered. "If you'll follow me I'll help you find it, but you must leave your cage."

It's tough to find meaning in a caged world. But that doesn't keep us from trying. Mine deep enough in every heart and you'll find it: a longing for meaning, a quest for purpose. As surely as a child breathes, he will someday wonder, "What is the purpose of my life?"

Some search for meaning in a career. "My purpose is to be a dentist." Fine vocation but hardly a justification for existence. They opt to be a human "doing" rather than a human "being." Who they are is what they do; consequently they do a lot. They work many hours because if they don't work, they don't have an identity.

For others, who they are is what they have. They find meaning in a new car or a new house or new clothes. These people are great for the economy and rough on the budget because they are always seeking meaning in something they own.

Still others seek meaning in who they sire. They live vicariously through their kids. Woe be unto these kids. It's hard enough being a youngster without also being someone's reason for living.

Some try sports, entertainment, cults, sex, you name it.

All mirages in the desert of purpose. "Claiming themselves to be wise without God, they became utter fools instead" (Rom. 1:22 TLB).

Shouldn't we face the truth? If we don't acknowledge God, we are flotsam in the universe. At best we are developed animals. At worst we are rearranged space dust. In the final analysis secularists have only one answer to the question, "What is the meaning of life?" Their answer? "We don't know."

Or as paleontologist Stephen J. Gould concluded:

> We are because one odd group of fishes had a peculiar fin anatomy that could transform into legs for terrestrial creatures; because the earth never froze entirely during an ice age; because a small and tenuous species, arising in Africa a quarter of million years ago, had managed, so far, to survive by hook and by crook. We may yearn for a 'higher' answer—but none exists.[2]

Sacrificed upon the altar of godlessness is the purpose of man.

Contrast that to God's vision for life: "We are God's handiwork, created in Christ Jesus to devote ourselves to the good deeds for which God has designed us" (Eph. 2:10 NEB).

With God in your world, you aren't an accident or an incident; you are a gift to the world, a divine work of art, signed by God.

One of the finest gifts I ever received is a football signed by thirty former professional quarterbacks. There is nothing unique about this ball. For all I know it was bought at a discount sports store. What makes it unique is the signatures.

The same is true with us. In the scheme of nature *Homo sapiens* are not unique. We aren't the only creatures with flesh and hair and blood and hearts. What makes us special is not our body but the signature of God on our lives. We are his works of art. We are created in his image to do good deeds. We are significant, not because of what we do, but because of whose we are.

3. *We Lose Our Worship*

You've heard the story of the man searching for his keys under the street light? His friend sees him and stops to help. After some minutes he asks, "Exactly where did you drop your keys?"

"In my house," the man answers.

"In your house? Then why are we looking out here?"

"Because the light is better out here."

You'll never find what you need if you don't look in the right place. If you're looking for keys, go where you lost them. If you're looking for truth and purpose, go outside the rafters. And if you're looking for the sacred, once again, you won't find it by thinking like a cricket.

"They traded the glory of God who holds the whole world in his hands for any cheap figurines you can buy at any roadside stand" (Rom. 1:21 MSG).

Let's return to the crickets for a moment. Assume that these crickets are quite advanced and often engage in the philosophical question, "Is there life beyond the rafters?"

Some crickets believe there is. There must be a creator of this place. How else would the lights come on? How else could air blow through the vents? How else could music fill the room? Out of their amazement for what they see, they worship what they can't see.

But other crickets disagree. Upon study they find the lights come on because of electricity. The air blows because of air conditioners, and music is the result of stereos and speakers. "There is no life beyond this room," they declare. "We have figured out how everything works."

Would we let the crickets get by with that? Of course not! "Just because you understand the system," we'd tell them, "that doesn't deny the presence of someone outside the system. After all, who built it? Who installed the switch? Who diagrammed the compressor and engineered the generator?

But don't we make the same mistake? We understand how storms are created. We map solar systems and transplant hearts. We measure the depths of the oceans and send signals to distant planets. We crickets have studied the system and are learning how it works.

And, for some, the loss of mystery has led to the loss of majesty. The more we know, the less we believe. Strange, don't you think? Knowledge of the workings shouldn't negate wonder. Knowledge should stir wonder. Who has more reason to worship than the astronomer who has seen the stars? Than the surgeon who has held a heart? Than the oceanographer who has pondered the depths? The more we know, the more we should be amazed.

Ironically, the more we know, the less we worship. We are more impressed with our discovery of the light switch than with the one who invented electricity. Call it cricket-brained logic. Rather than worship the Creator, we worship the creation (see Rom. 1:25).

No wonder there is no wonder. We've figured it all out.

One of the most popular attractions at Disney World is the Jungle Cruise. People will spend forty-five minutes waiting in the Florida heat for the chance to board the boat and wind through snake-infested forests. They come for the thrills. You never know when a native will jump out of the trees or a crocodile will peek out of the water. The waterfalls drench you, the rainbow inspires you, and the baby elephants playing in the water amuse you.

It's quite a trip—the first few times. But after four or five runs down the river, it begins to lose its zest. I should know. During the three years I lived in Miami, Florida, I made nearly twenty trips to Orlando. I was single and owned a van and was a sucker for anybody who wanted to spend a day at the Magic Kingdom. By the eighth or ninth trip I could tell you the names of the guides and the jokes they told.

A couple of times I actually dozed off on the journey. The trail had lost its secrets. Ever wonder why people sleep in on Sunday mornings (whether in the bed or in the sanctuary)? Now you know. They've seen it all. Why get excited? They know it all. There is nothing sacred. The holy becomes humdrum. Rather than dashing into life like kids to the park, we doze through our days like commuters on a train.

Can you see why people become "full of sexual sin, using our bodies wrongly with each other"? (Rom. 1:24). You've got to get excitement somewhere.

According to Romans 1, godlessness is a bad swap. In living for today, the hut-building hedonist destroys his hope of living in a castle tomorrow.

What was true in Paul's day is still true in ours, and we would do well to heed his warning. Otherwise, what is to keep us from destroying ourselves? If there is no standard in this life, no purpose to this life, and nothing sacred about this life, what is to keep us from doing whatever we want?"

"Nothing," said one cricket to the other.

How does God feel about such a view of life? Let me give you a hint. How would you feel if you saw your children settling for crumbs when you'd prepared for them a feast?

4 Godless Judging

Romans 2:1–11

If you think you can judge others, you are wrong. When you judge them, you are really judging yourself guilty, because you do the same things they do. God judges those who do wrong things, and we know that his judging is right. ROMANS 2:1

You know what disturbs me most about Jeffrey Dahmer?

What disturbs me most are not his acts, though they are disgusting. Dahmer was convicted of seventeen murders. Eleven corpses were found in his apartment. He cut off arms. He ate body parts. My thesaurus has 204 synonyms for *vile*, but each falls short of describing a man who kept skulls in his refrigerator and hoarded a human heart. He redefined the boundary for brutality. The Milwaukee monster dangled from the lowest rung of human conduct and then dropped. But that's not what troubles me most.

Can I tell you what troubles me most about Jeffrey Dahmer? Not his trial, as disturbing as it was, with all those pictures of him sitting serenely in court, face frozen, motionless. No sign of remorse, no hint of regret. Remember his steely eyes and impassive face? But I don't speak of him because of his trial. There is another reason. Can I tell you what really troubles me about Jeffrey Dahmer?

Not his punishment, though life without parole is hardly an exchange for his actions. How many years would satisfy justice? A lifetime in jail for every life he took? But that's another matter, and that's not what troubles me most about Jeffrey Dahmer. May I tell you what does?

His conversion.

Months before an inmate murdered him, Jeffrey Dahmer became a Christian. Said he repented. Was sorry for what he did. Profoundly sorry. Said he put his faith in Christ. Was baptized. Started life over. Began reading Christian books and attending chapel.

Sins washed. Soul cleansed. Past forgiven.

That troubles me. It shouldn't, but it does. Grace for a cannibal?

Maybe you have the same reservations. If not about Dahmer perhaps about someone else. Ever wrestled with the deathbed conversion of a rapist or the eleventh-hour conversion of a child molester? We've sentenced them, maybe not in court, but in our hearts. We've put them behind bars and locked the door. They are forever imprisoned by our disgust. And then, the impossible happens. They repent.

Our response? (Dare we say it?) We cross our arms and furrow our brows and say, "God won't let you off that easy. Not after what you did. God is kind, but he's no wimp. Grace is for average sinners like me, not deviants like you."

And for proof we might turn to Romans 1. "*God's anger is being shown against . . .*" And then Paul lists it all: sexual sin, evil, selfishness, hatred, jealousy, murder (see 1:26–30). We want to shout,

"Go get 'em, Paul! It's about time someone spoke out against sin! It's high time someone pulled back the blanket on adultery and turned the light on dishonesty. Nail those perverts. String up those porn peddlers. We'll stand by you, Paul! We decent, law-abiding folk are with you!"

Paul's response?

"If you think that leaves you on the high ground where you can point your finger at others, think again. Every time you criticize someone, you condemn yourself. It takes one to know one" (Rom. 2:1 MSG).

Whoops!

Having addressed the hut-building tomcat, he turns his torch on the hillside watchdog.

We Don't Hold the Gavel

In Romans 1 Paul confronts the hedonists. In chapter 2 he deals with another group, the judgmental moralists: those who, "pass judgment on someone else" (2:1 NIV). Somewhere between the escort service and the church service there is the person who "points [his] finger at others" (2:1 MSG).

"Therefore you have no excuse, O man, whoever you are, when you judge another; for in passing judgment upon him you condemn yourself, because you, the judge, are doing the very same things" (2:1 RSV).

Who is this person? It could be anyone ("O man, whoever you are") who filters God's grace through his own opinion. Anyone who dilutes God's mercy with his own prejudice. He is the prodigal son's elder brother who wouldn't attend the party (see Luke 15:11–32). He is the ten-hour worker, upset because the one-hour worker got the same wage (see Matt. 20:1–16). He is the fault-finding brother obsessed by his brother's sins and oblivious to his own.

If you "think you can judge others" (Rom. 2:1), Paul has a stern reminder for you. It's not your job to hold the gavel. "God judges those who do wrong things, and we know that his judging is right" (v. 2).

The key word here is *judges*. It's one thing to have an opinion. It's quite another to pass a verdict. It's one thing to have a conviction; it's another to convict the person. It's one thing to be repulsed at the acts of a Jeffrey Dahmer (and I am.) It's another entirely to claim that I am superior (I'm not) or that he is beyond the grace of God (no one is.)

As John Stott writes: "This [verse] is not a call either to suspend our critical faculties or to renounce all criticism and rebuke of others as illegitimate: it is rather a prohibition of standing in judgment on other people and condemning them (which as human beings we have no right to do), especially when we fail to condemn ourselves."[1]

It's our job to hate the sin. But it's God's job to deal with the sinner. God has called us to despise evil, but he's never called us to despise the evildoer.

But, oh, how we would like to. Is there any act more delightful than judging others? There is something smug and self-satisfying about donning the robe, stepping behind the bench, and slamming down the gavel. "Guilty!"

Besides, judging others is the quick and easy way to feel good about ourselves. A convenience-store ego-boost. Standing next to all the Mussolinis and Hitlers and Dahmers of the world, we boast, "Look, God, compared to them, I'm not too bad."

But that's the problem. God doesn't compare us to them. They aren't the standard. God is. And compared to him, Paul will argue, "There is no one who does anything good" (Rom. 3:12). In fact, that is one of two reasons why God is the One who judges.

Reason #1: We Aren't Good Enough

Suppose God simplified matters and reduced the Bible to one command: "Thou must jump so high in the air that you touch the moon." No need to love your neighbor or pray or follow Jesus; just touch the moon by virtue of a jump, and you'll be saved.

We'd never make it. There may be a few who jump three or four feet, even fewer who jump five or six; but compared to the distance we have to go, no one gets very far. Though you may jump six inches higher than I do, it's scarcely reason to boast.

Now, God hasn't called us to touch the moon, but he might as well have. He said, "You must be perfect, just as your Father in heaven is perfect" (Matt. 5:48). None of us can meet God's standard. As a result, none of us deserves to don the robe and stand behind the bench and judge others. Why? We aren't good enough. Dahmer may jump six inches, and you may jump six feet, but compared to the 230,000 miles that remain, who can boast?

The thought of it is almost comical. We who jump three feet look at the fellow who jumped one inch and say, "What a lousy jump." Why do we engage in such accusations? It's a ploy. As long as I am thinking of your weaknesses, then I don't have to think about mine. As long as I am looking at your puny jump, then I don't have to be honest about my own. I'm like the man who went to see the psychiatrist with a turtle on his head and a strip of bacon dangling from each ear and said, "I'm here to talk to you about my brother."

It's the universal strategy of impunity. Even kids use it. *If I can get Dad more angry at my brother than me, I'm off scot-free.* So I accuse. I compare. Rather than admit my own faults, I find faults in others. The easiest way to justify the mistakes in my house is to find worse ones in my neighbor's house.

Such scams don't work with God. Read carefully Paul's words.

> God isn't so easily diverted. He sees right through all smoke screens and holds you to what *you've* done. You didn't think, did you, that just by pointing your finger at others you would distract God from coming down on you hard? Or did you think that just because he's such a nice God he'd let you off the hook? Better think this one through from the beginning. God is kind, but he's not soft. In kindness he takes us firmly by the hand and leads us into a radical life change. (Rom. 2:2–4 MSG)

We aren't good enough to judge. Can the hungry accuse the beggar? Can the sick mock the ill? Can the blind judge the deaf? Can the sinner condemn the sinner? No. Only One can judge, and that One is neither writing nor reading this book.

Reason #2: We Don't Know Enough

Not only are we unworthy, we are unqualified. We don't know enough about the person to judge him. We don't know enough about his past. We condemn a man for stumbling this morning, but we didn't see the blows he took yesterday. We judge a woman for the limp in her walk but cannot see the tack in her shoe. We mock the fear in their eyes but have no idea how many stones they have ducked or darts they have dodged.

Are they too loud? Perhaps they fear being neglected again. Are they too timid? Perhaps they fear failing again. Too slow? Perhaps they fell the last time they hurried. You don't know. Only one who has followed yesterday's steps can be their judge.

Not only are we ignorant about yesterday, we are ignorant about tomorrow. Dare we judge a book while chapters are yet unwritten? Should we pass a verdict on a painting while the artist still holds the brush? How can you dismiss a soul until God's work is complete? "God began doing a good work in you, and I am sure he will continue it until it is finished when Jesus Christ comes again" (Phil. 1:6).

Be careful! The Peter who denies Jesus at tonight's fire may proclaim him with fire at tomorrow's Pentecost. The Samson who is blind and weak today may use his final strength to level the pillars of godlessness. A stammering shepherd in this generation may be the mighty Moses of the next. Don't call Noah a fool, you may be asking him for a lift. "Do not judge before the right time; wait until the Lord comes" (1 Cor. 4:5).

A condemned criminal was sent to his death by his country. In his final moments, he asked for mercy. Had he asked for mercy from the people, it would have been denied. Had he asked it of the government, it would have been declined. Had he asked it of his victims, they would have turned a deaf ear. But it wasn't to these he turned for grace. He turned instead to the bloodied form of the One who hung on the cross next to his and pleaded, "Jesus, remember me when you come into your kingdom." And Jesus answered by saying, "I tell you the truth, today you will be with me in paradise" (Luke 23:43).

As far as we know, Jeffrey Dahmer did the same thing. And as far as we know, Jeffrey Dahmer got the same response. And when you think about it, the request Dahmer made is no different than yours or mine. He may make it from a prison bunk and you may make it from a church pew, but from heaven's angle we're all asking for the moon.

And by heaven's grace we all receive it.

5

Godless Religion

Romans 2:17–3:18

You call yourself a Jew. You trust in the law of Moses and brag that you are close to God. . . . You think you know everything and have all truth. You teach others, so why don't you teach yourself? ROMANS 2:17, 20–21

Suppose I invite you to go sailing with me.

"I didn't know you were a sailor," you observe.

"You bet your barnacles I am," I answer.

"Tell me, where did you learn to sail?"

I flash a cocky smile and pull a faded photo out of my pocket. You look at the sai[illegible] standing on the bow of a schooner. "Th[illegible] my great-grandpa. He sailed Cape Horn. Sailing is in my blood. I got saltwater in my veins."

"Your great-grandpa taught you how to sail?"

"Of course not. He died before I was born."

"Then who taught you to sail?"

I produce a leather-bound book and boast, "I read the manual."

"You read a book on sailing?"

"More than that. I took a course at the community college. I can tell you the difference between fore and aft, and I can show you the stern and the bow. I can tie a square knot. You ought to see me hoist a mast."

"You mean, 'hoist a sail'?"

"Whatever. We even went on a field trip, and I met a real captain. I shook his hand! Come on, you want to sail?"

"Honestly, Max, I don't think you are a sailor."

"You want the proof? You want the *real* proof? Take a look, matey, I've got a gen-u-ine tattoo." I roll up my sleeve revealing a mermaid sitting on an anchor. "Watch how she jumps when I flex."

You aren't impressed. "That's all the proof you have?"

"What else do I need? I've got the pedigree. I've got the book. And I've got the tattoo. All aboard!"

Chances are you'd stay on shore. Even a landlubber knows it takes more than a family tree, a night course, and ink-stained skin to be seaworthy. You wouldn't trust a fellow like me to sail your boat, and Paul wouldn't trust a fellow like me to navigate the church.

Apparently some were trying. Oh, they weren't the seafaring type, they were the religious type. Their ancestors weren't shipmates; they were pew mates. They didn't have a book on boats, but they had a book called the Torah. And most of all, they'd been tattooed; they'd been circumcised. And they were proud; proud of their lineage, their law, and their initiation.

My hunch is they were also proud of Paul's letter. Imagine the congregation listening to this epistle. Jews on one side, Gentiles on the other. Can't you see the Jews beaming? Paul speaks out against the godless deviants, and they nod. Paul warns of the divine wrath directed at hedonist hut-builders, and they smile. As Paul, their fellow Jew, lambastes the evil uncircumcised, they erupt in a chorus, "Amen! Paul. Preach it!"

But then Paul surprises them.

He pokes his finger at their puffy chests and asks,

> What about you? You call yourself a Jew. You trust in the law of Moses and brag that you are close to God. You know what he wants you to do and what is important, because you have learned the law. You think you are a guide for the blind and a light for those who are in darkness. You think you can show foolish people what is right and teach those who know nothing. You have the law; so you think you know everything and have all truth. (Rom. 2:17–20)

Don't Put Pride in Your Pedigree

Those aren't fireworks you are hearing; they are bombshells. Seven bombshells to be exact. Seven heat-seeking verbs launched into the midst of legalism. Listen as they explode.

> "You *call* yourself a Jew."
>
> "You *trust* in the law of Moses and *brag* that you are close to God."
>
> "You *know* what he wants you to do and what is important because you have learned the law."
>
> "You *think* you are a guide for the blind and a light for those who are in darkness."
>
> "You *think* you can show foolish people what is right and teach those who know nothing."
>
> ". . . you *think* you know everything" (see 2:17–20).

Boom. Boom. Boom. Just when the deacons thought they were going to get praised, they got blasted. Paul tells them, "Some Jews you are. You trust in the law rather than the lawgiver and brag that you have a monopoly on God. You're convinced you are a part of a prized few who 'know' (beyond a shadow of a doubt) what God wants you to do. If that's not bad enough, you 'think' you are God's gift to the confused and the foolish. In fact, you 'think' you know everything."

Something tells me Paul just blew his shot at the "Clergyman of the Year" award. The apostle, however, is more concerned about making a point than about scoring points, and his point for religious rock-stackers is clear: "Don't put pride in your pedigree." Being born with a silver mezuzah in your mouth means nothing in heaven. Faith is intensely personal. There is no royal lineage or holy bloodline in God's kingdom.

The story of the lumberjack's son comes to mind. Somehow the youngster became convinced that there were ghosts in the forest. This disturbed his father, who made a living among the trees and wanted his son to do the same. To comfort his son the father gave him his scarf, saying, "The ghosts are afraid of me, my son. Wear this scarf, and the ghosts will be afraid of you. The scarf will make you a lumberjack."

And so the son did. He wore the scarf proudly, telling all who would listen that he was a lumberjack. Still, he never entered the forest, and he never cut a tree, but since he had his father's scarf, he considered himself a lumberjack.

The father would have been wiser to teach his son there were no ghosts rather than to teach him to trust in a scarf.

The Jews trusted the scarves of their fathers. They rode on the coattails of their heritage. Didn't matter that they were thieves, adulterers, and extortionists (see Rom. 2:22–23); they still considered themselves God's chosen few. Why? Because they had the scarf.

Maybe you were given a scarf. Perhaps the branches of your family tree are heavy with saints and seers. Perhaps you were born in a church basement and cut your teeth on a pew. If so, be grateful, but don't be lazy. Better to trust the truth than the scarf.

Or maybe you have no pedigree. Your ancestry is more like a lineup at the county jail than a roster of Sunday school teachers. If so, don't worry. Just as religious heritage brings no bonus points, a secular heritage brings no deficits. Family trees can't save you or condemn you; the ultimate decision is yours.

Don't Trust a Symbol

Having dealt with the problem of pedigree, Paul now addresses the problem of the tattoo. He turns his attention to the most sacred badge of the Jew: circumcision. Circumcision symbolized the nearness God desires with his people. God puts a knife to our self-sufficiency. He wants to be a part of our identity, our intimacy, and even our potency. Circumcision proclaimed that there is no part of our life too private or too personal for God.

Yet, rather than see circumcision as a sign of submission, the Jews had come to see it as a sign of superiority. With time they began to trust the symbol more than the Father. Paul shatters this illusion by proclaiming, "True circumcision is not only on the outside of the body. A person is a Jew only if he is a Jew inside; true circumcision is done in the heart by the Spirit, not by the written law. Such a person gets praise from God rather than from people" (Rom. 2:28–29).

Later Paul asks, "Did God accept Abraham before or after he was circumcised?" (Rom. 4:10). Important question. If God only accepted Abraham after the circumcision, then Abraham was accepted according to his merit and not according to his faith.

What is Paul's answer? Abraham was accepted "before his circumcision" (v. 10). Abraham was accepted by God in Genesis 15 and circumcised in Genesis 17. Fourteen years separate the two events!

If Abraham was already accepted by God, then why was he circumcised? Paul answers the question in the next verse: "Abraham was circumcised to show that he was right with God through faith before he was circumcised" (v. 11).

Paul point is crucial: Circumcision was symbolic. Its purpose was to show what God had already done.

I see a great example of this as I type these words. On my left hand is a symbol—a gold ring. Though not elaborate, it's priceless. It cost a pretty, young fourth-grade schoolteacher two hundred dollars. She gave it to me the day we married. The ring is a symbol of our love, a statement of our love, a declaration of our love, but it is not the source of our love.

When we have spats or trouble, I don't take off the ring and set it on a pedestal and pray to it. I don't rub it and seek wisdom. Were I to lose the ring, I'd be disappointed, but our marriage would continue. It is a symbol, nothing more.

Suppose I tried to make the ring more than it is. Suppose I became a jerk of a husband, cruel and unfaithful. Imagine that I failed to provide for Denalyn's needs or care for our children. What if one day she reached the breaking point and said, "You are not a husband to me. There is no love in your heart or devotion in your life. I want you to leave."

How do you think she'd respond if I countered, "How dare you say that? I'm wearing the ring you gave me. I've never removed it one minute! Sure I beat you and cheated on you, but I wore the ring. Isn't that enough?"

How many of you think such a defense would move her to apologize and weep, "Oh, Max, how forgetful of me. You have been so sacrificial wearing that ring all these years. Sure you have beaten me, abandoned me, neglected me, but I'll dismiss all that because you have worn the ring"?

Hogwash. She'd never say that. Why? Because apart from love, the ring means nothing. The symbol represents love, but it cannot replace love. Paul is accusing the Jews of trusting the symbol of circumcision while neglecting their souls. Could he accuse us of the same error?

Substitute a contemporary symbol such as baptism or communion or church membership.

"God, I know I never think about you. I know I hate people and cheat my friends. I abuse my body and lie to my spouse. But you don't mind, do you? I mean after all, I was baptized at that Christian camp when I was ten years old."

Or, "Every Easter I take communion."

Or, "My father and mother were fifth generation Presbyterians, you know."

Do you think God would say, "You're right. You never think of me or respect me. You hate your neighbor and abuse your kids, but since you were baptized, I will overlook your rebellion and evil ways"?

Hogwash. A symbol has no power apart from the ones who share it.

In my closet is a varsity football jacket. I earned it by playing two years of high-school football. It, too, is a symbol. It's symbolic of sweat and work and long hours on the practice field. The jacket and a sore knee are reminders of something I could do twenty years ago. Do you think if I put the jacket on now I'd instantly be twenty pounds lighter and a whole lot faster? Do you think if I wore that jacket into the office of a coach he'd extend his hand and say, "We've been waiting for a player like you. Go out there and suit up!"?

Hogwash. That jacket is merely a memoir of something I once did. It says nothing about what I could do today. It alone doesn't transform me, empower me, or enable me.

Neither does your heritage, even if you're a descendant of John Wesley.

Neither does your communion service, even if you double up on the wafers.

Neither does your baptism, even if you got dunked in the Jordan River.

Please understand. Symbols are important. Some of them, like communion and baptism, illustrate the cross of Christ. They symbolize salvation, demonstrate salvation, even articulate salvation. But they do not impart salvation.

Putting your trust in a symbol is like claiming to be a sailor because you have a tattoo or claiming to be a good husband because you have a ring or claiming to be a football player because you have a letter jacket.

Do we honestly think God would save his children based upon a symbol?

What kind of God would look at a religious hypocrite and say, "You've never loved me, sought me or obeyed me, but because your name was on the roll of a church in the right denomination I will save you"?

On the other hand, what kind of God would look at the sincere seeker and say, "You dedicated your life to loving me and loving my children. You surrendered your heart and confessed your sins. I want to save you so badly. I'm so sorry, your church took communion one time a month too many. Because of a technicality, you are forever lost in hell"?

Hogwash. Our God is abundant in love and steadfast in mercy. He saves us, not because we trust in a symbol, but because we trust in a Savior.

Please note Paul hasn't changed subjects; he's just changed audiences. His topic is still the tragedy of a godless life. "The wrath of God is being revealed from heaven against all the godlessness" (Rom. 1:18 NIV).

From God's perspective there is no difference between the ungodly party-goer, the ungodly finger-pointer, and the ungodly pew-sitter. The *Penthouse* gang, the courthouse clan, and the church choir need the same message: Without God all are lost.

Or as Paul summarizes:

> All of us, whether insiders or outsiders, start out in identical conditions, which is to say we all start out as sinners. Scripture leaves no doubt about it: "There's nobody living right, not even one, nobody who knows the score, nobody alert for God." (Rom. 3:10 MSG)

Just as lineage, laws, and tattoos don't make me a sailor, heritage, rituals, and ceremonies don't make me a Christian. "God justifies the believer, not because of the worthiness of his belief, but because of [Christ's] worthiness."[1]

Don't Try to Do What Only God Can Do

Let's go back to my sailing invitation. I know I said you probably wouldn't go, but let's pretend that you aren't as smart as you look, and you accept and board the boat.

You begin to worry when you notice that I lift the sail only a few inches on the mast. You think it even stranger that I position myself behind the partially raised sail and begin to blow.

"Why don't you raise the sail?" you ask.

"Because I can't blow on the whole thing," I pant.

"Let the wind blow it," you urge.

"Oh, I can't do that. I'm sailing this boat by myself."

Those are the words of a legalist, huffing and puffing to push his vessel to heaven. (Ever wonder why so many religious folk seem out of breath?)

With time we drift out to sea, and a powerful storm hits. Rain splatters on the deck, and the little vessel bounces on the waves. "I'm going to set the anchor!" I yell. You're relieved that I at least know where the anchor is, but then you are stunned at where I put it.

First, I take the anchor and set it up near the bow. "That should steady the boat!" I shout. But, of course, it doesn't. Next I carry the anchor to the stern. "Now we are secure!" But the bouncing continues. I hang the anchor on the mast, but it doesn't help. Finally, in fear and frustration, you take the anchor and throw it out to the deep and scream, "Don't you know you have to anchor to something other than yourself!"

A legalist doesn't know that. He anchors only to himself. His security comes from what he does; his lineage, his law, and his tattoo. When the storm blows the legalist casts his anchor on his own works. He will save himself. After all, isn't he in the right group? Doesn't he have the right law? And hasn't he passed through the right initiation? (Ever wonder why so many religious people have such stormy lives?)

Here is the point: Salvation is God's business.

Remember the parable of the river? The first brother, the hedonist, built a hut and called it a mansion. The second brother, the judgmentalist, watched him and called him a deviant. A legalist, the third brother stacked rocks and relied upon his own strength. He represents the godless religionist who stacks his good deeds against the current, thinking they will make a path upstream. In the end all three reject the invitation of the firstborn son, and all are equally distant from the father.

The message of the parable and Paul's message in Romans are

the same: God is the One who saves his children. There is only one name under heaven that has the power to save, and that name is not yours.

Regardless of the mermaid on your tattoo.

PART TWO

WHAT A GOD!

Ponder the achievement of God.

He doesn't condone our sin, nor does he compromise his standard.

He doesn't ignore our rebellion, nor does he relax his demands.

Rather than dismiss our sin, he assumes our sin and, incredibly, sentences himself.

God's holiness is honored. Our sin is punished . . . and we are redeemed.

God does what we cannot do so we can be what we dare not dream: perfect before God.

6

Calling the Corpses

Romans 3:21–26

All have turned away.
Together, everyone has become useless.
There is no one who does good;
there is not even one. . . .
This stops all excuses and brings the whole world under God's judgment. ROMANS 3:12, 19

A few weeks ago I traveled to the Midwest to pick up my two oldest daughters. They'd spent a week at camp. This wasn't their first time at camp, but it was their first time so far from home. The camp was great and the activities outstanding, but their hearts were heavy. They missed their mom and dad. And Mom and Dad weren't doing so well either.

Not wanting to risk any delayed flights, I flew up a day early. Parents weren't allowed to see their kids until 5:00 P.M., so I enjoyed the area, visited a few sights, and kept an eye on the time. My purpose wasn't to sightsee. My purpose was my kids.

I arrived at the camp at 3:00 P.M. A rope was stretched across the dirt road, and a sign dangling from the rope reminded me, "Parents may not enter until 5:00 P.M."

I wasn't alone at the rope. Other parents were already present. There was a lot of glancing at wristwatches. No in-depth conversations, just the expected, "How are you?" "Where are you from?" "And how many kids?" Nothing much beyond that. Our minds were down that dirt road. At about 4:30, I noticed a few dads positioning themselves near the rope. Not to be outdone, I did the same. Though most of the slots were taken, there was room for one more parent. I squeezed past one mother who was unaware that the horses had been called to the track. I felt sorry for her, but not enough to give her my spot.

With five minutes to go, conversation ended. No more playing games; this was serious stuff. The cars were on the track. The runners were in the blocks. The countdown was on. All we needed was someone to lower the rope.

Two camp counselors appeared to perform the honors. They knew better than to take one end of the rope and cross the road to allow the parents to enter. Such a move would have been fatal; they wouldn't have survived the stampede. Rather than endanger their lives, each took one end of the rope and, on a prearranged signal, lowered it to the ground. (They had done this before.)

We were off!

I was ready for this moment. I had waited long enough. I began with a brisk walk, but out of the corner of my eye I saw a dad starting to trot. *So that's what it's going to take, eh?* Good thing I was wearing jogging shoes. I broke into a run. Enough preliminaries. The hour had struck and the rope was down, and I was willing to do what it took to see my kids.

God feels the same.

God is ready to see his own. He, too, is separated from his children. He, too, will do whatever is necessary to take them home.

Yet, his desire leaves ours in the dust. Forget plane trips and rental cars; we're talking incarnation and sacrifice. Forget a night in a hotel; how about a lifetime on earth! I went from the state of Texas to the state of Missouri. He went from the state of being worshiped in heaven to being a baby in Bethlehem.

Why? He knows his children are without their father. And he knows we are powerless to return without his help.

Sin, the Universal Problem

But what separates us from God is not a rope and a camp policy. What separates us from God is sin. We aren't strong enough to remove it, and we aren't good enough to erase it. For all of our differences, there is one problem we all share. We are separated from God.

"There is *no one* who always does what is right, *not even one*. There is *no one* who understands. There is *no one* who looks to God for help. All have turned away. Together, everyone has become useless. There is *no one* who does anything good; there is *not even one*" (Rom. 3:10–11, italics mine).

Get the impression that Paul is trying to tell us something?

Every person on God's green earth has blown it. The hedonists blew it because they were pleasure-centered and not God-centered. The judgmentalists blew it because they were high-minded and not God-minded. The legalists blew it because they were work-driven and not grace-driven.

The hut-builders sought pleasure, the fault-finders sought impunity, the rock-stackers sought piety. The first disregards God, the second seeks to distract God, and the third hopes to reimburse God. But each one misses God. All are godless.

None are like the fourth son, who depended upon the father's plan to bring him home.

Death, the Universal Condition

This is the great shortfall of humanity. We're a long way from our Father and don't have a clue about how to get home.

Listen as Paul assumes the role of county coroner and describes the cadaver of the sinner.

> "Their throats are like open graves."
>
> "They use their tongues for telling lies."
>
> "The poison of vipers is on their lips."
>
> "Their mouths are full of cursing and hate."
>
> "Their feet are swift to shed blood" (see Rom. 3:13, 14, 16).

What a repulsive anatomy! Throats like open graves. Deceitful tongues. Viper lips. Mouths full of vulgarity. Feet that march toward violence. And to sum it up, Paul presents the cause of it all, "There is no fear of God before their eyes" (v. 18 NIV).

Sin infects the entire person, from eyes to feet. Not only does sin contaminate every human being, it contaminates the being of every human. Paul will say it most clearly later in the letter to the Romans. "The wages of sin is death . . ." (6:23 NIV).

Sin is a fatal disease.

Sin has sentenced us to a slow, painful death.

Sin does to a life what shears do to a flower. A cut at the stem separates a flower from the source of life. Initially the flower is attractive, still colorful and strong. But watch that flower over a period of time, and the leaves will wilt and the petals will drop. No matter what you do, the flower will never live again. Surround it with water. Stick the stem in soil. Baptize it with fertilizer. Glue the flower back on the stem. Do what you wish. The flower is dead.

When the Chinese dictator Mao Zedong died in 1976, his physician, Dr. Li Zhisui, was given an impossible task. The Politburo demanded, "The chairman's body is to be permanently preserved." The staff objected. The doctor objected. He had seen the dry and shrunken remains of Lenin and Stalin. He knew a body with no life was doomed to rot.

But he had his commands. Twenty-two liters of formaldehyde were pumped into the body. The result was horrifying. Mao's face swelled up like a ball, and his neck was as thick as his head. His ears stuck out in right angles, and the chemical oozed from his pores. A team of embalmers worked for five hours with towels and cotton balls to force the liquids down into his body. Finally the face looked normal, but the chest was so swollen that his jacket had to be slit in the back and his body covered with the red Communist Party flag.

That sufficed for the funeral, but the powers above wanted the body permanently preserved to lie in state at Tiananmen Square. For a year Dr. Zhisui supervised a team working in an underground hospital as they tried to preserve the remains. Because of the futility of the task, a government official ordered that an identical wax dummy be made. Both the body and the replica were taken to the mausoleum in Tiananmen Square. Tens of thousands came to file past a crystal casket and pay their respects to the man who'd ruled China for twenty-seven years. But even the doctor didn't know if they were seeing Mao or a waxwork dummy.[1]

Don't we do the same? Isn't that the occupation of humanity? Isn't that the hope of the workaholic? Isn't that the aspiration of the greedy, the power-monger, and the adulterer? Not to pump formaldehyde into a corpse but to pump life into a soul?

We fool just enough people to keep ourselves trying a bit longer. Sometimes, even we don't know if people are seeing the real self or a wax figure.

A dead flower has no life.

A dead body has no life.

A dead soul has no life.

Cut off from God, the soul withers and dies. The consequence of sin is not a bad day or a bad mood but a dead soul. The sign of a dead soul is clear: poisoned lips and cursing mouths, feet that lead to violence and eyes that don't see God.

Now you know how people can be so vulgar. Their souls are dead. Now you see how some religions can be so oppressive. They have no life. Now you understand how the drug peddler can sleep at night and the dictator can live with his conscience. He has none.

The finished work of sin is to kill the soul.

We Need a Miracle

Upon seeing the problem, can't we see the solution? The solution is not more government or education, not more formaldehyde in the corpse. Nor is the solution more religion; man-made rituals and doctrines may seem to reattach the flower to the stem but they can't. We don't need more religion; we need a miracle. We don't need someone to disguise the dead; we need someone to raise the dead.

That "someone" is introduced in Romans 3:22.

But before we read the verse, I have to pause and warn you: Prepare yourself for its simplicity. No need to brew mystical concoctions. Elaborate ceremonies are unnecessary. Complicated treatments are unneeded. Tortuous hours of rehabilitation are not required. God's solution for our malady is starkly simple.

Before we read the verse, I also have to pause and ask: Aren't you glad the letter didn't stop with verses 19 and 20? "This stops all excuses and brings the whole world under God's judgment, because no one can be made right with God by following the law. The law only shows us our sin."

Aren't you relieved Paul didn't leave the corpse on the table? Aren't you happy that the apostle didn't describe the condition without showing God's solution? Don't worry. Of that there was no danger. A freight train couldn't have kept Paul from writing the next verse. These words are the ones he's been waiting to write. The next lines are the reason for the epistle, even his reason for living.

For sixty-one verses we have sat with Paul in a darkened room as he described the fatality of sin. Every candle is down to the wick. Every lamp is empty of oil. There is a hearth, but it has no wood. There is a lantern, but it has no flame. We have groped in every corner and found no light. Unable to see even our hand before our faces, all we can do is stare into the night. We are unaware that Paul has crept next to a window and placed his hand on the latch. Just when we wonder if there is any light to be found, Paul throws open the shutters and announces: "But God has a way!" (v. 21).

> But God has a way to make people right with him without the law, and he has now shown us that way. . . . God makes people right with himself through their faith in Jesus Christ. This is true for all who believe in Christ, because all people are the same: All have sinned and are not good enough for God's glory, and all need to be made right with God by his grace, which is a free gift. They need to be made free from sin through Jesus Christ. God gave him as a way to forgive sin through faith in the blood of Jesus' death. This showed that God always does what is right and fair, as in the past when he was patient and did not punish people for their sins. (vv. 21–25)

Man's Windfall

As youngsters, we neighborhood kids would play street football. The minute we got home from school, we'd drop the books and hit the pavement. The kid across the street had a dad with a great arm and a strong addiction to football. As soon as he'd pull in the driveway from work we'd start yelling for him to come and play ball. He couldn't resist. Out of fairness he'd always ask, "Which team is losing?" Then he would join that team, which often seemed to be mine.

His appearance in the huddle changed the whole ball game. He was confident, strong, and most of all, he had a plan. We'd circle around him, and he'd look at us and say, "OK boys, here is what we are going to do." The other side was groaning before we left the huddle. You see, we not only had a new plan, we had a new leader.

He brought new life to our team. God does precisely the same. We didn't need a new play; we needed a new plan. We didn't need to trade positions; we needed a new player. That player is Jesus Christ, God's firstborn son.

"Though we were spiritually dead because of the things we did against God, he gave us new life with Christ" (Eph. 2:5). God's solution is not to preserve the dead—but to raise the dead. "Therefore, if anyone is in Christ, he is a new creation; the old has gone; the new has come!" (2 Cor. 5:17 NIV).

What Jesus did with Lazarus, he is willing to do with us. Which is good to know, for what Martha said about Lazarus can be said about us, "But, Lord, it has been four days since he died. There will be a bad smell" (John 11:39). Martha was speaking for us all. The human race is dead, and there is a bad smell. We have been dead and buried a long time. We don't need someone to fix us up; we need someone to raise us up. In the muck and mire of what we call life, there is death, and we have been in it so long we've grown accustomed to the stink. But Christ hasn't.

And Christ can't stand the thought of his kids rotting in the cemetery. So he comes in and calls us out. We are the corpse, and he is the corpse-caller. We are the dead, and he is the dead-raiser.

Our task is not to get up but to admit we are dead. The only ones who remain in the grave are the ones who don't think they are there.

The stone has been moved. "Lazarus!" he yells. "Larry! Sue! Horatio! Come out!" He calls.

"Andrea! Jenna! I'm here!" I shouted as I ran down the camp road. (I won the race.) I spotted Andrea first. She was under a canopy preparing to practice gymnastics. I called her name again. "Daddy!" she yelled and jumped into my arms.

There was no guarantee she'd respond. Though I had flown a thousand miles, rented a car, and waited an hour, she could have seen me and—heaven forbid!—ignored me. Some kids are too grown up to run to their parent in front of their friends.

But then there are those who have had enough camp food and mosquito repellent to make them jump for joy at the sight of their father. Such was the case with Andrea.

All of a sudden, Andrea had gone from feeling homesick to feeling happy. Why? Only one difference. Her father had come to take her home.

7 Where Love and Justice Meet

Romans 3:21–25

God has a way to make people right with him without the law, and he has now shown us that way which the law and the prophets told us about. God makes people right with himself through their faith in Jesus Christ. ROMANS 3:21–22

I'm glad the letter wasn't sent from heaven. It came from my automobile insurance company, my *former* automobile insurance company. I didn't drop them; they dropped me. Not because I didn't pay my premiums; I was on time and caught up. Not because I failed to do the paperwork; every document was signed and delivered.

I was dropped for making too many mistakes.

The letter begins by politely telling me that my record has been under review.

> *We have secured Motor Vehicle Records which indicate a speed violation by Max Lucado in December and January and a not-at-fault accident by Denalyn Lucado in December. Additional*

records indicate additional speed violations by Mr. Lucado in April and by Mrs. Lucado in December of the next year.

Now, I'm the first to admit that Denalyn and I tend to get a bit heavy-footed and careless. In fact, that is the reason we have insurance. Aren't the blemishes on my record an indication that I am a worthy client? Wasn't the whole insurance business invented for people like me? Don't my fender-benders and bumps put food on some adjuster's table? If not for my blunders, what would the actuaries actuate?

My initial thought was that the company was writing to congratulate me on being a good customer. *Maybe they're writing to invite me to a banquet or to tell me I've won an award*, I thought.

The letter continued, documenting other secrets of our past:

Our records indicate that on November 18 we paid to fix damage to another vehicle when Max Lucado backed into another car in a parking lot.

The twofold appearance of the word *another* alarmed me. "Another" vehicle. "Another" car. Somebody is counting! Perhaps I need to urge them to read 1 Corinthians 13:5, "Love . . . keeps no record of wrongs" (NIV). The letter continued with another set of "anothers".

In April we paid to fix another vehicle when Denalyn Lucado hit the rear of another car at a stop sign.

"But she was giving the baby a bottle!" I said in her defense to no one listening. Denalyn was at a stoplight. Sara dropped her bottle in the floorboard and was crying, so Denalyn leaned over and picked it up and bumped the car ahead of her. Honest mistake. Could have happened to anyone.

And that time I backed into another car? I reported it! I was the one who walked into the building, found the owner, and told him what I had done. Confessed my fault. I did my part. I could have backed into the car and driven off, which, to be honest, I did consider but didn't do. Should I also share with them 1 John 1:9? "If we confess our sins, he will forgive our sins . . ."

Don't I get some credit for being honest?

Apparently not. Read the conclusion of the letter.

> *In view of the above information, we are not willing to reinstate your automobile insurance policy. The policy will terminate at 12:01* A.M. *Standard Time January 4. I'm sorry our reply could not have been more favorable. For your protection, you are urged to obtain other insurance to prevent any lapse in coverage.*

Wait a minute. Let me see if I get this right. I bought insurance to cover my mistakes. But then I get dropped for making mistakes. Hello. Did I miss something? Did I fail to see a footnote? Did I skip some fine print in the contract?

Did I overlook a paragraph that read, "We, the aforesaid company will consider one Max Lucado insurable until he shows himself to be one who needs insurance upon which time his coverage ceases"?

Isn't that like a doctor treating healthy patients only? Or a dentist hanging a sign in the window, "No cavities, please"? Or a teacher penalizing you for asking too many questions? Isn't that like qualifying for a loan by proving you don't need one? What if the fire department said it would protect you *until* you had a fire? What if a bodyguard said he'd protect you *unless* someone was after you? Or a lifeguard said she'd watch over you unless you started to drown?

Or what if, perish the thought, heaven had limitations to its coverage? What if you got a letter from the Pearly Gate Underwriting Division that read:

Dear Mrs. Smith,

I'm writing in response to this morning's request for forgiveness. I'm sorry to inform you that you have reached your quota of sins. Our records show that, since employing our services, you have erred seven times in the area of greed, and your prayer life is substandard when compared to others of like age and circumstance.

Further review reveals that your understanding of doctrine is in the lower 20 percentile and you have excessive tendencies to gossip. Because of your sins you are a high-risk candidate for heaven. You understand that grace has its limits. Jesus sends his regrets and kindest regards and hopes that you will find some other form of coverage.

Many fear receiving such a letter. Some worry they already have! If an insurance company can't cover my honest mistakes, can I expect God to cover my intentional rebellion?

Paul answers the question with what John Stott calls "the most startling statement in Romans."[1] God "makes even evil people right in his sight" (Rom. 4:5). What an incredible claim! It's one thing to make good people right, but those who are evil? We can expect God to justify the decent, but the dirty? Surely coverage is provided for the driver with the clean record, but the speeder? The ticketed? The high-risk client? How in the world can justification come for the evil?

The Direction of Grace

It can't. It can't come from the world. It must come from heaven. Man has no way, but *God has a way . . .*

Up until this point in Paul's letter all efforts at salvation have been from earth upward. Man has inflated his balloon with his own hot air and not been able to leave the atmosphere. Our pleas of ignorance are inexcusable (Rom. 1:20). Our comparisons with others are impermissible (2:1). Our religious merits are unacceptable

(2:29). The conclusion is unavoidable: self-salvation simply does not work. Man has no way to save himself.

But Paul announces that *God has a way*. Where man fails God excels. Salvation comes from heaven downward, not earth upward. "A new day *from* heaven will dawn upon us" (Luke 1:78). "Every good action and every perfect gift is *from* God" (James 1:17).

Please note: Salvation is God-given, God-driven, God-empowered, and God-originated. The gift is not from man to God. It is from God to man. "It is not our love for God; it is God's love for us in sending his Son to be the way to take away our sins" (1 John 4:10).

Grace is created by God and given to man. "Sky above, make victory fall like rain; clouds, pour down victory. Let the earth receive it, and let salvation grow, and let victory grow with it. I, the LORD, have created it" (Isa. 45:8).

On the basis of this point alone, Christianity is set apart from any other religion in the world. "No other system, ideology or religion proclaims a free forgiveness and a new life to those who have done nothing to deserve it but deserve judgment instead."[2]

To quote John MacArthur: "As far as the way of salvation is concerned, there are only two religions the world has ever known or will ever know—the religion of divine accomplishment, which is biblical Christianity, and the religion of human achievement, which includes all other kinds of religion, by whatever names they may go under."[3]

Every other approach to God is a bartering system; if I do this, God will do that. I'm either saved by works (what I do), emotions (what I experience), or knowledge (what I know).

By contrast, Christianity has no whiff of negotiation at all. Man is not the negotiator; indeed, man has no grounds from which to negotiate.

Those closest to God have understood this. Those nearest to

him have never boasted about their deeds; in fact, they were most disgusted by the thought of self-salvation. They describe legalism in repulsive terms. Isaiah said our righteous acts are "like filthy pieces of cloth," referring to menstrual cloth (Isa. 64:6). Paul equated our religious credentials with the pile of stink you avoid in the cow pasture. ("[I] do count them but dung" [Phil. 3:8 KJV]).

We can summarize the first three and one-half chapters of Romans with three words: *We have failed.*

We have attempted to reach the moon but scarcely made it off the ground. We tried to swim the Atlantic, but couldn't get beyond the reef. We have attempted to scale the Everest of salvation, but we have yet to leave the base camp, much less ascend the slope. The quest is simply too great; we don't need more supplies or muscle or technique; we need a helicopter.

Can't you hear it hovering?

"God has a way to *make people right with him*" (Rom. 3:21, italics mine). How vital that we embrace this truth. God's highest dream is not to make us rich, not to make us successful or popular or famous. God's dream is to make us right with him.

The Dilemma of Grace

How does God make us right with him? Let's return to the insurance company and ask a few questions: First, was it unjust in dismissing me as a client? No. I may find its decision distasteful, unenjoyable, even disheartening, but I cannot call it unfair. It only did what it said it would do.

So did our Father. He told Adam, "If you ever eat fruit from that tree, you will die" (Gen. 2:17). No fine print. No hidden agenda. No loophole or technicality. God has not played games with us. He has been fair. Since Eden, the wages of sin have been death (Rom. 6:23).

Just as reckless driving has its consequences, so does reckless living. Just as I have no defense before the insurance company, I have no defense before God. My record accuses me. My past convicts me.

Now, suppose the founder and CEO of the insurance company chose to have mercy upon me. Suppose, for some reason, he wanted to keep me as a client. What can he do? Can't he just close his eyes and pretend I made no mistakes? Why doesn't he take my driving record and tear it up? Two reasons.

First, the integrity of the company would be compromised. He would have to relax the standards of the organization, something he could not and should not do. The ideals of the organization are too valuable to be abandoned. The company cannot abandon its precepts and still maintain integrity.

Second, the mistakes of the driver would be encouraged. If there is no price for my mistakes, why should I drive carefully? If the president will dismiss my errors, then what's to keep me from driving however I want? If he is willing to ignore any blunders, then blunder on!

Is that the aim of the president? Is that the goal of his mercy? Lowered standards and poor driving? No. The president is faced with this dilemma. *How can I be merciful and fair at the same time? How can I offer grace without endorsing mistakes?*

Or, put in biblical terms, how can God punish the sin and love the sinner? Paul has made it clear, "The wrath of God is being revealed from heaven against all godlessness and wickedness" (Rom. 1:18 NIV). Is God going to lower his standard so we can be forgiven? Is God going to look away and pretend I've never sinned? Would we want a God who altered the rules and made exceptions? No. We want a God who "does not change like . . . shifting shadows" (James 1:17) and who "judges all people in the same way" (Rom. 2:11).

Besides, to ignore my sin is to endorse my sin. If my sin has no price, then sin on! If my sin brings no pain, then sin on! In fact, "We should do evil so that good will come" (Rom. 3:8). Is this the aim of God? To compromise his holiness and enable our evil?

Of course not. Then what is he to do? How can he be just and love the sinner? How can he be loving and punish the sin? How can he satisfy his standard *and* forgive my mistakes? Is there any way God could honor the integrity of heaven without turning his back on me?

The Decision of Grace

Holiness demands that sin be punished. Mercy compels that the sinner be loved. How can God do both? May I answer the question by returning to the insurance executive? Imagine him inviting me to his office and saying these words.

"Mr. Lucado, I have found a way to deal with your mistakes. I can't overlook them; to do so would be unjust. I can't pretend you didn't commit them; to do so would be a lie. But here is what I can do. In our records we have found a person with a spotless past. He has never broken a law. Not one violation, not one trespass, not even a parking ticket. He has volunteered to trade records with you. We will take your name and put it on his record. We will take his name and put it on yours. We will punish him for what you did. You, who did wrong, will be made right. He, who did right, will be made wrong."

My response? "You've got to be kidding! Who would do this for me? Who is this person?"

To which the president answers, "Me."

If you're waiting for an insurance executive to say that, don't hold your breath. He won't. He can't. Even if he wanted to he couldn't. He has no perfect record.

But if you're wanting God to say those words, you can sigh with relief. He has. He can. For "God was in Christ, making peace between the world and himself. . . . Christ had no sin, but God made him become sin so that in Christ we could become right with God" (2 Cor. 5:19, 21).

The perfect record of Jesus was given to you, and your imperfect record was given to Christ. Jesus was "not guilty, but he suffered for those who are guilty to bring you to God" (1 Peter 3:18). As a result, God's holiness is honored and his children are forgiven.

By his perfect life Jesus fulfilled the commands of the law. By his death he satisfied the demands of sin. Jesus suffered not like a sinner, but as a sinner. Why else would he cry, "My God, my God, why have You forsaken Me?" (Matt. 27:46 NKJV).

Ponder the achievement of God. He doesn't condone our sin; nor does he compromise his standard. He doesn't ignore our rebellion; nor does he relax his demands. Rather than dismiss our sin he assumes our sin and, incredibly, sentences himself. God's holiness is honored. Our sin is punished. And we are redeemed. God is still God. The wages of sin is still death. And we are made perfect.

That's right, *perfect*. "With one sacrifice he made perfect forever those who are being made holy" (Heb. 10:14).

God justifies (makes perfect) then sanctifies (makes holy). God does what we cannot do so we can be what we dare not dream, perfect before God. He justly justifies the unjust.

And what did he do with your poor driving record? "He canceled the debt, which listed all the rules we failed to follow. He took away that record with its rules and nailed it to the cross" (Col. 2:14).

And what should be your response? Let's go one more time to the insurance company. I return to my agent and ask him to call up my file. He does and stares at the computer screen in disbelief. "Mr. Lucado, you have a perfect past. Your performance is spotless."

My response? If I'm dishonest and ungrateful, I will deepen my voice and cross my arms and say, "You are right. It's not easy to be great."

If I'm honest and grateful, I will simply smile and say, "I don't deserve that compliment. In fact, I don't deserve that record. It was and is an unspeakable gift of grace."

By the way, I have a new automobile-insurance company. They charge me a little more since I've been bumped from a competitor. And who knows? I may get a few more letters before it's all over.

My eternal soul is under heavenly coverage, and Jesus isn't known for dismissing clients. He is known, however, for paying premiums and I'm paid up for life. I'm in good hands with him.

Before moving to the next chapter, let me field a question. There's a fellow who's had his hand up ever since the last paragraph on page 74. Yes sir? You're finding this all too . . . what?

I'm sorry, I still didn't understand . . . too good to be what? Too good to be *true*? Ah . . . well. You're not the first. In fact, Paul knew many of us would question the issue. That's why he wrote Romans 4. That's why I wrote the next chapter.

Excuse me? You have another question? Yes, you do look familiar. You sold me what? The insurance policy? The one you later canceled? Hmmm. I bet you do have a hard time understanding grace.

8

Credit Where Credit Is Not Due

Romans 3:27–4:25

A person is made right with God through faith, not through obeying the law. ROMANS 3:28

Remember the good ol' days when credit cards were imprinted by hand? The clerk would take your plastic and place it in the imprint machine, and *rrack-rrack,* the numbers would be registered and the purchase would be made. I learned to operate such a device in a gasoline station on the corner of Broadway and Fourth when I was fourteen years old. For a dollar an hour I cleaned windshields, pumped gas, and checked the oil. (Yes, Virginia, gas-station attendants did those things back then.)

My favorite task, however, was imprinting credit cards. There's nothing like the surge of power you feel when you run the imprinter over the plastic. I'd always steal a glance at the customer to watch him wince as I *rrack-rracked* his card.

Credit-card purchases today aren't nearly as dramatic. Nowadays the magnetic strip is swiped through the slot, or the numbers are entered on the keyboard. No noise. No drama. No pain. Bring back the *rrack-rrack* days when the purchase was announced for all to hear.

You buy gas, *rrack-rrack.*

You charge some clothes, *rrack-rrack.*

You pay for dinner, *rrack-rrack.*

If the noise didn't get you, the statement at the end of the month would. Thirty days is ample time to *rrack* up enough purchases to *rrack* your budget.

And a lifetime is enough to *rrack* up some major debt in heaven.

You yell at your kids, *rrack-rrack.*

You covet a friend's car, *rrack-rrack.*

You envy your neighbor's success, *rrack-rrack.*

You break a promise, *rrack-rrack.*

You lie, *rrack-rrack.*

You lose control, *rrack-rrack.*

You doze off reading this book, *rrack-rrack, rrack-rrack, rrack-rrack.*

Further and further in debt.

Initially, we attempt to repay what we owe. (Remember the rock-stacker?) Every prayer is a check written, and each good deed is a payment made. If we can do one good act for every bad act, then won't our account balance out in the end? If I can counter my cussing with compliments, my lusts with loyalties, my complaints with contributions, my vices with victories—then won't my account be justified?

It would, except for two problems.

First, I don't know the *cost* of each sin. The price of gas is easy to find. Would that it were so clear with sin. It's not. What, for example, is the charge for getting mad in traffic? I get ticked off at some fellow who cuts in front of me, what do I do to pay for my crime? Drive fifty in a fifty-five zone? Give a wave and a smile to ten consecutive cars? Who knows? Or what if I wake up in a bad mood? What's the charge for a couple of mopey hours? Will one church service next Sunday offset one grumpy morning today? And what qualifies for a bad mood? Is the charge for grumpiness less on cloudy days than clear? Or am I permitted a certain number of grouchy days per year?

This can get confusing, you know.

And not only don't I know the cost of my sins, I don't always know the *occasion* of my sins. There are times when I sin and I don't even know it! I was twelve years old before I realized it was a sin to hate your enemy. My bike was stolen when I was eight. I hated the thief for four years! How do I pay for those sins? Do I get an exemption based on ignorance?

And what about the sins I'm committing now without realizing it? What if somebody somewhere discovers it is a sin to play golf? Or what if God thinks the way I play golf is a sin? Oh, boy. I'll have some serious settling up to do.

And what about our secret sins? Even as I write this chapter, I'm sinning. I'd like to think I'm writing to the glory of God, but am I? Am I free of vanity? Does this vessel have only concern for contents and no concern for the container? Hardly. I wonder if people will agree, if they'll approve, if they'll appreciate all the long, painstaking, tedious, exhausting, tortuous hours I am humbly putting into these watershed, historic thoughts.

And what of you? Any sins of omission on this month's statement? Did you miss any chance to do good? Overlook an opportunity to forgive? Neglect an open door to serve? Did you seize *every* chance to encourage your friends?

Rrack-rrack, rrack-rrack, rrack-rrack.

And there are other concerns. The grace period, for example.

My credit card allows a minimal payment and then rolls the debt into the next month. Does God? Will he let me pay off today's greed next year? What about interest? If I leave a sin on my statement for several months, does it incur more sin? And speaking of the statement . . . where is it? Can I see it? Who has it? How do I pay the blasted thing off?

There it is. That's the question. How do I deal with the debt I owe to God?

Deny it? My conscience won't let me.

Find worse sins in others? God won't fall for that.

Claim lineage immunity? Family pride won't help.

Try to pay it off? I could, but that takes us back to the problem. We don't know the cost of sin. We don't even know how much we owe.

Then what do we do? Listen to Paul's answer in what one scholar says is "possibly the most important single paragraph ever written."[1]

> All need to be made right with God by his grace, which is a free gift. They need to be made free from sin through Jesus Christ. God gave him as a way to forgive sin through faith in the blood of Jesus. (Rom. 3:24–25)

Simply put: The cost of your sins is more than you can pay. The gift of your God is more than you can imagine. "A person is made right with God through faith," Paul explains, "not through obeying the law" (v. 28).

This may very well be the most difficult spiritual truth for us to embrace. For some reason, people accept Jesus as Lord before they accept him as Savior. It's easier to comprehend his power than his mercy. We'll celebrate the empty tomb long before we'll kneel at the cross. We, like Thomas, would die for Christ before we'd let Christ die for us.

We aren't alone. We aren't the first to struggle with Paul's presentation of grace. Apparently, the first ones to doubt the epistle to the Romans were the first to read it. In fact, you get the impression Paul can hear their questions. The apostle lifts his pen from the page and imagines his readers: some squirming, some doubting, some denying. Anticipating their thoughts, he deals with their objections.

Objection #1: Too Risky to Be True

The first objection comes from the pragmatist. "Do we destroy the law by following the way of faith?" (Rom. 3:31). The concern here is motivation. "If I'm not saved by my works, then why work? If I'm not saved by the law, then why keep the law? If I'm not saved by what I do, then why do anything?"

You've got to admit grace is risky. There *is* the chance that people will take it to an extreme. There *is* the possibility that people will abuse God's goodness.

A further word about credit cards might be helpful here. My father had a simple rule about them: Own as few as possible and pay them off as soon as possible. His salary as a mechanic was sufficient but not abundant, and he hated the thought of paying interest. He made it a point to pay the balance in full at the end of the month. You can imagine my surprise when he put a credit card in my hand the day I left for college.

Standing in the driveway with car packed and farewells said, he handed it to me. I looked at the name on the plastic; it wasn't mine, it was his. He had ordered an extra card for me. His only instructions to me were, "Be careful how you use it."

Pretty risky, don't you think? As I was driving to college it occurred to me that I was a free man. I could go anywhere I wanted to go. I had wheels and a tank of gas. I had my clothes. I had money in my pocket and a stereo in the trunk and, most of all, I had a credit card. I was a slave set free! The chains were off. I could be in Mexico before nightfall! What was to keep me from going wild?

Such is the question of the pragmatist. What is to keep us from going wild? If worshiping doesn't save me, why worship? If tithing doesn't save me, why give? If my morality doesn't save me, then watch out, ladies, here I come! Jude warns of this attitude when he speaks of people who "abuse his grace as an opportunity for immorality" (Jude 4 PHILLIPS).

Later Paul will counter his critics with the question, "So do you think we should continue sinning so that God will give us even more grace! No!" (Rom. 6:1). Or as one translator writes, "What a ghastly thought!" (PHILLIPS).

A ghastly thought, indeed. Grace promoting evil? Mercy endorsing sin? What a horrible idea! The apostle uses the strongest Greek idiom possible to repudiate the idea: *Me genoito!* The phrase literally means "may it never be!" As he has already said, God's "kindness is meant to lead you to repentance" (Rom. 2:4 TLB).

Get it straight: Someone who sees grace as permission to sin has missed grace entirely. Mercy understood is holiness desired. "[Jesus] gave himself for us so he might pay the price to free us from all evil and to make us pure people who belong only to him—*people who are always wanting to do good deeds*" (Titus 2:14, italics mine).

Note that last phrase: "people who are always wanting to do good deeds." Grace fosters an eagerness for good. Grace doesn't spawn a desire to sin. If one has truly embraced God's gift, he will not mock it. In fact, if a person uses God's mercy as liberty to sin, one might wonder whether the person ever knew God's mercy at all.

When my father gave me his card, he didn't attach a list of regulations. There was no contract for me to sign or rules for me to read. He didn't tell me to place my hand on the Bible and pledge to reimburse him for any expenses. In fact, he didn't ask for any payment at all. As things turned out, I went a few weeks into the semester without using it. Why? Because he gave me more than a card; he gave me his trust. And where I might break his rules, I wasn't about to abuse his trust.

God's trust makes us eager to do right. Such is the genius of grace. The law can show us where we do wrong, but it can't make us eager to do right. Grace can. Or as Paul answers, "Faith causes us to be what the law truly wants" (Rom. 3:31).

Objection #2: Too New to Be True

The second objection to grace comes from a man who is cautious of anything new. "Don't give me any of this newfangled teaching. Just give me the law. If it was good enough for Abraham, it is good enough for me."

"All right, let me tell you about the faith of your father, Abraham," Paul answers.

"If Abraham was made right by the things he did, he had a reason to brag. But this is not God's view, because the Scripture says, 'Abraham believed God, and God accepted Abraham's faith, and that faith made him right with God'" (4:2–3).

These words must have stunned the Jews. Paul points to Abraham as a prototype of grace. The Jews upheld Abraham as a man who was blessed *because* of his obedience. Not the case, argues Paul. The first book in the Bible says that Abraham "believed the LORD, and he credited it to him as righteousness" (Gen. 15:6 NIV). It was his faith, not his works, that made him right with God. *The Message* renders Romans 4:2, "[Abraham] trusted God to set him right instead of trying to be right on his own."

Five times in six verses Paul uses the word *credit*. The term is common in the financial world. To credit an account is to make a deposit. If I credit your account then I either increase your balance or lower your debt.

Wouldn't it be nice if someone credited your charge-card account? All month long you *rrack-rrack* up the bills, dreading the day the statement comes in the mail. When it comes you leave it on your desk for a few days, not wanting to see how much you owe. Finally, you force yourself to open the envelope. With one eye closed and the other open, you peek at the number. What you read causes the other eye to pop open. "A zero balance!"

There must be a mistake, so you call the bank that issued the card. "Yes," the bank manager explains, "your account is paid in full. A Mr. Max Lucado sent us a check to cover your debt."

You can't believe your ears. "How do you know his check is good?"

"Oh, there is no doubt. Mr. Lucado has been paying off people's debts for years."

By the way, I'd love to do that for you, but don't get your hopes up. I have a few bills of my own. But Jesus would love to, and he can! He has no personal debt at all. And, what's more, he has been doing it for years. For proof Paul reaches into the two-thousand-year-old file marked "Abram of Ur" and pulls out a statement. The statement has its share of charges. Abram was far from perfect. There were times when he trusted the Egyptians before he trusted God: He even lied, telling Pharaoh that his wife was his sister. But Abram made one decision that changed his eternal life: "He trusted God to set him right instead of trying to be right on his own" (Rom. 4:3 MSG).

Here is a man justified by faith before his circumcision (v. 10), before the law (v. 13), before Moses and the Ten Commandments. Here is a man justified by faith before the cross! The sin-covering blood of Calvary extends as far into the past as it does into the future.

Abraham is not the only Old Testament hero to cast himself

upon God's grace. "David said the same thing. He said that people are truly blessed when God, without paying attention to good deeds, makes people right with himself. 'Happy are they whose sins are forgiven, whose wrongs are pardoned. Happy is the person whom God does not consider guilty'" (vv. 6–8).

We must not see grace as a provision made after the law had failed. Grace was offered *before* the law was revealed. Indeed, grace was offered before man was created! "You were bought, not with something that ruins like gold or silver, but with the precious blood of Christ, who was like a pure and perfect lamb. Christ was chosen before the world was made, but he was shown to the world in these last times for your sake" (1 Pet. 1:18–20).

Why would God offer grace before we needed it? Glad you asked. Let's return one final time to the charge card my father gave me. Did I mention that I went several months without needing it? But when I needed it, I *really* needed it. You see, I wanted to visit a friend on another campus. Actually, the friend was a girl in another city, six hours away. On an impulse I skipped class one Friday morning and headed out. Not knowing whether my parents would approve, I didn't ask their permission. Because I left in a hurry, I forgot to take any money. I made the trip without their knowledge and with an empty wallet.

Everything went fine until I rear-ended a car on the return trip. Using a crowbar, I pried the fender off my front wheel so the car could limp to a gas station. I can still envision the outdoor phone where I stood in the autumn chill. My father, who assumed I was on campus, took my collect call and heard my tale. My story wasn't much to boast about. I'd made a trip without his knowledge, without any money, and wrecked his car.

"Well," he said after a long pause, "these things happen. That's why I gave you the card. I hope you learned a lesson."

Did I learn a lesson? I certainly did. I learned that my father's forgiveness predated my mistake. He had given me the card before my wreck in the event that I would have one. He had provided for my blunder before I blundered. Need I tell you that God has done the same? Please understand, Dad didn't want me to wreck the car. He didn't give me the card *so* that I would wreck the car. But he knew his son. And he knew his son would someday need grace.

Please understand, God doesn't want us to sin. He didn't give us grace *so* we would sin. But he knows his children. "He made their hearts and understands everything they do" (Ps. 33:15). "He knows how we were made" (Ps. 103:14). And he knew that we would someday need his grace.

Grace is nothing new. God's mercy predates Paul and his readers, predates David and Abraham; it even predates creation. It certainly predates any sin you've committed. God's grace is older than your sin and greater than your sin. Too good to be true? That's the third objection.

Objection #3: Too Good to Be True

Just as there was a pragmatist who said grace is too risky and a traditionalist who said grace is too new, there was likely a skeptic who said, "This is too good to be true."

This is by far the most common objection to grace. No one came into my office this week to ask me about Abraham and works and law and faith. But these walls did hear the question of the young woman who spent two university years saying yes to the flesh and no to God. I did talk to a young husband who wonders if God could forgive an abortion he funded a decade ago. There was the father who'd just realized he'd devoted his life to work and neglected his kids.

All are wondering if they've overextended their credit line with

God. They aren't alone. The vast majority of people simply state, "God may give grace to you, but not to me. You see, I've charted the waters of failure. I've pushed the envelope too many times. I'm not your typical sinner, I'm guilty of ____________." And they fill in the blank.

How would you fill in the blank? Is there a chapter in your biography that condemns you? A valley of your heart too deep for the firstborn Son to reach? If you think there is no hope for you, then Paul has a person he wants you to meet. Our barren past reminds the apostle of Sarah's barren womb.

God had promised Sarah and Abram a child. In fact, the name Abram meant "exalted father." God even changed Abram's name to Abraham (father of many) but still no son. Forty years passed before the promise was honored. Don't you think the conversation became dreadfully routine for Abraham?

"What is your name?"

"Abraham."

"Oh, 'father of many'! What a great title. Tell me, how many sons do you have?"

Abraham would sigh and answer, "None."

God had promised a child, but Abraham had no son. He left his home for an unknown land, but no son was born. He overcame famine, but still had no son. His nephew Lot came and went, but still no son. He would have encounters with angels and Melchizedek, but still be without an heir.

By now Abraham was ninety-nine, and Sarah was not much younger. She knitted and he played solitaire, and both chuckled at the thought of bouncing a boy on their bony knees. He lost his hair, she lost her teeth, and neither spent a lot of time lusting for the other. But somehow they never lost hope. Occasionally, he'd think of God's promise and give her a wink, and she'd give him a smile and think, *Well, God did promise us a child, didn't he?*

> When everything was hopeless, Abraham believed anyway, deciding to live not on the basis of what he saw he *couldn't* do, but on what God said he *would do*. . . .
>
> Abraham didn't focus on his own impotence and say, "It's hopeless. This hundred-year-old body could never have a child." Nor did he survey Sarah's decades of infertility and give up. He didn't tiptoe around God's promise cautiously asking skeptical questions. He plunged into the promise and came up strong, ready for God. That's why it is said, "Abraham was declared fit before God by trusting God to set him right." (Rom. 4:18–21 MSG)

Everything was gone. No youth. No vigor. No strength. The get-up-and-go had got up and gone. All old Abe and Sarah had was a social-security check and a promise from heaven. But Abraham decided to trust the promise rather than focus on the problems. As a result the Medicare couple were the first to bring a crib into the nursing home.

Do we have much more than they? Not really. There's not a one of us who hasn't *rrack-rracked* up more bills than we could ever pay. But there's not a one of us who must remain in debt. The same God who gave a child to Abraham has promised grace to us.

What's more incredible, Sarah telling Abraham that he was a daddy, or God calling you and me righteous? Both are absurd. Both are too good to be true. But both are from God.

9 Major League Grace

Romans 5:1–3

Since we have been made right with God by our faith, we have peace with God. This happened through our Lord Jesus Christ, who has brought us into that blessing of God's grace that we now enjoy. We are happy because of the hope we have of sharing God's glory. ROMANS 5:1–2

Batters hustling to the plate to take their swings? Questionable calls going uncontested? Umpires being thanked after the game? Fans returning foul balls?

This is Major League Baseball?

It was. For a few weeks during the spring of '95, professional baseball was a different game. The million-dollar arms were at home. The Cadillac bats were in the rack. The contracted players were negotiating for more money. The owners, determined to start the season, threw open the gates to almost anybody who knew how to scoop a grounder or run out a bunt.

These weren't minor-leaguers. The minor leagues were also on strike. These were fellows who went from coaching Little League one week to wearing a Red Sox uniform the next.

The games weren't fancy, mind you. Line drives rarely reached the outfield. One manager said his pitchers threw the ball so slowly the radar gun couldn't clock them. A fan could shell a dozen peanuts in the time it took to relay a throw from the outfield. The players huffed and puffed more than the "Little Engine That Could."

But, my, did the players have fun! The diamond was studded with guys who played the game for the love of the game. When the coach said run, they ran. When he needed a volunteer to shag flies, a dozen hands went up. They arrived before the park was open, greasing their gloves and cleaning their cleats. When it was time to go home they stayed until the grounds crew ran them off. They thanked the attendants for washing their uniforms. They thanked the caterers for the food. They thanked the fans for paying the dollar to watch. The line of players willing to sign autographs was longer than the line of fans wanting them.

These guys didn't see themselves as a blessing to baseball but baseball as a blessing to them. They didn't expect luxury; they were surprised by it. They didn't demand more playtime; they were thrilled to play at all.

It was baseball again!

In Cincinnati the general manager stepped out on the field and applauded the fans for coming out. The Phillies gave away free hot dogs and sodas. In the trade of the year, the Cleveland Indians gave five players to the Cincinnati Reds—for free!

It wasn't classy. You missed the three-run homers and frozen-rope pick-offs. But that was forgiven for the pure joy of seeing some guys play who really enjoyed the game. What made them so special? Simple. They were living a life they didn't deserve. These guys didn't make it to the big leagues on skill; they made it on luck. They weren't picked because they were good; they were picked because they were willing.

And they knew it! Not one time did you read an article about the replacement players arguing over poor pay. I did read a story about a fellow who offered a hundred grand if some owner would sign him. There was no jockeying for position. No second-guessing the management. No strikes. No lockouts or walkouts. Heavens, these guys didn't even complain that their names weren't stitched on the jerseys. They were just happy to be on the team.

Shouldn't we be, as well? Aren't we a lot like these players? If the first four chapters of Romans tell us anything, they tell us we are living a life we don't deserve. We aren't good enough to get picked, but look at us, suited up and ready to play! We aren't skillful enough to make the community softball league, but our names are on the greatest roster of history!

Do we deserve to be here? No. But would we trade the privilege? Not for the world. For if Paul's proclamation is true, God's grace has placed us on a dream team beyond imagination. Our past is pardoned, and our future secure. And lest we forget this unspeakable gift, Paul itemizes the blessings that God's grace brings into our world (see Rom. 5:1–12).

Blessing #1: We Have Peace with God

"Since we have been made right with God by our faith, we have peace with God" (v. 1).

Peace with God. What a happy consequence of faith! Not just peace between countries, peace between neighbors, or peace at home; salvation brings peace with God.

Once a monk and his apprentice traveled from the abbey to a nearby village. The two parted at the city gates, agreeing to meet the next morning after completing their tasks. According to plan, they met and began the long walk back to the abbey. The monk noticed that the younger man was unusually quiet. He asked him if anything was wrong. "What business is it of yours?" came the terse response.

Now the monk was sure his brother was troubled, but he said nothing. The distance between the two began to increase. The apprentice walked slowly, as if to separate himself from his teacher. When the abbey came in sight, the monk stopped at the gate and waited on the student. "Tell me, my son. What troubles your soul?"

The boy started to react again, but when he saw the warmth in his master's eyes, his heart began to melt. "I have sinned greatly," he sobbed. "Last night I slept with a woman and abandoned my vows. I am not worthy to enter the abbey at your side."

The teacher put his arm around the student and said, "We will enter the abbey together. And we will enter the cathedral together. And together we will confess your sin. No one but God will know which of the two of us fell."[1]

Doesn't that describe what God has done for us? When we kept our sin silent, we withdrew from him. We saw him as an enemy. We took steps to avoid his presence. But our confession of faults alters our perception. God is no longer a foe but a friend. We are at peace with him. He did more than the monk did, much more. More than share in our sin, Jesus was "crushed for the evil we did. The punishment, which made us well, was given to him" (Isa. 53:5). "He accepted the shame" (Heb. 12:2). He leads us into the presence of God.

Blessing #2: We Have a Place with God

Being ushered into God's presence is the second blessing Paul describes: "This happened through our Lord Jesus Christ, who has brought us into that blessing of God's grace that we now enjoy" (v. 2). Look at the phrase, "who has brought us into." The Greek word means "to usher into the presence of royalty." Twice in Ephesians Paul reminds us of our right to enter God's presence:

> It is through Christ that all of us are able to come into the presence of the Father. (Eph. 2:18 TEV)
>
> Now we can come fearlessly right into God's presence. . . . (Eph. 3:12 TLV)

Christ meets you outside the throne room, takes you by the hand, and walks you into the presence of God. Upon entrance we find grace, not condemnation; mercy, not punishment. Where we would never be granted an audience with the king, we are now welcomed into his presence.

If you are a parent you understand this. If a child you don't know appears on your doorstep and asks to spend the night, what would you do? Likely you would ask him his name, where he lives, find out why he is roaming the streets, and contact his parents. On the other hand, if a youngster enters your house escorted by your child, that child is welcome. The same is true with God. By becoming friends with the Son we gain access to the Father.

Jesus promised, "All who stand before others and say they believe in me, I will say before my Father in heaven that they belong to me" (Matt. 10:32). Because we are friends of his Son, we have entrance to the throne room. He ushers us into that "blessing of God's grace that we now enjoy" (Rom. 5:2).

This gift is not an occasional visit before God but rather a permanent "access by faith into this grace by which we now stand" (v. 2 NIV). Here is where my analogy with the replacement baseball players ceases. They knew their status was temporary. Their privilege lasted only as long as the strike continued. Not so with us.

Our privilege lasts as long as God is faithful, and his faithfulness has never been questioned. "If we are not faithful, he will still be faithful, because he cannot be false to himself" (2 Tim. 2:13). Isaiah described God's faithfulness as the "belt around his waist" (Isa. 11:5). David announces that the Lord's faithfulness "reaches to the heavens" (Ps. 36:5).

I suppose the baseball analogy would work if the team owner conferred upon us the status of lifetime team members. Upon doing so our position on the squad would not depend upon our performance but upon his power. Has an owner ever given such a gift? I don't know, but God has and God does.

Before moving on, note the sequence of these blessings. The first blessing deals with our past; we have peace with God because our past is pardoned. The second blessing deals with the present. We have a place with God because Jesus has presented us to his Father. Any guess what the next blessing will cover?

Blessing #3: We Share in His Glory

You got it: our future. "And we are happy because of the hope we have of sharing God's glory" (Rom. 5:2).

Because of God's grace we go from being people whose "throats are like open graves" (Ps. 5:9) to being participants of God's glory. We were washed up and put out; now we are called up and put in.

What does it mean to share in God's glory? May I devote a chapter to that question? (Why am I asking you? The book's already written.) Come with me from the world of baseball and replacement players to a scene of a king and a cripple. You'll understand what I mean in a few pages.

10 The Privilege of Paupers

Romans 5:6–8

But God shows his great love for us in this way: Christ died for us while we were still sinners. ROMANS 5:8

Warning: The content of this chapter is likely to cause hunger. You might want to read it in the kitchen.

My first ministry position was in Miami, Florida. In our congregation we had more than our share of southern ladies who loved to cook. I fit in well because I was a single guy who loved to eat. The church was fond of having Sunday evening potluck dinners, and about once a quarter they *feasted.*

Some church dinners live up to the "potluck" name. The cooks empty the pot, and you try your luck. Not so with this church. Our potlucks were major events. Area grocery stores asked us to advise them in advance so they could stock their shelves. Cookbook sales went up. People never before seen in the pews could be found in the food line. For the women it was an unofficial cookoff, and for the men it was an unabashed pigout.

My, it was good, a veritable cornucopia of Corningware. Juicy ham bathed in pineapple, baked beans, pickled relish, pecan pie . . . (Oops, I just drooled on my computer keyboard.) Ever wondered why there are so many hefty preachers? You enter the ministry for meals like those.

As a bachelor I counted on potluck dinners for my survival strategy. While others were planning what to cook, I was studying the storage techniques of camels. Knowing I should bring something, I'd make it a point to raid my kitchen shelves on Sunday afternoon. The result was pitiful: One time I took a half-empty jar of Planters peanuts; another time I made a half-dozen jelly sandwiches. One of my better offerings was an unopened sack of chips; a more meager gift was a can of tomato soup, also unopened.

Wasn't much, but no one ever complained. In fact, the way those ladies acted, you would've thought I brought the Thanksgiving turkey. They'd take my jar of peanuts and set it on the long table with the rest of the food and hand me a plate. "Go ahead, Max, don't be bashful. Fill up your plate." And I would! Mashed potatoes and gravy. Roast beef. Fried chicken. I took a little bit of everything, except the peanuts.

I came like a pauper and ate like a king!

Though Paul never attended a potluck, he would have loved the symbolism. He would say that Christ does for us precisely what those women did for me. He welcomes us to his table by virtue of his love and our request. It is not our offerings that grant us a place at the feast; indeed, anything we bring appears puny at his table.

Our admission of hunger is the only demand, for "Blessed are those who hunger and thirst for righteousness, for they shall be filled" (Matt. 5:6 NKJV).

Our hunger, then, is not a yearning to be avoided but rather a God-given desire to be heeded. Our weakness is not to be dismissed but to be confessed. Isn't this at the heart of Paul's words when he writes, "When we were unable to help ourselves, at the moment of our need, Christ died for us, although we were living against God. Very few people will die to save the life of someone else. Although perhaps for a good person someone might possibly die. But God shows his great love for us in this way: Christ died for us while we were still sinners" (Rom. 5:6–8).

The Portrait of a Pauper

Paul's portrait of us is not attractive. We were "unable to help ourselves," "living against God," "sinners," and "God's enemies" (Rom. 5:6, 8, 10). Such are the people for whom God died.

Family therapist Paul Faulkner tells of the man who set out to adopt a troubled teenage girl. One would question the father's logic. The girl was destructive, disobedient, and dishonest. One day she came home from school and ransacked the house looking for money. By the time he arrived, she was gone and the house was in shambles.

Upon hearing of her actions, friends urged him not to finalize the adoption. "Let her go," they said. "After all, she's not really your daughter." His response was simply. "Yes, I know. But I told her she was."[1]

God, too, has made a covenant to adopt his people. His covenant is not invalidated by our rebellion. It's one thing to love us when we are strong, obedient, and willing. But when we ransack his house and steal what is his? This is the test of love.

And God passes the test. "God shows his great love for us in this way: Christ died for us while we were still sinners" (5:8).

The ladies at our church didn't see me and my peanuts and say, "Come back when you've learned to cook."

The father didn't look at the wrecked house and say, "Come back when you've learned respect."

God didn't look at our frazzled lives and say, "I'll die for you when you deserve it."

Nor did David look at Mephibosheth and say, "I'll rescue you when you've learned to walk."

Mephibo-*what?*

Mephibosheth. When you hear his story you'll see why I mention his name. Blow the dust off the books of 1 and 2 Samuel, and there you'll see him.

> (Saul's son Jonathan had a son named Mephibosheth, who was crippled in both feet. He was five years old when the news came from Jezreel that Saul and Jonathan were dead. Mephibosheth's nurse had picked him up and run away. But as she hurried to leave, she dropped him, and now he was lame.) (2 Sam. 4:4)

The parentheses around the verse are not typos. Mephibosheth is bracketed into the Bible. The verse doesn't tell us much, just his name (Mephibosheth), his calamity (dropped by his nurse), his deformity (crippled), and then it moves on.

But that's enough to raise a few questions. Who was this boy? Why is this story in Scripture? Why is Lucado mentioning him in a book about grace? A bit of background would be helpful.

Mephibosheth was the son of Jonathan, the grandson of Saul, who was the first king of Israel. Saul and Jonathan were killed in battle, leaving the throne to be occupied by David. In those days the new king often staked out his territory by exterminating the family of the previous king.

David had no intention of following this tradition, but the family of Saul didn't know that. So they hurried to escape. Of special concern to them was five-year-old Mephibosheth, for upon the deaths of his father and uncle, he was the presumptive heir to the throne. If David was intent on murdering Saul's heirs, this boy would be first on his list. So the family got out of Dodge. But in the haste of the moment, Mephibosheth slipped from the arms of his nurse, permanently damaging both feet. For the rest of his life he would be a cripple.

If his story is beginning to sound familiar, it should. You and he have a lot in common. Weren't you also born of royalty? And don't you carry the wounds of a fall? And hasn't each of us lived in fear of a king we have never seen?

Mephibosheth would understand Paul's portrait of us paupers, "when we were unable to help ourselves . . . " (Rom. 5:6). For nearly two decades the young prince lived in a distant land, unable to walk to the king, too fearful to talk to the king. He was unable to help himself.

Meanwhile, David's kingdom flourished. Under his leadership, Israel grew to ten times its original size. He knew no defeat on the battlefield nor insurrection in his court. Israel was at peace. The people were thankful. And David, the shepherd made king, did not forget his promise to Jonathan.

The Promise of a King

David and Jonathan were like two keys on a piano keyboard. Alone they made music, but together they made harmony. Jonathan "loved David as much as he loved himself" (1 Sam. 20:17). Their legendary friendship met its ultimate test the day David learned that Saul was trying to kill him. Jonathan pledged to save David and asked his friend one favor in return: "You must never stop showing your kindness to my family, even when the LORD has destroyed all your enemies from the earth. So Jonathan made an agreement with David" (1 Sam. 20:15–16).

Don't you know this was a tender memory for David? Can't you imagine him reflecting on this moment years later? Standing on the balcony overlooking the safe city. Astride his steed riding through the abundant fields. Dressed in armor inspecting his capable army. Were there times when he was overwhelmed with gratitude? Were there times when he thought, *Had it not been for Jonathan saving my life, none of this would have happened?*

Perhaps such a moment of reflection prompted him to turn to his servants and ask, "Is anyone still left in Saul's family? I want to show kindness to that person for Jonathan's sake!" (2 Sam. 9:1).

Those in the grip of grace are known to ask such questions. Can't I do something for somebody? Can't I be kind to someone because others have been kind to me? This isn't a political maneuver. David isn't seeking to do good to be applauded by people. Nor is he doing something good so someone will do something for him. He is driven by the singular thought that he, too, was once weak. And in his weakness he was helped. David, while hiding from Saul, qualified for Paul's epitaph, "when we were unable to help ourselves" (Rom. 5:6).

David was delivered; now he desires to do the same. A servant named Ziba knows of a descendant. "'Jonathan has a son still living who is crippled in both feet.' The king asked Ziba, 'Where is this son?' Ziba answered, 'He is at the house of Makir son of Ammiel in Lo Debar'" (2 Sam. 9:3–4).

Just one sentence and David knew he had more than he bargained for. The boy was "crippled in both feet." Who would have blamed David for asking Ziba, "Are there any other options? Any healthy family members?"

Who would have faulted him for reasoning, *A cripple would not fit well into the castle crowd. Only the elite walk these floors; this kid can't even walk! And what service could he provide? No wealth, no education, no training. And who knows what he looks like? All these years he's been living in . . . what was it again? Lo Debar? Even the name means "barren place." Surely there is someone I can help who isn't so needy.*

But such words were never spoken. David's only response was, "Where is this son?" (v. 4).

This son. One wonders how long it had been since Mephibosheth was referred to as a son. In all previous references he was called a cripple. Every mention of him thus far is followed by his handicap. But the words of David make no mention of his affliction. He doesn't ask, "Where is Mephibosheth, this problem child?" but rather asks, "Where is this son?"

Many of you know what it's like to carry a stigma. Each time your name is mentioned, your calamity follows.

"Have you heard from John lately? You know, the fellow who got divorced?"

"We got a letter from Jerry. Remember him, the alcoholic?"

"Sharon is in town. What a shame that she has to raise those kids alone."

"I saw Melissa today. I don't know why she can't keep a job."

Like a pesky sibling, your past follows you wherever you go. Isn't there anyone who sees you for who you are and not what you did? Yes. There is One who does. Your King. When God speaks of you, he doesn't mention your plight, pain, or problem; he lets you share his glory. He calls you his child.

> He will not always accuse us,
>   and he will not be angry forever.
> He has not punished us as our sins should be punished;
>   he has not repaid us for the evil we have done.
> As high as the sky is above the earth,

so great is his love for those who respect him.
He has taken our sins away from us
as far as the east is from the west.
The LORD has mercy on those who respect him,
as a father has mercy on his children.
He knows how we were made;
he remembers that we are dust. (Ps. 103:9–14)

Mephibosheth carried his stigma for twenty years. When people mentioned his name, they mentioned his problem. But when the king mentioned his name, he called him "son." And one word from the palace offsets a thousand voices in the streets.

David's couriers journeyed to Mephibosheth's door, carried him to a chariot, and escorted him to the palace. He was taken before the king, where he bowed facedown on the floor and confessed, "I am your servant" (2 Sam. 9:6). His fear is understandable. Though he may have been told that David was kind, what assurance did he have? Though the emissaries surely told him that David meant no harm, he was afraid. (Wouldn't you be?) The anxiety was on the face that faced the floor. David's first words to him were, "Don't be afraid."

By the way, your king has been known to say the same. Are you aware that the most repeated command from the lips of Jesus was, "Fear not"? Are you aware that the command from heaven not to be afraid appears in every book of the Bible?

Mephibosheth had been called, found, and rescued, but he still needed assurance. Don't we all? Don't we, like the trembling guest, need assurance that we are bowing before a gracious king? Paul says we have that assurance. The apostle points to the cross as our guarantee of God's love. "God shows his great love for us in this way: Christ died for us while we were still sinners" (Rom. 5:8). God proved his love for us by sacrificing his Son.

Formerly God had sent prophets to preach: Now he has sent his son to die. Earlier God commissioned angels to aid, now he has offered his son to redeem. When we tremble he points us to the splattered blood on the splintered beams and says, "Don't be afraid."

During the early days of the Civil War a Union soldier was arrested on charges of desertion. Unable to prove his innocence, he was condemned and sentenced to die a deserter's death. His appeal found its way to the desk of Abraham Lincoln. The president felt mercy for the soldier and signed a pardon. The soldier returned to service, fought the entirety of the war, and was killed in the last battle. Found within his breast pocket was the signed letter of the president.[2]

Close to the heart of the soldier were his leader's words of pardon. He found courage in grace. I wonder how many thousands more have found courage in the emblazoned cross of their king.

The Privilege of Adoption

Just as David kept his promise to Jonathan, so God keeps his promise to us. The name Mephibosheth means "he who scatters shame." And that is exactly what David intended to do for the young prince.

In swift succession David returned to Mephibosheth all his land, crops, and servants and then insisted that the cripple eat at the king's table. Not just once but four times!

> "I will give you back all the land of your grandfather Saul, and *you will always eat at my table*."
>
> "Mephibosheth . . . *will always eat at my table*."
>
> "So *Mephibosheth ate at David's table* as if he were one of the king's sons."
>
> "Mephibosheth lived in Jerusalem, because *he always ate at the king's table. And he was crippled in both feet*." (2 Sam. 9:7, 10, 11, 13 *italics mine*)

Pause and envision the scene in the royal dining room. May I turn my pen over to Charles Swindoll to assist you?

> The dinner bell rings through the king's palace and David comes to the head of the table and sits down. In a few moments Amnon—clever, crafty, Amnon—sits to the left of David. Lovely and gracious Tamar, a charming and beautiful young woman, arrives and sits beside Amnon. And then across the way, Solomon walks slowly from his study; precocious, brilliant, preoccupied Solomon. The heir apparent slowly sits down. And then Absalom—handsome, winsome Absalom with beautiful flowing hair, black as a raven, down to his shoulders—sits down. That particular evening Joab, the courageous warrior and David's commander of the troops, has been invited to dinner. Muscular, bronzed Joab is seated near the king. Afterward they wait. They hear the shuffling of feet, the clump, clump, clump of the crutches as Mephibosheth rather awkwardly finds his place at the table and slips into his seat . . . and the tablecloth covers his feet. I ask you: Did Mephibosheth understand grace?[3]

And I ask you, do you see our story in his?

Children of royalty, crippled by the fall, permanently marred by sin. Living parenthetical lives in the chronicles of earth only to be remembered by the king. Driven not by our beauty but by his promise, he calls us to himself and invites us to take a permanent place at his table. Though we often limp more than we walk, we take our place next to the other sinners-made-saints and we share in God's glory.

May I share a partial list of what awaits you at his table?

> You are beyond condemnation (Rom. 8:1).
>
> You are delivered from the law (Rom. 7:6).
>
> You are near God (Eph. 2:13).
>
> You are delivered from the power of evil (Col. 1:13).
>
> You are a member of his kingdom (Col. 1:13).

You are justified (Rom. 5:1).

You are perfect (Heb. 10:14).

You have been adopted (Rom. 8:15).

You have access to God at any moment (Eph. 2:18).

You are a part of his priesthood (1 Pet. 2:5).

You will never be abandoned (Heb. 13:5).

You have an imperishable inheritance (1 Pet. 1:4).

You are a partner with Christ in life (Col. 3:4) and privilege (Eph. 2:6), suffering (2 Tim. 2:12), and service (1 Cor. 1:9).

You are a:

member of his body (1 Cor. 12:13),

branch in the vine (John 15:5),

stone in the building (Eph 2:19–22),

bride for the groom (Eph. 5:25–27),

priest in the new generation (1 Pet. 2:9), and a

dwelling place of the Spirit (1 Cor. 6:19).

You possess (get this!) every spiritual blessing possible. "In Christ, God has given us every spiritual blessing in the heavenly world" (Eph. 1:3). This is the gift offered to the lowliest sinner on earth. Who could make such an offer but God? "From him we all received one gift after another" (John 1:16).

Paul speaks for us all when he asks,

> Have you ever come on anything quite like this extravagant love of God, this deep, deep, wisdom? It's way over our heads. We'll never figure it out.
>
> "Is there anyone around who can explain God?
> Anyone smart enough to tell him what to do?

Anyone who has done him such a huge favor
that God has to ask his advice?"

Everything comes from him;
Everything comes through him;
Everything ends up in him.
Always glory! Always praise!
Yes. Yes. Yes. (Rom. 11:33–36 MSG)

Like Mephibosheth, we are sons of the King. And like me in Miami, our greatest offering is peanuts compared to what we are given.

PART THREE

WHAT A DIFFERENCE!

Where the grace of God is missed, bitterness is born.

But where the grace of God is embraced, forgiveness flourishes.

The longer we walk in the garden,

the more likely we are to smell like flowers.

The more we immerse ourselves in grace, the more likely we are to give grace.

Romans 6:11–12

11 Grace Works

How can we who died to sin still live in it? ROMANS 6:2 RSV

Sometimes I give away money at the end of a sermon. Not to pay the listeners (though some may feel they've earned it) but to make a point. I offer a dollar to anyone who will accept it. Free money. A gift. I invite anyone who wants the cash to come and take it.

The response is predictable. A pause. Some shuffling of feet. A wife elbows her husband, and he shakes his head. A teen starts to stand and then remembers her reputation. A five-year-old starts walking down the aisle, and his mother pulls him back. Finally some courageous (or impoverished) soul stands up and says, "I'll take it!" The dollar is given, and the application begins.

"Why didn't you take my offer?" I ask the

rest. Some say they were too embarrassed. The pain wasn't worth the gain. Others feared a catch, a trick. And then there are those whose wallets are fat. What's a buck to someone who has hundreds?

Then the obvious follow-up question. "Why don't people accept Christ's free gift?" The answers are similar. Some are too embarrassed. To accept forgiveness is to admit sin, a step we are slow to take. Others fear a trick, a catch. Surely there is some fine print in the Bible. Others think, *Who needs forgiveness when you're as good as I am?*

The point makes itself. Though grace is available to all, it's accepted by few. Many choose to sit and wait while only a few choose to stand and trust.

Usually that is the end of it. The lesson is over, I'm a dollar poorer, one person is a dollar richer, and all of us are a bit wiser. Something happened a couple of weeks back, however, that added a new dimension to the exercise. Myrtle was the one who said yes to the dollar. I'd made the offer and was waiting for a taker when she yelled, "I'll take it!" Up she popped and down she came and I gave her the dollar. She took her seat, I made my point, and we all went home.

I ran into her a few days later and kidded her about making money off my sermons. "Do you still have the dollar?" I asked.

"No."

"Did you spend it?"

"No, I gave it away," she answered. "When I returned to my seat a youngster asked me if he could have it, and I said, 'Sure, it was a gift to me; it's a gift to you.'"

My, isn't that something? As simply as she received, she gave. As easily as it came, it went. The boy didn't beg, and she didn't struggle. How could she, who had been given a gift, not give a gift in return? She was caught in the grip of grace.

We'll use these final chapters to discuss the impact of grace. Now that we've considered the mess we made and the God we have, let's ponder what a difference grace makes in our lives. Exactly what does a grace-driven Christian look like?

Grace Releases Us

In Romans 6 Paul asks a crucial question: "How can we who died to sin still live in it?" (v. 2 RSV). How can we who have been made right not live righteous lives? How can we who have been loved not love? How can we who have been blessed not bless? How can we who have been given grace not live graciously?

Paul seems stunned that an alternative would even exist! How could grace result in anything but gracious living? "So do you think we should continue sinning so that God will give us even more grace? No!" (v. 1).

The two-dollar term for this philosophy is antinomianism: *anti*, meaning "against" and *nomos* meaning "moral law." Promoters of the idea see grace as a reason to do bad rather than a reason to do good. Grace grants them a ticket for evil. The worse I act the better God seems. This isn't Paul's first reference to the teaching. Remember Romans 3:7? "A person might say, 'When I lie, it really gives him the glory, because my lie shows God's truth.'"

What a scam. You mothers wouldn't tolerate it. Can you imagine your teenager saying, "Mom, I'll keep my room messy so the whole neighborhood can see what a good housekeeper you are"? A boss wouldn't let the employee say, "The reason I'm lazy is to give you an opportunity to display your forgiveness." No one respects the beggar who refuses to work, saying, "I'm just giving the government an opportunity to demonstrate benevolence."

We'd scoff at such hypocrisy. We wouldn't tolerate it, and we wouldn't do it.

Or would we? Let's answer that one slowly. Perhaps we don't sin *so* God can give grace, but do we ever sin *knowing* God will give grace? Do we ever compromise tonight, knowing we'll confess tomorrow?

It's easy to be like the fellow visiting Las Vegas who called the preacher, wanting to know the hours of the Sunday service. The preacher was impressed. "Most people who come to Las Vegas don't do so to go to church."

"Oh, I'm not coming for the church. I'm coming for the gambling and parties and wild women. If I have half as much fun as I intend to, I'll need a church come Sunday morning."

Is that the intent of grace? Is God's goal to promote disobedience? Hardly. "Grace . . . teaches us not to live against God nor to do the evil things the world wants us to do. Instead, that grace teaches us to live now in a wise and right way and in a way that shows we serve God" (Titus 2:11–12). God's grace has released us from selfishness. Why return?

The Penalty Has Been Paid

Think of it this way. Sin put you in prison. Sin locked you behind the bars of guilt and shame and deception and fear. Sin did nothing but shackle you to the wall of misery. Then Jesus came and paid your bail. He served your time; he satisfied the penalty and set you free. Christ died, and when you cast your lot with him, your old self died too.

The only way to be set free from the prison of sin is to serve its penalty. In this case the penalty is death. Someone has to die, either you or a heaven-sent substitute. You cannot leave prison unless there is a death. But that death has occurred at Calvary. And when Jesus died, you died to sin's claim on your life. You are free.

Near the city of Sao José dos Campos, Brazil, is a remarkable facility. Twenty years ago the Brazilian government turned a prison over to two Christians. The institution was renamed Humaita, and the plan was to run it on Christian principles. With the exception of two full-time staff, all the work is done by inmates. Families outside the prison adopt an inmate to work with during and after his term. Chuck Colson visited the prison and made this report:

> When I visited Humaita I found the inmates smiling—particularly the murderer who held the keys, opened the gates and let me in. Wherever I walked I saw men at peace. I saw clean living areas, people working industriously. The walls were decorated with Biblical sayings from Psalms and Proverbs. . . . My guide escorted me to the notorious prison cell once used for torture. Today, he told me, that block houses only a single inmate. As we reached the end of a long concrete corridor and he put the key in the lock, he paused and asked, "Are you sure you want to go in?"
>
> "Of course," I replied impatiently, "I've been in isolation cells all over the world." Slowly he swung open the massive door, and I saw the prisoner in that punishment cell: a crucifix, beautifully carved by the Humaita inmates—the prisoner Jesus, hanging on a cross.
>
> "He's doing time for the rest of us," my guide said softly.[1]

Christ has taken your place. There is no need for you to remain in the cell. Ever heard of a discharged prisoner who wanted to stay? Nor have I. When the doors open, prisoners leave. The thought of a person preferring jail over freedom doesn't compute. Once the penalty is paid, why live under bondage? You are discharged from the penitentiary of sin. Why, in heaven's name, would you ever want to set foot in that prison again?

Paul reminds us: "Our old life died with Christ on the cross so that our sinful selves would have no power over us and we would not be slaves to sin. Anyone who has died is made free from sin's control" (Rom. 6:6–7).

He is not saying that it is impossible for believers to sin; he's saying it is stupid for believers to sin. "It's not the literal impossibility . . . . but the moral incongruity" of the saved returning to sin.[2]

What does the prison have that you desire? Do you miss the guilt? Are you homesick for dishonesty? Do you have fond memories of being lied to and forgotten? Was life better when you were dejected and rejected? Do you have a longing to once again see a sinner in the mirror?

It makes no sense to go back to prison.

The Vow Has Been Made

Not only has a price been paid, a vow has been made. "Did you forget that all of us became part of Christ when we were baptized?" (Rom. 6:2).

Baptism was no casual custom, no ho-hum ritual. Baptism was, and is, "a pledge made to God from a good conscience" (1 Pet. 3:21 TJB).

Paul's high regard for baptism is demonstrated in the fact that he knows all of his readers have been instructed in its importance. "*You have been taught* that when we were baptized into Christ we were baptized into his death" (Rom. 6:2 TJB, italics mine).

What form of amnesia is this? Like a bride horrified to see her new husband flirting with women at the wedding reception, Paul asks, "Did you forget your vows?"

Indeed, baptism is a vow, a sacred vow of the believer to follow Christ. Just as a wedding celebrates the fusion of two hearts, baptism celebrates the union of sinner with Savior. We "became part of Christ when we were baptized" (v. 2).

Do the bride and groom understand all of the implications of the wedding? No. Do they know every challenge or threat they will face? No. But they know they love each other and vow to be faithful to the end.

When a willing heart enters the waters of baptism, does he know the implications of the vow? No. Does she know every temptation or challenge? No. But both know the love of God and are responding to him.

Please understand, it is not the act that saves us. But it is the act that symbolizes how we are saved! The invisible work of the Holy Spirit is visibly dramatized in the water.

> That plunge beneath the running waters was like a death; the moment's pause while they swept overhead was like a burial; the standing erect once more in air and sunlight was a species of resurrection.[3]

Remove your shoes, bow your head, and bend your knees; this is a holy event. Baptism is not to be taken lightly.

To return to sin after sealing our souls in baptism is like committing, well, it's like committing adultery on your honeymoon. Can you imagine the distraught bride discovering her husband in the arms of another woman only days after hearing his vow at the altar? Among her many sizzling words will likely be the question, "Have you forgotten what you said to me?"

Similarly God asks, "Does our union mean nothing to you? Is our covenant so fragile that you would choose the arms of a harlot over mine?"

Who, in their right mind, would want to abandon these vows? Who will care for you more than Christ? Have we forgotten what life was like before our baptism? Have we forgotten the mess we were in before we were united with him? I choose the word *mess* intentionally. May I share a mess I'm glad I am out of? My bachelor's apartment.

Exposed to a Higher Standard

Of all the names I've been called, no one has ever accused me of being a neat freak. Some people have a high threshold of pain; I have a high threshold of sloppiness. Not that my mom didn't try. And not that she didn't succeed. As long as I was under her roof, I stacked my plate and picked up my shorts. But once I was free, I was free indeed.

Most of my life I've been a closet slob. I was slow to see the logic of neatness. Why make up a bed if you are going to sleep in it again tonight? Does it make sense to wash dishes after only one meal? Isn't it easier to leave your clothes on the floor at the foot of the bed so they'll be there when you get up and put them on? Is anything gained by putting the lid on the toothpaste tube tonight only to remove it again tomorrow?

I was as compulsive as anyone, only I was compulsive about being messy. Life was too short to match your socks; just buy longer pants!

Then I got married.

Denalyn was so patient. She said she didn't mind my habits . . . if I didn't mind sleeping outside. Since I did, I began to change.

I enrolled in a twelve-step program for slobs. ("My name is Max, I hate to vacuum.") A physical therapist helped me rediscover the muscles used for hanging shirts and placing toilet paper on the holder. My nose was reintroduced to the fragrance of Pine Sol. By the time Denalyn's parents came to visit, I was a new man. I could go three days without throwing a sock behind the couch.

But then came the moment of truth. Denalyn went out of town for a week. Initially I reverted to the old man. I figured I'd be a slob for six days and clean on the seventh. But something strange happened, a curious discomfort. I couldn't relax with dirty dishes in the sink. When I saw an empty potato-chip sack on the floor I—

hang on to your hat—bent over and picked it up! I actually put my bath towel back on the rack. What had happened to me?

Simple. I'd been exposed to a higher standard.

Isn't that what has happened with us? Isn't that the heart of Paul's argument? How could we who have been freed from sin return to it? Before Christ our lives were out of control, sloppy, and indulgent. We didn't even know we were slobs until we met him.

Then he moved in. Things began to change. What we threw around we began putting away. What we neglected we cleaned up. What had been clutter became order. Oh, there were and still are occasional lapses of thought and deed, but by and large he got our house in order.

Suddenly we find ourselves wanting to do good. Go back to the old mess? Are you kidding? "In the past you were slaves to sin—sin controlled you. But thank God, you fully obeyed the things that you were taught. You were made free from sin, and now you are slaves to goodness" (Rom. 6:17–18).

Can a discharged prisoner return to confinement? Yes. But let him remember the gray walls and the long nights. Can a newlywed forget his vows? Yes. But let him remember his holy vow and his beautiful bride. Can a converted slob once again be messy? Yes. But let him consider the difference between the filth of yesterday and the purity of today.

Can one who has been given a free gift not share that gift with others? I suppose. But let him remember Myrtle. Let him remember that he, like she, received a free gift. Let him remember that all of life is a gift of grace. And let him remember that the call of grace is to live a gracious life.

For that is how grace works.

12 Turning Yourself In

Luke 22:54–62

What a wretched man I am! ROMANS 7:24

Charles Robertson should have turned himself in. Not that he would've been acquitted; he robbed a bank. But at least he wouldn't have been the laughingstock of Virginia Beach.

Cash-strapped Robertson, nineteen, went to Jefferson State Bank on a Wednesday afternoon, filled out a loan application, and left. Apparently he changed his mind about the loan and opted for a quicker plan. He returned within a couple of hours with a pistol, a bag, and a note demanding money. The teller complied, and all of a sudden Robertson was holding a sack of loot.

Figuring the police were fast on their way, he dashed out the front door. He was halfway to the car when he realized he'd left the note. Fearing it could be used as evidence against him, he ran back into the bank and snatched it from the teller. Now holding the note and the money, he ran a block to his parked car. That's when he realized he'd left his keys on the counter when he'd returned for the note.

"At this point," one detective chuckled, "total panic set in."

Robertson ducked into the restroom of a fast-food restaurant. He dislodged a ceiling tile and hid the money and the .25 caliber handgun. Scampering through alleys and creeping behind cars, he finally reached his apartment where his roommate, who knew nothing of the robbery, greeted him with the words, "I need my car."

You see, Robertson's getaway vehicle was a loaner. Rather than confess to the crime and admit the bungle, Robertson shoveled yet another spade of dirt deeper into the hole. "Uh, uh, your car was stolen," he lied.

While Robertson watched in panic, the roommate called the police to inform them of the stolen vehicle. About twenty minutes later an officer spotted the "stolen" car a block from the recently robbed bank. Word was already on the police radio that the robber had forgotten his keys. The officer put two and two together and tried the keys on the car. They worked.

Detectives went to the address of the person who'd reported the missing car. There they found Robertson. He confessed, was charged with robbery, and put in jail. No bail. No loan. No kidding.

Some days it's hard to do anything right. It's even harder to do anything *wrong* right. Robertson's not alone. We've done the same. Perhaps we didn't take money but we've taken advantage or taken control or taken leave of our senses and then, like the thief, we've taken off. Dashing down alleys of deceit. Hiding behind buildings of work to be done or deadlines to be met. Though we try to act normal, anyone who looks closely at us can see we are on the lam:

Eyes darting and hands fidgeting, we chatter nervously. Committed to the cover-up, we scheme and squirm, changing the topic and changing direction. We don't want anyone to know the truth, especially God.

But from the beginning God has called for honesty. He's never demanded perfection, but he has expected truthfulness. As far back as the days of Moses, God said:

> If they will confess their sins and the sins of their fathers—their treachery against me and their hostility toward me, which made me hostile toward them so that I sent them into the land of their enemies—then . . . I will remember my covenant with Jacob and my covenant with Isaac and my covenant with Abraham, and I will remember the land. (Lev. 26:40–42 NIV)

Honest Hearts Lead to Honest Worship

Nehemiah knew the value of honesty. Upon hearing of the crumbled walls in Jerusalem, did he fault God? Did he blame heaven? Hardly. Read his prayer: "I confess the sins we Israelites have done against you. My father's family and I have sinned against you. We have been wicked toward you and have not obeyed the commands, rules, and laws you gave your servant Moses" (Neh. 1:6–7).

Here is the second most powerful man in the kingdom turning himself in, accepting responsibility for the downfall of his people. The scene of his personal confession, however, is nothing compared to the day the entire nation repented. "They stood and confessed their sins and their ancestors' sins. For a fourth of the day they stood where they were and read from the Book of Teachings of the Lord their God. For another fourth of the day they confessed their sins and worshiped the Lord their God" (Neh. 9:2–4).

Can you picture the event? Hundreds of people spending hours in prayer, not making requests but making confessions. "I'm guilty, God." "I've failed you, Father."

Such public honesty is common in Scripture. God instructed the high priest to "put both his hands on the head of the living goat, and he will confess over it all the sins and crimes of Israel. In this way Aaron will put the people's sins on the goat's head. . . . The goat will carry on itself all the people's sins to a lonely place in the desert. The man who leads the goat will let it loose there" (Lev. 16:21–22).

By virtue of this drama the people learned that God despises sin and God deals with sin. Before there could be honest worship, there had to be honest hearts.

The Motivation of Truth

Confession does for the soul what preparing the land does for the field. Before the farmer sows the seed he works the acreage, removing the rocks and pulling the stumps. He knows that seed grows better if the land is prepared. Confession is the act of inviting God to walk the acreage of our hearts. "There is a rock of greed over here Father, I can't budge it. And that tree of guilt near the fence? Its roots are long and deep. And may I show you some dry soil, too crusty for seed?" God's seed grows better if the soil of the heart is cleared.

And so the Father and the Son walk the field together; digging and pulling, preparing the heart for fruit. Confession invites the Father to work the soil of the soul.

Confession seeks pardon from God, not amnesty. Pardon presumes guilt; amnesty, derived from the same Greek word as *amnesia*, "forgets" the alleged offense without imputing guilt. Confession admits wrong and seeks forgiveness; amnesty denies wrong and claims innocence.

Many mouth a prayer for forgiveness while in reality claiming amnesty. Consequently our worship is cold (why thank God for a grace we don't need?) and our faith is weak (I'll handle my mistakes myself, thank you). We are better at keeping God out than we are at inviting God in. Sunday mornings are full of preparing the body for worship, preparing the hair for worship, preparing the clothes for worship . . . but preparing the soul?

Am I missing the mark when I say that many of us attend church on the run? Am I out of line when I say many of us *spend life on the run?*

Am I overstating the case when I announce, "Grace means you don't have to run anymore!"? It's the truth. Grace means it's finally safe to turn ourselves in.

A Model of Truth

Peter did. Remember Peter? "Flash the sword and deny the Lord" Peter? The apostle who boasted one minute and bolted the next? He snoozed when he should have prayed. He denied when he should have defended. He cursed when he should have comforted. He ran when he should have stayed. We remember Peter as the one who turned and fled, but do we remember Peter as the one who returned and confessed? We should.

I've got a question for you.

How did the New Testament writers know of his sin? Who told them of his betrayal? And, more importantly, how did they know the details? Who told them of the girl at the gate and the soldiers starting the fire? How did Matthew know it was Peter's accent that made him a suspect? How did Luke learn of the stare of Jesus? Who told all four of the crowing rooster and flowing tears?

The Holy Spirit? I suppose. Could be that each writer learned of the moment by divine inspiration. Or, more likely, each learned of the betrayal by an honest confession. Peter turned himself in. Like the bank robber, he bungled it and ran. Unlike the robber, Peter stopped and thought. Somewhere in the Jerusalem shadows he quit running, fell to his knees, buried his face in his hands, and gave up.

But not only did he give up, he opened up. He went back to the room where Jesus had broken the bread and shared the wine. (It says a lot about the disciples that they let Peter back in the door.)

There he is, every burly bit of him filling the doorframe. "Fellows, I've got something to get off my chest." And that's when they learn of the fire and the girl and the look from Jesus. That's when they hear of the cursing mouth and the crowing rooster. That's how they heard the story. He turned himself in.

How can I be so sure? Two reasons.

1. *He couldn't stay away*. When word came that the tomb was empty, who was first out of the room? Peter. When word came that Jesus was on the shore, who was first out of the boat? Peter. He was on the run again. Only now he was running in the right direction.

Here is a good rule of thumb: Those who keep secrets from God keep their distance from God. Those who are honest with God draw near to God.

This is nothing novel. It happens between people. If you loan me your car and I wreck it, will I look forward to seeing you again? No. It is no coincidence that the result of the very first sin was to duck into the bushes. Adam and Eve ate the fruit, heard God in the garden, and crept behind the leaves.

"Where are you?" God asked, not for his benefit. He knew exactly where they were. The question was spiritual, not geographical. "Examine where you are, children. You aren't where you were. You were at my side; now you have hidden from me."

Secrets erect a fence while confession builds a bridge.

Once there were a couple of farmers who couldn't get along with each other. A wide ravine separated their two farms, but as a sign of their mutual distaste for each other, each constructed a fence on his side of the chasm to keep the other out.

In time, however, the daughter of one met the son of the other, and the couple fell in love. Determined not to be kept apart by the folly of their fathers, they tore down the fence and used the wood to build a bridge across the ravine.

Confession does that. Confessed sin becomes the bridge over which we can walk back into the presence of God.

There is a second reason I'm confident of Peter's confession.

2. *He couldn't stay silent*. Only fifty days after denying Christ, Peter is preaching Christ. Peter cursed his Lord at the Passover. He proclaimed his Lord at the feast. This is not the action of a fugitive. What took him from traitor to orator? He let God deal with the secrets of his life. "Confess your sins to each other and pray for each other so that God can heal you" (James 5:16).

"If we confess our sins, he will forgive our sins, because we can trust God to do what is right. He will cleanse us from all the wrongs we have done" (1 John 1:9).

The fugitive lives in fear, but the penitent lives in peace.

The Moment of Truth

Again, Jesus has never demanded that we be perfect, only that we be honest. "You want me to be completely truthful" wrote David (Ps. 51:6). But honesty is a stubborn virtue for most. "Me, a thief?" we ask with revolver in one hand and bag of loot in the other.

It wasn't easy for Peter. He considered himself the MVA (most valuable apostle). Wasn't he one of the early draft picks? Wasn't he one of the chosen three? Didn't he confess Christ while the others were silent? Peter never thought he needed help until he lifted his eyes from the fire and saw the eyes of Jesus. "While Peter was still speaking a rooster crowed. Then the Lord turned and looked straight at Peter" (Luke 22:60–61).

Jesus and Peter are not the only two in the midnight street, but they might as well be. Jesus is surrounded by accusers, but he doesn't respond. He's encircled by enemies, but he doesn't react. The night air is full of taunts, but Jesus doesn't hear. But let one follower slip when he should have stood and the Master's head pops up and his eyes search through the shadows and the disciple knows.

"The Lord looks down from heaven and sees every person. From his throne he watches all who live on earth. He made their hearts and understands everything they do" (Ps. 33:13–15).

You know when God knows. You know when he is looking. Your heart tells you. Your Bible tells you. Your mirror tells you. The longer you run, the more complicated life gets. But the sooner you confess, the lighter your load becomes. David knew this. He wrote:

> When I kept things to myself,
>   I felt weak deep inside me.
>   I moaned all day long.
> Day and night you punished me.
>   My strength was gone as in the summer heat.
> Then I confessed my sins to you
>   and didn't hide my guilt.
> I said, "I will confess my sins to the LORD,"
>   and you forgave my guilt. (Ps. 32:3–5)

These verses remind me of a mistake I made in high school. (My mother says I shouldn't use my juvenile foibles for illustrations. But I have so many!) Our baseball coach had a firm rule against chewing tobacco. We had a couple of players who were known to sneak a chew, and he wanted to call it to our attention.

He got our attention, all right. Before long we'd all tried it. A sure test of manhood was to take a chew when the pouch was passed down the bench. I had barely made the team; I sure wasn't going to fail the test of manhood.

One day I'd just popped a plug in my mouth when one of the players warned, "Here comes the coach!" Not wanting to get caught, I did what came naturally, I swallowed. *Gulp*.

I added new meaning to the scripture, "I felt weak deep inside me. I moaned all day long. . . . My strength was gone as in the summer heat." I paid the price for hiding my disobedience.

My body was not made to ingest tobacco. Your soul was not made to ingest sin.

May I ask a frank question? Are you keeping any secrets from God? Any parts of your life off limits? Any cellars boarded up or attics locked? Any part of your past or present that you hope you and God never discuss?

Learn a lesson from the robber: The longer you run, the worse it gets. Learn a lesson from Peter: The sooner you speak to Jesus, the more you'll speak for Jesus. And take a pointer from a nauseated third baseman. You'll feel better if you get it out.

Once you're in the grip of grace, you're free to be honest. Turn yourself in before things get worse. You'll be glad you did.

Honest to God, you will.

13

Sufficient Grace

2 Corinthians 12:7–9

To keep me from becoming conceited because of these surpassingly great revelations, there was given me a thorn in my flesh, a messenger of Satan to torment me. Three times I pleaded with the Lord to take it away from me. But he said to me, 'My grace is sufficient for you, my power is made perfect in weakness.'"

2 CORINTHIANS 12:7–9 NIV

Here is the scene: You and I and a half-dozen other folks are flying across the country in a chartered plane. All of a sudden the engine bursts into flames, and the pilot rushes out of the cockpit.

"We're going to crash!" he yells. "We've got to bail out!"

Good thing he knows where the parachutes are because we don't. He passes them out, gives us a few pointers, and we stand in line as he throws open the door. The first passenger steps up to the door and shouts over the wind, "Could I make a request?"

"Sure, what is it?"

"Any way I could get a pink parachute?"

The pilot shakes his head in disbelief. "Isn't it enough that I gave you a parachute at all?" And so the first passenger jumps.

The second steps to the door. "I'm wondering if there is any way you could ensure that I won't get nauseated during the fall?"

"No, but I can ensure that you will have a parachute for the fall."

Each of us comes with a request and receives a parachute.

"Please captain," says one, "I am afraid of heights. Would you remove my fear?"

"No," he replies, "but I'll give you a parachute."

Another pleads for a different strategy, "Couldn't you change the plans? Let's crash with the plane. We might survive."

The pilot smiles and says, "You don't know what you are asking" and gently shoves the fellow out the door. One passenger wants some goggles, another wants boots, another wants to wait until the plane is closer to the ground.

"You people don't understand," the pilot shouts as he "helps" us, one by one. "I've given you a parachute; that is enough."

Only one item is necessary for the jump, and he provides it. He places the strategic tool in our hands. The gift is adequate. But are we content? No. We are restless, anxious, even demanding.

Too crazy to be possible? Maybe in a plane with pilots and parachutes, but on earth with people and grace? God hears thousands of appeals per second. Some are legitimate. We, too, ask God to remove the fear or change the plans. He usually answers with a gentle shove that leaves us airborne and suspended by his grace.

The Problem: When God Says No

There are times when the one thing you want is the one thing you never get. You're not being picky or demanding; you're only obeying his command to "ask God for everything you need" (Phil. 4:6).

All you want is an open door or an extra day or an answered prayer, for which you will be thankful.

And so you pray and wait.

No answer.

You pray and wait.

No answer.

You pray and wait.

May I ask a very important question? What if God says no?

What if the request is delayed or even denied? When God says no to you, how will you respond? If God says, "I've given you my grace, and that is enough," will you be content?

Content. That's the word. A state of heart in which you would be at peace if God gave you nothing more than he already has. Test yourself with this question: What if God's only gift to you were his grace to save you. Would you be content? You beg him to save the life of your child. You plead with him to keep your business afloat. You implore him to remove the cancer from your body. What if his answer is, "My grace is enough." Would you be content?

You see, from heaven's perspective, grace *is* enough. If God did nothing more than save us from hell, could anyone complain? If God saved our souls and then left us to spend our lives leprosy-struck on a deserted island, would he be unjust? Having been given eternal life, dare we grumble at an aching body? Having been given heavenly riches, dare we bemoan earthly poverty?

Let me be quick to add, God has not left you with "just salvation." If you have eyes to read these words, hands to hold this book, the means to own this volume, he has already given you grace upon grace. The vast majority of us have been saved and then blessed even more!

But there are those times when God, having given us his grace, hears our appeals and says, "My grace is sufficient for you." Is he being unfair?

In *God Came Near* I've told how our oldest daughter fell into a swimming pool when she was two years old. A friend saw her and pulled her to safety.[1] What I didn't tell was what happened the next morning in my prayer time. I made a special effort to record my gratitude in my journal. I told God how wonderful he was for saving her. As clearly as if God himself were speaking, this question came to mind: *Would I be less wonderful had I let her drown? Would I be any less a good God for calling her home? Would I still be receiving your praise this morning had I not saved her?*

Is God still a good God when he says no?

The Plea: Remove the Thorn

Paul wrestled with that one. He knew the angst of unanswered prayer. At the top of his prayer list was an unidentified request that dominated his thoughts. He gave the appeal a code name: "a thorn in my flesh" (2 Cor. 12:7 NIV). Perhaps the pain was too intimate to put on paper. Maybe the request was made so often he reverted to shorthand. "I'm here to talk about the thorn again, Father." Or could it be that by leaving the appeal generic, Paul's prayer could be our prayer? For don't we all have a thorn in the flesh?

Somewhere on life's path our flesh is pierced by a person or a problem. Our stride becomes a limp, our pace is slowed to a halt, we try to walk again only to wince at each effort. Finally we plead with God for help.

Such was the case with Paul. (By the way, don't you find it encouraging that even Paul had a thorn in the flesh? There is comfort in learning that one of the writers of the Bible wasn't always on the same page with God.)

You don't get a thorn unless you're on the move, and Paul never stopped. Thessalonica, Jerusalem, Athens, Corinth—if he wasn't preaching he was in prison because of his preaching. But his walk was hampered by this thorn. The barb pierced through the sole of his sandal and into the soul of his heart and soon became a matter of intense prayer. "I begged the Lord three times to take this problem away from me" (2 Cor. 12:8).

This was no casual request, no P.S. in a letter. It was the first plea of the first sentence. "Dear God, I need some help!"

Nor was this a superficial prickle. It was a "stabbing pain" (PHILLIPS). Every step he took sent a shudder up his leg. Three different times he limped over to the side of the trail and prayed. His request was clear, and so was God's response, "My grace is sufficient" (v. 9 NIV).

What was this thorn in the flesh? No one knows for sure, but here are the top candidates.

1. *Sexual temptation.* Paul battling the flesh? Maybe. After all, Paul was a single man. He describes the temptress like one who knew her firsthand. "I want to do the things that are good, but I do not do them. I do not do the good things I want to do, but I do the bad things I do not want to do" (Rom. 7:18–19). Is Paul asking God to once and for all deliver him from the thirst for forbidden waters?

2. Perhaps the problem was not the flesh but *foes*; not temptation but opposition. The passage hints at this possibility. "This problem was a messenger from Satan," (2 Cor. 12:7). Paul had his share of opponents. There were those who questioned his apostleship (2 Cor. 12:12). There were some who undermined his message of grace (Gal. 1:7). By the way, when Paul wrote that this "messenger of Satan" was sent "to beat me," he wasn't exaggerating. Remove his robe and look at the scars. Or, since you can't do that, read of his attacks.

> I have been near death many times. Five times the Jews have given me their punishment of thirty-nine lashes with a whip. Three different times I was beaten with rods. One time I was almost stoned to death. Three times I was in ships that wrecked, and one of those times I spent

> a night and a day in the sea. I have gone on many travels and have been in danger from rivers, thieves, my own people, the Jews, and those who are not Jews. I have been in danger in cities, in places where no one lives, and on the sea. And I have been in danger with false Christians. (2 Cor. 11:23–26)

Could anyone fault Paul for asking for a reprieve? A body can endure only so much. One grows weary living in the cross hairs of Satan's scope. "God, what if we limit this year to verbal attacks and let my sores heal? Or could we stagger the whippings and the stonings so they don't come at the same time? I've got a bruise on my neck that wakes me up each time I roll over. And remember the night in the jail in Philippi? My back hasn't recovered yet."

3. Of course, there were those who thought Paul deserved every lash, which leads us to a third option. Some think the thorn was his *abrasive nature*. Whatever he learned at the feet of Gamaliel, he may have dozed off the day they discussed the topic of tact. Before he knew grace, he had killed Christians. After he knew grace, he grilled the Christians. Example? "When Peter came to Antioch, I challenged him to his face, because he was wrong" (Gal. 2:11). Written like a true diplomat. In Paul's view you were on God's side or Satan's side, and should you slide from the first to the second he didn't keep it a secret, "Hymenaeus and Alexander have done that, and I have given them to Satan so they will learn not to speak against God" (1 Tim. 1:20).

Everyone within range of his tongue and pen knew how he felt and knew when to duck.

4. On the other hand, a case can be made that the thorn was not temptation, opposition, or public relation skills; it could have been *his body*. Remember his words at the end of one of his letters? "See what large letters I use to write this myself" (Gal. 6:11). Maybe his

eyes were bad. Could be he never got over that trip to Damascus. God got his attention with a light so bright Paul was left blind for three days. Maybe he never fully recovered. His clear vision of the cross may have come at the cost of a clear vision of anything else. He wrote of the Galatians that, "you would have taken out your eyes and given them to me if that were possible" (4:15).

In Paul's profession poor eyesight could be an occupational hazard. It's hard to travel if you can't see the trail. Not easy to write epistles if you can't see the page. Poor vision leads to strained eyes, which leads to headaches, which leads to long nights and long prayers for relief. "God, any chance I could see?"

It's hard to impress the crowd if you're making eye contact with a tree thinking it's a person. Which brings to mind one final possibility.

5. We assume Paul was a dynamic speaker, but those who heard him might disagree. "His speaking is nothing," he overheard them say in Corinth (2 Cor. 10:10). The apostle didn't argue with them. "When I came to you, I was weak and fearful and trembling. My teaching and preaching were not with words of wisdom that persuade people but proof of the power that the spirit gives" (1 Cor. 2:3–4). Translation? *I was so scared that I stuttered, so nervous that I forgot my point, and the fact that you heard anything at all is testimony to God.*

Let's back away for a minute and tally this up. (I don't know how you envisioned Paul, but that image may be about to change.) Tempted often. Beaten regularly. Opinionated. Dim-sighted. Thick-tongued. Is this the apostle Paul? (Could be he never got married because he couldn't get a date.) No wonder some questioned if he were an apostle.

And no wonder he prayed.

The Principle: Grace Is Enough

Are any of these requests inappropriate? Wouldn't he have been a better apostle with no temptation, no enemies, a calm demeanor, good eyes, and a glib tongue?

Maybe, but then again, maybe not.

Had God removed temptation, Paul may never have embraced God's grace. Only the hungry value a feast, and Paul was starving. The self-given title on his office door read, "Paul, Chief of Sinners." No pen ever articulated grace like Paul's. That may be because no person ever appreciated grace like Paul.

Had God stilled the whips, Paul may have never known love. "If I were burned alive for preaching the Gospel but didn't love others, it would be no value whatsoever" (1 Cor. 13:3 TLB). Persecution distills motives. In the end Paul's motives were distilled to one force, "the love of Christ controls us" (2 Cor. 5:14).

Had God made him meek and mild, who would have faced the legalists and confronted the hedonists and challenged the judgmentalists? The reason the letter of Galatians is in your Bible is because Paul couldn't stomach a diluted grace. Attribute the letters to Corinth to Paul's intolerance of sloppy faith. Paul's honesty may not have made many friends, but it sure made many disciples.

And Paul's eyes. If God had healed his eyesight, would Paul have had such insights? While the rest of the world was watching the world, Paul was seeing visions too great for words (2 Cor. 12:3–4).

And public speaking? Nothing intoxicates like the approval of the crowd. God may have just been keeping his apostle sober. Whatever the affliction, it was there for a purpose. And Paul knew it: "To keep me from becoming conceited." The God who despises pride did whatever necessary to keep Paul from becoming proud.

In this case, he simply told him, "My grace is sufficient." In your case, he may be saying the same thing.

You wonder why God doesn't remove temptation from your life? If he did, you might lean on your strength instead of his grace. A few stumbles might be what you need to convince you: His grace is sufficient for your sin.

You wonder why God doesn't remove the enemies in your life? Perhaps because he wants you to love like he loves. Anyone can love a friend, but only a few can love an enemy. So what if you aren't everyone's hero? His grace is sufficient for your self-image.

You wonder why God doesn't alter your personality? You, like Paul, are a bit rough around the edges? Say things you later regret or do things you later question? Why doesn't God make you more like him? He is. He's just not finished yet. Until he is, his grace is sufficient to overcome your flaws.

You wonder why God doesn't heal you? He *has* healed you. If you are in Christ, you have a perfected soul and a perfected body. His plan is to give you the soul now and the body when you get home. He may choose to heal parts of your body before heaven. But if he doesn't, don't you still have reason for gratitude? If he never gave you more than eternal life, could you ask for more than that? His grace is sufficient for gratitude.

Wonder why God won't give you a skill? If only God had made you a singer or a runner or a writer or a missionary. But there you are, tone-deaf, slow of foot and mind. Don't despair. God's grace is still sufficient to finish what he began. And until he's finished, let Paul remind you that the power is in the message, not the messenger. His grace is sufficient to speak clearly even when you don't.

For all we don't know about thorns, we can be sure of this. God would prefer we have an occasional limp than a perpetual strut. And if it takes a thorn for him to make his point, he loves us enough not to pluck it out.

God has every right to say no to us. We have every reason to say thanks to him. The parachute is strong, and the landing will be safe. His grace is sufficient.

14 The Civil War of the Soul

Romans 7:7–26

I was alive before I knew the law. But when the law's command came to me, then sin began to live and I died. The command was meant to bring life, but for me it brought death. . . . When I want to do good, evil is there with me. In my mind, I am happy with God's law. But I see another law working in my body, which makes war against the law that my mind accepts. That other law working in my body is the law of sin, and it makes me its prisoner. What a miserable man I am! Who will save me from this body that brings me death? ROMANS 7:9–10, 21–24

The following paragraphs document the degeneration of this author into criminal activity. The facts are true, and no names have been changed. I confess. I have violated the law. What's worse, I don't want to stop!

My felonious actions began innocently. My route to the office takes me south to an intersection where I and every other person in Texas turn east. Each morning I wait *long* minutes in a *long* line at a *long* light, always mumbling, "There must be a better way." A few days back I found it. While still a half-mile from the light, I spotted a shortcut, an alley behind a shopping center. It was worth a try. I turned on my blinker, made a quick left, bid farewell to the crawling commuters, and took my chances. I weaved in between the dumpsters and over the speed bumps and *voila*. It worked! The alley led me to my eastbound avenue several minutes faster than the rest of society.

Lewis and Clark would have been proud. I certainly was. From then on, I was ahead of the pack. Every morning while the rest of the cars waited in line, I veered onto my private autobahn and smugly applauded myself for seeing what others missed. I was surprised that no one had discovered it earlier, but then again, few have my innate navigational skills.

One morning Denalyn was with me in the car. "I'm about to remind you why you married me," I told her as we drew near to the intersection. "See that long line of cars? Hear that dirge from the suburbs? See that humdrum of humanity? It's not for me. Hang on!"

Like a hunter on a safari, I swerved from the six-lane onto the one-lane and shared with my sweetheart my secret expressway to freedom. "What do you think?" I asked her, awaiting her worship.

"I think you broke the law."

"What?"

"You just went the wrong way on a one-way street."

"I did not."

"Go back and see for yourself."

I did. She was right. Somehow I'd missed the sign. My road-less-taken was a route-not-permitted. Next to the big orange dumpster was a "Do Not Enter" sign. No wonder people gave me those looks when I turned into the alley. I thought they were envious; they thought I was deviant.

But my problem is not what I did before I knew the law. My

problem is what I want to do now, after I know the law. You'd think that I would have no desire to use the alley, but I do! Part of me still wants the shortcut. Part of me wants to break the law. (Forgive me all you patrolmen who are reading this book). Each morning the voices within me have this argument:

My "ought to" says, "It's illegal."

My "want to" answers, "But I've never been caught."

My "ought to" reminds, "The law is the law."

My "want to" counters, "But the law isn't for careful drivers like me. Besides, the five minutes I save I'll dedicate to prayer."

My "ought to" doesn't buy it. "Pray in the car."

Before I knew the law, I was at peace. Now that I know the law, an insurrection has occurred. I'm a torn man. On one hand I know what to do, but I don't want to do it. My eyes read the sign "Do Not Enter," but my body doesn't want to obey. What I should do and end up doing are two different matters. I was better off not knowing the law.

Sound familiar? It could. For many it is the itinerary of the soul. Before coming to Christ we all had our share of shortcuts. Immorality was a shortcut to pleasure. Cheating was a shortcut to success. Boasting was a shortcut to popularity. Lying was a shortcut to power.

Then we found Christ, we found grace, and we saw the signs. Hasn't it happened to you? You've got a hot temper and then read, "If you are angry with a brother or sister, you will be judged" (Matt. 5:22). *Wow, I never knew that.*

You've got wandering eyes and then read, "If anyone looks at a woman and wants to sin sexually with her, in his mind he has already done that sin with the woman" (Matt. 5:28). *Oh my, now what do I do?*

You tend to exaggerate to make your point and then discover, "Say only yes if you mean yes, and no if you mean no. If you say more than yes or no, it is from the Evil One" (Matt. 5:37). *But I've been talking like this for years.*

You enjoy letting people see your generosity and then read, "So when you give to the poor, don't let anyone know what you are doing" (Matt. 6:3). *Oh boy, I didn't know that was wrong.*

You have a habit of categorizing people into neat boxes and then hear Jesus say, "Don't judge other people, or you will be judged" (Matt. 7:1). *Son of a gun, no one ever told me judging was a sin.*

All these years you've been taking shortcuts, never seeing the "Do Not Enter" sign. But now you see it. Now you know it. I know, I know . . . it would have been easier had you never seen the sign, but now the law has been revealed. So what do you do?

Your battle is identical to the one within the heart of Paul.

> But I need something *more!* For if I know the law but still can't keep it, and if the power of sin within me keeps sabotaging my best intentions, I obviously need help! I realize that I don't have what it takes. I can will it, but I can't *do* it. I decide to do good, but I don't *really* do it; I decide not to do bad, but then I do it anyway. My decisions, such as they are, don't result in actions. Something has gone wrong deep within me and gets the better of me every time.
>
> It happens so regularly that it's predictable. The moment I decide to do good, sin is there to trip me up. I truly delight in God's commands, but it's pretty obvious that not all of me joins in that delight. Parts of me covertly rebel, and just when I least expect it, they take charge. (Rom. 7:14–23 MSG)

The civil war of the soul.

How *welcome* is Paul's confession! How good to know he struggled like the rest of us. Those who have been amazed by grace have been equally amazed by their sin. Why do I say yes to God one day and yes to Satan the next? Once I know God's commands, why am I not eager to obey them? Shouldn't these conflicts cease now that I see the sign? Does my struggle mean I'm not saved?

These are the questions of Romans 7. And these are the questions of many Christians. Some years ago I witnessed one man's inner war and chronicled these thoughts:

From where I sit I can see a redbird. He is on the roof across from my office. He has been there for three days. A splendid sight: deep crimson chest, crown of feathers which stands upon command. He sings the same song over and over—a long chirp followed by four short ones. The rhythm never varies. The pattern never changes.

He flies to the top of the building and perches on the highest point of the roof. He opens the feathered fan on the back of his neck, cocks his head back, and calls, "Chiiirrrup, chirp, chirp, chirp, chirp." Then he stands as if looking for the one he called to respond. But there is never an answer.

He will repeat the effort. The feathers will flash and the call will sound and he will wait. But there is never a reply.

After a few moments he will nosedive into the patio. He will see his reflection in a plate-glass window and fly into it—beak first. The crash will echo in the patio, and he will retreat. For just a moment. He gathers himself, then sees his reflection and off he goes . . . *slap!* Backward he staggers, scrambling to keep control, only to open his eyes and see the reflection and "*Pop!*" the sad drama is repeated.

I shake my head. "Why won't you learn?" I wonder. "How many times will it take for you to learn that the bird in the window is only an illusion?"

But he remains . . . flying into windows.

Minutes later a young man walks into my office. Sharp, well-dressed. Firm handshake, tanned face, flashy smile. Small talk about basketball, busy work schedules, and airports. I'm tempted to cut the chatter short . . . but don't. He needs time to gather courage. We know why he is here. We've had this talk before. He has a wife. He has a lover. He abandoned the first and lives with the second.

"Have you gone home?" I ask.

"No," he sighs, looking through the window into the patio. "I tried, but I didn't."

"Have you spoken to your wife?"

"I haven't got the nerve."

"He's just a kid," I say to myself. Underneath the Italian suit and sharp talk, he's a frightened six-year-old who knows he shouldn't but doesn't know how to stop. What is this vacuum within him that can't be filled by marriage? What is this passion which takes him to other beds?

I look out the window over his shoulder and see the redbird slap his beak against the pane. I look across my desk and see the man bury his face in his hands. "I know what I should do, but I can't."

What will it take for both to stop? How long will they hurt themselves before they wake up?

The next day I came to the office and the bird was gone. Soon after I called the man and he was gone. I think the bird learned a lesson. I'm not sure the man ever did.

Maybe you've hit your head against the wall. Are there weaknesses within you that stun you? Your words? Your thoughts? Your temper? Your greed? Your grudge? Your gossip? Things were better before you knew the law existed. But now you know. And now you have a war to wage. And I have two truths about grace for you to take into battle.

1. He Still Claims You

First of all, remember your position—you are a child of God. Some interpret the presence of the battle as the abandonment of God. Their logic goes something like this: "I am a Christian. My desires, however, are anything but Christian. No child of God would have these battles. I must be an orphan. God may have given me a place back then, but he has no place for me now."

That's Satan sowing those seeds of shame. If he can't seduce you with your sin, he'll let you sink in your guilt. Nothing pleases him more than for you to cower in the corner, embarrassed that you're still dealing with some old habit. "God's tired of your struggles," he whispers. "Your father is weary of your petitions for forgiveness," he lies.

And many believe him, spending years convinced that they are disqualified from the kingdom. *Can I go to the well of grace too many times? I don't deserve to ask for forgiveness again.*

Forgive my abrupt response, but who told you that you deserved forgiveness the first time? When you came to Christ did he know every sin you'd committed up until that point? Yes. Did Christ know every sin you would commit in the future? Yes, he knew that too. So Jesus saved you, knowing all the sins you would ever commit until the end of your life? Yes. You mean he is willing to call you his child even though he knows each and every mistake of your past and future? Yes.

Sounds to me like God has already proven his point. If your sin were too great for his grace, he never would have saved you in the first place. Your temptation isn't late-breaking news in heaven. Your sin doesn't surprise God. He saw it coming. Is there any reason to think that the One who received you the first time won't receive you every time?

Besides, the very fact that you are under attack must mean that you're on the right side. Did you notice who else had times of struggle? Paul did. Note the tense in which Paul is writing:

I *do* not understand . . ."

". . . it *is* sin living in me . . ."

"I *do* not *do* the good things I *want* . . ."

"I *see* another law working in my body . . ."

"What a miserable man I *am*" (see Rom. 7:14–25, italics mine).

Paul is writing in the present tense. He is not describing a struggle of the past, but a struggle in the present. For all we know, Paul was engaged in spiritual combat even as he wrote this letter. *You mean the apostle Paul battled sin while he was writing a book in the Bible?* Can you think of a more strategic time for Satan to attack?

Is it possible that Satan feared the fruit of this epistle to the Romans?

Could it be that he fears the fruits of your life? Could it be that you are under attack—not because you are so weak but because you might become so strong? Perhaps he hopes that in defeating you today he will have one less missionary or writer or giver or singer to fight with tomorrow.

2. *He Still Guides You*

Let me give you a second truth to take to the battlefield. The first was your position: You are a child of God. The second is your principle: the Word of God.

When under attack, our tendency is to question the validity of God's commands; we rationalize like I do with the one-way street. *The law is for others, not for me. I'm a good driver.* By questioning the validity of the law, I decrease in my mind the authority of the law.

For that reason Paul is quick to remind us, "the law is holy, and the command is holy and right and good" (7:12). The root word for *holy* is *hagios*, which means "different." God's commands are holy because they come from a different world, a different sphere, a different perspective.

In a sense the "Do Not Enter" sign on my forbidden alley was from a different sphere. Our city lawmakers' thoughts are not like my thoughts. They are concerned for the public good. I am concerned with personal convenience. They want what is best for the city. I want what is best for me. They know what is safe. I know what is quick. But they don't create laws for my pleasure; they make laws for my safety.

The same is true with God. What we consider shortcuts God sees as disasters. He doesn't give laws for our pleasure. He gives them for our protection. In seasons of struggle we must trust his wisdom, not ours. He designed the system; he knows what we need.

But since I am stubborn, I think *I* do. My disrespect for the "Do Not Enter" sign reveals an ugly, selfish side of me. Had I never seen the law, I would have never seen how selfish I am.

A poignant example of this was penned seventeen hundred years ago by Augustine in his book *Confessions:*

> There was a pear tree near our vineyard, laden with fruit. One stormy night we rascally youths set out to rob it and carry our spoils away. We took off a huge load of pears—not to feast upon ourselves, but to throw them to the pigs, though we ate just enough to have the pleasure of forbidden fruit. They were nice pears, but it was not the pears that my wretched soul coveted for I had plenty better at home. I picked them simply in order to become a thief . . . the desire to steal was simply awakened by the prohibition of stealing.[1]

Augustine wasn't lured by the pears; he was lured by the fence. Isn't there within each of us a voice which says, "I wonder how many pears I can pick without being seen. I wonder how many times I can go down this one-way street without getting caught"?

The moment we begin asking those questions we have crossed an invisible line into the arena of fear. Grace delivered us from fear, but watch how quickly we return. Grace told us we didn't have to spend our lives looking over our shoulders, but look at us glancing backward. Grace told us that we were free from guilt, but look at us with pear stains on our cheeks and guilt on our consciences.

Don't we know better? What has happened to us? Why are we so quick to revert back to our old ways? Or as Paul so candidly writes, "What a miserable man I am! Who will save me from this body that brings me death?" (Rom. 7:24).

Simply stated: We are helpless to battle sin alone. Aren't we glad Paul answered his own question?

"I thank God for saving me through Jesus Christ our Lord!" (v. 25).

The same One who saved us first is there to save us still.

There is never a point at which you are any less saved than you were the first moment he saved you. Just because you were grumpy at breakfast doesn't mean you were condemned at breakfast. When you lost your temper yesterday, you didn't lose your salvation. Your name doesn't disappear and reappear in the book of life according to your moods and actions. Such is the message of grace. "There is now no condemnation for those who are in Christ Jesus" (Rom. 8:1 NIV).

You are saved, not because of what you do, but because of what Christ did. And you are special, not because of what you do, but because of whose you are. And you are his.

And because we are his, let's forget the shortcuts and stay on the main road. He knows the way. He drew the map. He knows the way home.

15

The Heaviness of Hatred

Matthew 18:21–35

Be kind and loving to each other, and forgive each other just as God forgave you in Christ. EPHESIANS 4:32

Each week Kevin Tunell is required to mail a dollar to a family he'd rather forget. They sued him for $1.5 million but settled for $936, to be paid a dollar at a time. The family expects the payment each Friday so Tunell won't forget what happened on the first Friday of 1982.

That's the day their daughter was killed. Tunell was convicted of manslaughter and drunken driving. He was seventeen. She was eighteen. Tunell served a court sentence. He also spent seven years campaigning against drunk driving, six years more than his sentence required. But he keeps forgetting to send the dollar.

The weekly restitution is to last until the

year 2000. Eighteen years. Tunell makes the check out to the victim, mails it to her family, and the money is deposited in a scholarship fund.

The family has taken him to court four times for failure to comply. After the most recent appearance, Tunell spent thirty days in jail. He insists that he's not defying the order but rather is haunted by the girl's death and tormented by the reminders. He offered the family two boxes of checks covering the payments until the year 2001, one year more than required. They refused. It's not money they seek, but penance.

Quoting the mother, "We want to receive the check every week on time. He must understand we are going to pursue this until August of the year 2000. We will go back to court every month if we have to."[1]

Few would question the anger of the family. Only the naive would think it fair to leave the guilty unpunished. But I do have one concern. Is 936 payments enough? Not for Tunell to send, mind you, but for the family to demand? When they receive the final payment, will they be at peace? In August 2000, will the family be able to put the matter to rest? Is eighteen years' worth of restitution sufficient? Will 196 months' worth of remorse be adequate?

How much is enough? Were you in the family and were Tunell your target, how many payments would you require? Better stated, how many payments *do* you require?

No one—I repeat, *no one*—makes it through life free of injury. Someone somewhere has hurt you. Like the eighteen-year-old, you've been a victim. She died because someone drank too much. Part of you has died because someone spoke too much, demanded too much, or neglected too much.

The Habit of Hatred

Everyone gets wounded; hence everyone must decide: how many payments will I demand? We may not require that the offender write checks, but we have other ways of settling the score.

Silence is a popular technique. (Ignore them when they speak.) *Distance* is equally effective. (When they come your way, walk the other.) *Nagging* is a third tool for revenge. ("Oh, I see you still have fingers on your hand. Funny you never use them to dial my number." "Oh, Joe, nice of you to drop in on us *unpromoted* peons.")

Amazing how creative we can be at getting even. If I can soil one evening, spoil one day, foil one Friday, then justice is served and I'm content.

For now. Until I think of you again. Until I see you again. Until something happens that brings to mind the deed you did, then I'll demand another check. I'm not about to let you heal before I do. As long as I suffer, you suffer. As long as I hurt, you hurt. You cut me, and I'm going to make you feel bad as long as I bleed, even if I have to reopen the wound myself.

Call it a bad addiction. We start the habit innocently enough, indulging our hurts with doses of anger. Not much, just a needle or two of rancor. The rush numbs the hurt, so we come back for more and up the dosage; we despise not only what he did, but who he is. Insult him. Shame him. Ridicule him. The surge energizes. Drugged on malice, the roles are reversed; we aren't the victim, we're the victor. It feels good. Soon we hate him and anyone like him. ("All men are jerks." "Every preacher is a huckster." "You can't trust a woman.") The progression is predictable. Hurt becomes hate, and hate becomes rage as we become junkies unable to make it through the day without mainlining on bigotry and bitterness.

How will the score be settled? How do I break the cycle? How many payments do I demand? Peter had a similar question for Jesus: "Master, how many times do I forgive a brother or sister who hurts me? Seven?" (Matt. 18:21 MSG).

Peter is worried about over-forgiving an offender. The Jewish law stipulated that the wounded forgive three times. Peter is willing to double that and throw in one more for good measure. No doubt he thinks Jesus will be impressed. Jesus isn't. The Master's answer still stuns us. "Seven! Hardly. Try seventy times seven" (v. 22 MSG).

If you're pausing to multiply seventy times seven, you're missing the point. Keeping tabs on your mercy, Jesus is saying, is not being merciful. If you're calibrating your grace, you're not being gracious. There should never be a point when our grace is exhausted.

The Cause of Hatred

By this point Jesus' listeners are thinking of the Kevin Tunells in the world. "But what about the father who abandoned me as a kid?"

"And my wife who dumped me for a newer model?"

"And the boss who laid me off even though my child was sick?"

The Master silences them with a raised hand and the story of the forgetful servant.

> The kingdom of heaven is like a king who decided to collect the money his servants owed him. When the king began to collect his money, a servant who owed several million dollars was brought to him. But the servant did not have enough money to pay the master, the king. So the master ordered that everything the servant owned should be sold, even the servant's wife and children. Then the money would be used to pay the king what the servant owed.
>
> But the servant fell on his knees and begged, "Be patient with me, and I will pay you everything I owe." The master felt sorry for his servant and told him he did not have to pay it back. Then he let the servant go free. (Matt. 18:23–28)

This servant had a serious problem. Somehow he had amassed a bill worth millions of dollars. If he could pay a thousand dollars a day for thirty years, he'd be debt free. Fat chance. He didn't make a grand a day. His debt was far greater than his power to repay.

And unless you skipped the first half of this book, you know the same is true of us. Our debt is far greater than our power to repay.

Our pockets are empty while our debt is millions. We don't need a salary; we need a gift. We don't need swimming lessons; we need a lifeguard. We don't need a place to work; we need someone to work in our place. That "someone" is Jesus Christ. "God makes people right with himself through their faith in Jesus Christ. . . . God gave him as a way to forgive sin through faith in the blood of Jesus' death" (Rom. 3:22, 25).

Our Master has forgiven an insurmountable debt. Does God demand reimbursement? Does he insist on his pound of flesh? When your feet walk the wrong road, does he demand that you cut them off? When your eyes look twice where they should never look once, does he blind you? When you use your tongue for profanity instead of praise, does he cut it out?

If he did, we would be one maimed civilization. He demands no payment, at least not from us.

And those promises we make, "Just get me through this mess, God. I'll never disappoint you again." We're as bad as the debtor. "Be patient with me," he pledged. "I will pay you everything I owe." The thought of pleading for mercy never entered his mind. But though he never even begs for grace, he receives it. He leaves the king's chamber a debt-free man.

But he doesn't believe it.

> Later, that same servant found another servant who owed him a few dollars. The servant grabbed him around the neck and said, "Pay me the money you owe me!"
>
> The other servant fell on his knees and begged him, "Be patient with me, and I will pay you everything I owe."

> But the first servant refused to be patient. He threw the other servant into prison until he could pay everything he owed. (Matt. 18:28–29)

Something is wrong with this picture. Are these the actions of a man forgiven millions? Choking a person who owes him a few bucks? Are these the words of a man who has been set free? "Pay me the money you owe me!"

Remember the finger-pointer from the parable at the beginning of the book? Here he is! So occupied with the mistake of his brother that he misses the grace of the Father.

He demands that his debtor be put in jail until he can repay the debt. How bizarre! Not only is he ungrateful, he is irrational. How can he expect the man to earn money while in prison? If he has no funds out of jail, will he discover some money in jail? Of course not. What's he going to do? Sell magazines to the inmates? The decision makes no sense.

But hatred never does.

How could this happen? How can one forgiven not forgive? How could a free man not be quick to free others?

Part of the answer is found in the words of Jesus. "The person who is forgiven only a little will love only a little" (Luke 7:47).

To believe we are totally and eternally debt free is seldom easy. Even if we've stood before the throne and heard it from the king himself, we still doubt. As a result, many are forgiven only a little, not because the grace of the king is limited, but because the faith of the sinner is small. God is willing to forgive all. He's willing to wipe the slate completely clean. He guides us to a pool of mercy and invites us to bathe. Some plunge in, but others just touch the surface. They leave feeling unforgiven.

Apparently that was the problem of the servant. He still *felt* in debt. How else can we explain his behavior? Rather than forgive his transgressor, he chokes him! "I'll squeeze it out of you." He hates the very sight of the man. Why? Because the man owes him so much? I don't think so. He hates the man because the man reminds him of his debt to the master.

The king forgave the debt, but the servant never truly accepted the grace of the king. Now we understand why the Hebrew writer insisted, "See to it that no one misses the grace of God and that no bitter root grows up to cause trouble and defile many" (Heb. 12:15 NIV).

The Cure for Hatred

Where the grace of God is missed, bitterness is born. But where the grace of God is embraced, forgiveness flourishes. In what many believe to be Paul's final letter, he urges Timothy to "be strong in the grace we have in Christ Jesus" (2 Tim. 2:1).

How insightful is this last exhortation. Paul doesn't urge Timothy to be strong in prayer or Bible study or benevolence, as vital as each may be. He wants his son in the faith to major in grace. Claim *this* territory. Dwell on *this* truth. If you miss anything, don't miss the grace of God.

The longer we walk in the garden, the more likely we are to smell like flowers. The more we immerse ourselves in grace, the more likely we are to give grace. Could this be the clue for coping with anger? Could it be the secret is not in demanding payment but in pondering the payment of your Savior?

Your friend broke his promises? Your boss didn't keep her word? I'm sorry, but before you take action, answer this question: How did God react when you broke your promises to him?

You've been lied to? It hurts to be deceived. But before you double your fists, think: How did God respond when you lied to him?

You've been neglected? Forgotten? Left behind? Rejection hurts. But before you get even, get honest with yourself. Have you ever neglected God? Have you always been attentive to his will? None of us have. How did he react when you neglected him?

The key to forgiving others is to quit focusing on what they did to you and start focusing on what God did for you.

But, Max, that's not fair! Somebody has to pay for what he did.

I agree. Someone must pay, and Someone already has.

You don't understand, Max, this guy doesn't deserve grace. He doesn't deserve mercy. He's not worthy of forgiveness.

I'm not saying he is. But are you?

Besides, what other choice do you have? Hatred? The alternative is not appealing. Look what happens when we refuse to forgive, "The master was very angry and put the servant in prison to be punished until he could pay everything he owed" (Matt. 18:34).

Unforgiving servants always end up in prison. Prisons of anger, guilt, and depression. God doesn't have to put us in a jail; we create our own. "Some men stay healthy till the day they die . . . others have no happiness at all; they live and die with bitter hearts" (Job 21:23–25 TEV).

Oh, the gradual grasp of hatred. Its damage begins like the crack in my windshield. Thanks to a speeding truck on a gravel road, my window was chipped. With time the nick became a crack, and the crack became a winding tributary. Soon the windshield was a spider web of fragments. I couldn't drive my car without thinking of the jerk who drove too fast. Though I've never seen him, I could describe him. He is some deadbeat bum who cheats on his wife, drives with a six-pack on the seat, and keeps the television so loud the neighbors can't sleep. His carelessness blocked my vision. (Didn't do much for my view out the windshield either.)

Ever heard the expression "blind rage"?

Let me be very clear. Hatred will sour your outlook and break your back. The load of bitterness is simply too heavy. Your knees will buckle under the strain, and your heart will break beneath the weight. The mountain before you is steep enough without the heaviness of hatred on your back. The wisest choice—the *only* choice—is for you to drop the anger. You will never be called upon to give anyone more grace than God has already given you.

During World War I, a German soldier plunged into an out-of-the-way shell hole. There he found a wounded enemy. The fallen soldier was soaked with blood and only minutes from death. Touched by the plight of the man, the German soldier offered him water. Through this small kindness a bond was developed. The dying man pointed to his shirt pocket; the German soldier took from it a wallet and removed some family pictures. He held them so the wounded man could gaze at his loved ones one final time. With bullets raging over them and war all around them, these two enemies were, but for a few moments, friends.[2]

What happened in that shell hole? Did all evil cease? Were all wrongs made right? No. What happened was simply this: Two enemies saw each other as humans in need of help. This is forgiveness. Forgiveness begins by rising above the war, looking beyond the uniform, and choosing to see the other, not as a foe or even as a friend, but simply as a fellow fighter longing to make it home safely.

16

Life Aboard the Fellow-Ship

Romans 15:7

Welcome with open arms fellow believers who don't see things the way you do.
ROMANS 14:1 MSG

Accept one another, then, just as Christ accepted you, in order to bring praise to God. ROMANS 15:7 NIV

Grace makes three proclamations.

First, only God can forgive my godlessness. "Only God can forgive sins" (Mark 2:7). Dealing with my sins is God's responsibility. I repent, I confess, but only God can forgive. (And he does.)

Second, only God can judge my neighbor. "You cannot judge another person's servant. The master decides if the servant is doing well or not" (Rom. 14:4). Dealing with my neighbor is God's responsibility. I must speak; I must pray. But only God can convince. (And he does.)

Third, I must accept who God accepts. "Christ accepted you, so you should accept each other, which will bring glory to God"

(Rom. 15:7). God loves me and makes me his child. God loves my neighbor and makes him my brother. My privilege is to complete the triangle, to close the circuit by loving who God loves.

Easier said than done. "To live above with those we love, oh, how that will be glory. To live below with those we know, now that's another story."[1] Best I can figure the situation reads something like this . . .

Rocking the Boat

God has enlisted us in his navy and placed us on his ship. The boat has one purpose—to carry us safely to the other shore.

This is no cruise ship; it's a battleship. We aren't called to a life of leisure; we are called to a life of service. Each of us has a different task. Some, concerned with those who are drowning, are snatching people from the water. Others are occupied with the enemy, so they man the cannons of prayer and worship. Still others devote themselves to the crew, feeding and training the crew members.

Though different, we are the same. Each can tell of a personal encounter with the captain, for each has received a personal call. He found us among the shanties of the seaport and invited us to follow him. Our faith was born at the sight of his fondness, and so we went.

We each followed him across the gangplank of his grace onto the same boat. There is one captain and one destination. Though the battle is fierce, the boat is safe, for our captain is God. The ship will not sink. For that, there is no concern.

There is concern, however, regarding the disharmony of the crew. When we first boarded we assumed the crew was made up of others like us. But as we've wandered these decks, we've encountered curious converts with curious appearances. Some wear uniforms we've never seen, sporting styles we've never witnessed. "Why do you look the way you do?" we ask them.

"Funny," they reply. "We were about to ask the same of you."

The variety of dress is not nearly as disturbing as the plethora of opinions. There is a group, for example, who clusters every morning for serious study. They promote rigid discipline and somber expressions. "Serving the captain is serious business," they explain. It's no coincidence that they tend to congregate around the stern.

There is another regiment deeply devoted to prayer. Not only do they believe in prayer, they believe in prayer by kneeling. For that reason you always know where to locate them; they are at the bow of the ship.

And then there are a few who staunchly believe real wine should be used in the Lord's Supper. You'll find them on the port side.

Still another group has positioned themselves near the engine. They spend hours examining the nuts and bolts of the boat. They've been known to go below deck and not come up for days. They are occasionally criticized by those who linger on the top deck, feeling the wind in their hair and the sun on their face. "It's not what you learn," those topside argue. "It's what you feel that matters."

And, oh, how we tend to cluster.

Some think once you're on the boat, you can't get off. Others say you'd be foolish to go overboard, but the choice is yours.

Some believe you volunteer for service; others believe you were destined for the service before the ship was even built.

Some predict a storm of great tribulation will strike before we dock; others say it won't hit until we are safely ashore.

There are those who speak to the captain in a personal language. There are those who think such languages are extinct.

There are those who think the officers should wear robes, there are those who think there should be no officers at all, and there are those who think we are all officers and should all wear robes.

And, oh, how we tend to cluster.

And then there is the issue of the weekly meeting at which the captain is thanked and his words are read. All agree on its importance, but few agree on its nature. Some want it loud, others quiet. Some want ritual, others spontaneity. Some want to celebrate so they can meditate; others meditate so they can celebrate. Some want a meeting for those who've gone overboard. Others want to reach those overboard but without going overboard and neglecting those on board.

And, oh, how we tend to cluster.

The consequence is a rocky boat. There is trouble on deck. Fights have broken out. Sailors have refused to speak to each other. There have even been times when one group refused to acknowledge the presence of others on the ship. Most tragically, some adrift at sea have chosen not to board the boat because of the quarreling of the sailors.

"What do we do?" we'd like to ask the captain. "How can there be harmony on the ship?" We don't have to go far to find the answer.

On the last night of his life Jesus prayed a prayer that stands as a citadel for all Christians:

> I pray for these followers, but I am also praying for all those who will believe in me because of their teaching. Father, I pray that they can be one. As you are in me and I am in you, I pray that they can also be one in us. Then the world will believe that you sent me. (John 17:20)

How precious are these words. Jesus, knowing the end is near, prays one final time for his followers. Striking, isn't it, that he prayed not for their success, their safety, or their happiness.

He prayed for their unity. He prayed that they would love each other.

As he prayed for them, he also prayed for "those who will believe because of their teaching." That means us! In his last prayer Jesus prayed that you and I be one.

The Command of Acceptance

Of all the lessons we can draw from this verse, don't miss the most important: Unity matters to God. The Father does not want his kids to squabble. Disunity disturbs him. Why? Because "all people will know that you are my followers if you love each other" (John 13:35). Unity creates belief. How will the world believe that Jesus was sent by God? Not if we agree with each other. Not if we solve every controversy. Not if we are unanimous on each vote. Not if we never make a doctrinal error. But if we love one another.

Unity creates belief. Disunity fosters disbelief. Who wants to board a ship of bickering sailors? Life on the ocean may be rough, but at least the waves don't call us names.

Paul Billheimer may very well be right when he says:

> The continuous and widespread fragmentation of the Church has been the scandal of the ages. It has been Satan's master strategy. The sin of disunity probably has caused more souls to be lost than all other sins combined."[2]

"All people will know that you are my followers if you love each other." Stop and think about this verse for a minute. Could it be that *unity* is the key to reaching the world for Christ?

If unity is the key to evangelism, shouldn't it have precedence in our prayers? Shouldn't we, as Paul said, "make every effort to keep the unity of the Spirit through the bond of peace" (Eph. 4:3 NIV)? If unity matters to God, then shouldn't unity matter to us?

If unity is a priority in heaven, then shouldn't it be a priority on earth?

Nowhere, by the way, are we told to *build* unity. We are told simply to *keep* unity. From God's perspective there is but "one flock and one shepherd" (John 10:16). Unity does not need to be created; it simply needs to be protected.

How do we do that? How do we make every effort to keep the unity? Does that mean we compromise our convictions? No. Does that mean we abandon the truths we cherish? No. But it does mean we look long and hard at the attitudes we carry.

A Case Study in Capernaum

Sometime ago Denalyn bought a monkey. I didn't want a monkey in our house, so I objected.

"Where is he going to eat?" I asked.

"At our table."

"Where is he going to sleep?" I inquired.

"In our bed."

"What about the odor?" I demanded.

"I got used to you; I guess the monkey can too."

Unity doesn't begin in examining others but in examining self. Unity begins, not in demanding that others change, but in admitting that we aren't so perfect ourselves.

For a great example of this, go to a village called Capernaum and enter a small house occupied by Jesus and the disciples. Listen as the Master asks them a question. "What were you arguing about on the road?" (Mark 9:33).

The disciples' faces flush, not red with anger but pink with embarrassment. They had argued. About doctrine? No. Over strategy? Not that either. Ethics and values? Sorry. They had argued about which of them was the greatest.

Peter thought he was (he'd walked on water). John laid claim to the top slot (he was Jesus' favorite). Matthew boasted he was the best (after all, his book would be first in the New Testament). Power plays and one-upmanship. Is that where division usually begins?

> Where jealousy and selfishness are, there will be confusion and every kind of evil. (James 3:16)
>
> Do you know where your fights and arguments come from? They come from the selfish desires that wage war within you. (James 4:1)

Remarkable. Jockeying for position in the very presence of Christ. But not as remarkable as Jesus' response to them.

"Whoever *accepts* a child like this in my name *accepts* me. And whoever *accepts* me *accepts* the One who sent me" (Mark 9:37 italics mine).

Jesus felt so strongly about acceptance that he used the word four times in one sentence.

The answer to arguments? Acceptance. The first step to unity? Acceptance. Not agreement, acceptance. Not unanimity, acceptance. Not negotiation, arbitration, or elaboration. Those might come later but only after the first step, acceptance.

Such an answer troubles John. Too simplistic. The Son of Thunder was unacquainted with tolerance. Why, you just don't go around "accepting" people! Fences have to be built. Boundaries are a necessary part of religion. Case in point? John has one.

The Test of Divergence

"Teacher, we saw someone using your name to force demons out of a person. We told him to stop, because he does not belong to our group" (Mark 9:38).

John has a dilemma. He and the other disciples ran into

someone who was doing great work. This man was casting out demons (the very act the disciples had trouble doing in Mark 9:20). He was changing lives. And, what's more, the man was giving the credit to God. He was doing it in the name of Christ.

Everything about him was so right. Right results. Right heart. But there was one problem. He was from the wrong group.

So the disciples did what any able-bodied religious person would do with someone from the wrong group. They escorted him to the hull of the boat and put him in confinement. "We told him to stop, because he does not belong to our group" (v. 38).

John wants to know if they did the right thing. John's not cocky; he's confused. So are many people today. What do you do about good things done in another group? What do you do when you like the fruit but not the orchard?

I've asked that question. I am deeply appreciative of my heritage. It was through a small, West Texas Church of Christ that I came to know the Nazarene, the cross, and the Word. The congregation wasn't large, maybe two hundred on a good Sunday. Most of the families were like mine, blue-collar oil-field workers. But it was a loving church. When our family was sick, the members visited us. When we were absent, they called. And when this prodigal returned, they embraced me.

I deeply appreciate my heritage. But through the years, my faith has been supplemented by people of other groups. I wasn't long on God's ship before I found encouragement in other staterooms.

A Brazilian Pentecostal taught me about prayer. A British Anglican by the name of C. S. Lewis put muscle in my faith. A Southern Baptist helped me understand grace.

One Presbyterian, Steve Brown, taught me about God's sovereignty while another, Frederick Buechner, taught me about God's passion. A Catholic, Brennan Manning, convinced me that Jesus is relentlessly tender. I'm a better husband because I read James

Dobson and a better preacher because I listened to Chuck Swindoll and Bill Hybels.

And only when I get home will I learn the name of a radio preacher whose message steered me back to Christ. I was a graduate student who'd lost his bearings. Needing some money over Christmas break, I took a job driving an oil-field delivery truck. The radio only picked up one station. A preacher was preaching. On a cold December day in 1978 I heard him describe the cross. I don't know his name. I don't know his heritage. He could have been a Quaker or an angel or both for all I know. But something about what he said caused me to pull the pickup onto the side of the road and rededicate my life to Christ.

Examine the Fruit and the Faith

What do you do when you see great works done by folks of other groups? Not divisive acts, not heretical teachings, but good works that give glory to God? Let's return to the conversation between Jesus and the disciples.

Before you note what Jesus said to John, note what he didn't say.

Jesus did not say, "John, if the people are nice, they are in." Generous gestures and benevolent acts are not necessarily a sign of a disciple. Just because a group is distributing toys at Christmas doesn't mean they are Christians. Just because they are feeding the hungry does not mean they are the honored ones of God. Jesus doesn't issue a call for blind tolerance.

Nor does he endorse blanket rejection. If unanimity of opinion were necessary for fellowship, this would have been a perfect time for Jesus to say so. But he didn't. Jesus didn't hand John a book of regulations by which to measure every candidate. Were such a checklist necessary, this would have been the ideal time to give it. But he didn't.

Look at what Jesus did say: "Don't stop him, because anyone who uses my name to do powerful things will not easily say evil things about me" (Mark 9:39).

Jesus was impressed with the man's *pure faith* (". . . who uses my name") and his *powerful fruit* (". . . to do powerful things"). His answer offers us a crucial lesson on studied tolerance. How should you respond to a good heart from a different religious heritage?

First, look at the fruit. Is it good? Is it healthy? Is he or she helping or hurting people? Production is more important than pedigree. The fruit is more important than the name of the orchard. If the person is bearing fruit, be grateful! A good tree cannot produce bad fruit (see Matt. 7:17), so be thankful that God is at work in other groups than yours.

But also look at the faith. In whose name is the work done? Jesus was accepting of this man's work because it was done in the name of Christ. What does it mean to do something "in the name of Jesus"? It means you are under the authority of and empowered by that name.

If I go to a car dealership and say I want a free car, the salespeople are going to laugh at me. If, however, I go with a letter written and signed by the owner of the dealership granting me a free car, then I drive off in a free car. Why? Because I am there under the authority of and empowered by the owner.

The Master says examine the person's faith. If he or she has faith in Jesus and is empowered by God, grace says that's enough. This is an important point. There are some who do not work in God's name. Remember the rock-stackers and the finger-pointers in the parable? They present a salvation of works rather than a salvation of grace. They are not working in the name of God, indeed they do not need God. They are working under the banner of human-merit self-righteousness. Just as Paul was intolerant of self-salvation, we must be as well.

But there are believers in many different heritages who cast their hope in God's firstborn Son and put their faith in the cross of Christ. If they, like you, are trusting him to carry them to the father's castle, don't you share a common Savior? If their trust, like yours, is in the all-sufficient sacrifice of Christ, aren't you covered with the same grace?

You mean they don't have to be in my group? No.

They don't have to share my background? They don't.

They don't have to see everything the way I do? Does anyone?

What is important is their fruit and their faith. Later, a much more tempered Son of Thunder would reduce it to this. "Whoever confesses that Jesus is the Son of God has God living inside, and that person lives in God" (1 John 4:15).

Ironic. The one who challenged the simple answer of the Master eventually rendered the simplest answer himself.

It should be simple. Where there is faith, repentance, and a new birth, there is a Christian. When I meet a man whose faith is in the cross and whose eyes are on the Savior, I meet a brother. Wasn't that Paul's approach? When he wrote the church in Corinth, he addressed a body of Christians guilty of every sin from abusing the Lord's Supper to arguing over the Holy Spirit. But how does he address them? "I beg you, brothers and sisters" (1 Cor. 1:10).

When the church in Rome was debating whether to eat meat offered to idols, did Paul tell them to start two churches? One for the meat-eaters and one for the non-meat-eaters? No, on the contrary, he urged, "Christ accepted you, so you should accept each other, which will bring glory to God" (Rom. 15:7).

Is God asking us to do anything more than what he has already done? Hasn't he gone a long way in accepting us? If God can tolerate my mistakes, can't I tolerate the mistakes of others? If God allows me, with my foibles and failures, to call him Father, shouldn't I extend the same grace to others? In fact, who can offer grace except those secure in the grip of grace? If God doesn't demand perfection, should I?

"They are God's servants," Paul reminds us, "not yours. They are responsible to him, not to you. Let him tell them whether they are right or wrong. And God is able to make them do as they should" (Rom. 14:4 TLB).

God's ship is a grand vessel. Just as a ship has many rooms, so God's kingdom has room for many opinions. But just as a ship has one deck, God's kingdom has a common ground: the all-sufficient sacrifice of Jesus Christ.

Will you pray with me for the day when Jesus' prayer is answered?

Will you pray with me for the day when the world is won because the church is one?

Will you pray with me for the day when we come out of our rooms and stand together to salute our captain? When clusters cease and the chorus commences?

Jesus' final prayer before the cross was for the unity of his followers. Would he offer a prayer that couldn't be answered? I don't think so either.

17 What We Really Want to Know

Romans 8:31–39

Can anything separate us from the love Christ has for us? ROMANS 8:35

It was her singing that did it. At first I didn't notice. Had no reason to. The circumstances were commonplace. A daddy picking up his six-year-old from a Brownie troop meeting. Sara loves Brownies; she loves the awards she earns and the uniform she wears. She'd climbed in the car and shown me her new badge and freshly baked cookie. I'd turned onto the road, turned on her favorite music, and turned my attention to more sophisticated matters of schedules and obligations.

But only steps into the maze of thought I stepped back out. Sara was singing. Singing about God. Singing to God. Head back, chin up, and lungs full, she filled the car with music. Heaven's harps paused to listen.

Is that my daughter? She sounds older. She looks older, taller, even prettier. Did I sleep through something? What happened to the chubby cheeks? What happened to the little face and pudgy fingers? She is becoming a young lady. Blonde hair down to her shoulders. Feet dangling over the seat. Somewhere in the night a page had turned and, well, look at her!

If you're a parent you know what I mean. Just yesterday diapers, today the car keys? Suddenly your child is halfway to the dormitory, and you're running out of chances to show your love, so you speak.

That's what I did. The song stopped and Sara stopped, and I ejected the tape and put my hand on her shoulder and said, "Sara, you're something special." She turned and smiled tolerantly. "Someday some hairy-legged boy is going to steal your heart and sweep you into the next century. But right now, you belong to me."

She tilted her head, looked away for a minute, then looked back and asked, "Daddy, why are you acting so weird?"

I suppose such words would sound strange to a six-year-old. The love of a parent falls awkwardly on the ears of a child. My burst of emotion was beyond her. But that didn't keep me from speaking.

There is no way our little minds can comprehend the love of God. But that didn't keep him from coming.

And we, too, have tilted our heads. Like Sara, we have wondered what our Father was doing. From the cradle in Bethlehem to the cross in Jerusalem, we've pondered the love of our Father. What *can* you say to that kind of emotion? Upon learning that God would rather die than live without you, how do you react? How can you begin to explain such passion? If you're Paul the apostle, you don't. You make no statements. You offer no explanations. You ask a few questions. Five questions, to be exact.

Paul's response to God's grace is a quintet of queries, launched like fireworks, not to bring answers, but to bring amazement. "[Paul] challenges anybody and everybody, in heaven, earth or hell, to answer them and deny the truth which they contain."[1]

These questions are not new to you. You've asked them. In the night you've asked them; in anger you've asked them. The doctor's diagnosis brought them to the surface, as did the court's decision and the phone call from the bank. The questions are probes of pain and problem and circumstance. No, the questions are not new, but maybe the answers are.

The Question of Protection

"If God is for us, who can be against us?" (Rom 8:31 NIV).

The question is not simply, "Who can be against us?" You could answer that one. Who is against you? Disease, inflation, corruption, exhaustion. Calamities confront, and fears imprison. Were Paul's question, "Who can be against us?" we could list our foes much easier than we could fight them. But that is not the question. The question is, *If GOD IS FOR US, who can be against us?*

Indulge me for a moment. Four words in this verse deserve your attention. Read slowly the phrase, "God is for us." Please pause for a minute before you continue. Read it again, aloud. (My apologies to the person next to you.) *God is for us*. Repeat the phrase four times, this time emphasizing each word. (Come on, you're not in that big of a hurry.)

God is for us.

God *is* for us.

God is *for* us.

God is for *us*.

God is for you. Your parents may have forgotten you, your teachers may have neglected you, your siblings may be ashamed of you;

but within reach of your prayers is the maker of the oceans. God!

God *is* for you. Not "may be," not "has been," not "was," not "would be," but "God is!" He *is* for you. Today. At this hour. At this minute. As you read this sentence. No need to wait in line or come back tomorrow. He is with you. He could not be closer than he is at this second. His loyalty won't increase if you are better nor lessen if you are worse. He *is* for you.

God is *for* you. Turn to the sidelines; that's God cheering your run. Look past the finish line; that's God applauding your steps. Listen for him in the bleachers, shouting your name. Too tired to continue? He'll carry you. Too discouraged to fight? He's picking you up. God is *for* you.

God is for *you*. Had he a calendar, your birthday would be circled. If he drove a car, your name would be on his bumper. If there's a tree in heaven, he's carved your name in the bark. We know he has a tattoo, and we know what it says. "I have written your name on my hand," he declares (Isa. 49:16).

"Can a mother forget the baby at her breast and have no compassion on the child she has borne?" God asks in Isaiah 49:15 (NIV). What a bizarre question. Can you mothers imagine feeding your infant and then later asking, "What was that baby's name?" No. I've seen you care for your young. You stroke the hair, you touch the face, you sing the name over and over. Can a mother forget? No way. But "even if she could forget, . . . I will not forget you," God pledges (Isa. 49:15).

God is with you. Knowing that, who is against you? Can death harm you now? Can disease rob your life? Can your purpose be taken or your value diminished? No. Though hell itself may set itself against you, no one can defeat you. You are protected. God is with you.

The Question of Provision

"He who did not spare his own Son, but gave him up for us all—how will he not also, along with him, graciously give us all things?" (Rom. 8:32 NIV).

Suppose a man comes upon a child being beaten by thugs. He dashes into the mob, rescues the boy, and carries him to a hospital. The youngster is nursed to health. The man pays for the child's treatment. He learns that the child is an orphan and adopts him as his own and gives the boy his name. And then, one night, months later, the father hears the son sobbing into his pillow. He goes to him and asks about the tears.

"I'm worried, Daddy. I'm worried about tomorrow. Where will I get food to eat? How am I going to buy clothes to stay warm? And where will I sleep?"

The father is rightfully troubled. "Haven't I shown you? Don't you understand? I risked my life to save you. I gave my money to treat you. You wear my name. I've called you my son. Would I do all that and then not meet your needs?"

This is Paul's question. *Would he who gave his Son not meet our needs?*

But still we worry. We worry about the IRS and the SAT and the FBI. We worry about education, recreation, and constipation. We worry that we won't have enough money, and when we have money we worry that we won't manage it well. We worry that the world will end before the parking meter expires. We worry what the dog thinks if he sees us step out of the shower. We worry that someday we'll learn that fat-free yogurt was fattening.

Honestly, now. Did God save you so you would fret? Would he teach you to walk just to watch you fall? Would he be nailed to the cross for your sins and then disregard your prayers? Come on. Is

Scripture teasing us when it reads, "He has put his angels in charge of you to watch over you wherever you go"? (Ps. 91:11)

I don't think so either.

Two Questions about Guilt and Grace

"Who can accuse the people God has chosen? No one, because God is the One who makes them right. Who can say God's people are guilty? No one, because Christ Jesus died, but he was also raised from the dead, and now he is on God's right side, begging God for us" (Rom. 8:33–34).

Sometime ago I read a story of a youngster who was shooting rocks with a slingshot. He could never hit his target. As he returned to Grandma's backyard, he spied her pet duck. On impulse he took aim and let fly. The stone hit, and the duck was dead. The boy panicked and hid the bird in the woodpile, only to look up and see his sister watching.

After lunch that day, Grandma told Sally to help with the dishes. Sally responded, "Johnny told me he wanted to help in the kitchen today. Didn't you Johnny?" And she whispered to him, "Remember the duck!" So, Johnny did the dishes.

What choice did he have? For the next several weeks he was at the sink often. Sometimes for his duty, sometimes for his sin. "Remember the duck," Sally'd whisper when he objected.

So weary of the chore, he decided that any punishment would be better than washing more dishes, so he confessed to killing the duck. "I know, Johnny," his grandma said, giving him a hug. "I was standing at the window and saw the whole thing. Because I love you, I forgave you. I wondered how long you would let Sally make a slave out of you."[2]

He'd been pardoned, but he thought he was guilty. Why? He had listened to the words of his accuser.

You have been accused as well. You have been accused of dishonesty. You've been accused of immorality. You've been accused of greed, anger, and arrogance.

Every moment of your life, your accuser is filing charges against you. He has noticed every error and marked each slip. Neglect your priorities, and he will jot it down. Abandon your promises, and he will make a note. Try to forget your past; he'll remind you. Try to undo your mistakes; he will thwart you.

This expert witness has no higher goal than to take you to court and press charges. Even his name, Diabolos, means "slanderer." Who is he? The devil.

He is "the accuser of our brothers and sisters, who accused them day and night before our God" (Rev. 12:10). Can't you see him? Pacing back and forth before God's bench. Can't you hear him? Calling your name, listing your faults.

He rails: "This one you call your child, God. He is not worthy. Greed lingers within. When he speaks, he thinks often of himself. He'll go days without an honest prayer. Why, even this morning he chose to sleep rather than spend time with you. I accuse him of laziness, egotism, worry, distrust . . ."

As he speaks, you hang your head. You have no defense. His charges are fair. "I plead guilty, your honor," you mumble.

"The sentence?" Satan asks.

"The wages of sin is death," explains the judge, "but in this case the death has already occurred. For this one died with Christ."

Satan is suddenly silent. And you are suddenly jubilant. You realize that Satan cannot accuse you. No one can accuse you! Fingers may point and voices may demand, but the charges glance off like arrows hitting a shield. No more dirty dishwater. No more penance. No more nagging sisters. You have stood before the judge and heard him declare, "Not guilty."

"The Lord God helps me, so I will not be ashamed. I will be

determined, and I know I will not be disgraced. He shows that I am innocent, and he is close to me. So who can accuse me? If there is someone, let us go to court together" (Isa. 50:7–8).

Once the judge has released you, you need not fear the court.

The Question of Endurance

"Can anything separate us from the love Christ has for us?" (Rom. 8:35).

There it is. This is the question. Here is what we want to know. We want to know how long God's love will endure. Paul could have begun with this one. Does God really love us forever? Not just on Easter Sunday when our shoes are shined and our hair is fixed. We want to know (deep within, don't we really want to know?), how does God feel about me when I'm a jerk? Not when I'm peppy and positive and ready to tackle world hunger. Not then. I know how he feels about me then. Even I like me then.

I want to know how he feels about me when I snap at anything that moves, when my thoughts are gutter-level, when my tongue is sharp enough to slice a rock. How does he feel about me then?

That's the question. That's the concern. That's the reason most of you read this book. Oh, you don't say it; you may not even know it. But I can see it on your faces. I can hear it in your words. Did I cross the line this week? Last Tuesday when I drank vodka until I couldn't walk . . . last Thursday when my business took me where I had no business being . . . last summer when I cursed the God who made me as I stood near the grave of the child he gave me?

Did I drift too far? Wait too long? Slip too much?

That's what we want to know.

Can anything separate us from the love Christ has for us?

God answered our question before we asked it. So we'd see his answer, he lit the sky with a star. So we'd hear it, he filled the night with a choir; and so we'd believe it, he did what no man had ever dreamed. He became flesh and dwelt among us.

He placed his hand on the shoulder of humanity and said, "You're something special."

Untethered by time, he sees us all. From the backwoods of Virginia to the business district of London; from the Vikings to the astronauts, from the cave-dwellers to the kings, from the hut-builders to the finger-pointers to the rock-stackers, he sees us. Vagabonds and ragamuffins all, he saw us before we were born.

And he loves what he sees. Flooded by emotion. Overcome by pride, the Starmaker turns to us, one by one, and says, "You are my child. I love you dearly. I'm aware that someday you'll turn from me and walk away. But I want you to know, I've already provided you a way back."

And to prove it, he did something extraordinary.

Stepping from the throne, he removed his robe of light and wrapped himself in skin: pigmented, human skin. The light of the universe entered a dark, wet womb. He who angels worship nestled himself in the placenta of a peasant, was birthed into the cold night, and then slept on cow's hay.

Mary didn't know whether to give him milk or give him praise, but she gave him both since he was, as near as she could figure, hungry and holy.

Joseph didn't know whether to call him Junior or Father. But in the end called him Jesus, since that's what the angel said and since he didn't have the faintest idea what to name a God he could cradle in his arms.

Neither Mary nor Joseph said it as bluntly as my Sara, but don't you think their heads tilted and their minds wondered, "What in the world are you doing, God?" Or, better phrased, "God, what are you doing in the world?"

"Can anything make me stop loving you?" God asks. "Watch me

speak your language, sleep on your earth, and feel your hurts. Behold the maker of sight and sound as he sneezes, coughs, and blows his nose. You wonder if I understand how you feel? Look into the dancing eyes of the kid in Nazareth; that's God walking to school. Ponder the toddler at Mary's table; that's God spilling his milk.

"You wonder how long my love will last? Find your answer on a splintered cross, on a craggy hill. That's me you see up there, your maker, your God, nail-stabbed and bleeding. Covered in spit and sin-soaked. That's your sin I'm feeling. That's your death I'm dying. That's your resurrection I'm living. That's how much I love you."

"Can anything come between you and me?" asks the firstborn Son.

Hear the answer and stake your future on the triumphant words of Paul: "I am sure that neither death, nor life, nor angels, nor ruling spirits, nothing now, nothing in the future, no powers, nothing above us, nothing below us, nor anything else in the whole world will ever be able to separate us from the love of God that is in Christ Jesus our Lord" (Rom. 8:38–39).

Conclusion
"Don't Forget to Look After Me"

"Good, I'm glad you're sitting by me. Sometimes I throw up."

Not exactly what you like to hear from the airline passenger in the next seat. Before I had time to store my bag in the overhead compartment, I knew his name, age, and itinerary. "I'm Billy Jack. I'm fourteen, and I'm going home to see my daddy." I started to tell him my name, but he spoke first.

"I need someone to look after me. I get confused a lot."

He told me about the special school he attended and the medication he took. "Can you remind me to take my pill in a few minutes?" Before we buckled up he stopped the airline attendant. "Don't forget about me," he told her. "I get confused."

Once we were airborne, Billy Jack ordered a soft drink and dipped his pretzels in it. He kept glancing at me as I drank and asked if he could drink what I didn't. He spilled some of his soda and apologized.

"No problem," I said, wiping it up.

Billy Jack showed me his cassette player and asked if I'd like to listen to one of his tapes. "I brought my favorites," he smiled, handing me the sound tracks from *The Little Mermaid*, *Aladdin*, and *The Lion King*.

When he started playing with his Nintendo Game Boy, I tried to doze off. That's when he started making noises with his mouth, imitating a trumpet. "I can sound like the ocean, too," he bragged, swishing spit back and forth in his cheeks.

(Didn't sound like the ocean, but I didn't tell him.)

Billy Jack was a little boy in a big body. "Can clouds hit the ground?" he asked me. I started to answer, but he looked back out the window like he'd never asked. Unashamed of his needs, he didn't let a flight attendant pass without a reminder: "Don't forget to look after me."

When they brought the food: "Don't forget to look after me."

When they brought more drinks: "Don't forget to look after me."

When any attendant would pass, Billy Jack would urge: "Don't forget to look after me."

I honestly can't think of one time Billy Jack didn't remind the crew that he needed attention. The rest of us didn't. We never asked for help. We were grownups. Sophisticated. Self-reliant. Seasoned travelers. Most of us didn't even listen to the emergency landing instructions. (Billy Jack asked me to explain them to him.)

Midway through the writing of this book I remembered Billy Jack. He would have understood the idea of grace. He knew what it was like to place himself totally in the care of someone else. I didn't share with him "The Parable of the River" (it wasn't written yet), but I know which brother he would have liked.

The youngest. The one who let the elder brother carry him up the river. He wouldn't have understood the three who refused the offer of the firstborn son. Why *not* place your care in the hands of someone stronger?

Have you?

Many haven't. We are sophisticated, mature. An epistle to challenge the self-sufficient, Romans was written for folks like us. Confession of need is admission of weakness, something we are slow to do. That's why I think Billy Jack would have understood grace. It occurred to me that he was the safest person on the flight. Had the plane encountered trouble, he would have received primary assistance. The flight attendants would have bypassed me and gone to him. Why? He had placed himself in the care of someone stronger.

Again I ask, have you?

One thing's for sure: You cannot save yourself. The river is too strong; the distance is too great. God has sent his firstborn Son to carry you home. Are you firmly in the grip of his grace? I pray that you are. I *earnestly* pray that you are.

Before we conclude our time together, would you spend some time with the following questions? May the Holy Spirit use them to reveal any resistance you might have to God's grace.

Are you quick to tell others of the rocks you've stacked? Or do you prefer boasting about the strength of your elder brother?

Do you live in fear of never doing enough? Or do you live in gratitude, knowing enough has already been done?

Do you have a small circle, accepting only the few who work like you? Or do you have a large circle, accepting all who love who you love?

Do you worship to impress God? Or do you worship to thank God?

Do you do good deeds in order to be saved? Or do you do good deeds because you are saved?

Do you pray, "God, I thank you that I am not like other people who steal, cheat, or take part in adultery"?[1]

Or do you confess, "God, have mercy on me, a sinner"?

* * *

One last thought. Billy Jack spent the final hour of the flight with his head on my shoulder, his hands folded between his knees. Just when I thought he was asleep, his head popped up and he said, "My dad is going to meet me at the airport. I can't wait to see him because he watches after me."

Paul would have liked Billy Jack.

Notes

INTRODUCTION

1. Edward Mote, "The Solid Rock."
2. Martin Luther, "Preface to the Epistle of St. Paul to the Romans," *Luther's Works*, vol. 35, ed. J. Pelikan and H. Lehmann: Muhlenburg Press, 1960), page 365.

CHAPTER 2 GOD'S GRACIOUS ANGER

1. Anders Nygren, *Commentary on Romans*, (Philadelphia: Fortress Press, 1949), 98.
2. Carthaginian theologian Tertullian, quoted in William Barclay, *The Letter to the Romans*, (Louisville, Ky.: Westminster Press, 1975, 27.

CHAPTER 3 GODLESS LIVING

1. Ravi Zacharias, *Can Man Live Without God?* (Dallas: Word, 1994), 23.
2. Stephen Jay Gould, quoted in Donald McCullough, *The Trivialization of God* (Colorado Springs: NavPress, 1995), 16.

CHAPTER 4 GODLESS JUDGING

1. John Stott, *Romans: God's Good News for the World* (Downers Grove, IL: InterVarsity Press, 1994), 82.

CHAPTER 5 GODLESS RELIGION

1. From "Definition of Justification," in Richard Hooker's *Ecclesiastical Policy*, as quoted in Stott, *Romans: God's Good News for the World*, 118.

CHAPTER 6 CALLING THE CORPSES

1. Dr. Li Zhisui, "The Private Life of Chairman Mao," *US News and World Report*, 10 October 1994, 55–90.

CHAPTER 7 WHERE LOVE AND JUSTICE MEET

1. Stott, *Romans: God's Good News for the World*, 112.
2. Ibid., 118.
3. John MacArthur, *The New Testament Commentary of Romans* (Chicago: Moody 1991, 199.

CHAPTER 8 CREDIT WHERE CREDIT IS NOT DUE

1. Dr. Leon Morris, *The Epistle to the Romans* (Grand Rapids, Mich.: Eerdmans and InterVarsity, 1988), as quoted in Stott, *Romans: God's Good News for the World*, 109.

CHAPTER 9 MAJOR LEAGUE GRACE

1. I heard this story at a ministers retreat featuring Gordon MacDonald in February 1990.

CHAPTER 10 THE PRIVILEGE OF PAUPERS

1. Dr. Paul Faulkner, *Achieving Success without Failing Your Family* (W. Monroe La.: Howard Publishing, 1994), 14–15.
2. *1041 Sermon Illustrations, Ideas and Expositions* (Grand Rapids, Mich.: Baker, 1953), 244.
3. Charles R. Swindoll, *The Grace Awakening* (Waco, Tex.: Word, 1990), 70.

CHAPTER 11 GRACE WORKS

1. Charles Colson, "Making the World Safe for Religion," *Christianity Today*, 8 November 1993, 33.
2. Stott, *Romans: God's Good News for the World*, 169.
3. William Sanday and Arthur C. Headlam, "A Critical and Exegetical Commentary on the Epistle to the Romans," in the *The International Commentary*.

CHAPTER 13 SUFFICIENT GRACE

1. Max Lucado, *God Came Near* (Portland, Oreg.: Multnomah Press, 1987), 151–52.

CHAPTER 14 THE CIVIL WAR OF THE SOUL

1. Augustine, *Confessions*, as quoted by William Barclay, *The Letter to the Romans* (Philadelphia: Westminster Press, 1977), 98.

CHAPTER 15 THE HEAVINESS OF HATRED

1. "Drunken Driver Skips $1 Weekly Payments to Victim's Parents," *San Antonio Light*, 31 March 1990.

CHAPTER 16 LIFE ABOARD THE FELLOW-SHIP

1. Source unknown.
2. Paul Billheimer, *Love Covers* (Minneapolis: Bethany House, 1981), 7.

CHAPTER 17 WHAT WE REALLY WANT TO KNOW

1. Stott, *Romans: God's Good News for the World*, 254.
2. Steven Cole, "Forgiveness," *Leadership Magazine*, 1983, 86.

CONCLUSION: "DON'T FORGET TO LOOK AFTER ME"

1. Luke 18:11–13.

Study Guide

Written by Steve Halliday

Each of these short studies is designed not only to help you think through and apply the ideas developed in *In The Grip Of Grace*, but also to help you interact with the biblical passages that prompted those ideas.

The first section of each study, "Looking Back," excerpts portions of each chapter and supplies questions for personal or group study. The second section, "Looking Deep," helps you dig a little deeper into Scripture's perspective on the topic under discussion.

Introduction:

The Greatest Discovery of My Life

Looking Back

1. An epistle for the self-sufficient, Romans contrasts the plight of people who choose to dress in self-made garments with those who gladly accept the robes of grace.
   - A. What do you think Max means by "self-made garments"? Have you ever worn such "garments"? If so, explain.
   - B. What do you think Max means by "the robes of grace"? Are these "robes" in your wardrobe? Explain.
2. God used the book of Romans to change the lives (and the wardrobes) of Luther, John Wesley, John Calvin, William Tyndale, St. Augustine, and millions of others. There is every reason to think he'll do the same for you.
   - A. What comes to mind when you think of the book of Romans?
   - B. What do you know of the men Max mentions in this paragraph—Luther, Wesley, Calvin, Tyndale, Augustine? How did Romans change their lives?
   - C. How can the book of Romans change your own life? Do you think it will? Explain.

Looking Deep

1. Read Romans 1:16–17.
   - A. How do these two verses explain the theme of Romans?

B. How does Paul use these verses to describe what he plans to unfold in the rest of his book?
C. Do you believe you have a good understanding of the topic described in these verses? Explain.
D. Are these verses being "lived out" in your daily life? Explain.

2. Read Galatians 3:26.
   A. How does this verse compare to Romans 1:16–17?
   B. What is common to each?

1

The Parable of the River

Looking Back

1. Though they did not know where they were, of one fact they were sure: They were not intended for this place.
   A. How did the sons know they were not intended for their new surroundings?
   B. In what way is this statement a description of our own circumstances?
2. One chose to indulge, the other to judge, and the third to work. None of them chose his father.
   A. With which of the three brothers are you most likely to identify? Explain.
   B. What is wrong with the responses of each of the three sons?
3. All four brothers heard the same invitation. Each had an opportunity to be carried home by the elder brother. The first said no, choosing a grass hut over his father's house. The second said no, preferring to analyze the mistakes of his brother rather than admit his own. The third said no, thinking it wiser to make a good impression than an honest confession. And the fourth said yes, choosing gratitude over guilt.
   A. What reasons did each of the three brothers give for refusing the offer of the eldest brother? Have you ever heard people give similar reasons for refusing Jesus' offer of salvation? If so, describe them.

B. How did the fourth brother choose "gratitude over guilt"?

4. As you read of the brothers, which describes your relationship to God? Have you, like the fourth son, recognized your helplessness to make the journey home alone? Do you take the extended hand of your father? Are you caught in the grip of his grace?
   A. Answer the questions above.
   B. How does someone know whether he or she is "caught in the grip of [God's] grace"?
5. What does Max mean by each of the following, and what do they all have in common?
   A. The Hut-Building Hedonist
   B. The Fault-Finding Judgmentalist
   C. The Rock-Stacking Legalist
6. I might as well prepare you: The first chapters of Romans are not exactly upbeat. Paul gives us the bad news before he gives the good news. He will eventually tell us that we are all equal candidates for grace, but not before he proves that we are all desperately sinful.
   A. Why do you think Paul began with the bad news before he explained the good news?
   B. When we explain the gospel to someone, do we usually follow Paul's pattern? Explain.

Looking Deep

1. Read Ephesians 1:7–8
   A. According to verse 7, what do we have in Christ?
   B. According to what measure were we given these things, according to verses 7–8?
2. Read Ephesians 2:4–9
   A. How are love, mercy and grace related to each other in verses 4–5? What do these three work together to achieve?

B. What future grace will we experience, according to verse 7?

C. What do you learn about grace in verses 8–9? How does this affect you personally?

2

God's Gracious Anger

Looking Back

1. God does not sit silently while his children indulge in perversion. He lets us go our sinful way and reap the consequences. Every broken heart, every unwanted child, every war and tragedy can be traced back to our rebellion against God.
   A. Why do you think God doesn't stop us before we "go our sinful way"?
   B. Do you agree that "every war and tragedy can be traced back to our rebellion against God"? Explain.
2. God is angry at evil. For many, this is a revelation.
   A. What does it mean that God is "angry" at evil?
   B. Was this a revelation to you? If so, explain.
3. Many don't understand God's anger because they confuse the wrath of God with the wrath of man. The two have little in common.
   A. How is the wrath of God different from the wrath of man?
   B. Do the two kinds of "wrath" have anything in common? If so, what?
4. Every star is an announcement. Each leaf a reminder. The glaciers are megaphones, the seasons are chapters, the clouds are banners. Nature is a song of many parts but one theme and one verse: *God is*.

A. How does nature proclaim that God exists?
B. If this is true, then why are there atheists?

5. The question is not, "How dare a loving God be angry?", but rather "How could a loving God feel anything less?"
   A. Have you ever met someone who thought love and anger couldn't co-exist? If so, why did they believe this?
   B. Why does Max believe that God must demonstrate both love and anger? Do you agree? Why or why not?

Looking Deep

1. Read Romans 1:18–20
   A. Against whom is the "wrath of God" being revealed, according to verse 18? How is it being revealed?
   B. Why is the "wrath of God" being revealed, according to verse 19?
   C. Why are men "without excuse," according to verse 20?
2. Read Psalm 19:1–6
   A. What do these verses teach us about God's creation?
   B. What does God's creation teach us about God?

3

Godless Living

Looking Back

1. If there is no ultimate good behind the world, then how do we define "good" within the world? If the majority opinion determines good and evil, what happens when the majority is wrong?
   A. How would you answer Max's two questions above?
   B. Without God, can there be any truly "good" or "evil"? Explain.
2. What dike does the God-denying thinker have to stop the flood? What anchor will the secularist use to keep society from being sucked out to sea? If a society deletes God from the human equation, what sandbags will they stack against the swelling tide of barbarism and hedonism?
   A. What kind of anchor is society's trust in?
   B. What biblical examples of godlessness serve as wake-up calls for our society?
3. Mine deep enough in every heart and you'll find it: a longing for meaning, a quest for purpose. As surely as a child breathes, he will someday wonder, "What is the purpose of my life?"
   A. Have you ever struggled with a longing for meaning or a sense of purpose? If so, describe the struggle. If not, why not?
   B. What is the purpose of your life?
4. With God in your world, you aren't an accident nor an incident, you are a gift to the world, a divine work of art, signed by God.

A. Do you ever feel like an "accident" or an "incident"? If so, when are such feelings most likely to occur?

B. Do you believe you are a "gift to the world, a divine work of art, signed by God"? Explain.

5. Ironically, the more we know the less we worship. We are more impressed with our discovery of the light switch than with the one who invented electricity.

A. Do you agree that the more we know, the less we worship? Explain.

B. Why do you think it seems so easy to forget God?

6. According to Romans 1, godlessness is a bad swap. In living for today, the hut-building hedonist destroys his hope of living in a castle tomorrow.

A. How do people make this "bad swap" today?

B. Did you ever choose a "hut" over a "castle"? If so, describe the situation. What caused you to make a change?

Looking Deep

1. Read Romans 1:21–32.

A. What is the awful sin described in verse 21? What happens to those who commit such a sin?

B. What is the sin described in verses 22–23? How is this related to the sin of verse 21?

C. What is the sin described in verse 24? Does this seem related to the sin of verses 22–23? Explain.

D. How does verse 25 summarize verses 21–24?

E. Work through verses 26–32, noting how the passage intensifies as it progresses. What is the significance of this?

2. Read Ephesians 2:10.

A. How are believers described in this verse? What task are they given to do?

B. How firm is God in his intention for believers?

4

Godless Judging

Looking Back

1. Ever wrestled with the deathbed conversion of a rapist or the eleventh hour conversion of a child molester? We've sentenced them, maybe not in court, but in our hearts. We put them behind bars and locked the door. They are forever imprisoned by our disgust. And then, the impossible happens. They repent. Our response? (Dare we say it?) We cross our arms and furrow our brows, "God won't let you off that easy. Not after what you did. God is kind but he's no wimp. Grace is for average sinners like me, not deviants like you."
   A. What did you think when you read of Jeffrey Dahmer's reported conversion? Be honest.
   B. What would you say to a person who told you, "If your God could forgive Jeffrey Dahmer or Adolf Hitler, I want no part of him"?
2. It's one thing to be repulsed at the acts of a Jeffrey Dahmer (and I am). It's another entirely to claim that I am superior (I'm not), or that he is beyond the grace of God (no one is).
   A. What repulses us about the acts of a Jeffrey Dahmer? Why does one set of sins seem worse than another?
   B. Why is it so easy for us to believe we are superior to others?
   C. Why can Max say that no one is beyond the grace of God?
3. The easiest way to justify the mistakes in my house is to find worse ones in my neighbor's house.

   A. What does Max mean by the statement above?
   B. Do you agree with him? Why or why not?
4. The request Dahmer made is no different than yours or mine. He may make it from a prison bunk, you may make it from a church pew, but from heaven's angle we're all asking for the moon. And by heaven's grace we all receive it.
   A. Why was Dahmer's request no different than yours or mine?
   B. What does Max mean that "from heaven's angle we're all asking for the moon"?

Looking Deep

1. Read Romans 2:1–11.
   A. Why do those who pass judgment on others have no excuse? What are they actually doing when they pass judgment (verse 1)?
   B. What warning is given in verses 3–4?
   C. How can someone show "contempt" for God's kindness and patience, according to verse 5?
   D. Both a warning and a promise are given in verses 6–10. Describe each of them, and to whom each are given.
   E. What is the purpose of verse 11? Why is this important to say here?
2. Read Matthew 20:1–16.
   A. In a single sentence, what do you think the point of Jesus' parable is?
   B. What does he want us to know?
3. Read 1 Corinthians 4:5.
   A. What does this verse tell us *not* to do? What does it tell us to do?
   B. What does it say God will do? What does it say will be the result?

5

Godless Religion

Looking Back

1. Faith is intensely personal. There is no royal lineage or holy bloodline in God's kingdom.
   A. Why is faith "intensely personal"?
   B. What does Max mean that "there is no royal lineage or holy bloodline in God's kingdom"? Are you glad for this? Explain.
2. Paul is accusing the Jews of trusting the symbol of circumcision while neglecting their souls. Could he accuse us of the same error?
   A. How is it possible to trust a symbol while ignoring the spiritual reality the symbol represents?
   B. Answer Max's question above and explain your answer.
3. Symbols are important. Some of them, like communion and baptism, illustrate the cross of Christ. They symbolize salvation, demonstrate salvation, even articulate salvation. But they do not impart salvation.
   A. How do communion and baptism illustrate the cross of Christ?
   B. Why can't symbols impart salvation?
4. From God's perspective there is no difference between the ungodly partygoer, the ungodly finger-pointer, and the ungodly pew-sitter. The Penthouse gang, the courthouse clan, and the

church choir need the same message: Without God all are lost.

A. Why is there no difference between the three groups mentioned above?

B. What is the remedy for all three groups mentioned above?

5. There is only one name under heaven that has the power to save, and that name is not yours.

A. How is the modern world apt to respond to Max's statement above?

B. How would you respond to someone who objected to Max's statement?

Looking Deep

1. Read Romans 2:17–3:18.

A. What claims of superiority does Paul say Jews were making (2:17–20)?

B. What questions does Paul ask of the Jews (2:21–23)? What answers does he assume?

C. What is the connection of verse 24 to the preceding passage? In what way is this verse a conclusion?

D. What value does circumcision have, according to 2:25–29? What two kinds of people are contrasted?

E. What advantages does Paul say Jews have (3:1–4)?

F. What major problem is being discussed in 3:5–8? How would you answer the apostle's questions?

G. What major teaching is developed in 3:9–18? How does Paul do this? What does he conclude?

2. Read Acts 4:10–12.

A. How was the lame man healed according to verse 10?

B. How does Peter describe Jesus according to verses 10–11?

C. What claim does Peter make in verse 12? How is this significant?

6

Calling the Corpses

Looking Back

1. For all of our differences, there is one problem we all share. We are separated from God.
   A. What does it mean to be "separated from God"?
   B. What are some of the evidences that a person is separated from God?
   C. How did we all come to be separated from God?
2. A dead flower has no life. A dead body has no life. A dead soul has no life. Cut off from God, the soul withers and dies. The consequence of sin is not a bad day or a bad mood, but a dead soul.
   A. What does Max mean by "a dead soul"?
   B. Why is the consequence of sin "a dead soul"?
3. We don't need more religion, we need a miracle. We don't need someone to disguise the dead, we need someone to raise the dead.
   A. How is religion different from a miracle?
   B. Who needs to be raised from the dead?
4. We are the corpse and he is the corpse-caller. We are the dead and he is the dead-raiser. Our task is not to get up but to admit we are dead. The only ones who remain in the grave are the ones who don't think they are there.
   A. What does it mean to "admit we are dead"? What are the

consequences if we don't admit this?

B. How can someone not know they are "in the grave"? Do you know anyone like this? If so, explain.

Looking Deep

1. Read Romans 3:21–26.
   A. What two kinds of "righteousness" are contrasted in verses 21–22? What kind does God endorse?
   B. What does verse 23 tell us about ourselves? How is this significant?
   C. How does verse 24 solve the problem of verse 23?
   D. How do verses 25–26 explain how God can be perfectly just and yet declare us not guilty?
2. Read 2 Corinthians 5:17–18.
   A. What does it mean to be "in Christ"? How does one get to be "in Christ"?
   B. What is true of someone who is "in Christ"? Is this true of you? Explain.

7

Where Love and Justice Meet

Looking Back

1. What if, perish the thought, heaven had limitations to its coverage?
   - A. Answer Max's question above.
   - B. Do you know of anyone who believes heaven has "limitations to its coverage"? If so, describe what they believe these limitations to be.
2. It's one thing to make good people right, but those who are evil? We can expect God to justify the decent, but the dirty? Surely coverage is provided for the driver with the clean record, but the speeder? The ticketed? The high-risk client? How in the world can justification come for the evil?
   - A. In God's eyes, are there any "good people" (see Luke 18:19)? Any "decent" people? Any with a "clean record"? Explain.
   - B. How *can* justification come for the evil?
3. Salvation is God-given, God-driven, God-empowered, and God-originated. The gift is not from man to God. It is from God to man.
   - A. Why is it important to emphasize that salvation begins and ends with God?
   - B. Why is it important to remember that salvation is a gift?

4. Is God going to lower his standard so we can be forgiven? Is God going to look away and pretend that I've never sinned? Would we want a God who altered the rules and made exceptions?
   A. What would be bad about God lowering his standard so we could be forgiven?
   B. Would you want a God who altered the rules and made exceptions? Explain.
5. Ponder the achievement of God. He doesn't condone our sin, nor does he compromise his standard. He doesn't ignore our rebellion, nor does he relax his demands. Rather than dismiss our sin he assumes our sin and, incredibly, sentences himself. God's holiness is honored. Our sin is punished. And we are redeemed.
   A. How did God "sentence himself"? What does this mean?
   B. How does the cross both honor God's holiness and secure our redemption?

Looking Deep

1. Read Romans 4:4–8.
   A. What two things are contrasted in verses 4 and 5? How are they different?
   B. How does Paul use the words of David to support his contention in verse 5?
   C. What does it mean to "trust God"? Is this a one-time event, or an ongoing action? Explain.
2. Read 2 Corinthians 5:19, 21.
   A. What did God do, according to verse 19? How did he do this? What was the result?
   B. What did God do, according to verse 21? Why did he do this? What was the result?

3. Read Colossians 2:13–15.
   A. How were we described in verse 13? How did God respond to this condition?
   B. How did God do this, according to verse 14?
   C. In what way does the cross show God's "triumph"? How is this possible?

8

Credit Where Credit Is Not Due

Looking Back

1. I don't always know the *occasion* of my sins. There are times when I sin and I don't even know it!
   A. How is it possible to sin and not be aware of it?
   B. Describe any instances you can think of in which you belatedly realized that you had committed some sin.
2. The cost of your sins is more than you can pay. The gift of your God is more than you can imagine.
   A. Suppose you only sinned once in your entire life. Could you pay that kind of debt? Explain.
   B. In what way is the gift of God more than we can imagine?
3. Grace is risky. There *is* the chance that people will take it to an extreme. There *is* the possibility that people will abuse God's goodness.
   A. Do you agree that "grace is risky"? Why or why not?
   B. In what ways have you seen that grace is risky? How have you seen people abuse God's goodness? Have you ever done so? Explain.
4. Grace fosters an eagerness for good. Grace doesn't spawn a desire to sin. If one has truly embraced God's gift, he will not mock it. In fact, if a person uses God's mercy as liberty to sin, one might wonder whether the person ever knew God's mercy at all.

A. Why does grace foster "an eagerness for good"? How does this work?

B. Do you agree with Max's last statement? Why or why not?

5. The vast majority of people simply state, "God may give grace to you, but not to me. You see, I've charted the waters of failure. I've pushed the envelope too many times. I'm not your typical sinner, I'm guilty of ________________" and they fill in the blank.

A. Have you ever heard someone make a statement like that above? If so, describe what was said. How did you respond?

B. Do you ever feel as though you could make such a statement? How would you "fill in the blank"? What does God's Word say about this?

Looking Deep

1. Read Romans 4:13–24.

A. According to verse 13, how did Abraham receive God's promise? Why is this important (v. 14)?

B. Who may receive the benefits of the promise (vv. 16–17)?

C. Why is Abraham a particularly good example of a man who lived by faith (vv. 18–22)?

D. What part of Abraham's example do verses 23–24 encourage us to follow? Have you followed this example? Explain.

2. Read Galatians 3:2–14.

A. Paul asks at least five questions in Galatians 3:2–5. What are they, and what answer does the apostle expect for each?

B. What does Abraham illustrate in this passage (vv. 6–9)?

How does this compare to the Romans text above?

C. How many people are justified through the law according to 3:10–12?

D. How can we appropriate the promise to Abraham according to 3:13–14? What benefit does this bring?

9

Major League Grace

Looking Back

1. These guys didn't make it to the big leagues on skill, they made it on luck. They weren't picked because they were good, they were picked because they were willing.
   A. How does Max compare the striking ballplayers with the replacement players?
   B. Did the replacement players recognize their good fortune? How do we know?
2. If the first four chapters of Romans tell us anything, they tell us we are living a life we don't deserve. We aren't good enough to get picked, but look at us, suited up and ready to play!
   A. In what way are we "living a life we don't deserve"? How is this like the replacement ballplayers?
   B. How did we come to be "suited up and ready to play"? How did this happen? Who is responsible?
3. Peace with God. What a happy consequence of faith! Not just peace between countries, peace between neighbors, or peace at home; salvation brings peace with God.
   A. How would you describe "peace with God"? Of what does it consist?
   B. How is peace with God better than other kinds of peace?
4. Christ meets you outside the throne room, takes you by the

hand, and walks you into the presence of God. Upon entrance we find grace, not condemnation; mercy, not punishment.

A. Imagine yourself being led into the throne room of God by Jesus. How do you feel?

B. On what basis can we expect to find grace, not condemnation; and mercy, not punishment?

5. Because of God's grace we go from being people whose "throats are open graves" (v. 13) to being participants of God's glory. We were washed up and put out, now we are called up and put in.

A. In what ways are people whose "throats are open graves" different from those who are "participants in God's glory"?

B. In what way were we "washed up and put out"? In what way are we now "called up and put in"?

Looking Deep

1. Read Romans 5:1–3.

A. How are we "justified," according to 5:1? What does it mean to be "justified"? What result does this produce?

B. What does it mean to "stand" in "grace"? What result does this "standing" produce?

C. What two things don't seem to go together in 5:3? In what way does Paul put them together?

2. Read Isaiah 53:4–6.

A. What did Jesus do for us according to verse 4? What does this mean?

B. What happened to Jesus, according to verse 5? For what purpose did this happen?

C. How are we pictured in verse 6? What did the Lord do about this situation? Are you glad for this? Explain.

10

The Privilege of Paupers

Looking Back

1. Christ welcomes us to his table by virtue of his love and our request. It is not our offerings which grant us a place at the feast; indeed, anything we bring appears puny at his table. Our admission of hunger is the only demand.
   A. Why do our offerings appear puny at God's table? Why do we so often bring them anyway?
   B. What does Max mean by admitting our "hunger"? How do we do this? Have you done this? Explain.
2. God didn't look at our frazzled lives and say, "I'll die for you when you deserve it."
   A. Had God said such a thing, how would that affect you right now?
   B. Has anyone ever deserved for God to die for them? Explain.
3. Isn't there anyone who sees you for who you are and not what you did? Yes. There is one who does. Your king. When God speaks of you, he doesn't mention your plight, pain, or problem; he lets you share his glory. He calls you his child.
   A. Are you ever tempted to think of yourself by what you have done in life? What is wrong about such thinking?
   B. What does it mean to share God's glory? How does this affect you in practical terms?

4. Are you aware that the most repeated command from the lips of Jesus was, "Fear not"? Are you aware that the only phrase to appear in every book of the Bible is the one from heaven, "Don't be afraid?"
   A. How is it significant that Jesus' most common command was "fear not"? What does this assume?
   B. Why would God so often tell us not to be afraid? What is the best way to overcome such fear?
5. Consider the list of blessings at God's table found on pp. 104–105.
   A. Which of these blessings is most precious to you? Why?
   B. Which of these blessings seems most distant to you? Why?
   C. How can knowledge of these blessings practically affect the way you live?

Looking Deep

1. Read Romans 5:6–8.
   A. For whom did Christ die, according to verse 6? When did he die? Why did he die?
   B. What contrast does Paul play up in verses 7–8? By doing this, who and what does he wish to exalt? Explain.
2. Read Matthew 5:6.
   A. What group of people does Jesus describe in this verse? What promise does he give to them?
   B. Do you believe you are included in this group? Explain.
3. Read Psalm 103:8–18.
   A. List the characteristics of God described in this passage. How is each important to you personally?
   B. List the characteristics of human beings described in this passage. How does this list mesh with the first list?

11

Grace Works

Looking Back

1. How can we who have been made right not live righteous lives? How can we who have been loved, not love? How can we who have been blessed, not bless? How can we who have been given grace, not live graciously?
   A. How would you answer Max's questions above?
   B. In your own life, what are the greatest hindrances to living righteously, loving, blessing, and living graciously?
2. Perhaps we don't sin *so* God can give grace, but do we ever sin *knowing* God will give grace? Do we ever compromise tonight, knowing we'll confess tomorrow?
   A. How would you answer Max's questions above?
   B. What is wrong with compromising tonight if we know we'll confess tomorrow?
3. Christ has taken your place. There is no need for you to remain in the cell.
   A. What "cell" is Max talking about?
   B. What specific kinds of "cells" are you most likely to enter? Explain.
4. Baptism is a vow; a sacred vow of the believer to follow Christ. Just as a wedding celebrates the fusion of two hearts, baptism celebrates the union of sinner with Savior.
   A. What parallels do you see between baptism and marriage? What differences are there?

B. In what way does baptism celebrate the union of sinner with Savior? What kind of union is this?

5. Before Christ our lives were out of control, sloppy, and indulgent. We didn't even know we were slobs until we met him. Then he moved in. Things began to change. Not overnight, but gradually. What we threw around we began putting away. What we neglected we cleaned up. What had been clutter became order.

   A. Did you know you were a "slob" before you met Christ? Explain.

   B. How have things changed in your own life since Christ moved in? Could an outsider notice the changes? Explain.

Looking Deep

1. Read Romans 6:1–12.

   A. What is the problem Paul addresses in 6:1? Is this still a problem today? Explain.

   B. How does Paul answer his own question (vv. 2–4)?

   C. What truth does Paul lay out in verses 5–7? Is this truth helpful in a practical sense? Why or why not?

   D. What promise is given in verse 8? How does this connect with verse 11? What practical admonition does Paul then give in verse 12?

2. Read Titus 2:11–12 (cf. 1:16).

   A. What has appeared "to all men"? What did this do (2:11)?

   B. What does grace teach us to do (2:12)? How does it do this?

   C. In what way is Titus 1:16 the flip side of 2:12?

3. Read Acts 26:20.

   A. How does this verse reinforce the message of Titus 1:16 ?

   B. How does this verse reinforce the message of Titus 2:12?

12

Turning Yourself In

Looking Back

1. From the beginning God has called for honesty. He's never demanded perfection, but he has expected truthfulness.
   A. If God knows everything already, why would he demand honesty from us?
   B. If God knows everything already, why is it foolish not to be completely honest with him?
2. Confession does for the soul what preparing the land does for the field. Before the farmer sows the seed he works the acreage, removing the rocks and pulling the stumps. He knows that seed grows better if the land is prepared. Confession is the act of inviting God to walk the acreage of our hearts.
   A. In what ways is confession like a farmer preparing his land for crops?
   B. Is confession a regular practice of yours? Why or why not?
3. Confession seeks pardon from God, not amnesty. Pardon presumes guilt; amnesty, derived from the same Greek word as *amnesia*, "forgets" the alleged offense without imputing guilt. Confession admits wrong and seeks forgiveness; amnesty denies wrong and claims innocence.
   A. Why should we seek pardon, not amnesty? In your own words, what is the difference?
   B. How can we admit wrong and guilt without beginning to loathe ourselves?

4. Those who keep secrets from God, keep their distance from God. Those who are honest with God, draw near to God.
   A. Is it really possible to keep secrets from God? Explain.
   B. Why does honesty draw a person close to God?
5. May I ask a frank question? Are you keeping any secrets from God? Any parts of your life off limits? Any cellars boarded up or attics locked? Any part of your past or present that you hope you and God never discuss?
   A. How would you answer Max's question above?
   B. What areas of life are hardest for you to discuss with God? Why?

Looking Deep

1. Read Romans 6:18–23.
   A. From what have believers been set free (v. 18)? To what have they become slaves?
   B. What choice is laid out in verse 19? What choice are you making in this regard?
   C. What question does Paul ask in verse 21? How would you answer him?
   D. What contrast is made between verses 21 and 22?
   E. What contrasts are made in verse 23? How are these crucial?
2. Read James 4:7–10.
   A. What commands are given in this passage?
   B. What promises are made in this passage?
   C. In your own words, what is the main point of this passage?
3. Read James 5:16.
   A. What does this verse instruct us to do? How often do we comply? Explain.
   B. What promise is given here for those who do what they are instructed?

13

Sufficient Grace

Looking Back

1. There are times when the one thing you want is the one thing you never get.
   - A. What one thing do you want that you've never received? How do you react to this?
2. When God says no to you, how will you respond? If God says, "I've given you my grace and that is enough," will you be content?
   - A. Why do you think God sometimes tells us no?
   - B. Are there any specific things you can do to be content with God's grace when he denies a request? If so, what are they?
3. Don't you find it encouraging that even Paul had a thorn in the flesh? There is comfort in learning that one of the writers of the Bible wasn't always on the same page with God.
   - A. Do you find it encouraging that even Paul had a thorn in the flesh? Explain.
   - B. Why does it help to remember that the writers of the Bible were real people with real problems?
4. You wonder why God doesn't remove temptation from your life? If he did, you might lean on your strength instead of his grace.
   - A. What kind of temptations regularly give you the most difficulty? How do you deal with them?

B. In what areas are you tempted to lean on your own strength rather than his grace? When you do so, what is usually the result?

5. For all we don't know about thorns, we can be sure of this. God would prefer we have an occasional limp than a perpetual strut.

   A. What "thorns" keep you from strutting?

   B. Why is it better to "have an occasional limp than a perpetual strut"?

Looking Deep

1. Read 2 Corinthians 12:7–9.

   A. Why was the "thorn" given to Paul (v. 7)? Who gave it to him? What was the "thorn's" task?

   B. What was the apostle's response to the thorn (v. 8)?

   C. What was God's response to Paul's request (v. 9)? How did Paul react to God's response? Do you think you would have reacted like this? Explain.

2. Read Philippians 4:6–7.

   A. What should be our attitude toward anxiety, according to verse 6? How are we to respond to it? Is this usually your attitude? Explain.

   B. What is the result of complying with the apostle's instruction of verse 6 (v. 7)? Have you experienced this result? Explain.

14

The Civil War of the Soul

Looking Back

1. You'd think that I would have no desire to use the alley, but I do! Part of me still wants the shortcut. Part of me wants to break the law.
   A. Have you ever felt the way Max said he does about the alley? If so, explain.
   B. Why do you think our struggle often intensifies when we hear that a desirable course of action is not allowed?
2. Those who have been amazed by grace have been equally amazed by their sin. Why do I say yes to God one day and yes to Satan the next?
   A. What amazes you about grace? What amazes you about your own sin?
   B. How would you answer Max's question above?
3. Are there weaknesses within you which stun you? Your words? Your thoughts? Your temper? Your greed? Your grudge? Your gossip? Things were better before you knew the law existed. But now you do. And now you have a war to wage.
   A. How would you answer Max's questions above?
   B. What internal war do you most often have to wage? Describe it.
4. Your temptation isn't late-breaking news in heaven. Your sin doesn't surprise God. He saw it coming. Is there any reason to

think that the one who received you the first time won't receive you every time?

A. Do you find it ironic that your sin surprises you, but not God? Explain.

B. How would you answer Max's question above?

5. What we consider shortcuts, God sees as disasters. He doesn't give laws for our pleasure. He gives them for our protection. In seasons of struggle we must trust his wisdom, not ours.

A. In what ways are God's laws for our protection? Do they exist for any other reason? Explain.

B. How can we practically learn to trust God's wisdom? How do you practice this habit? What tempts you away from it?

6. There is never a point in which you are any less saved than you were the first moment he saved you. Just because you were grumpy at breakfast doesn't mean you were condemned at breakfast. Your name doesn't disappear and reappear in the book of life according to your moods and actions. Such is the message of grace.

A. What do you think about Max's statements above? Do you agree with him? Why or why not?

B. If you *could* be condemned at breakfast because you were grumpy, what would that do to grace? What would "grace" mean in a world like that?

Looking Deep

1. Read Romans 7:7–25.

A. Is the law good or bad (vv. 7–12)? Yet what effect does the law have on us?

B. What is it that "kills" us (v. 13)?

C. What is Paul's struggle as described in verses 14–19? Do you see a similar struggle in yourself? If so, describe it.

D. What conclusion does Paul make in verse 20? What is the significance of this conclusion?
E. What general principle does Paul develop in verses 21–23? Is this principle at work in you? Explain.
F. How does Paul respond to this general principle in verse 24? Can you identify with this reaction? Explain.
G. Describe Paul's final reaction in verse 25. What is the reason for this joyful outburst?

2. Read Romans 8:1.
   A. What does it mean to be in Christ Jesus?
   B. How does the truth of this verse change everything for us? Explain.

15

The Heaviness of Hatred

Looking Back

1. No one, I repeat *no one*, makes it through life free of injury. Someone, somewhere has hurt you. Part of you has died because someone spoke too much, demanded too much, or neglected too much.
   A. What have been the biggest "hurts" you've received through the years? How did you respond?
   B. What are the biggest hurts you've caused someone else? How did they respond?
2. Everyone gets wounded, hence everyone must decide: How many payments will I demand? We may not require that the offender write checks, but we have other ways of settling the score.
   A. What are some of the ways you've seen that people use to even the score?
   B. What are some of the ways you've used to try to even the score? How did these ways work out?
3. Keeping tabs on your mercy is not being merciful. If you're calibrating your grace, you're not being gracious. There should never be a point when our grace is exhausted.
   A. Why is it a contradiction to keep tabs on your mercy or calibrate your grace?
   B. What kinds of situations are most likely to exhaust your

grace? How do you deal with these situations?

4. To believe we are totally and eternally debt free is seldom easy. Even if we've stood before the throne and heard it from the king himself, we still doubt. As a result many are forgiven only a little, not because the grace of the king is limited, but because the faith of the sinner is small.
   A. Why isn't it easy to believe we are "totally and eternally debt free"?
   B. Have you been forgiven a little or a lot? Explain.
5. The longer we walk in the garden, the more likely we are to smell like flowers. The more we immerse ourselves in grace, the more likely we are to give grace.
   A. Who is the most gracious person you know? Describe him or her. What makes the person so gracious?
   B. How can we immerse ourselves in grace? What does that mean?
6. The key to forgiving others is to quit focusing on what they did to you and start focusing on what God did for you.
   A. What can you do to make it easier to quit focusing on what someone did to you?
   B. Take some time to make a list of the good things God did for you just this week. How many items are on your list?

Looking Deep

1. Read Romans 8:5–17.
   A. What two classes of people do verses 5–8 describe? Which one most describes you? Explain.
   B. How does Paul define a Christian in verse 9?
   C. What conclusion does Paul make in verses 10–11?
   D. Based on the conclusion he makes in verses 10–11, what kind of lifestyle does Paul say we should be living in verses 12–16?

   E. What kind of future does Paul lay out for believers in verse 17? Should this make any difference in the way we live today? Explain.

2. Read Matthew 18:21–34.
   A. How does the parable of verses 23–34 answer Peter's question in verse 21?
   B. Have you ever failed to extend grace to another—one who owes you less than you owe Jesus?

3. Read Hebrews 12:15.
   A. How is it possible to "miss" the grace of God, according to this verse?
   B. What power does bitterness have, according to this verse? Why is it to be avoided? Are you avoiding it? Explain.

16

Life Aboard the Fellow-Ship

Looking Back

1. God has enlisted us in his navy and placed us on his ship. The boat has one purpose—to carry us safely to the other shore.
   A. Are you in God's navy? Are you aboard ship? How do you know?
   B. What part of the ship do you stay in?
2. We aren't called to a life of leisure, we are called to a life of service. Each of us has a different task.
   A. What is the specific task to which God has called you?
   B. How are you serving God on the "ship"?
3. Unity matters to God. The Father does not want his kids to squabble. Disunity disturbs him.
   A. As you honestly look at your own life, would you say you have more often helped to keep unity or to create disunity?
   B. Give an example of what you mean.
4. Nowhere, by the way, are we told to build unity. We are told simply to *keep* unity.
   A. What is the difference between "building" unity and "keeping" unity?
   B. How is this difference significant?
5. Unity doesn't begin in examining others, but in examining

self. Unity begins, not in demanding that others change, but in admitting that we aren't so perfect ourselves.

   A. What kind of self-examination do you think Max is calling for here?
   B. Reflect on personal examples and results of engaging in this kind of self-examination.

6. The answer to arguments? Acceptance. The first step to unity? Acceptance. Not agreement, acceptance. Not unanimity, acceptance.
   A. What is the difference between acceptance and agreement?
   B. What is the difference between acceptance and unanimity?
7. Just because a group is distributing toys at Christmas that doesn't mean they are Christians. Just because they are feeding the hungry that does not mean they are the honored ones of God. Jesus doesn't issue a call for blind tolerance.
   A. Why is discernment an important part of unity?
   B. What is the difference between acceptance and blind tolerance?
8. First, look at the fruit. Is it good? Is it healthy? Is he or she helping or hurting people? Production is more important than pedigree. The fruit is more important than the name of the orchard.
   A. What does Max mean by "fruit" here?
   B. What kind of "fruit" are you producing? Would others agree? Explain.
9. Also look at the faith. In whose name is the work done? Jesus was accepting of this man's work because it was done in the name of Christ.
   A. Should we judge someone's faith? If so, what does this mean and how can it be done?

   B. Just because someone uses the name "Jesus," does that mean they believe in the Jesus of the Bible?

10. Where there is faith, repentance, and a new birth, there is a Christian. When I meet a man whose faith is in the cross and eyes are on the Savior, I meet a brother.
    A. Does Max's statement above make you pleased or uncomfortable?
    B. Explain your answer.

Looking Deep

1. Read Romans 14:1–13.
   A. What is the main topic of this passage? Give evidence to support your belief.
   B. What examples does Paul give to illustrate his main point? List them.
   C. Consider Paul's questions in verses 4 and 10. How do these questions relate to Paul's main point?
   D. How do verses 11–12 add strength to Paul's instruction?
   E. What conclusion does Paul make in verse 13? Why do you think the apostle spends so much time on this topic?
2. Read Ephesians 4:3–7.
   A. What command is given in verse 3? How is this to be accomplished?
   B. What reason for this command is given in verses 4–6?
   C. How does verse 7 explain the power to fulfill this command?

17

What We Really Want to Know

Looking Back

1. There is no way our little minds can comprehend the love of God. But that didn't keep him from coming.
   A. Do you understand God's love better today than you did five years ago? Explain.
   B. Why is it good news that God's love is beyond our full comprehension?
2. God is with you. Knowing that, who is against you? Can death harm you now? Can disease rob your life? Can your purpose be taken or your value diminished? No. Though hell itself may set itself against you, no one can defeat you. You are protected. God is with you.
   A. When are you most likely to fear that God is *not* with you? How do you respond to these instances?
   B. Answer Max's questions above. Why do you give these answers?
3. Did God save you so you would fret? Would he teach you to walk just to watch you fall? Would he be nailed to the cross for your sins and then disregard your prayers?
   A. Answer Max's questions above.
   B. What is the point of asking the questions above?
4. Satan cannot accuse you. No one can accuse you! Fingers may point and voices may demand, but the charges glance off like

arrows hitting a shield. No more dirty dishwater. No more penance. No more nagging sisters. You have stood before the judge and heard him declare, "Not guilty."

A. Why is Satan unable to make accusations against you that stick?

B. How could we have been declared "not guilty" by the judge?

5. "You wonder how long my love will last? Find your answer on a splintered cross, on a craggy hill. That's me you see up there, your maker, your God, nail-stabbed and bleeding. Covered in spit and sin-soaked. That's your sin I'm feeling. That's your death I'm dying. That's your resurrection I'm living. That's how much I love you."

A. Why is the cross God's final answer to how much he loves us?

B. How does the cross guarantee that God will always see to our welfare despite whatever hardships we may face?

Looking Deep

1. Read Romans 8:31–39.

A. What is Paul's question in verse 31? What does he intend to suggest by asking this question?

B. Explain the apostle's logic behind his statement in verse 32. Why is this statement so crucial to daily living?

C. In what way are the questions of verses 33–35 related? What is their function?

D. How can the quotation found in verse 36 actually be an encouragement? How is it intended to function in this way?

E. What is the connection of verse 37 to verse 36? What is the apostle's point?

F. Does Paul leave anything out of verses 38–39? What does

he intend for us to understand? How does he want these truths to encourage us?

2. Read Isaiah 49:15–16.
   A. What question is asked in verse 15? What answer is expected? What comparison is intended with the subsequent statement?
   B. What metaphor does God use in verse 16? What is his point? What does he want us to believe? Why?
3. Read Isaiah 50:7–10.
   A. What attitude does the writer adopt in verse 10? Why?
   B. How do verses 8–9 foreshadow Paul's words in Romans 8:31–39?
   C. Who is addressed in verse 10? What instruction is given? Do you follow this instruction? Explain.

Conclusion

"Don't Forget About Me"

Looking Back

1. Unashamed of his needs, Billy Jack didn't let a flight attendant pass without a reminder: "Don't forget to look after me." I honestly can't think of one time Billy Jack didn't remind the crew that he needed attention. The rest of us didn't. We never asked for help. We were grown-up. Sophisticated. Self-reliant.
   - A. In what way can Billy Jack be a good example for us?
   - B. Why didn't the rest of the people on this flight ask the crew for extra attention? In what way is this similar to those who refuse to ask God for help?
2. Midway through the writing of this book I remembered Billy Jack. He would have understood the idea of grace. He knew what it was like to place himself totally in the care of someone else.
   - A. Why does Max think Billy Jack would have understood the idea of grace?
   - B. How do you think Billy Jack might define grace?
3. It occurred to me that Billy Jack was the safest person on the flight. Had the plane encountered trouble, he would have received primary assistance. The flight attendants would have bypassed me and gone to him. Why? He had placed himself in the care of someone stronger.

A. Why would Billy Jack have been the safest person on the flight?

B. Have you placed yourself in the care of someone stronger? Explain.

4. One thing's for sure: You cannot save yourself. The river is too strong, the distance is too great. God has sent his firstborn son to carry you home. Are you firmly in the grip of his grace?

A. Why can't we save ourselves?

B. Answer Max's question above: Are you firmly in the grip of God's grace? How do you know?

Looking Deep

1. Read Romans 10:1–13.

A. What error did Paul say his countrymen made in verses 1–3?

B. How is verse 4 the answer to this error?

C. What two methods of justification are contrasted in verses 5–8? How does each work? Have you opted for either one? If so, which? Why?

D. According to verses 9–10, how is one saved? Have you done this? Explain.

E. What promise is given in verse 11? Why is this important?

F. What summary statement is made in verses 12–13? In what way does this sum up the message of *In The Grip Of Grace*? How?

2. Read Romans 11:33–36.

A. What prompted these verses of glowing praise? What got Paul so excited?

B. Does this excite you as well? Explain.

JOHN

INTRODUCTION

He's an old man, this one who sits on the stool and leans against the wall. Eyes closed and face soft, were it not for his hand stroking his beard, you'd think he was asleep.

Some in the room assume he is. He does this often during worship. As the people sing, his eyes will close and his chin will fall until it rests on his chest, and there he will remain motionless. Silent.

Those who know him well know better. They know he is not resting. He is traveling. Atop the music he journeys back, back, back until he is young again. Strong again. There again. There on the seashore with James and the apostles. There on the trail with the disciples and the women. There in the Temple with Caiaphas and the accusers.

It's been sixty years, but John sees him still. The decades took John's strength, but they didn't take his memory. The years dulled his sight, but they didn't dull his vision. The seasons may have wrinkled his face, but they didn't soften his love.

He had been with God. God had been with him. How could he forget?

- The wine that moments before had been water—John could still taste it.
- The mud placed on the eyes of the blind man in Jerusalem—John could still remember it.
- The aroma of Mary's perfume as it filled the room—John could still smell it.

And the voice. Oh, the voice. His voice. John could still hear it.

I am the light of the world, it rang . . . I am the door . . . I am the way, the truth, the life.

I will come back, it promised, and take you to be with me.

Those who believe in me, it assured, will have life even if they die.

John could hear him. John could see him. Scenes branded on his heart. Words seared into his soul. John would never forget. How could he? He had been there.

He opens his eyes and blinks. The singing has stopped. The teaching has begun. John looks at the listeners and listens to the teacher.

If only you could have been there, he thinks.

But he wasn't. Most weren't. Most weren't even born. And most who were there are dead. Peter is. So is James. Nathanael, Martha, Philip. They are all gone. Even Paul, the apostle who came late, is dead.

Only John remains.

He looks again at the church. Small but earnest. They lean forward to hear the teacher. John listens to him. What a task. Speaking of one he never saw. Explaining words he never heard. John is there if the teacher needs him.

But what will happen when John is gone? What will the teacher do then? When John's voice is silent and his tongue stilled? Who will tell them how Jesus silenced the waves? Will they hear how he fed the thousands? Will they remember how he prayed for unity?

How will they know? If only they could have been there.

Suddenly, in his heart he knows what to do.

Later, under the light of a sunlit shaft, the old fisherman unfolds the scroll and begins to write the story of his life . . .

In the beginning there was the Word . . .

LIFE LESSON

John 1:1-51

SITUATION The Greeks and the Jews were familiar with the concept of the *word.* For the Jews it was an expression of God's wisdom, and for the Greeks it meant reason and intellect.

OBSERVATION Leaving his heavenly home, Jesus put on human flesh to bring us God's Good News.

INSPIRATION It all happened in a moment, a most remarkable moment. . . . that was like none other. For through that segment of time a spectacular thing occurred. God became a man. While the creatures of earth walked unaware, Divinity arrived. Heaven opened herself and placed her most precious one in a human womb. . . .

God as a fetus. Holiness sleeping in a womb. The creator of life being created.

God was given eyebrows, elbows, two kidneys, and a spleen. He stretched against the walls and floated in the amniotic fluids of his mother.

God had come near. . . .

The hands that first held him were unmanicured, calloused, and dirty.

No silk. No ivory. No hype. No party. No hoopla.

Were it not for the shepherds, there would have been no reception. And were it not for a group of star-gazers, there would have been no gifts. . . .

Christ Comes to the World

In the beginning there was the Word.[n] The Word was with God, and
the Word was God. 2He was with God in the beginning. 3All
things were made by him, and nothing was made without him.
4In him there was life, and that life was the light of all people. 5The
Light shines in the darkness, and the darkness has not overpowered it.
6There was a man named John[n] who was sent by God. 7He came to tell
people the truth about the Light so that through him all people could hear
about the Light and believe. 8John was not the Light, but he came to tell
people the truth about the Light. 9The true Light that gives light to all was
coming into the world!
10The Word was in the world, and the world was made by him, but the
world did not know him. 11He came to the world that was his own, but his
own people did not accept him. 12But to all who did accept him and believe
in him he gave the right to become children of God. 13They did not become
his children in any human way—by any human parents or human desire.
They were born of God.
14The Word became a human and lived among us. We saw his glory—
the glory that belongs to the only Son of the Father—and he was full of
grace and truth. 15John tells the truth about him and cries out, saying,
"This is the One I told you about: 'The One who comes after me is greater
than I am, because he was living before me.'"
16Because he was full of grace and truth, from him we all received one gift
after another. 17The law was given through Moses, but grace and truth
came through Jesus Christ. 18No one has ever seen God. But God the only
Son is very close to the Father,[n] and he has shown us what God is like.

John Tells People About Jesus

19Here is the truth John[n] told when the Jews in Jerusalem sent priests
and Levites to ask him, "Who are you?"
20John spoke freely and did not refuse to answer. He said, "I am not the
Christ."
21So they asked him, "Then who are you? Are you Elijah?"[n]
He answered, "No, I am not."
"Are you the Prophet?"[n] they asked.
He answered, "No."
22Then they said, "Who are you? Give us an answer to tell those who sent
us. What do you say about yourself?"
23John told them in the words of the prophet Isaiah:
"I am the voice of one
calling out in the desert:
'Make the road straight for the Lord.'" *Isaiah 40:3*

Word The Greek word is "logos," meaning any kind of communication; it could be translated "message." Here, it means Christ, because Christ was the way God told people about himself.

John John the Baptist, who preached to people about Christ's coming (Matthew 3, Luke 3).

But . . . Father This could be translated, "But the only God is very close to the Father." Also, some Greek copies say, "But the only Son is very close to the Father."

John John the Baptist, who preached to people about Christ's coming (Matthew 3, Luke 3).

Elijah A man who spoke for God. He lived hundreds of years before Christ and was expected to return before Christ (Malachi 4:5-6).

Prophet They probably meant the prophet that God told Moses he would send (Deuteronomy 18:15-19).

24Some Pharisees who had been sent asked John: 25"If you are not the Christ or Elijah or the Prophet, why do you baptize people?"

26John answered, "I baptize with water, but there is one here with you that you don't know about. 27He is the One who comes after me. I am not good enough to untie the strings of his sandals."

28This all happened at Bethany on the other side of the Jordan River, where John was baptizing people.

29The next day John saw Jesus coming toward him. John said, "Look, the Lamb of God,[n] who takes away the sin of the world! 30This is the One I was talking about when I said, 'A man will come after me, but he is greater than I am, because he was living before me.' 31Even I did not know who he was, although I came baptizing with water so that the people of Israel would know who he is."

32-33Then John said, "I saw the Spirit come down from heaven in the form of a dove and rest on him. Until then I did not know who the Christ was. But the God who sent me to baptize with water told me, 'You will see the Spirit come down and rest on a man; he is the One who will baptize with the Holy Spirit.' 34I have seen this happen, and I tell you the truth: This man is the Son of God."

The First Followers of Jesus

35The next day John[n] was there again with two of his followers. 36When he saw Jesus walking by, he said, "Look, the Lamb of God!"[n]

37The two followers heard John say this, so they followed Jesus. 38When Jesus turned and saw them following him, he asked, "What are you looking for?"

They said, "Rabbi, where are you staying?" ("Rabbi" means "Teacher.")

39He answered, "Come and see." So the two men went with Jesus and saw where he was staying and stayed there with him that day. It was about four o'clock in the afternoon.

40One of the two men who followed Jesus after they heard John speak about him was Andrew, Simon Peter's brother. 41The first thing Andrew did was to find his brother Simon and say to him, "We have found the Messiah." ("Messiah" means "Christ.")

42Then Andrew took Simon to Jesus. Jesus looked at him and said, "You are Simon son of John. You will be called Cephas." ("Cephas" means "Peter."[n])

43The next day Jesus decided to go to Galilee. He found Philip and said to him, "Follow me."

44Philip was from the town of Bethsaida, where Andrew and Peter lived. 45Philip found Nathanael and told him, "We have found the man that Moses wrote about in the law, and the prophets also wrote about him. He is Jesus, the son of Joseph, from Nazareth."

46But Nathanael said to Philip, "Can anything good come from Nazareth?"

Philip answered, "Come and see."

47As Jesus saw Nathanael coming toward him, he said, "Here is truly an Israelite. There is nothing false in him."

Lamb of God Name for Jesus. Jesus is like the lambs that were offered for a sacrifice to God.
Peter The Greek name "Peter," like the Aramaic name "Cephas," means "rock."

For thirty-three years he would feel everything you and I have ever felt. He felt weak. He grew weary. He was afraid of failure. He was susceptible to wooing women. He got colds, burped, and had body odor. His feelings got hurt. His feet got tired. And his head ached.

To think of Jesus in such a light is—well, it seems almost irreverent, doesn't it? It's not something we like to do; it's uncomfortable. It is much easier to keep the humanity out of the incarnation. He's easier to stomach that way. . . .

But don't do it. For heaven's sake, don't. Let him be as human as he intended to be. Let him into the mire and muck of our world. For only if we let him in can he pull us out.

(From *God Came Near* by Max Lucado)

APPLICATION If people want to know what God is like, they can look at Jesus. If they want to know what Jesus is like, they should be able to look at his followers. Can people see Christ in you?

EXPLORATION The Word is Born—John 14:6-7; 1 Corinthians 8:5-6; Galatians 4:4; Philippians 2:7, 8; 1 Timothy 3:16; Hebrews 2:14; 13:8; 1 John 1:1-2; 4:2.